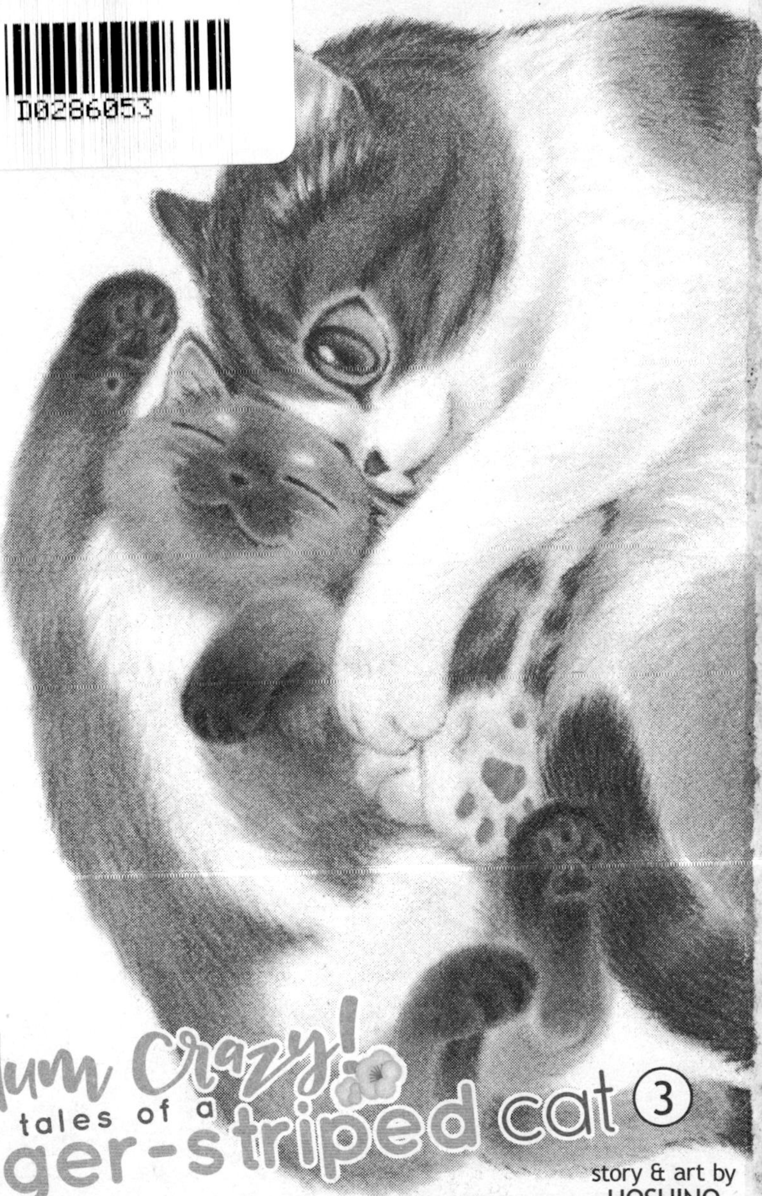

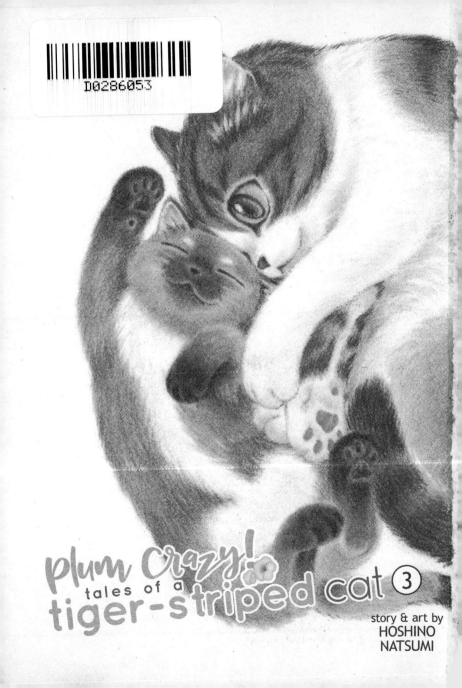

plum crazy! tales of a tiger-striped cat 3

story & art by
HOSHINO
NATSUMI

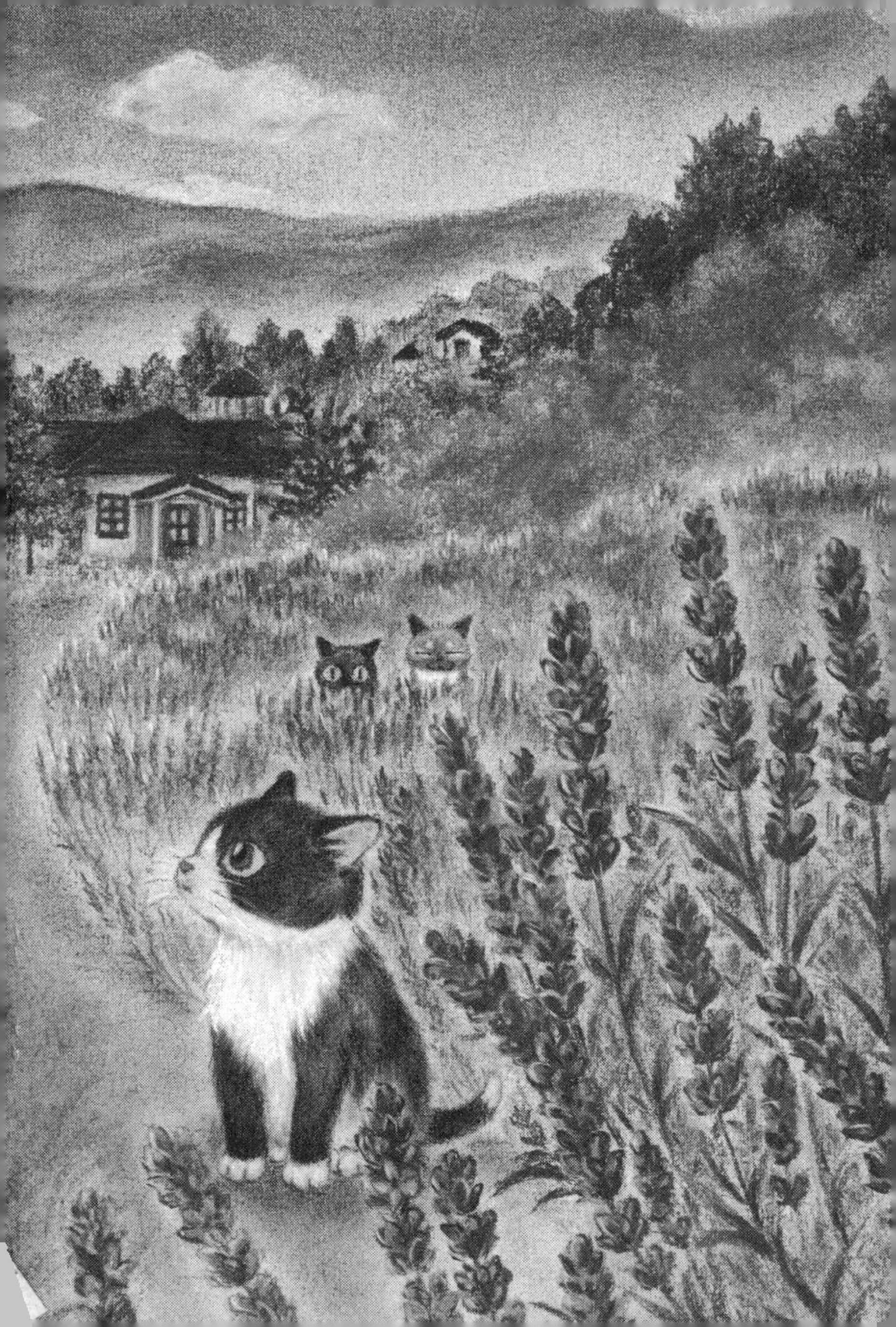

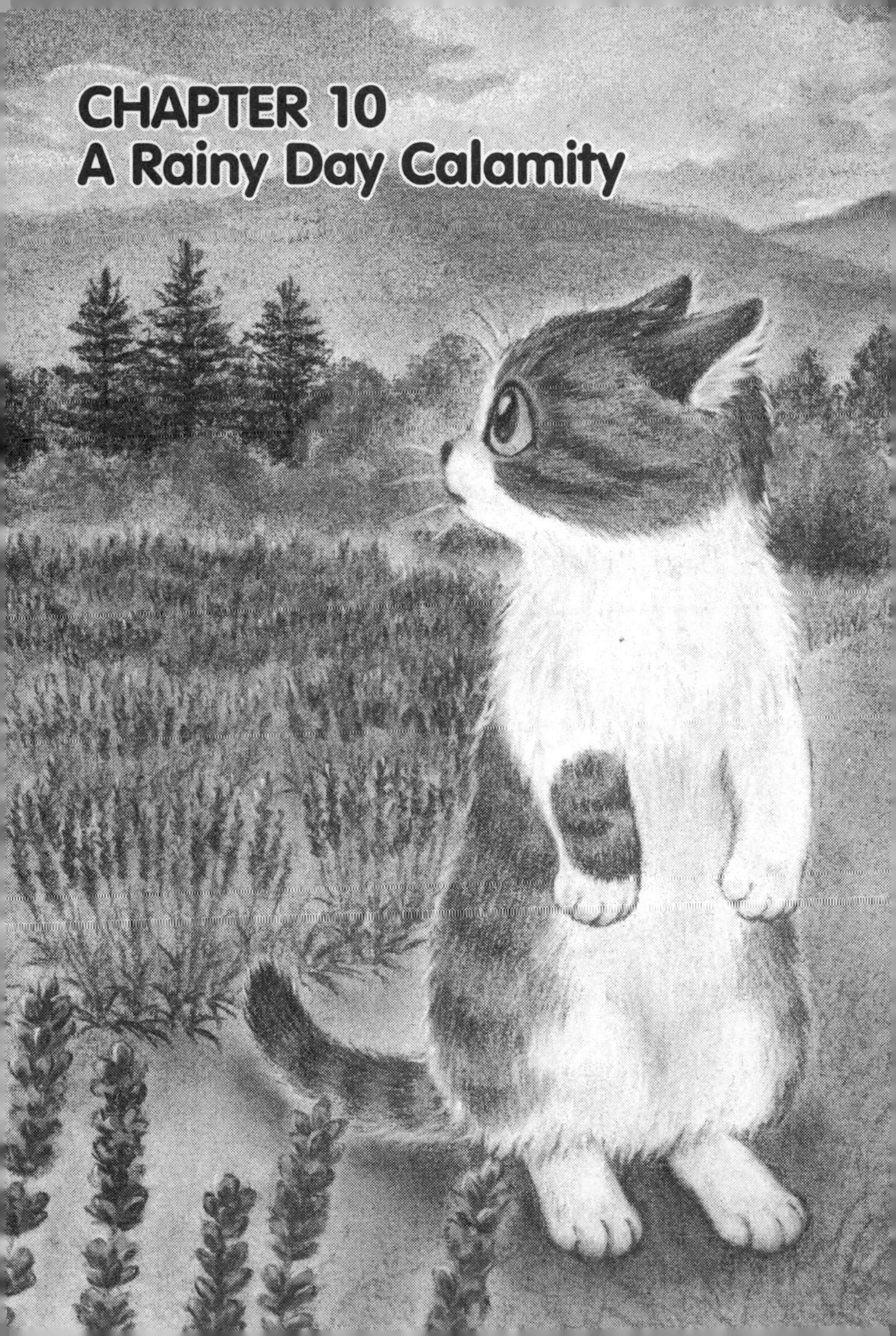
CHAPTER 10
A Rainy Day Calamity

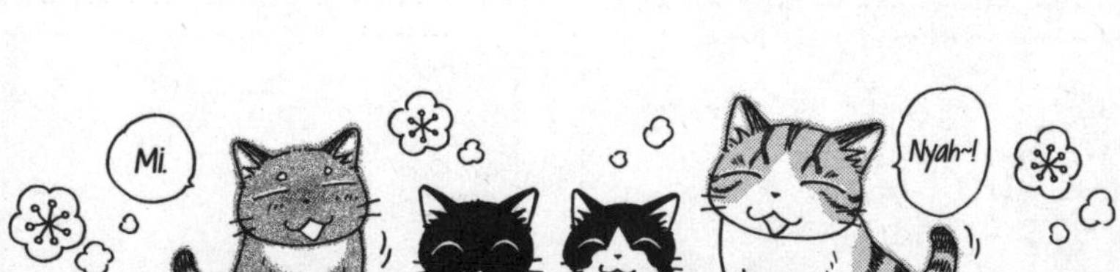
Mi.
Nyah~!

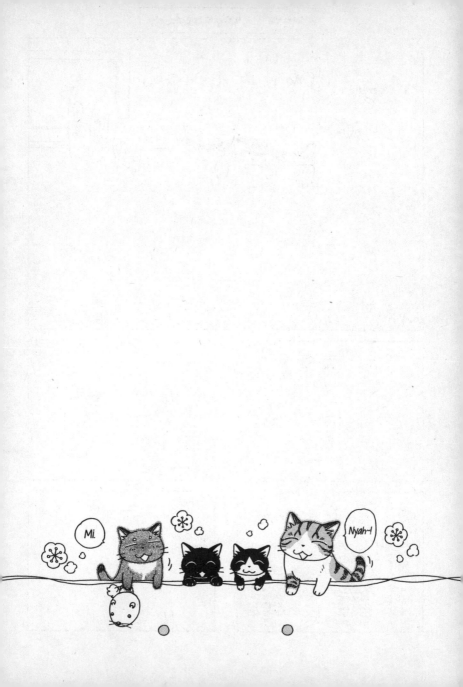

Short.10 A Rainy Day Calamity

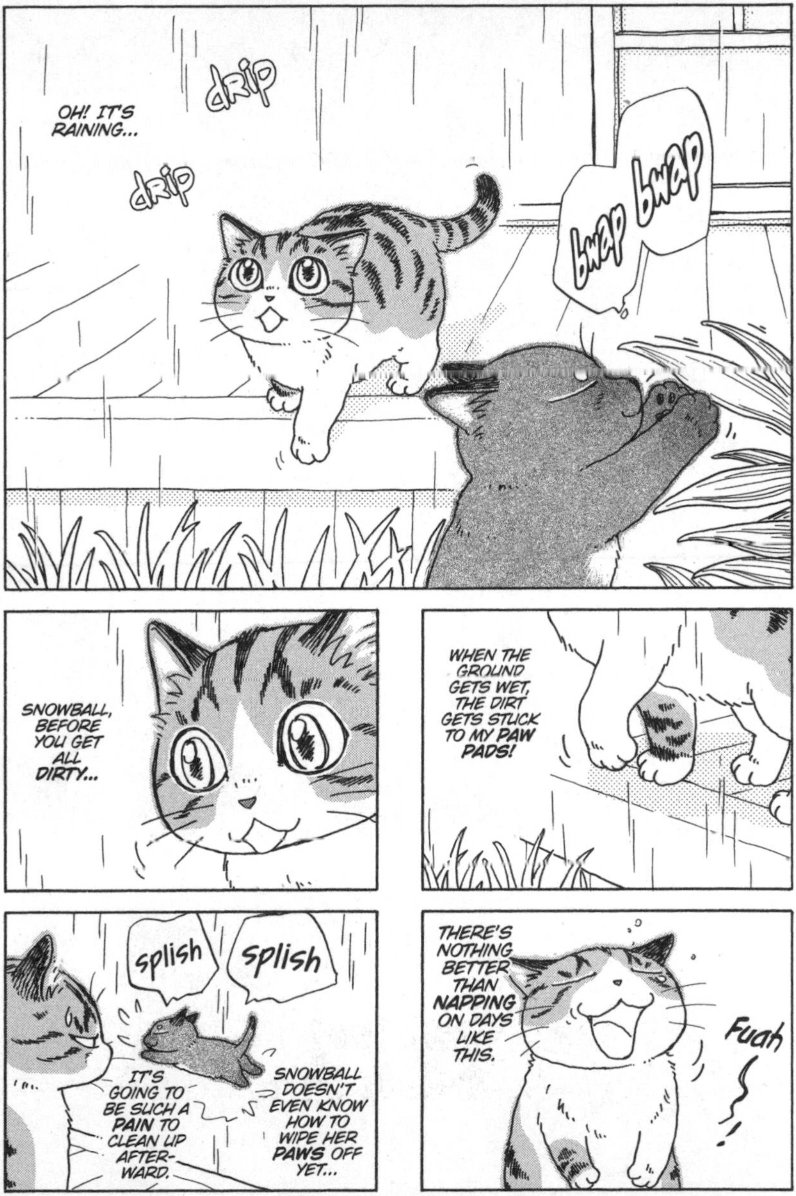

bwap bwap
drip
OH! IT'S RAINING...
drip
WHEN THE GROUND GETS WET, THE DIRT GETS STUCK TO MY PAW PADS!
SNOWBALL, BEFORE YOU GET ALL DIRTY...
THERE'S NOTHING BETTER THAN NAPPING ON DAYS LIKE THIS.
Fuah
splish
splish
SNOWBALL DOESN'T EVEN KNOW HOW TO WIPE HER PAWS OFF YET...
IT'S GOING TO BE SUCH A PAIN TO CLEAN UP AFTER-WARD.

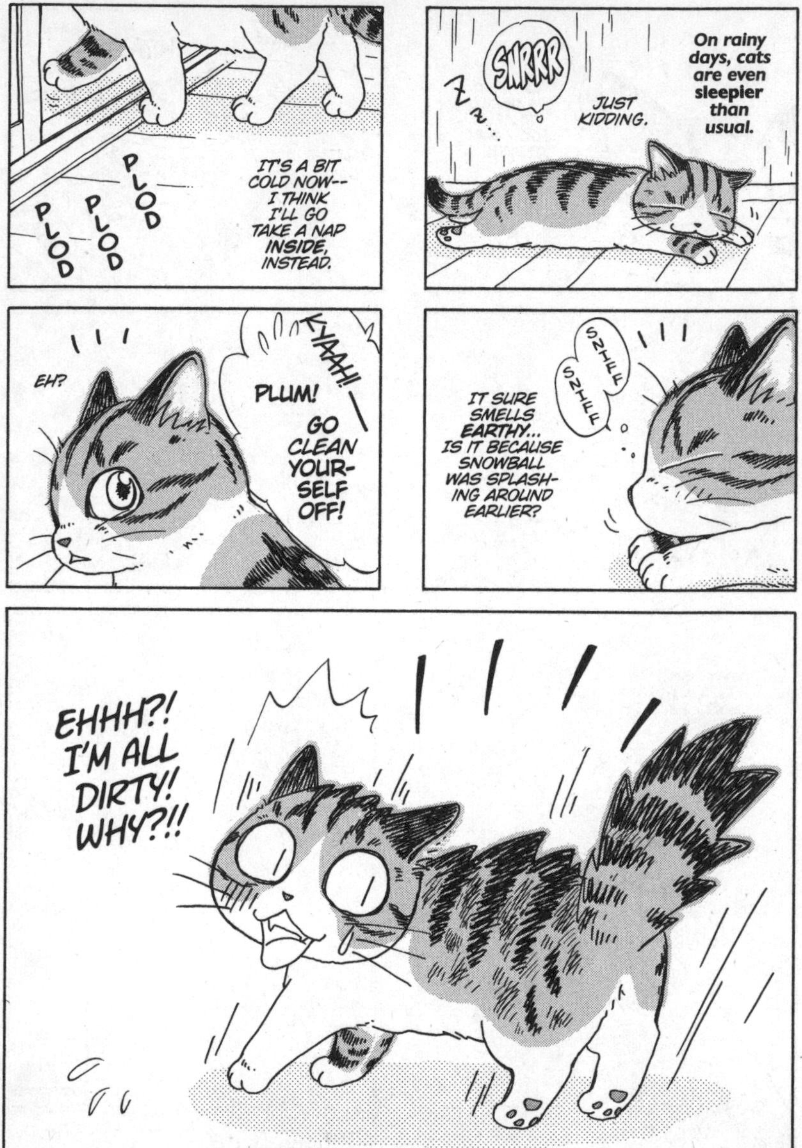
On rainy days, cats are even sleepier than usual.
SNRRR
Z z...
JUST KIDDING.
PLOD PLOD PLOD
IT'S A BIT COLD NOW-- I THINK I'LL GO TAKE A NAP INSIDE, INSTEAD.
SNIFF SNIFF
IT SURE SMELLS EARTHY... IS IT BECAUSE SNOWBALL WAS SPLASHING AROUND EARLIER?
KYAAAH!
PLUM!
GO CLEAN YOURSELF OFF!
EH?
EHHH?! I'M ALL DIRTY! WHY?!!

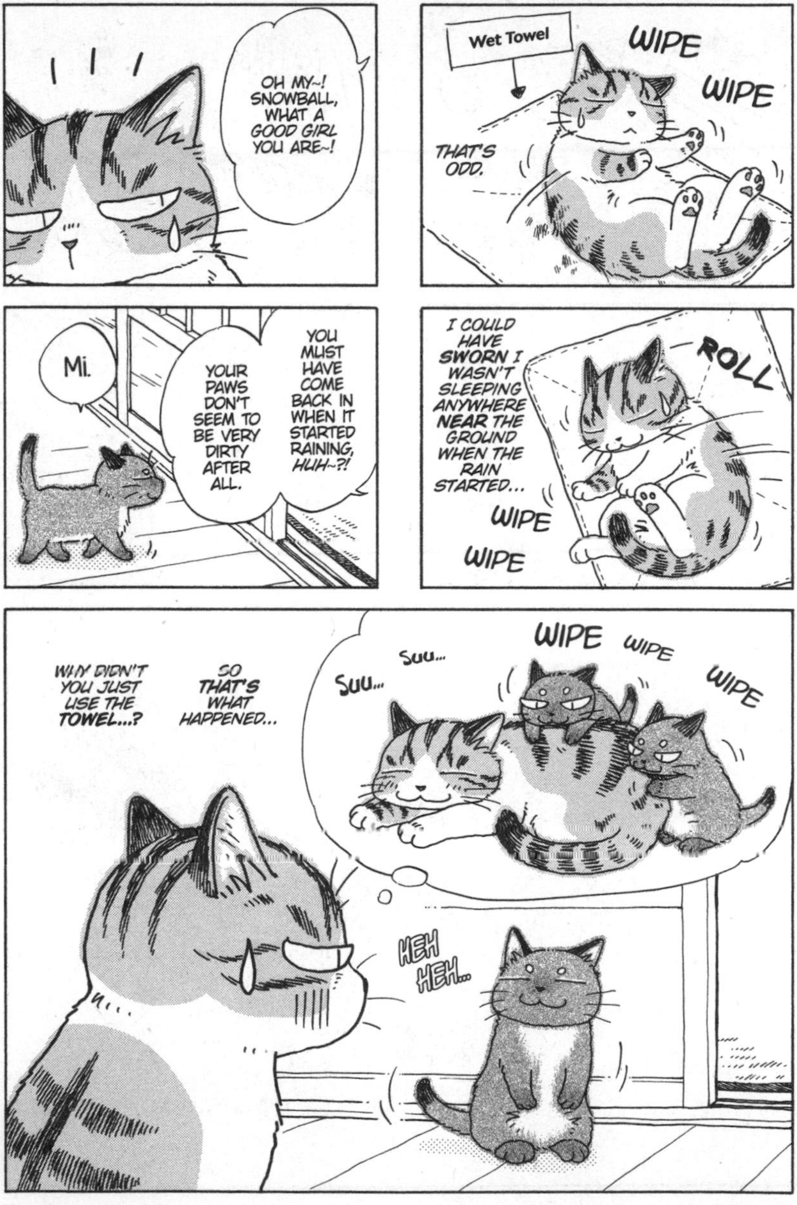
Wet Towel
WIPE
WIPE
THAT'S ODD.
OH MY~! SNOWBALL, WHAT A GOOD GIRL YOU ARE~!
ROLL
I COULD HAVE SWORN I WASN'T SLEEPING ANYWHERE NEAR THE GROUND WHEN THE RAIN STARTED...
WIPE
WIPE
YOU MUST HAVE COME BACK IN WHEN IT STARTED RAINING, HUH~?!
YOUR PAWS DON'T SEEM TO BE VERY DIRTY AFTER ALL.
Mi.
WIPE
WIPE
WIPE
Suu...
Suu...
SO THAT'S WHAT HAPPENED...
WHY DIDN'T YOU JUST USE THE TOWEL...?
HEH HEH...

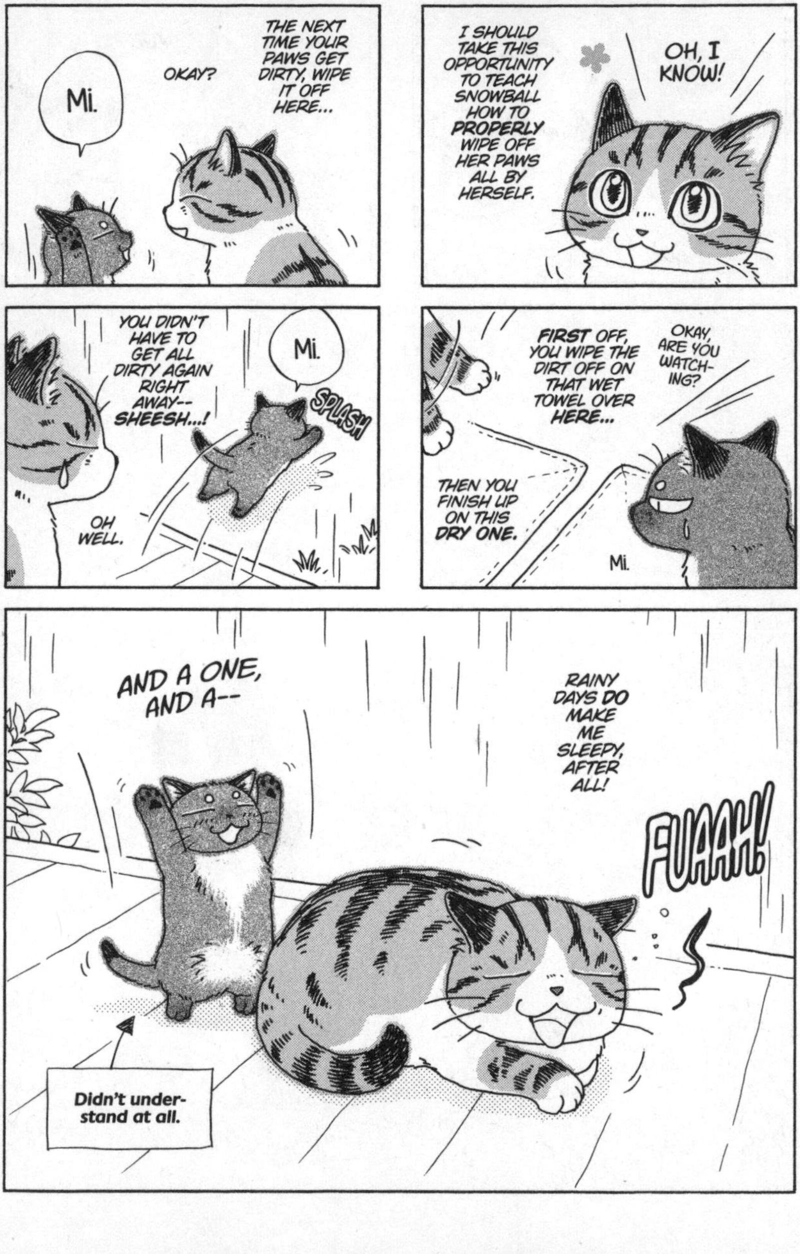
OH, I KNOW!
I SHOULD TAKE THIS OPPORTUNITY TO TEACH SNOWBALL HOW TO PROPERLY WIPE OFF HER PAWS ALL BY HERSELF.
THE NEXT TIME YOUR PAWS GET DIRTY, WIPE IT OFF HERE...
OKAY?
Mi.
OKAY, ARE YOU WATCHING?
FIRST OFF, YOU WIPE THE DIRT OFF ON THAT WET TOWEL OVER HERE...
THEN YOU FINISH UP ON THIS DRY ONE.
Mi.
Mi.
SPLASH
YOU DIDN'T HAVE TO GET ALL DIRTY AGAIN RIGHT AWAY-- SHEESH...!
OH WELL.
RAINY DAYS DO MAKE ME SLEEPY, AFTER ALL!
FUAAH!
AND A ONE, AND A--
Didn't understand at all.

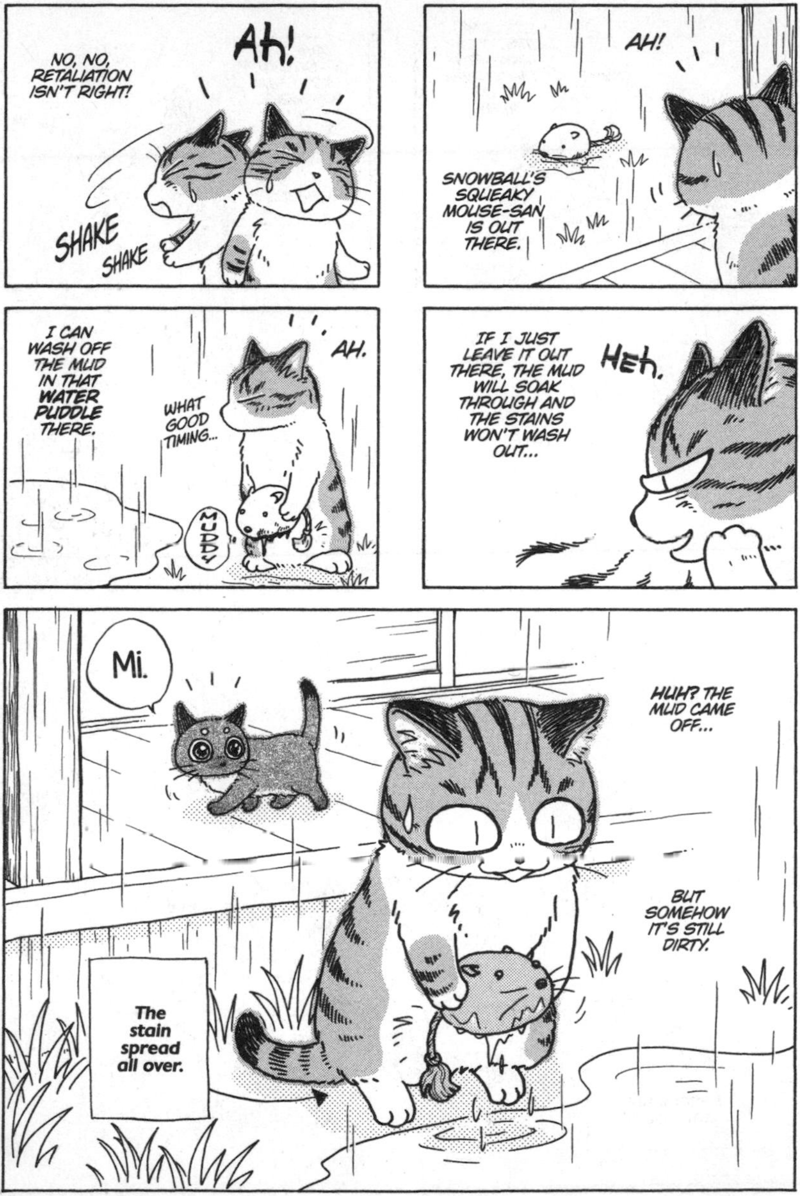
AH!
SNOWBALL'S SQUEAKY MOUSE-SAN IS OUT THERE.
Ah!
NO, NO, RETALIATION ISN'T RIGHT!
SHAKE
SHAKE
IF I JUST LEAVE IT OUT THERE, THE MUD WILL SOAK THROUGH AND THE STAINS WON'T WASH OUT...
Heh.
AH.
I CAN WASH OFF THE MUD IN THAT WATER PUDDLE THERE.
WHAT GOOD TIMING...
MUDDY
HUH? THE MUD CAME OFF...
BUT SOMEHOW IT'S STILL DIRTY.
Mi.
The stain spread all over.

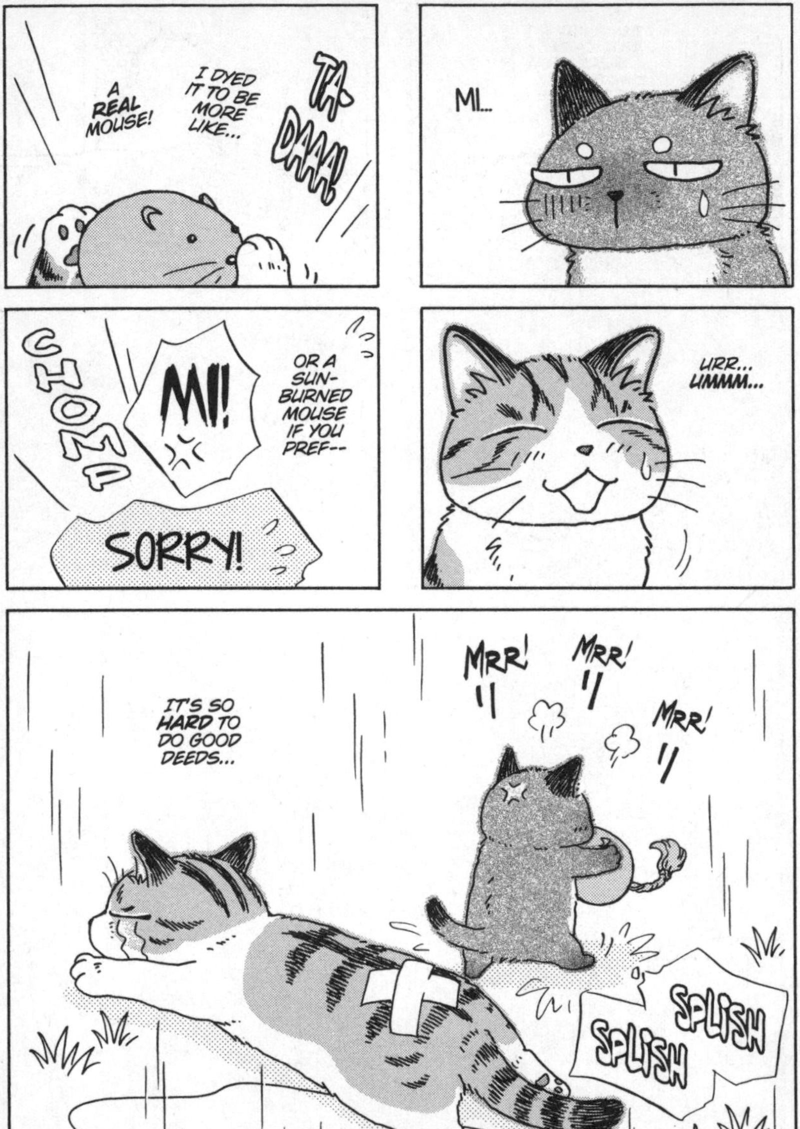
MI...
TA DAAA!
I DYED IT TO BE MORE LIKE...
A REAL MOUSE!
URR... UMMM...
OR A SUN-BURNED MOUSE IF YOU PREF--
MI!
CHOMP
SORRY!
MRR!
MRR!
MRR!
IT'S SO HARD TO DO GOOD DEEDS...
SPLISH
SPLISH

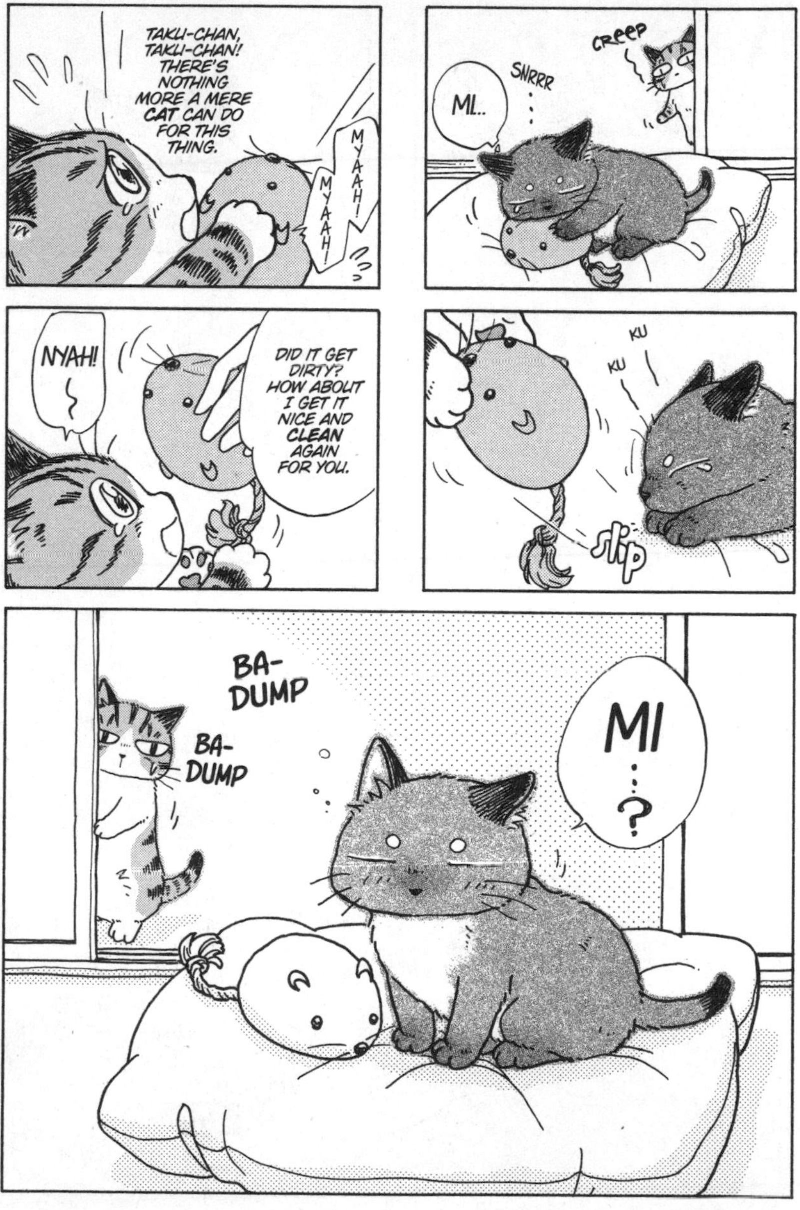
CREEP
SNRRR...
MI..
TAKU-CHAN, TAKU-CHAN! THERE'S NOTHING MORE A MERE CAT CAN DO FOR THIS THING.
MYAAH!
MYAAH!
KU
KU
slip
DID IT GET DIRTY? HOW ABOUT I GET IT NICE AND CLEAN AGAIN FOR YOU.
NYAH!
MI...?
BA-DUMP
BA-DUMP

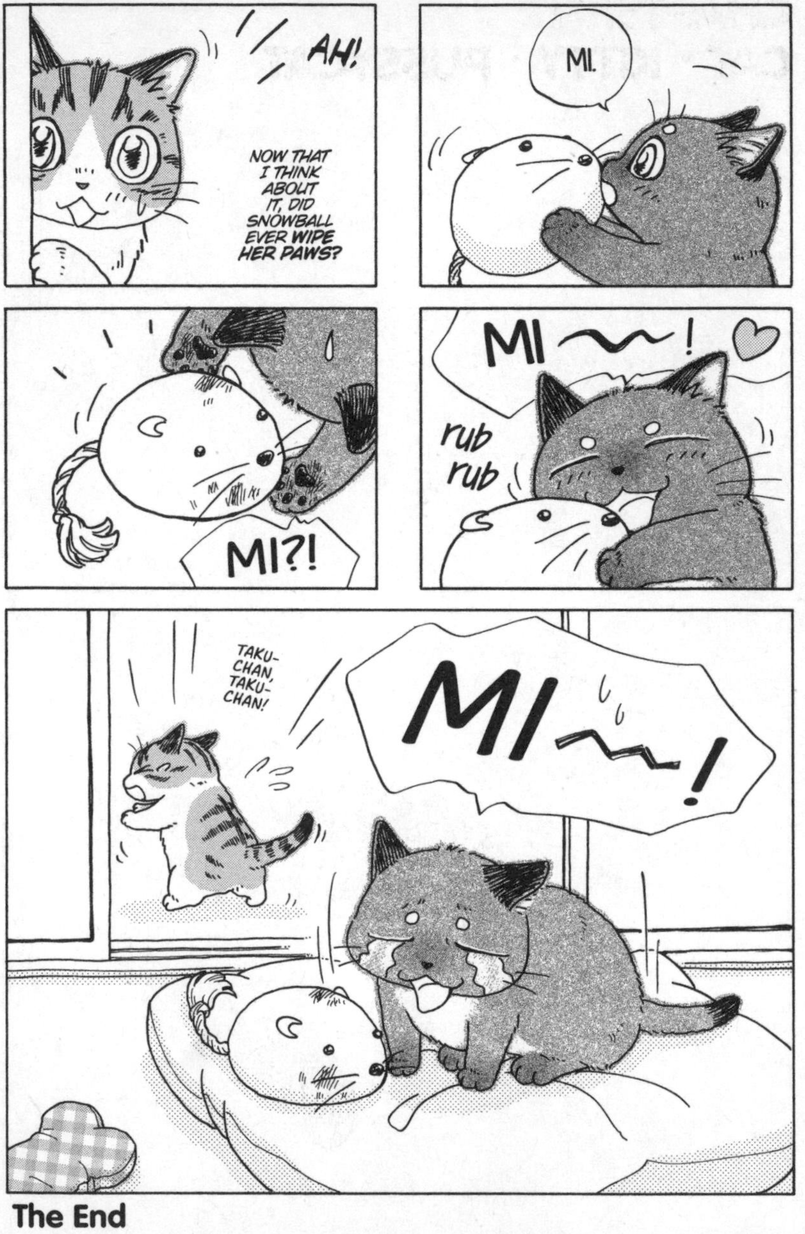
MI.
AH!
NOW THAT I THINK ABOUT IT, DID SNOWBALL EVER WIPE HER PAWS?
MI~!
rub rub
MI?!
MI~!
TAKU-CHAN, TAKU-CHAN!

The End

CHAPTER 15
CAT · KITTY · PUSSYCAT

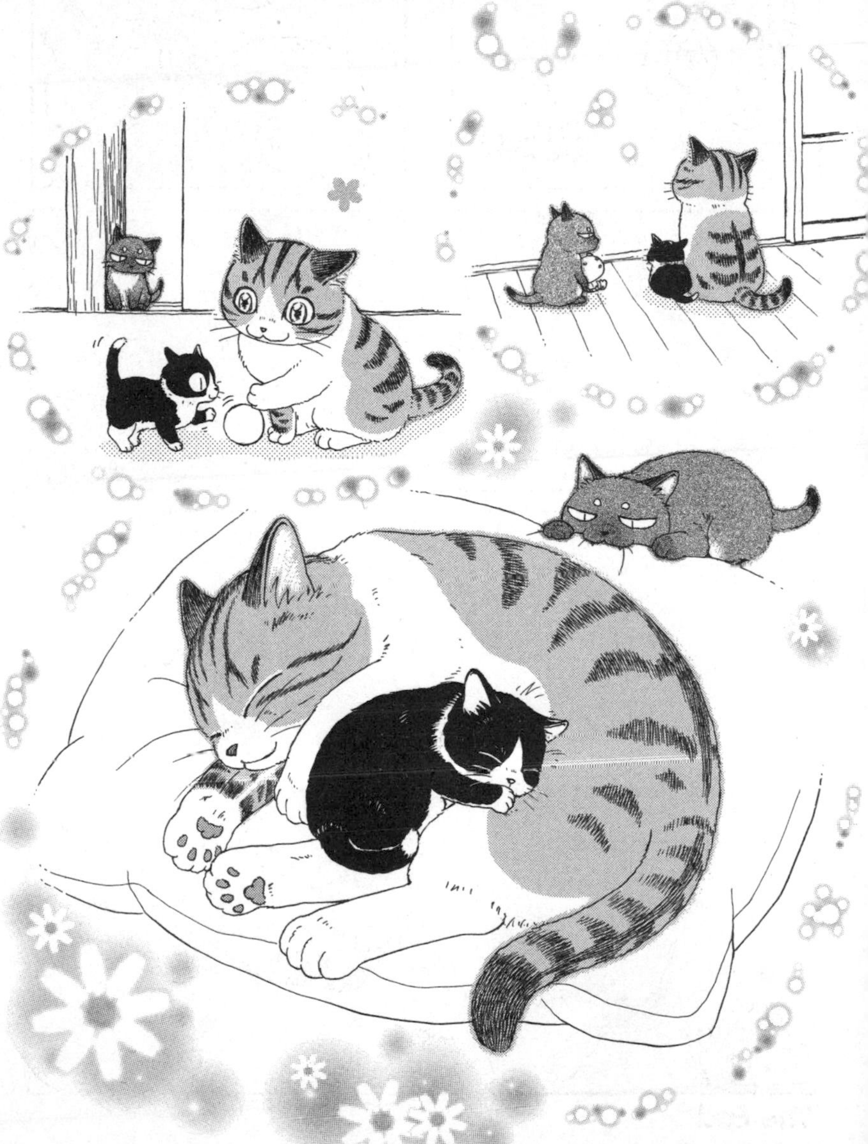

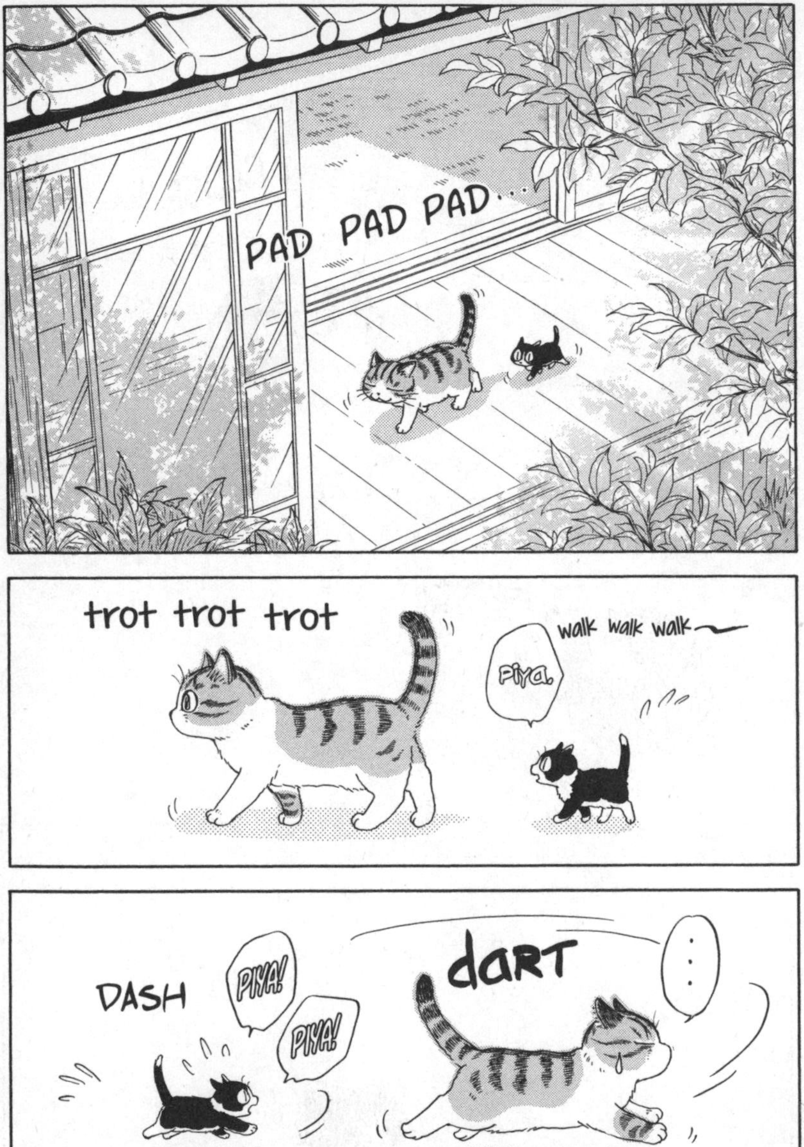
PAD PAD PAD...
walk walk walk~
Piya.
trot trot trot
...
dart
PIYA!
PIYA!
DASH

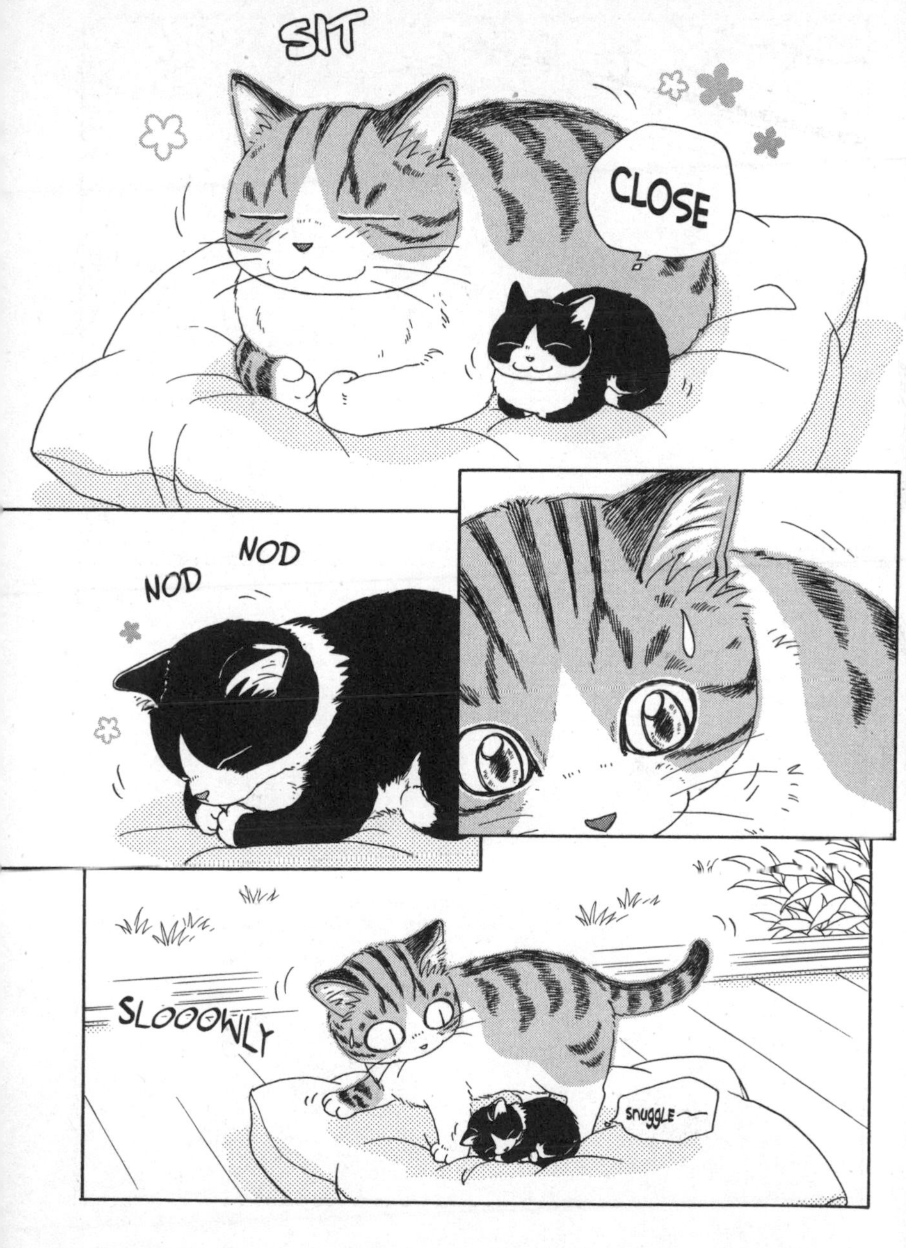
SIT
CLOSE
NOD
NOD
SLOOOWLY
snuggle~

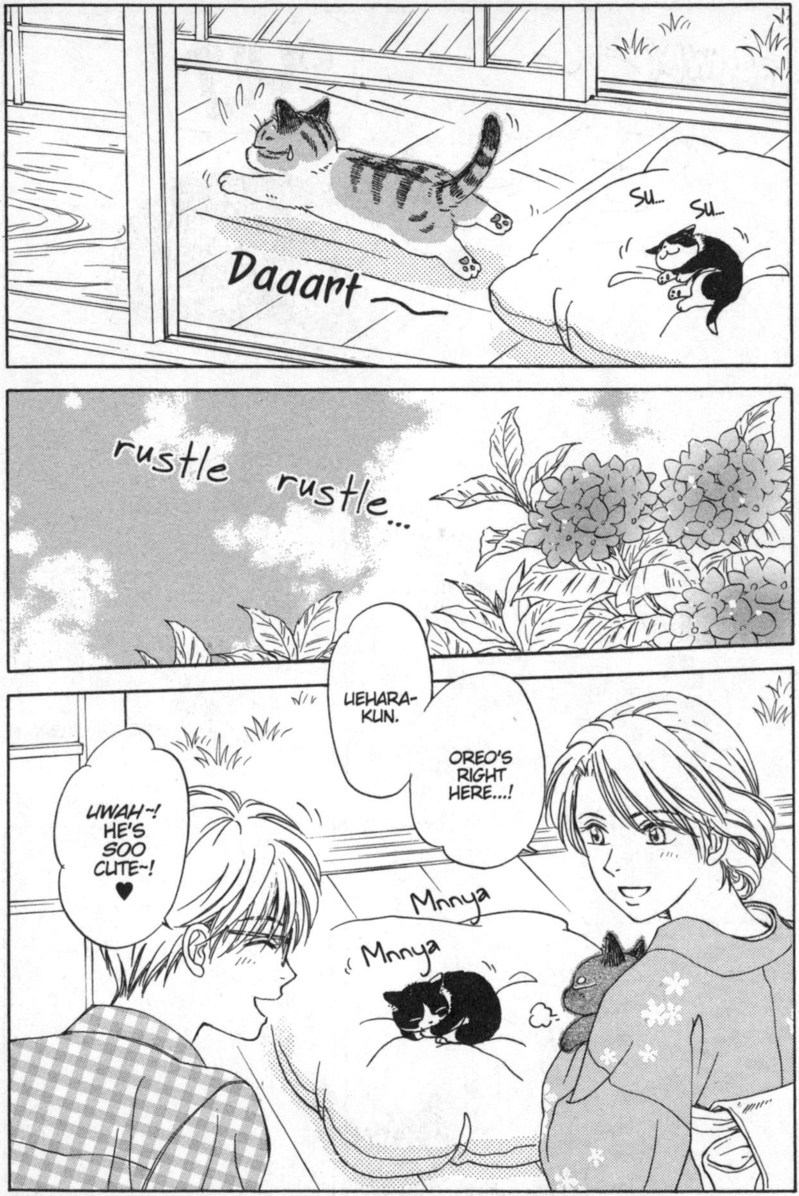
Su... Su...
Daaart
rustle rustle...
UEHARA-KUN.
OREO'S RIGHT HERE...!
UWAH~! HE'S SOO CUTE~! ♥
Mnnya
Mnnya

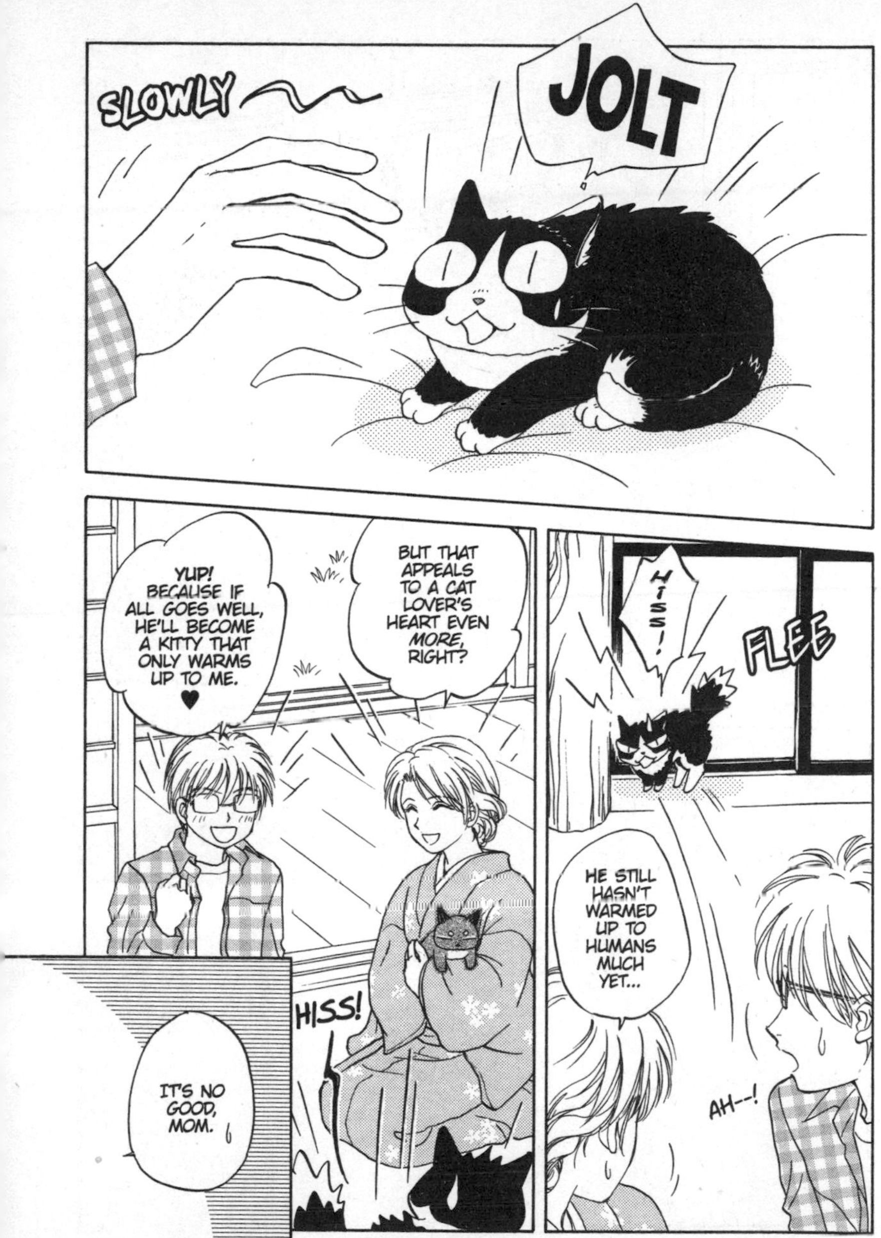
JOLT
SLOWLY
HISS!
FLEE
HE STILL HASN'T WARMED UP TO HUMANS MUCH YET...
AH--!
BUT THAT APPEALS TO A CAT LOVER'S HEART EVEN MORE, RIGHT?
YUP! BECAUSE IF ALL GOES WELL, HE'LL BECOME A KITTY THAT ONLY WARMS UP TO ME. ♥
HISS!
IT'S NO GOOD, MOM.

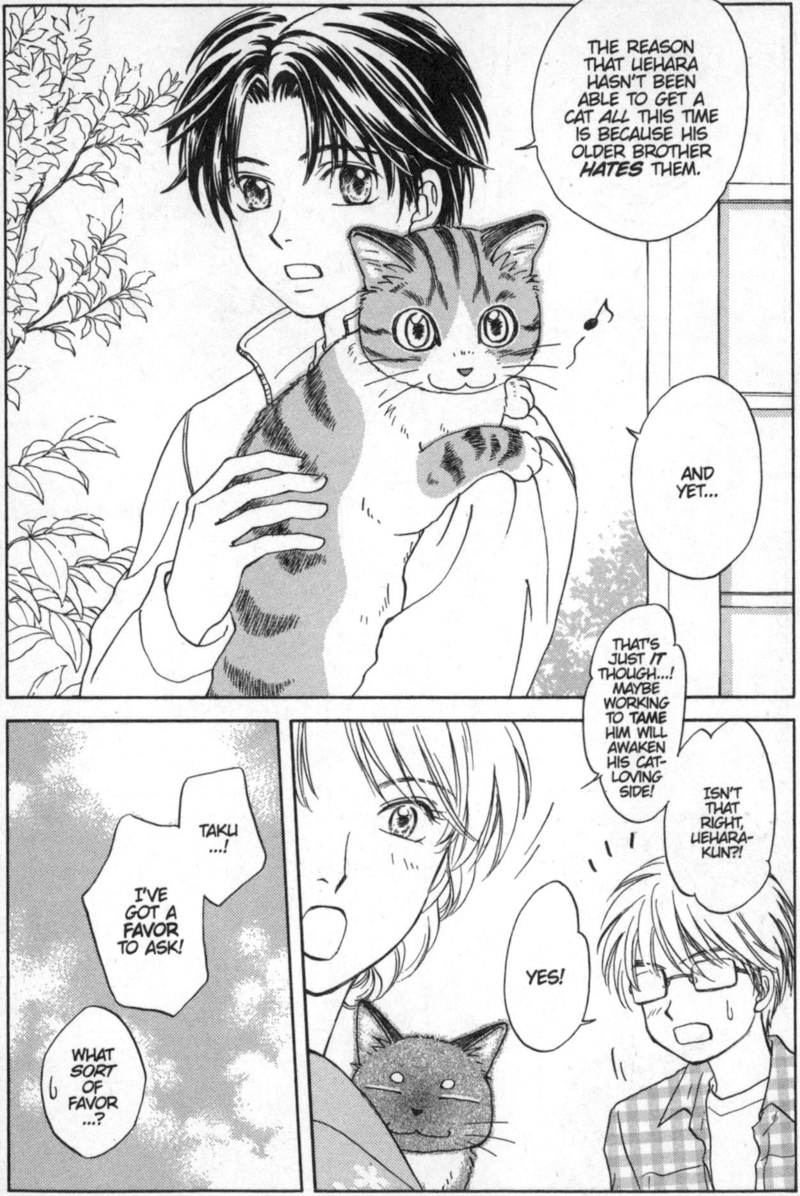
THE REASON THAT UEHARA HASN'T BEEN ABLE TO GET A CAT *ALL* THIS TIME IS BECAUSE HIS OLDER BROTHER ***HATES*** THEM.
AND YET...
THAT'S JUST *IT* THOUGH...! MAYBE WORKING TO TAME HIM WILL AWAKEN HIS CAT-LOVING SIDE!
ISN'T THAT RIGHT, UEHARA-KUN?!
YES!
TAKU ...!
I'VE GOT A FAVOR TO ASK!
WHAT SORT OF FAVOR ...?

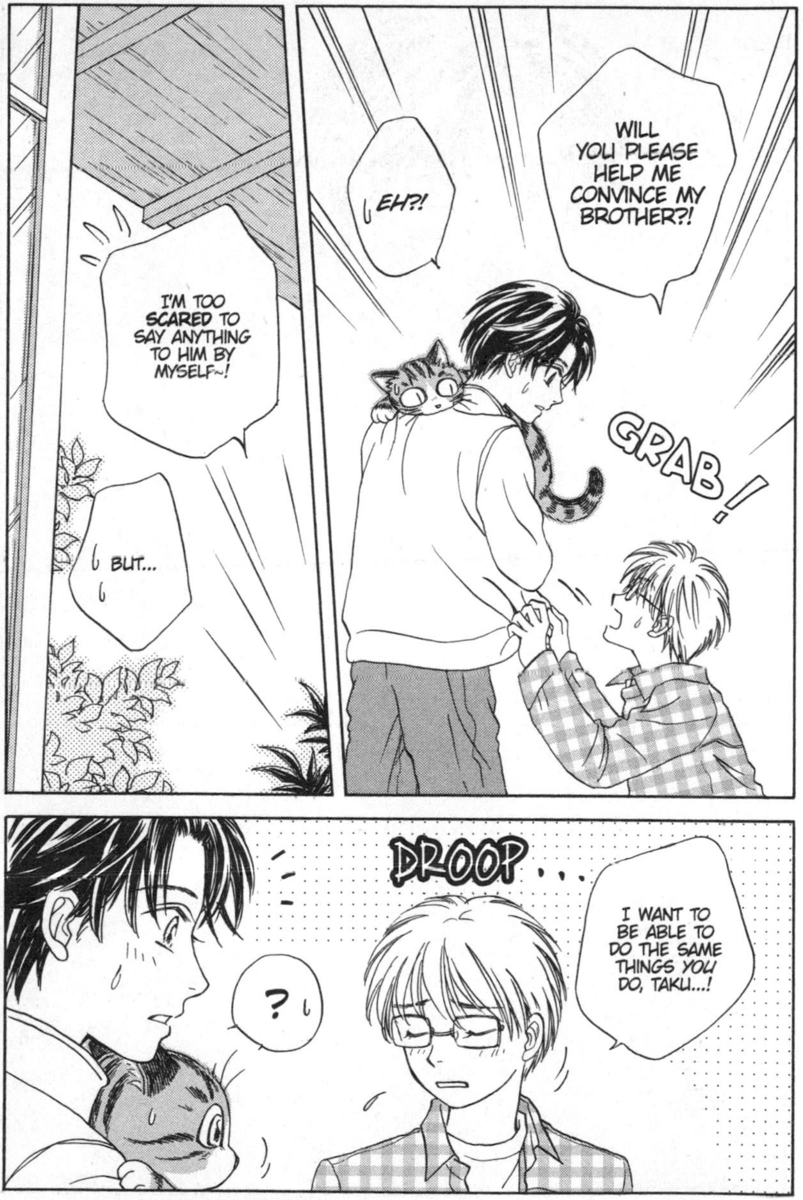
WILL YOU PLEASE HELP ME CONVINCE MY BROTHER?!
EH?!
GRAB!
I'M TOO SCARED TO SAY ANYTHING TO HIM BY MYSELF~!
BUT...
I WANT TO BE ABLE TO DO THE SAME THINGS YOU DO, TAKU...!
DROOP...
?

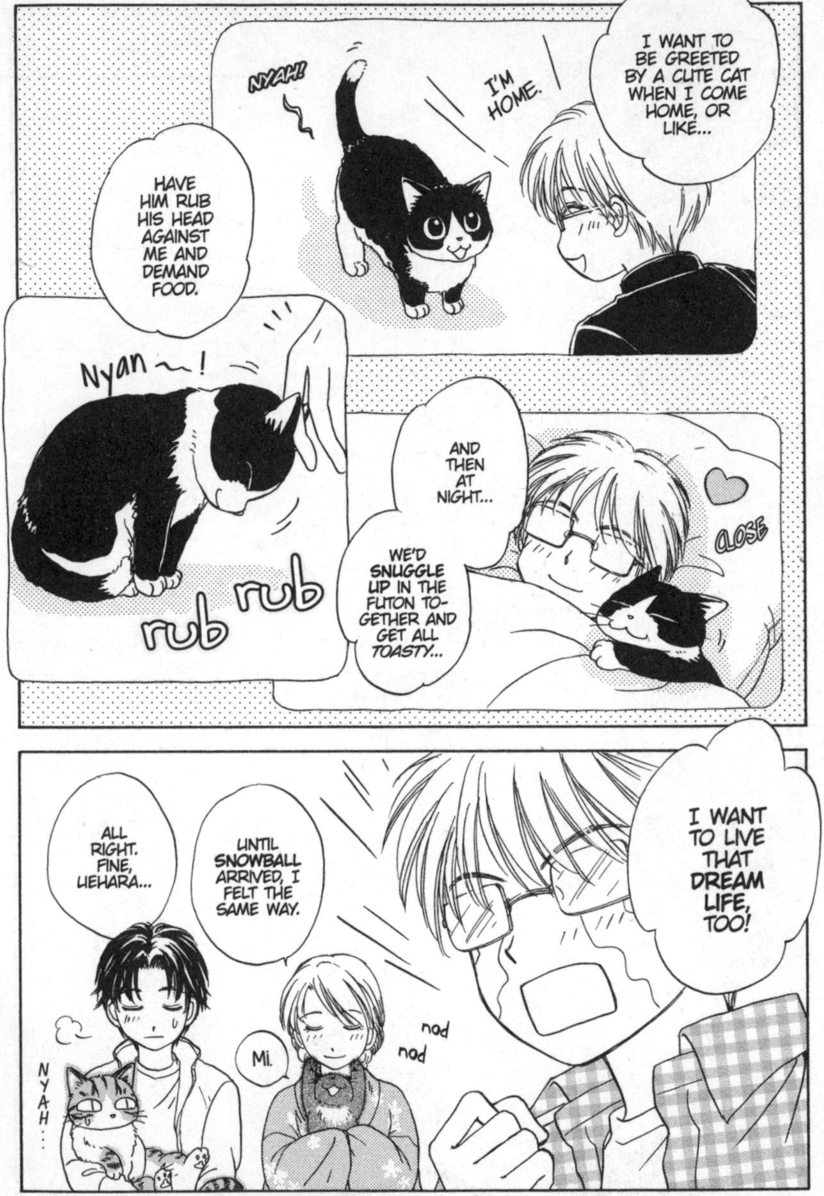
I WANT TO BE GREETED BY A CUTE CAT WHEN I COME HOME, OR LIKE...
I'M HOME.
NYAH!
HAVE HIM RUB HIS HEAD AGAINST ME AND DEMAND FOOD.
Nyan~!
rub rub
AND THEN AT NIGHT...
WE'D SNUGGLE UP IN THE FUTON TO-GETHER AND GET ALL TOASTY...
CLOSE
I WANT TO LIVE THAT DREAM LIFE, TOO!
UNTIL SNOWBALL ARRIVED, I FELT THE SAME WAY.
nod nod
Mi.
ALL RIGHT. FINE, UEHARA...
NYAH...

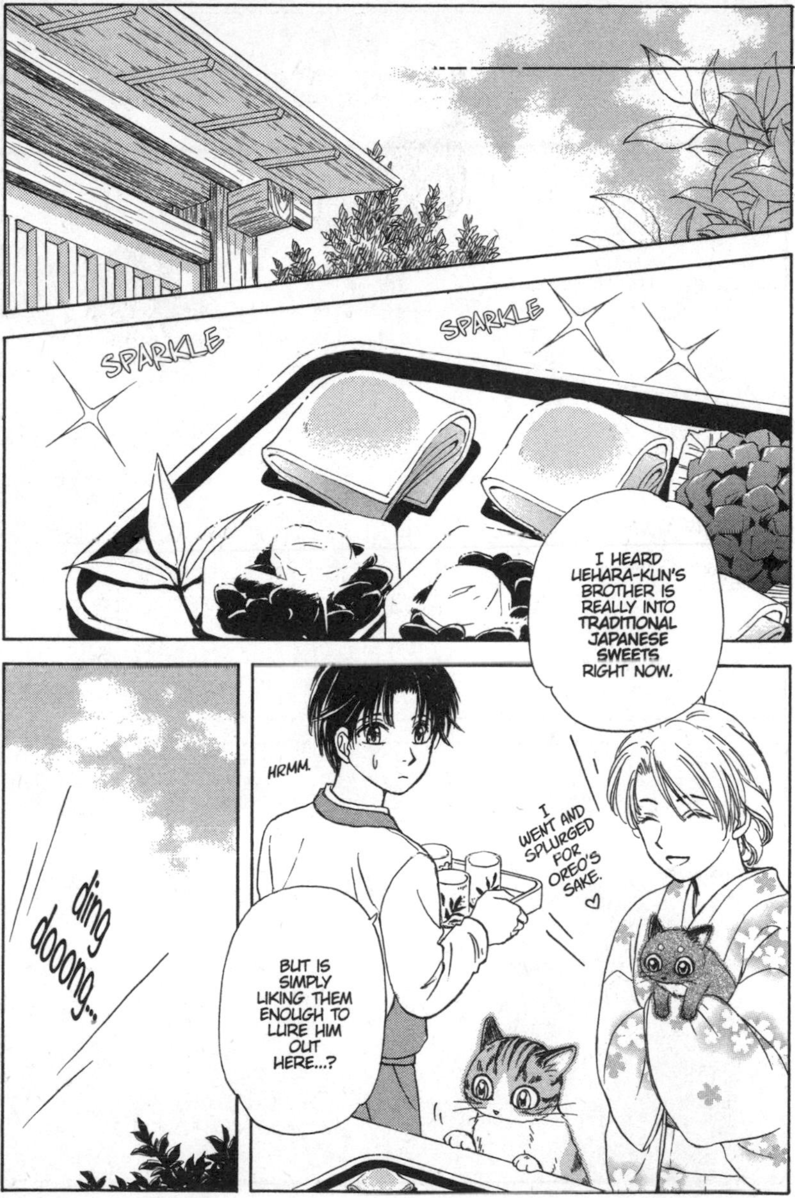
SPARKLE
SPARKLE
I HEARD UEHARA-KUN'S BROTHER IS REALLY INTO TRADITIONAL JAPANESE SWEETS RIGHT NOW.
I WENT AND SPLURGED FOR OREO'S SAKE. ♥
HRMM.
BUT IS SIMPLY LIKING THEM ENOUGH TO LURE HIM OUT HERE...?
ding dooong...

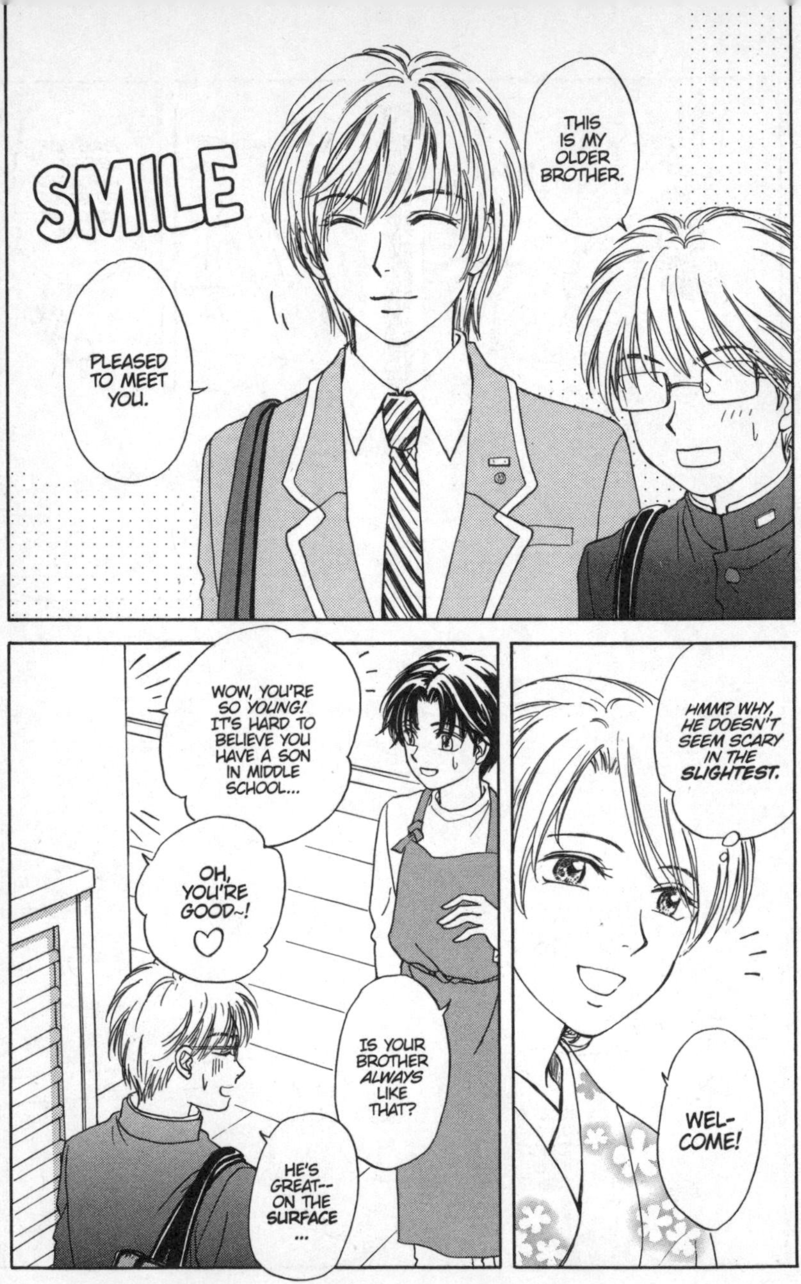
THIS IS MY OLDER BROTHER.
SMILE
PLEASED TO MEET YOU.
HMM? WHY, HE DOESN'T SEEM SCARY IN THE *SLIGHTEST.*
WEL-COME!
WOW, YOU'RE SO *YOUNG!* IT'S HARD TO BELIEVE YOU HAVE A SON IN MIDDLE SCHOOL...
OH, YOU'RE GOOD~! ♡
IS YOUR BROTHER *ALWAYS* LIKE THAT?
HE'S GREAT-- ON THE SURFACE ...

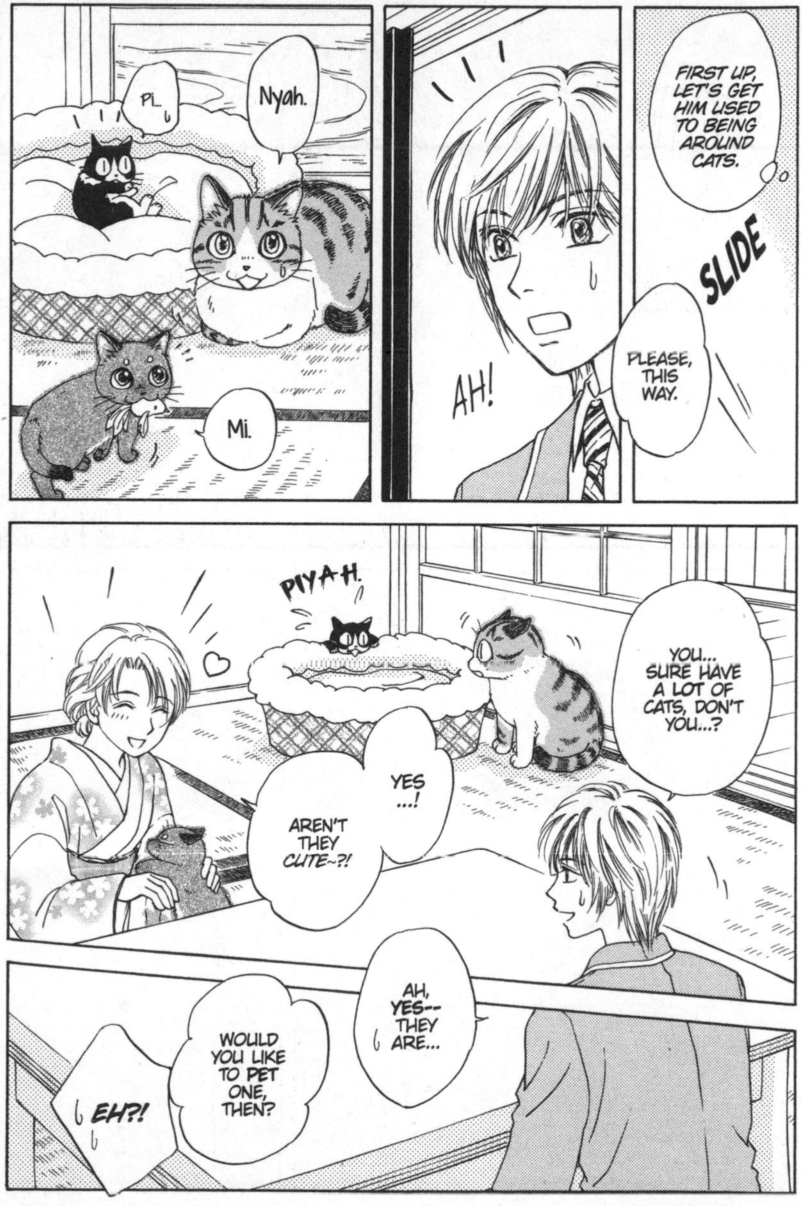
FIRST UP, LET'S GET HIM USED TO BEING AROUND CATS.
SLIDE
PLEASE, THIS WAY.
AH!
Nyah.
Pi..
Mi.
YOU... SURE HAVE A LOT OF CATS, DON'T YOU...?
PIYAH.
YES ...!
AREN'T THEY CUTE~?!
AH, YES-- THEY ARE...
WOULD YOU LIKE TO PET ONE, THEN?
EH?!

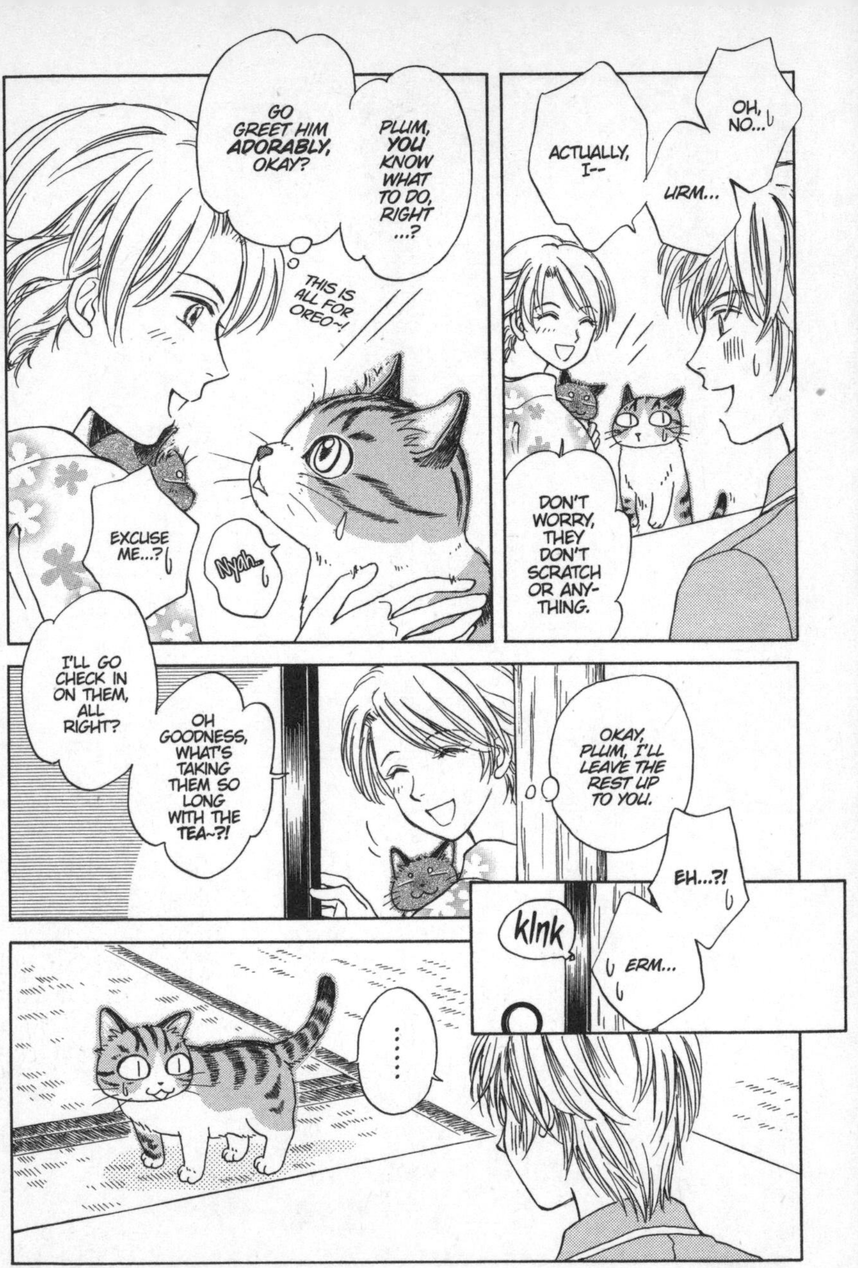

OH, NO...
ACTUALLY, I--
URM...
DON'T WORRY, THEY DON'T SCRATCH OR ANY-THING.
PLUM, YOU KNOW WHAT TO DO, RIGHT ...?
GO GREET HIM ADORABLY, OKAY?
THIS IS ALL FOR OREO~!
Nyah...
EXCUSE ME...?
OKAY, PLUM, I'LL LEAVE THE REST UP TO YOU.
OH GOODNESS, WHAT'S TAKING THEM SO LONG WITH THE TEA~?!
I'LL GO CHECK IN ON THEM, ALL RIGHT?
EH...?!
klnk
ERM...
......

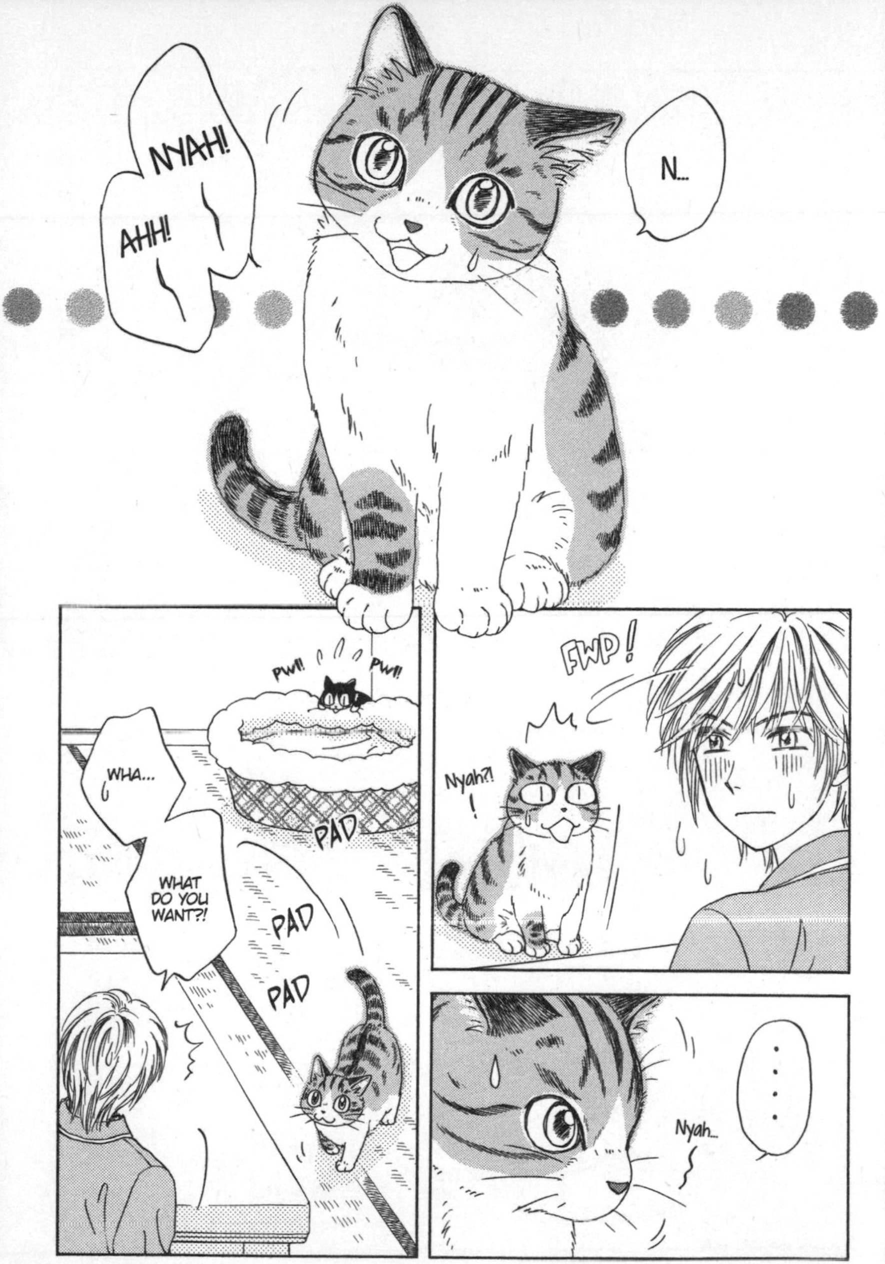
N...
NYAH! AHH!
FWP!
Nyah?!
....
Nyah...
PWI! PWI!
WHA...
PAD
WHAT DO YOU WANT?!
PAD
PAD

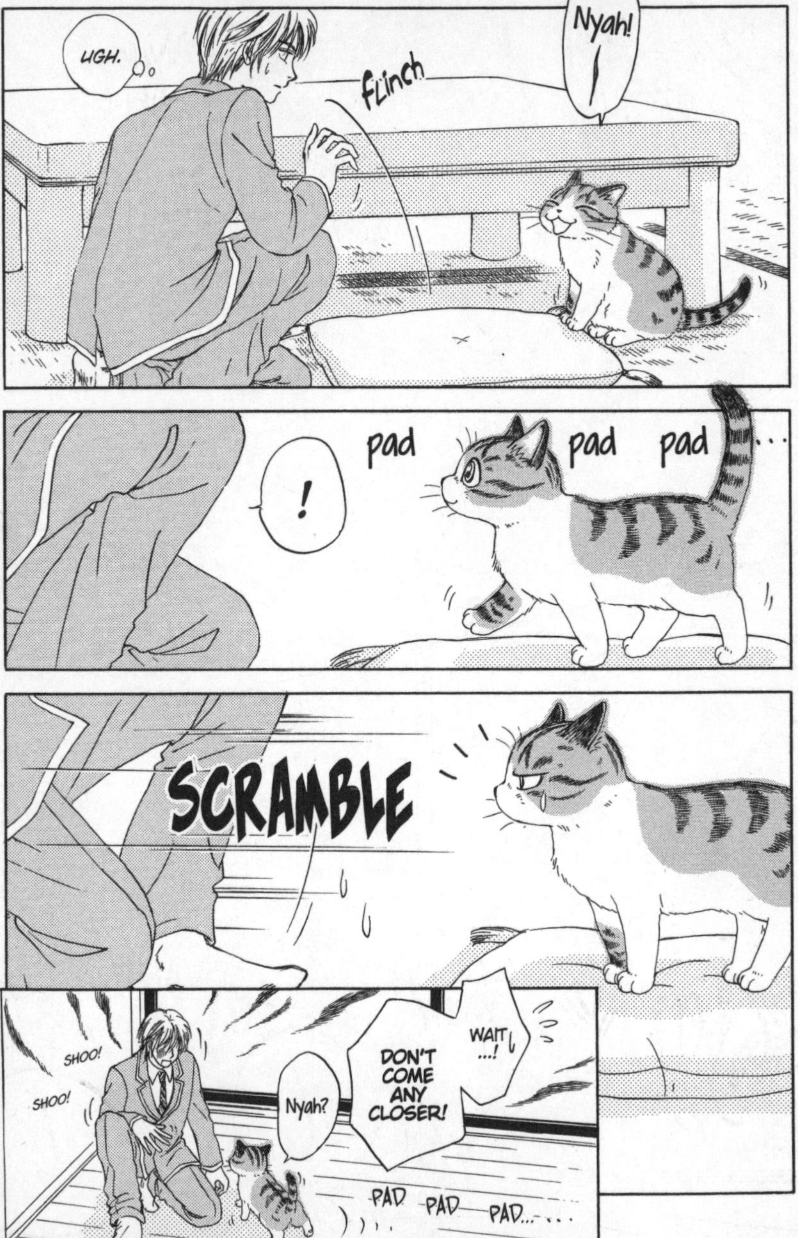
Nyah!
FLinch
UGH.
pad pad pad...
!
SCRAMBLE
WAIT ...!
DON'T COME ANY CLOSER!
Nyah?
SHOO!
SHOO!
PAD PAD PAD... ...

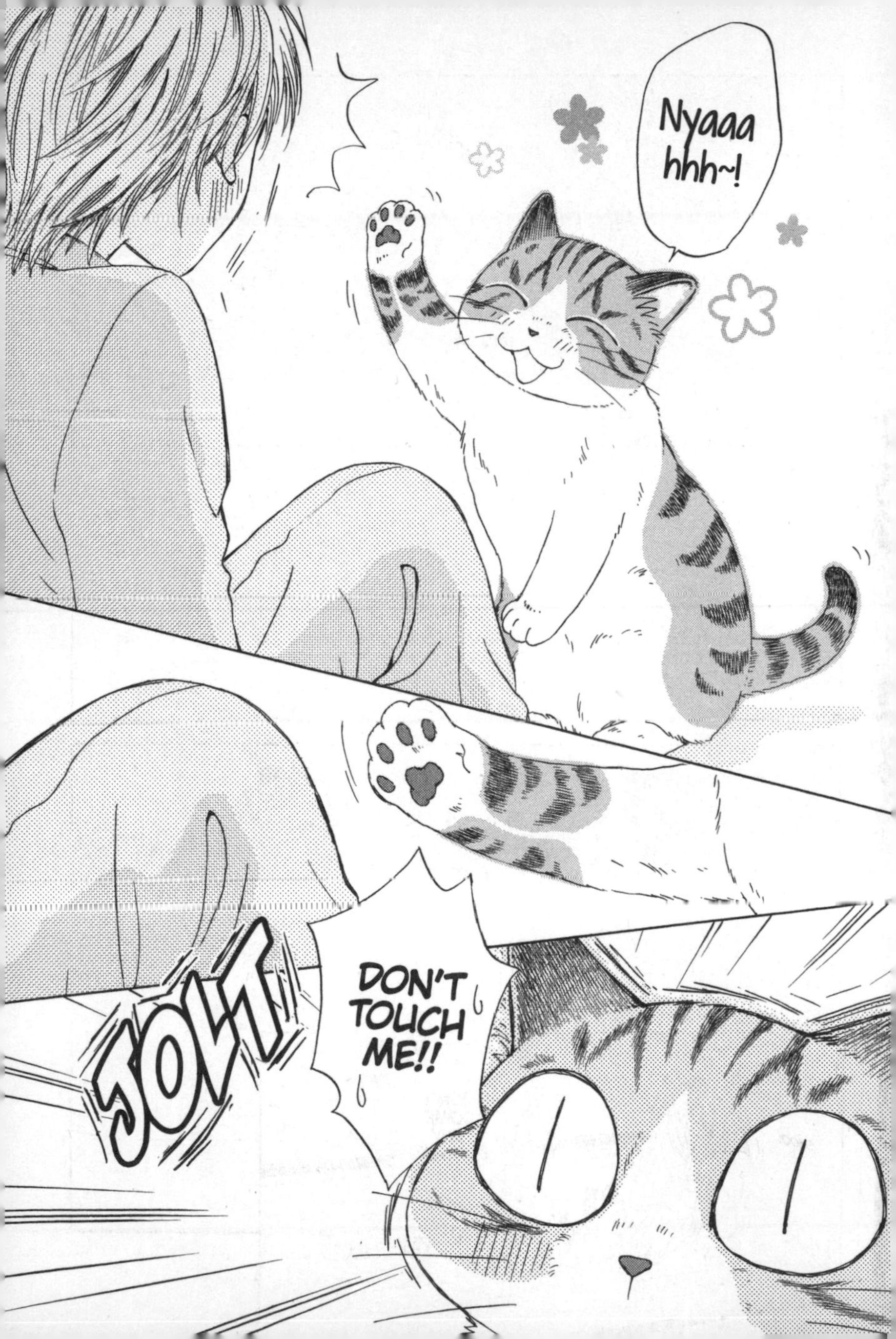
Nyaaa hhh~!
DON'T TOUCH ME!!
JOLT

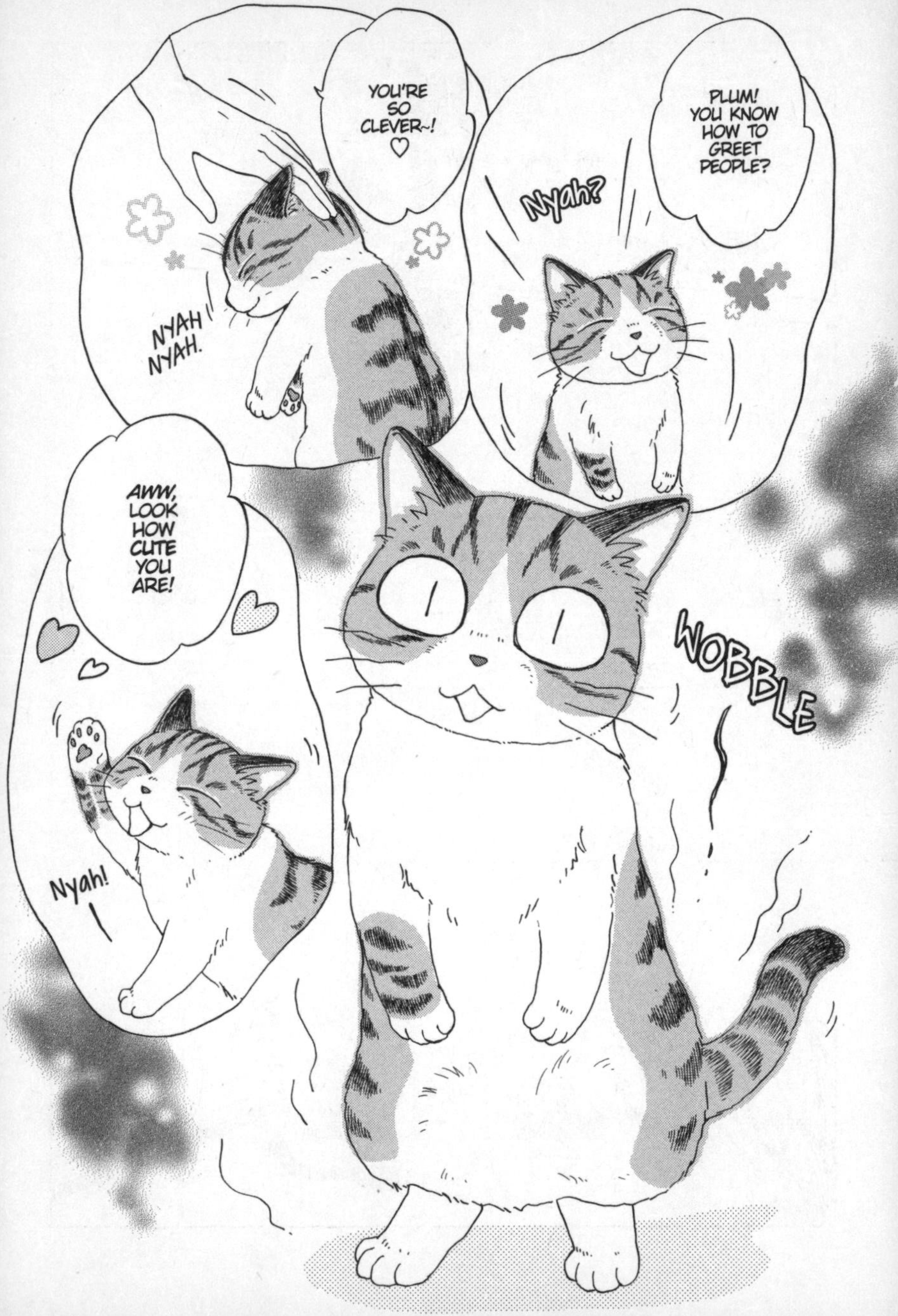
PLUM! YOU KNOW HOW TO GREET PEOPLE?
Nyah?
YOU'RE SO CLEVER~! ♡
NYAH NYAH.
AWW, LOOK HOW CUTE YOU ARE!
Nyah!
WOBBLE

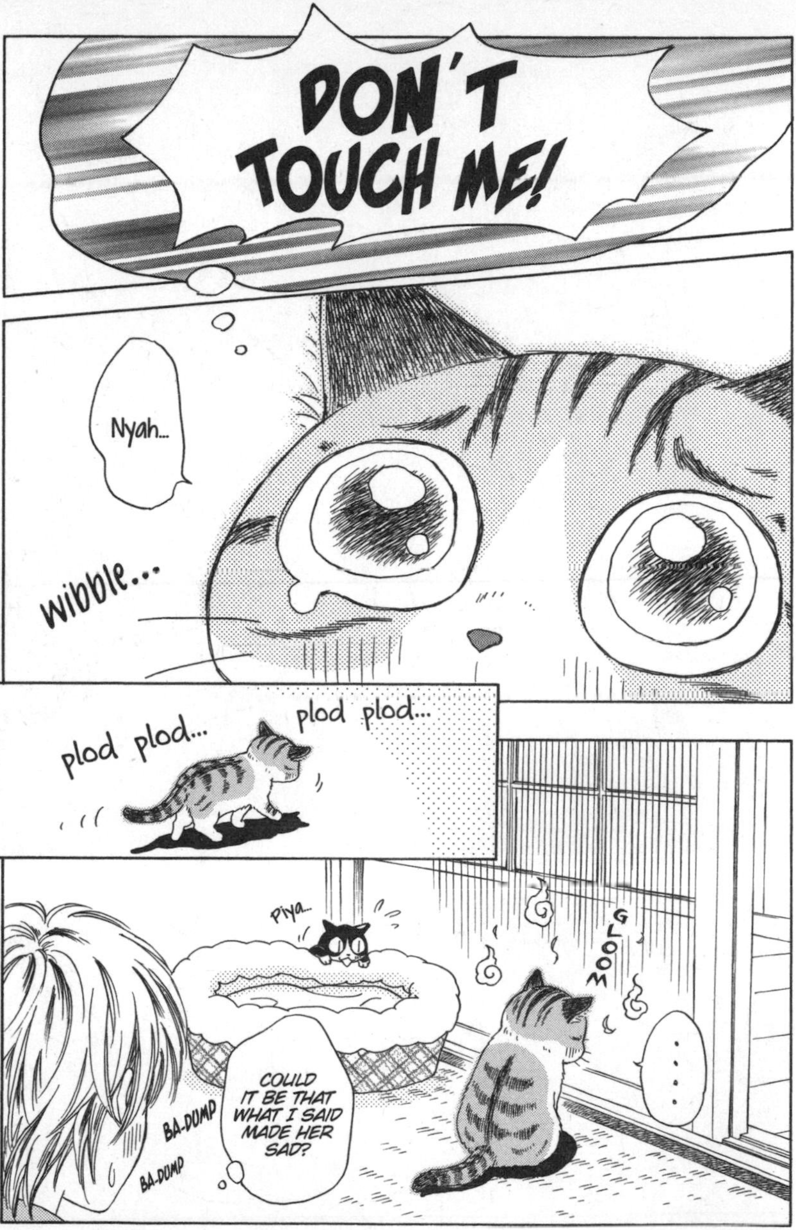
DON'T TOUCH ME!
Nyah...
wibble...
plod plod...
plod plod...
GLOOM
....
Piya...
COULD IT BE THAT WHAT I SAID MADE HER SAD?
BA-DUMP
BA-DUMP

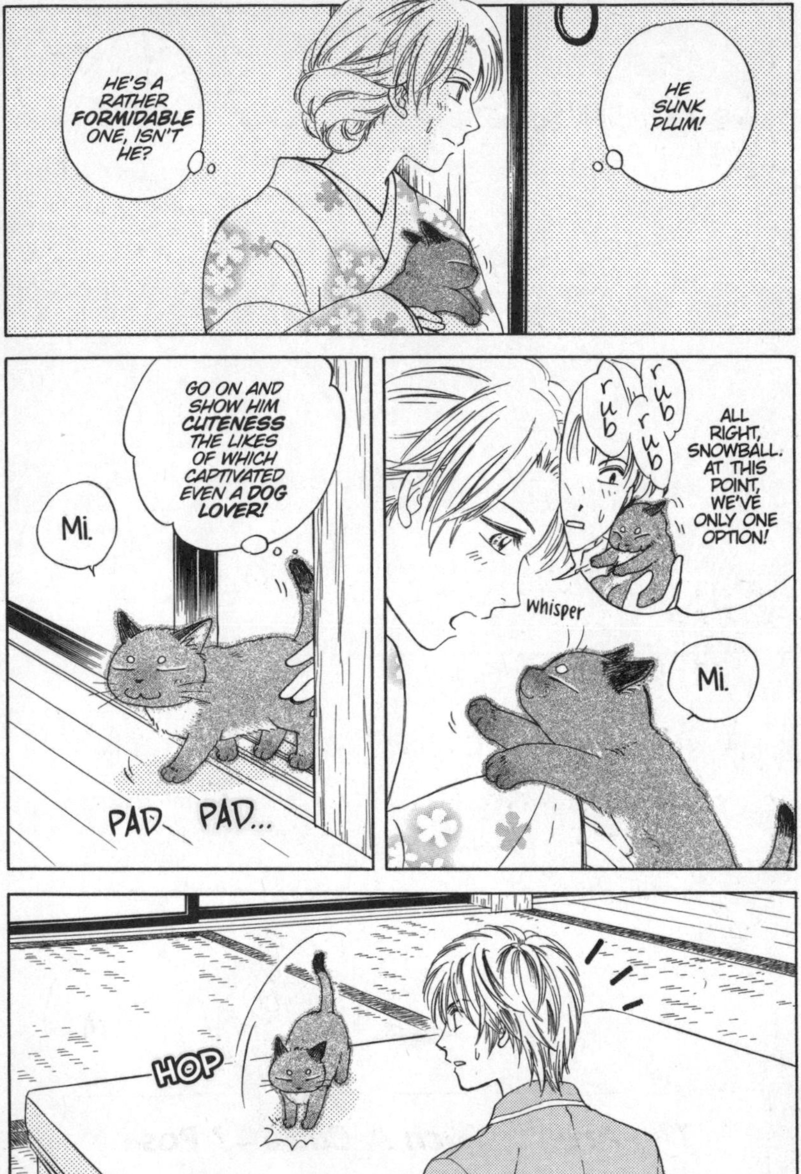
HE SUNK PLUM!
HE'S A RATHER FORMIDABLE ONE, ISN'T HE?
rub rub rub
ALL RIGHT, SNOWBALL. AT THIS POINT, WE'VE ONLY ONE OPTION!
whisper
Mi.
GO ON AND SHOW HIM CUTENESS THE LIKES OF WHICH CAPTIVATED EVEN A DOG LOVER!
Mi.
PAD PAD...
HOP

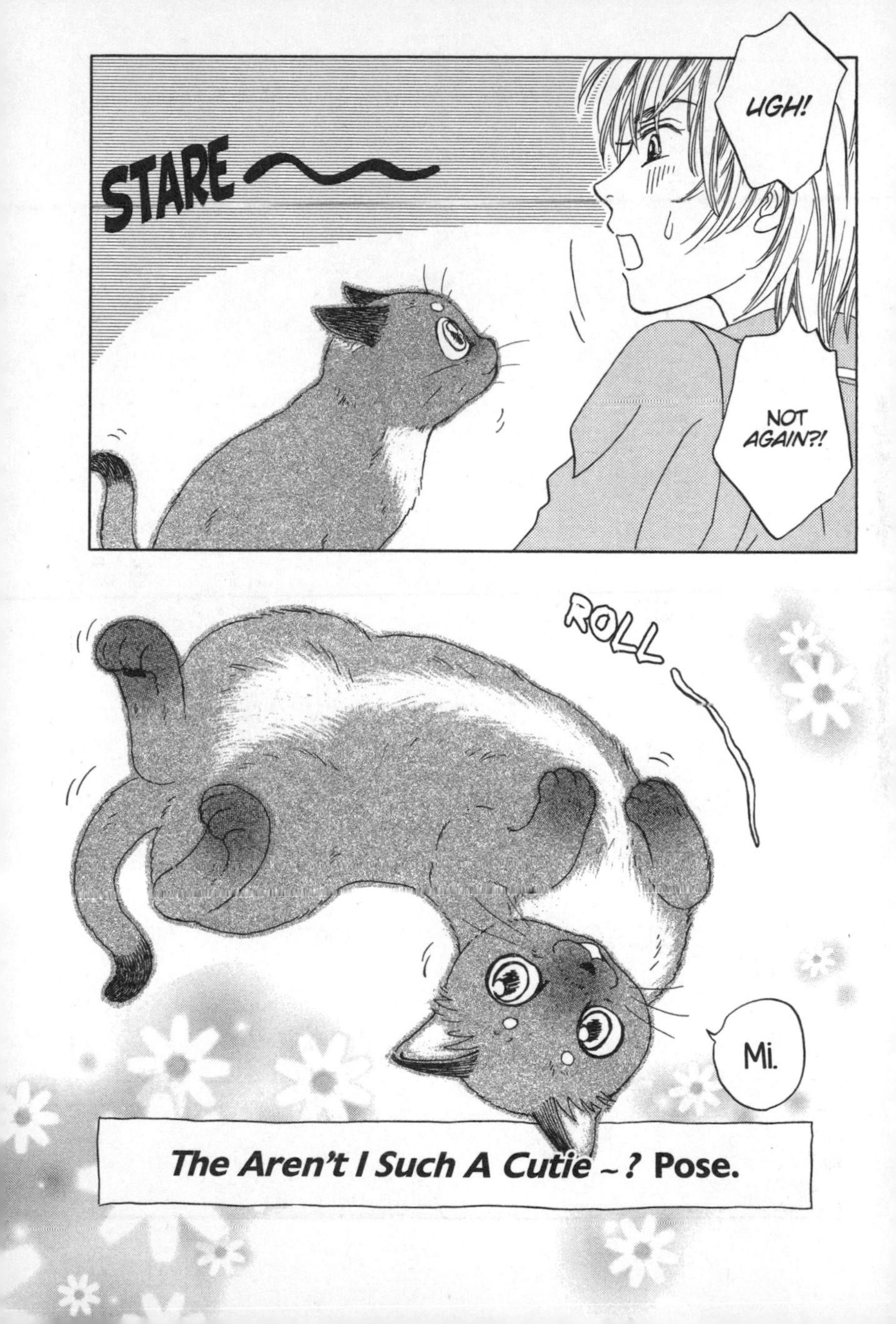
UGH!
NOT AGAIN?!
STARE~~
ROLL~
Mi.
The Aren't I Such A Cutie ~? Pose.

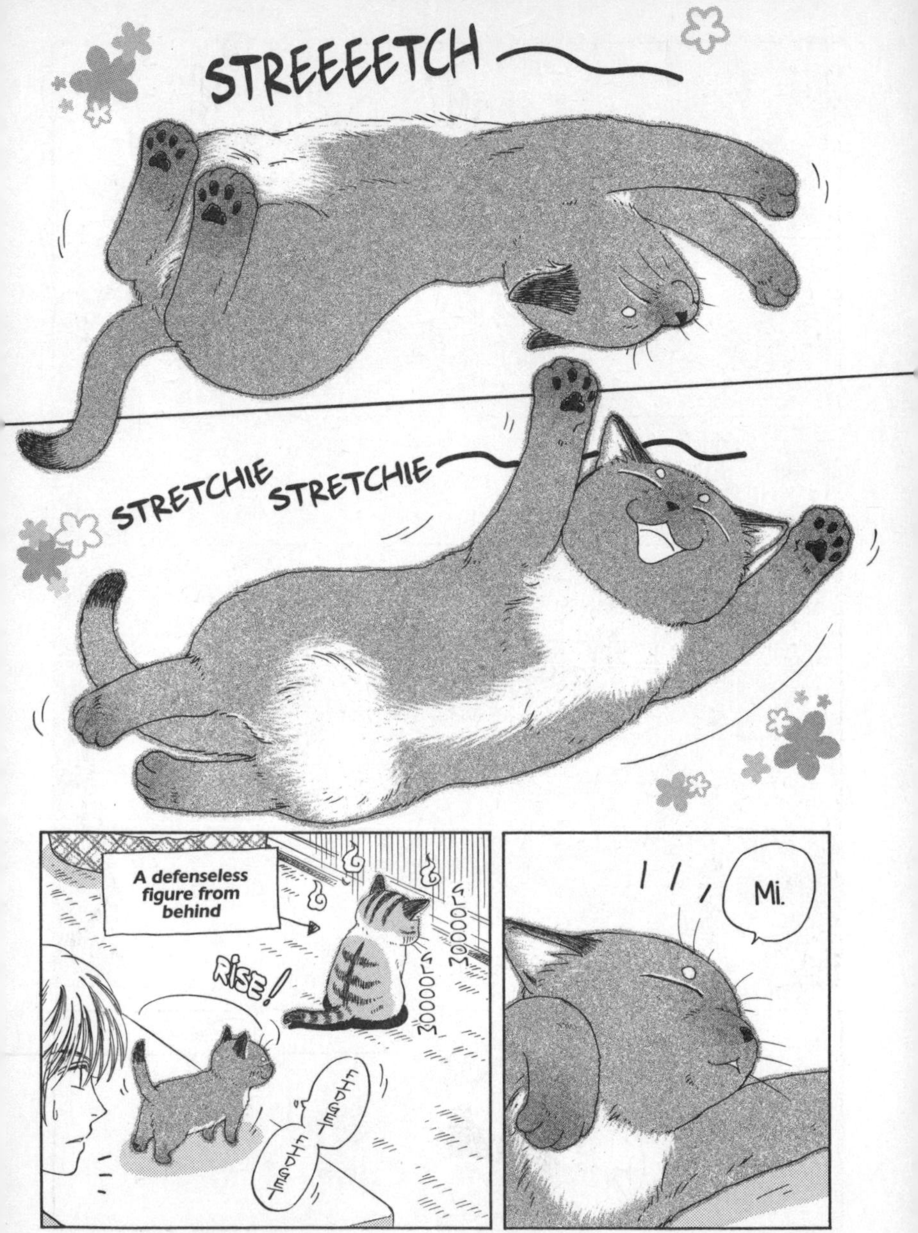
STREEEETCH
STRETCHIE STRETCHIE
Mi.
A defenseless figure from behind
GLOOOOOM
GLOOOOOM
RISE!
FIDGET FIDGET

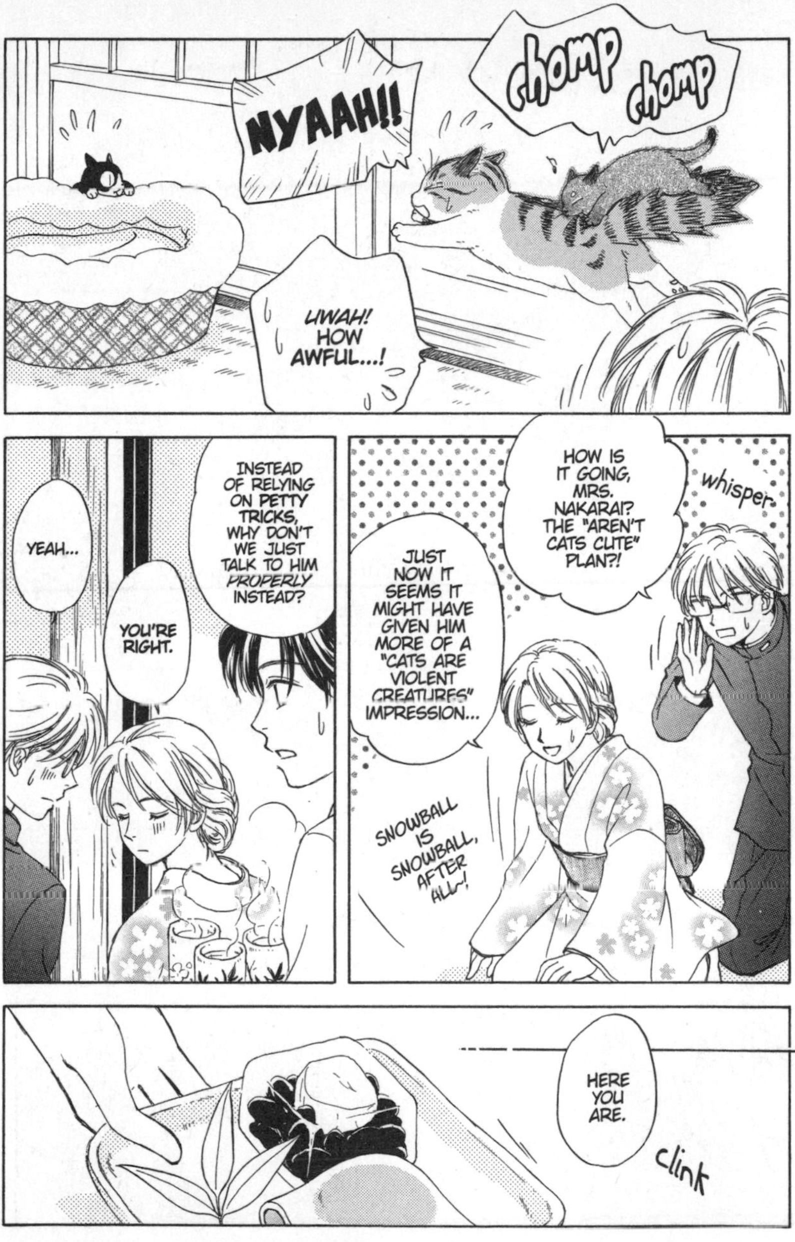
chomp chomp
NYAAH!!
UWAH! HOW AWFUL...!
whisper
HOW IS IT GOING, MRS. NAKARAI? THE "AREN'T CATS CUTE" PLAN?!
JUST NOW IT SEEMS IT MIGHT HAVE GIVEN HIM MORE OF A "CATS ARE VIOLENT CREATURES" IMPRESSION...
SNOWBALL IS SNOWBALL, AFTER ALL~!
INSTEAD OF RELYING ON PETTY TRICKS, WHY DON'T WE JUST TALK TO HIM PROPERLY INSTEAD?
YEAH...
YOU'RE RIGHT.
HERE YOU ARE.
clink

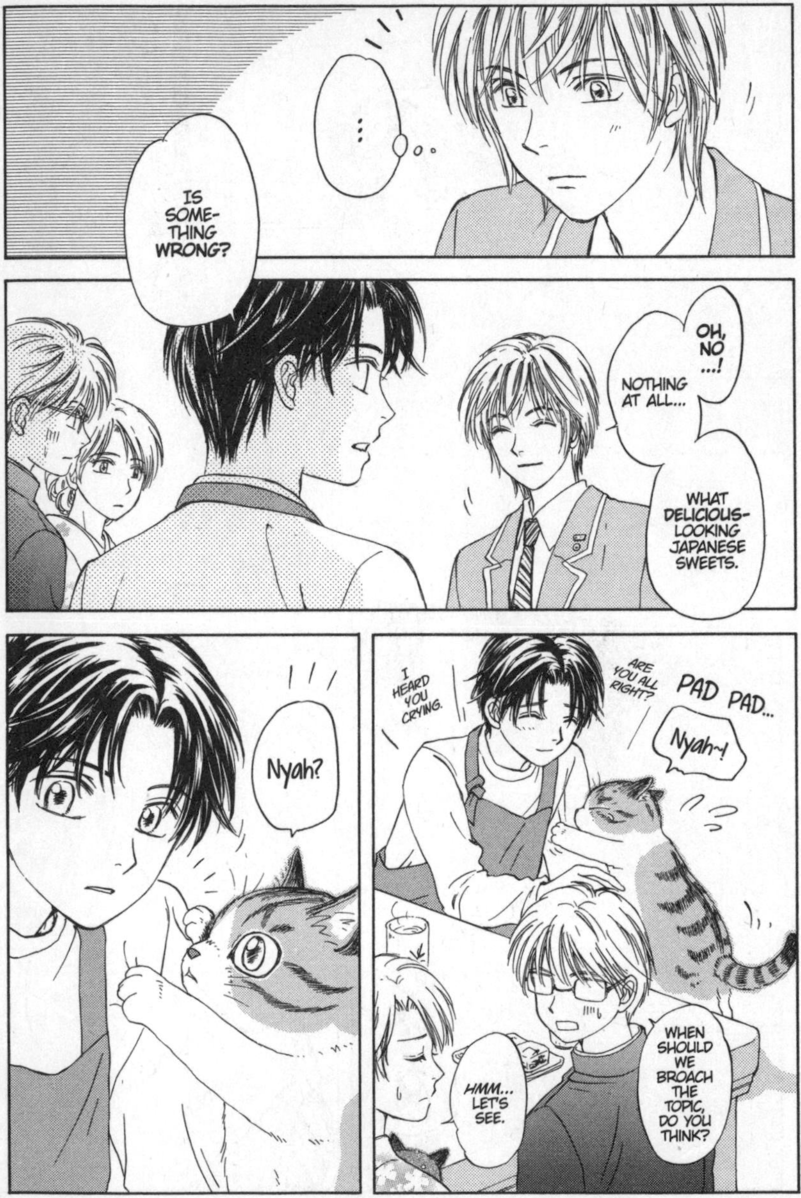
...
IS SOMETHING WRONG?
OH, NO ...! NOTHING AT ALL...
WHAT DELICIOUS-LOOKING JAPANESE SWEETS.
PAD PAD...
Nyah~!
ARE YOU ALL RIGHT?
I HEARD YOU CRYING.
WHEN SHOULD WE BROACH THE TOPIC, DO YOU THINK?
HMM... LET'S SEE.
Nyah?

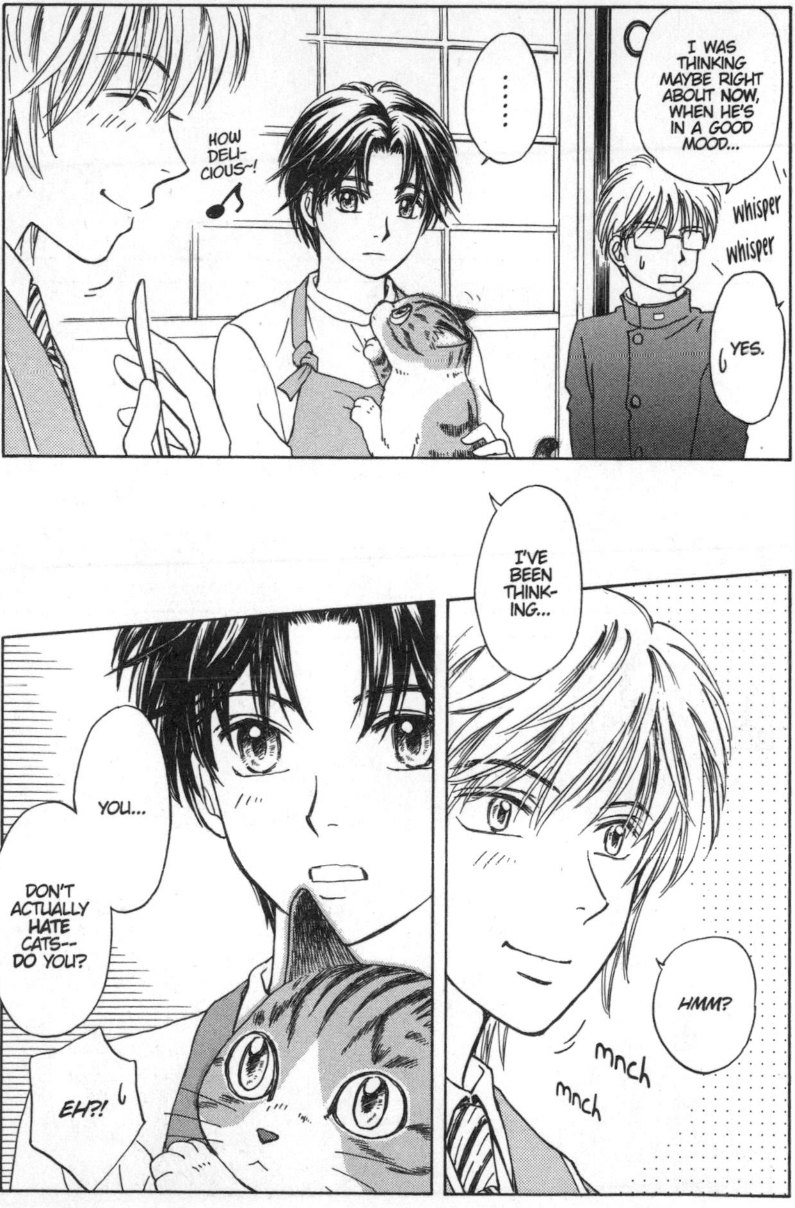
I WAS THINKING MAYBE RIGHT ABOUT NOW, WHEN HE'S IN A GOOD MOOD...
whisper
whisper
YES.
......
HOW DELICIOUS~!
I'VE BEEN THINKING...
HMM?
mnch
mnch
YOU...
DON'T ACTUALLY HATE CATS-- DO YOU?
EH?!

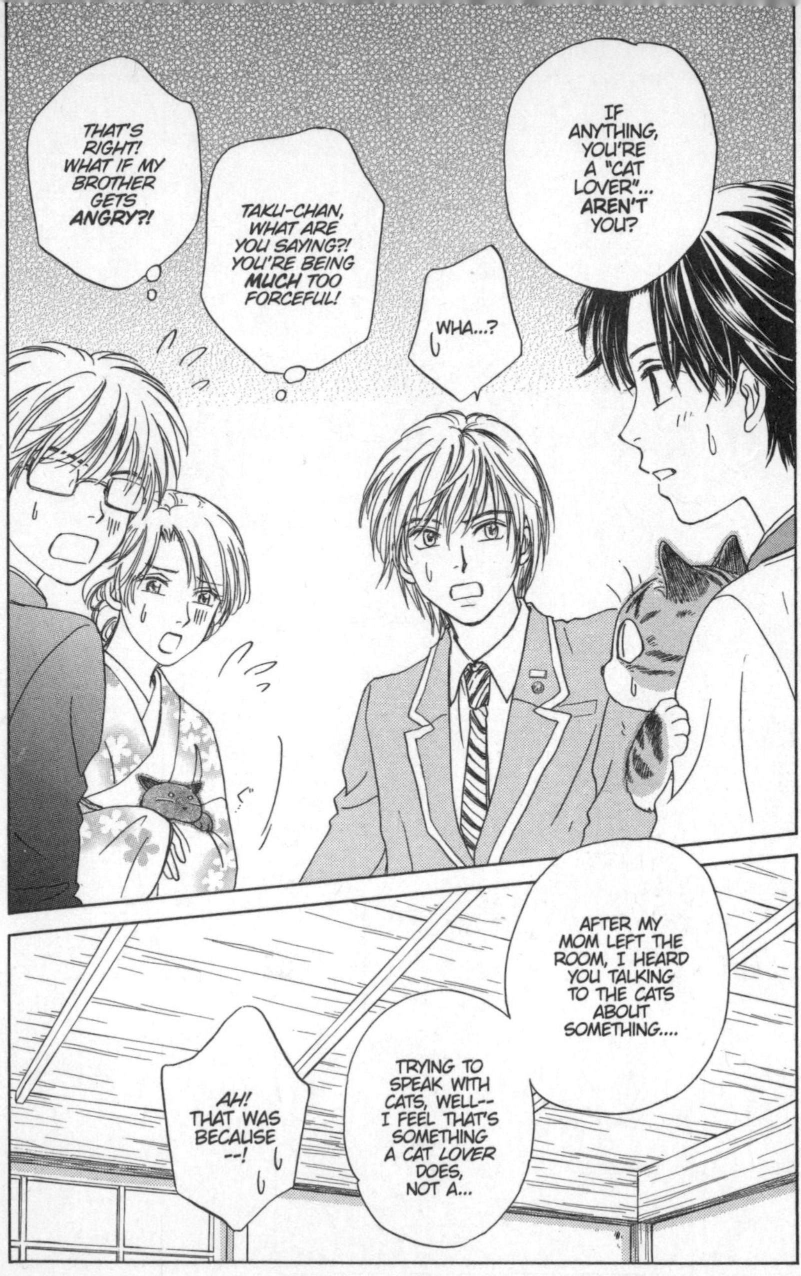
IF ANYTHING, YOU'RE A "CAT LOVER"... AREN'T YOU?
WHA...?
TAKU-CHAN, WHAT ARE YOU SAYING?! YOU'RE BEING *MUCH* TOO FORCEFUL!
THAT'S RIGHT! WHAT IF MY BROTHER GETS **ANGRY?!**
AFTER MY MOM LEFT THE ROOM, I HEARD YOU TALKING TO THE CATS ABOUT SOMETHING....
TRYING TO SPEAK WITH CATS, WELL-- I FEEL THAT'S SOMETHING A CAT *LOVER* DOES, NOT A...
AH! THAT WAS BECAUSE --!

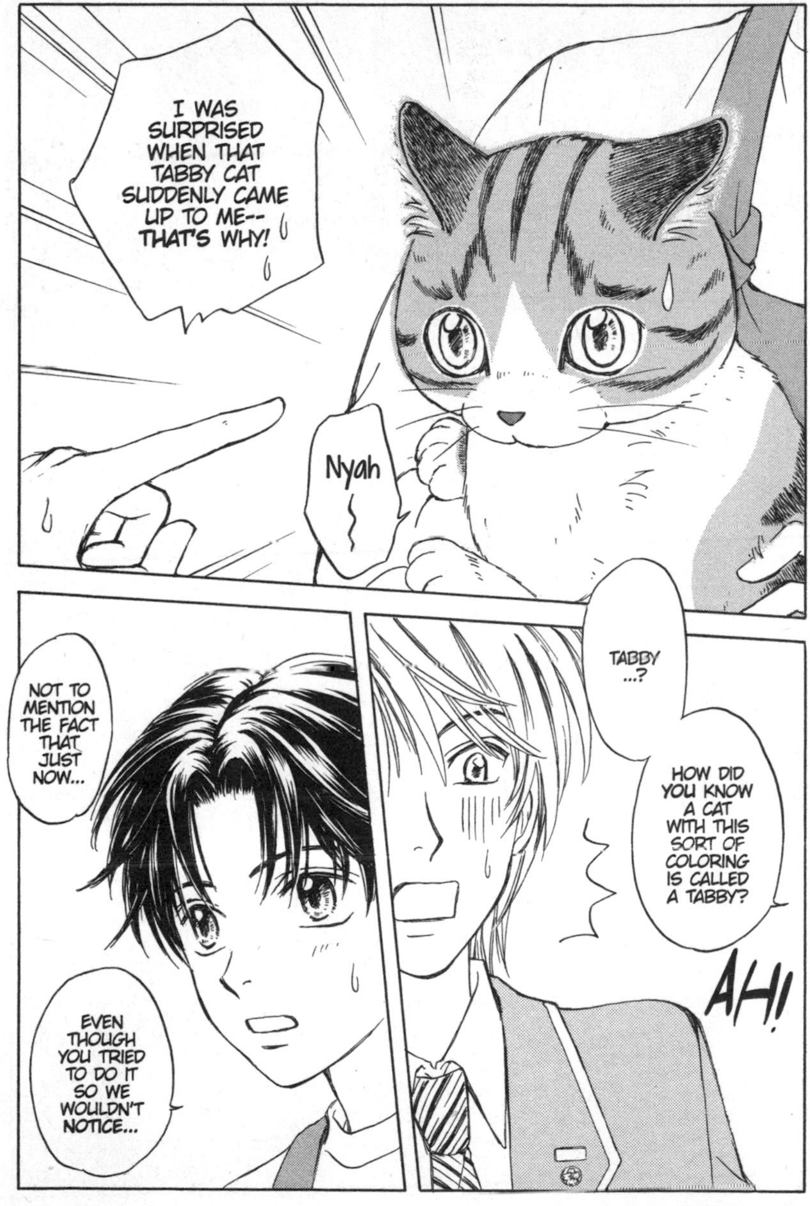
I WAS SURPRISED WHEN THAT TABBY CAT SUDDENLY CAME UP TO ME--THAT'S WHY!
Nyah
TABBY ...?
HOW DID YOU KNOW A CAT WITH THIS SORT OF COLORING IS CALLED A TABBY?
AH!
NOT TO MENTION THE FACT THAT JUST NOW...
EVEN THOUGH YOU TRIED TO DO IT SO WE WOULDN'T NOTICE...

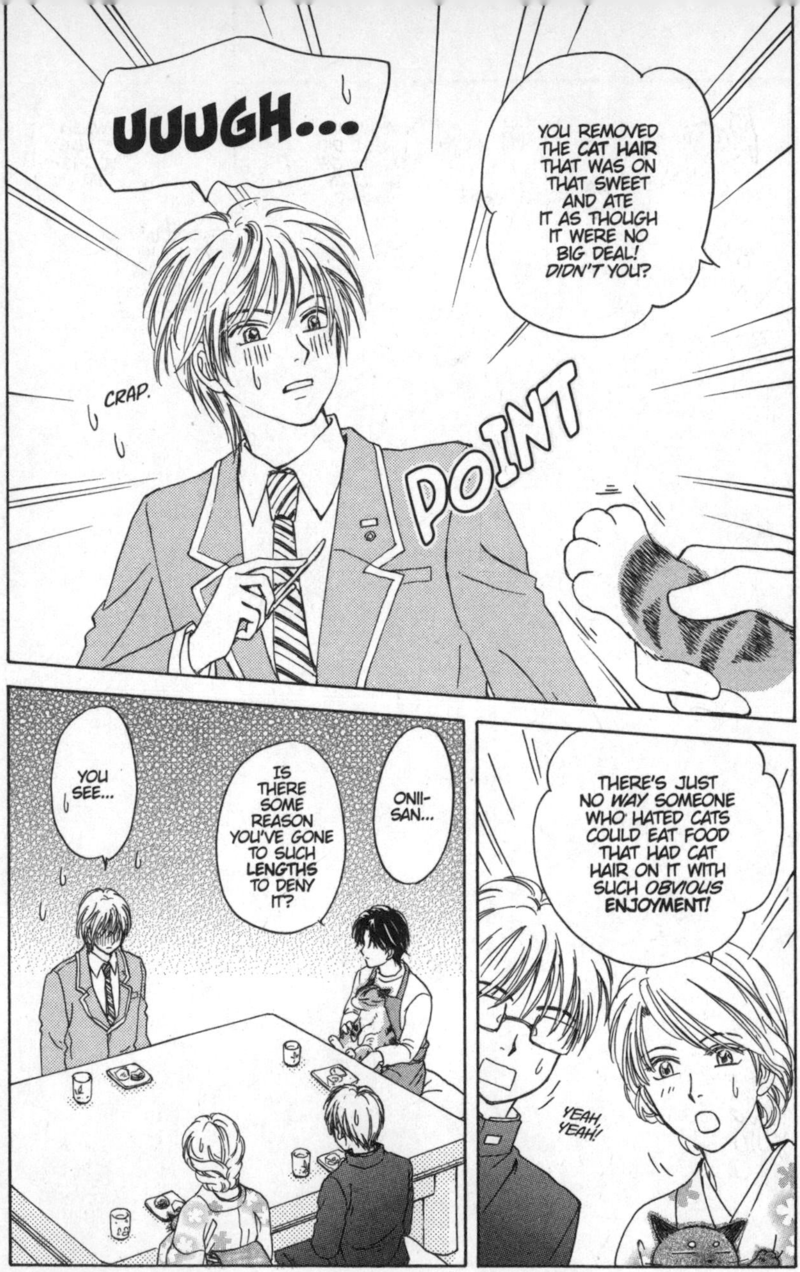
YOU REMOVED THE CAT HAIR THAT WAS ON THAT SWEET AND ATE IT AS THOUGH IT WERE NO BIG DEAL! DIDN'T YOU?
UUUGH...
POINT
CRAP.
THERE'S JUST NO WAY SOMEONE WHO HATED CATS COULD EAT FOOD THAT HAD CAT HAIR ON IT WITH SUCH OBVIOUS ENJOYMENT!
YEAH, YEAH!
ONII-SAN...
IS THERE SOME REASON YOU'VE GONE TO SUCH LENGTHS TO DENY IT?
YOU SEE...

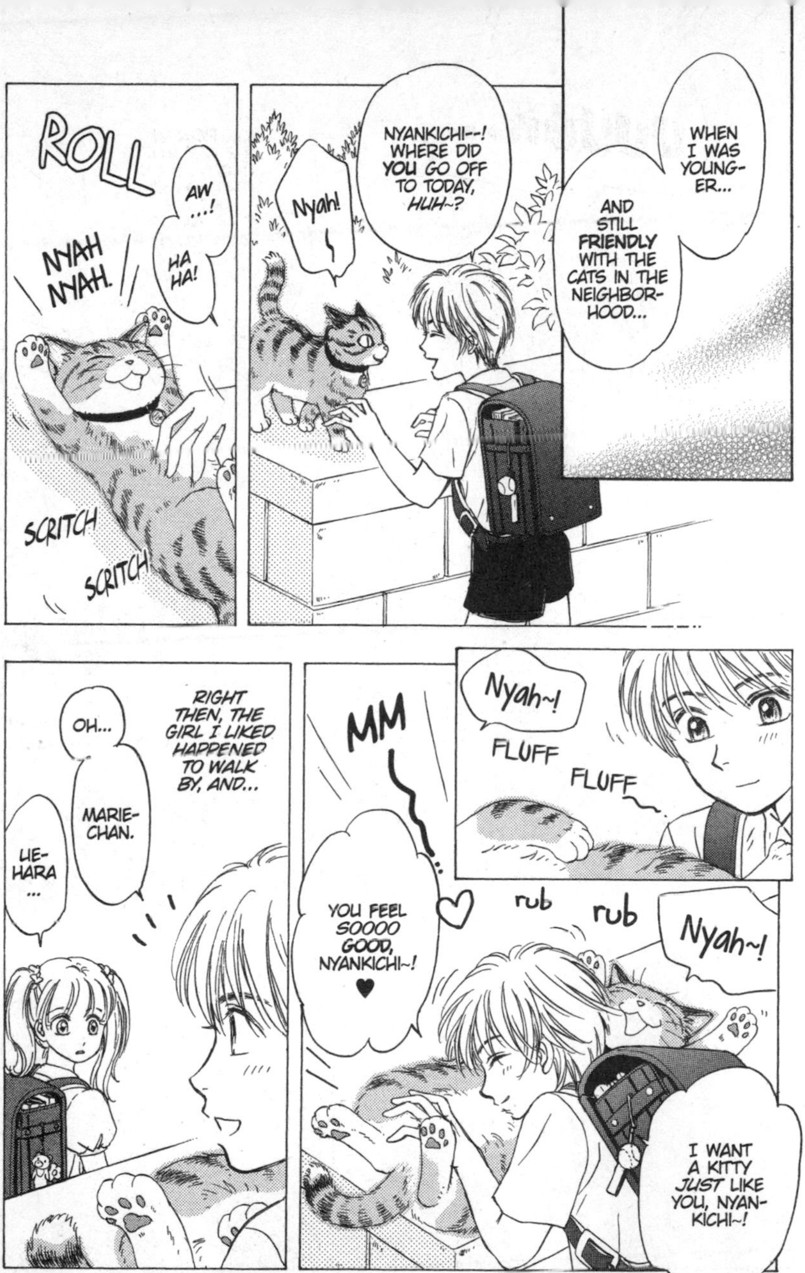
WHEN I WAS YOUNGER...
AND STILL FRIENDLY WITH THE CATS IN THE NEIGHBORHOOD...
NYANKICHI--! WHERE DID YOU GO OFF TO TODAY, HUH~?
Nyah!
ROLL
AW...! HA HA!
NYAH NYAH.
SCRITCH SCRITCH
Nyah~!
FLUFF FLUFF
MM
YOU FEEL SOOOO GOOD, NYANKICHI~! ♥
rub rub
Nyah~!
I WANT A KITTY JUST LIKE YOU, NYANKICHI~!
RIGHT THEN, THE GIRL I LIKED HAPPENED TO WALK BY, AND...
OH...
MARIE-CHAN.
UEHARA...

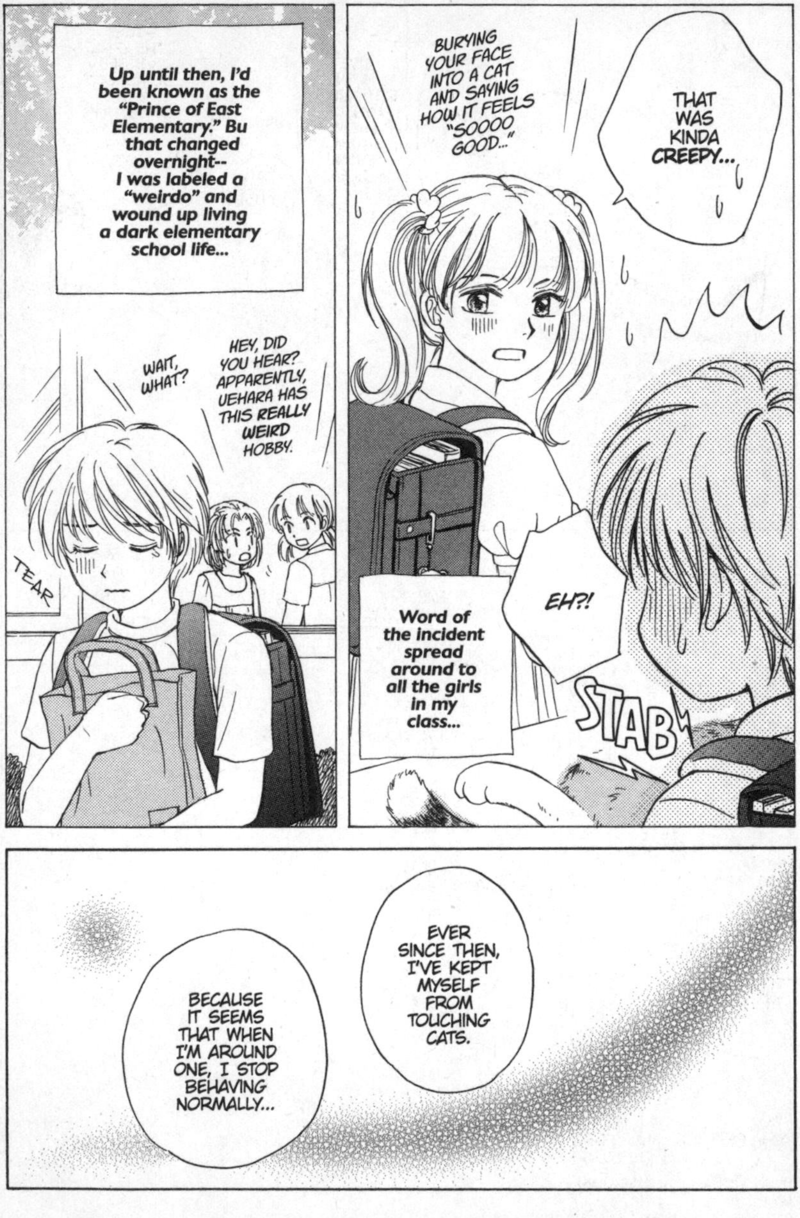

BURYING YOUR FACE INTO A CAT AND SAYING HOW IT FEELS "SOOOO GOOD..."
THAT WAS KINDA CREEPY...
EH?!
STAB
Word of the incident spread around to all the girls in my class...
Up until then, I'd been known as the "Prince of East Elementary." Bu that changed overnight-- I was labeled a "weirdo" and wound up living a dark elementary school life...
HEY, DID YOU HEAR? APPARENTLY, UEHARA HAS THIS REALLY WEIRD HOBBY.
WAIT, WHAT?
TEAR
EVER SINCE THEN, I'VE KEPT MYSELF FROM TOUCHING CATS.
BECAUSE IT SEEMS THAT WHEN I'M AROUND ONE, I STOP BEHAVING NORMALLY...

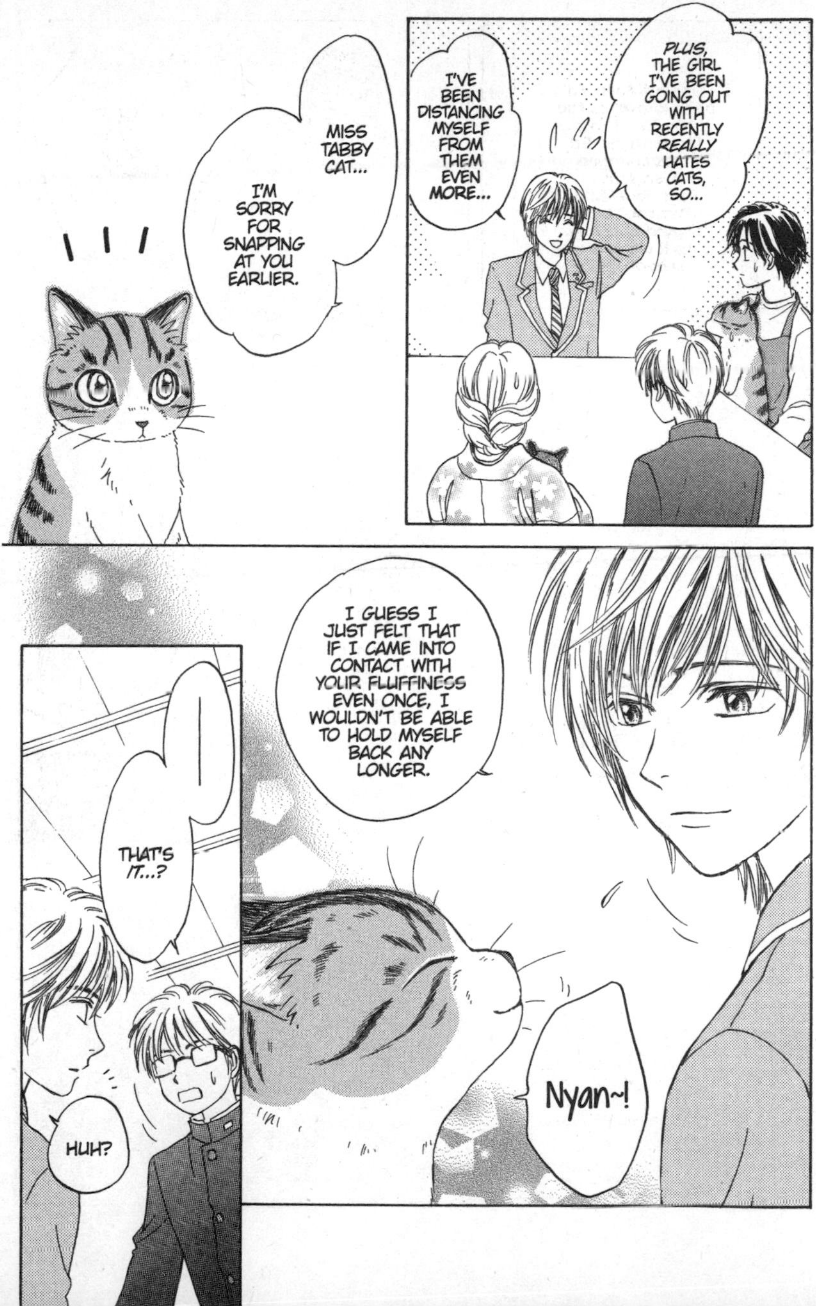
PLUS, THE GIRL I'VE BEEN GOING OUT WITH RECENTLY REALLY HATES CATS, SO...
I'VE BEEN DISTANCING MYSELF FROM THEM EVEN MORE...
MISS TABBY CAT...
I'M SORRY FOR SNAPPING AT YOU EARLIER.
I GUESS I JUST FELT THAT IF I CAME INTO CONTACT WITH YOUR FLUFFINESS EVEN ONCE, I WOULDN'T BE ABLE TO HOLD MYSELF BACK ANY LONGER.
Nyan~!
THAT'S IT...?
HUH?

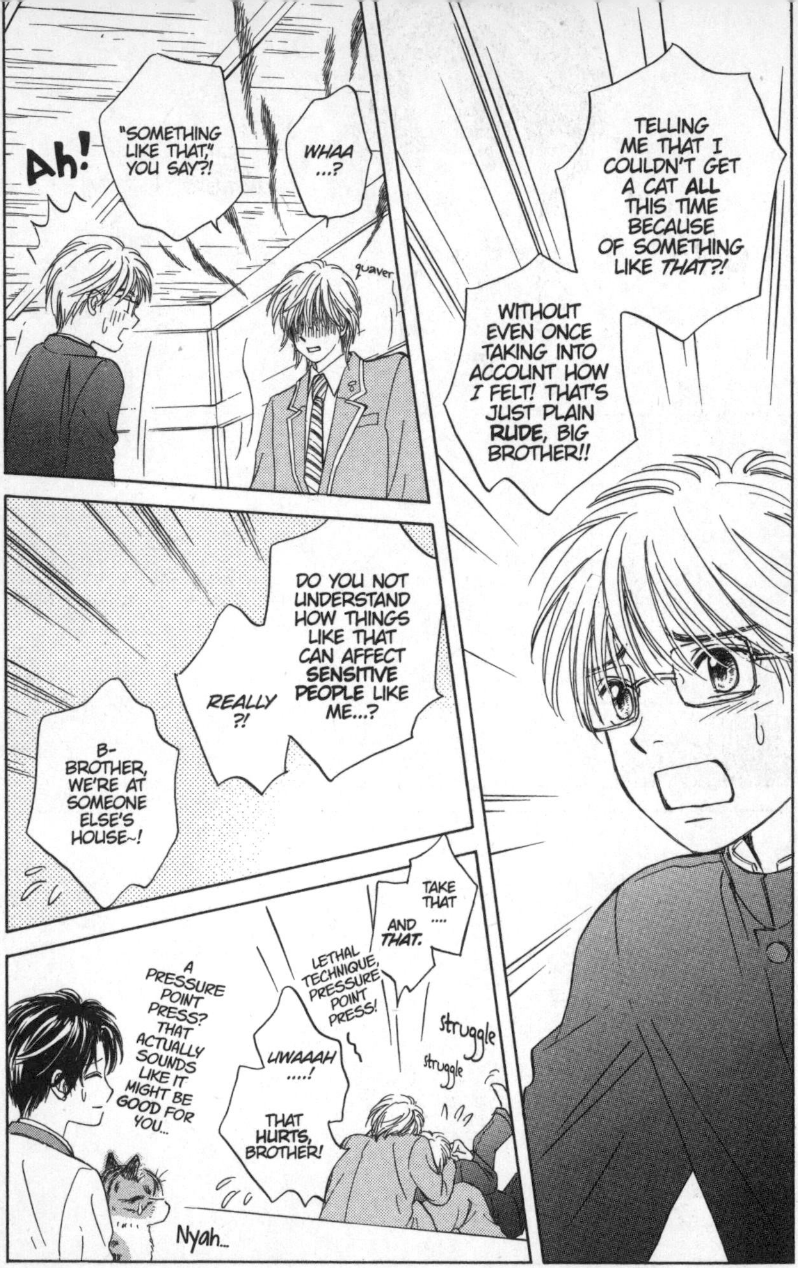
TELLING ME THAT I COULDN'T GET A CAT ALL THIS TIME BECAUSE OF SOMETHING LIKE THAT?!
WITHOUT EVEN ONCE TAKING INTO ACCOUNT HOW I FELT! THAT'S JUST PLAIN RUDE, BIG BROTHER!!
WHAA ...?
quaver
"SOMETHING LIKE THAT," YOU SAY?!
Ah!
DO YOU NOT UNDERSTAND HOW THINGS LIKE THAT CAN AFFECT SENSITIVE PEOPLE LIKE ME...?
REALLY ?!
B-BROTHER, WE'RE AT SOMEONE ELSE'S HOUSE~!
TAKE THAT ....
AND THAT.
LETHAL TECHNIQUE, PRESSURE POINT PRESS!
struggle
struggle
UWAAAH ....!
THAT HURTS, BROTHER!
A PRESSURE POINT PRESS? THAT ACTUALLY SOUNDS LIKE IT MIGHT BE GOOD FOR YOU...
Nyah...

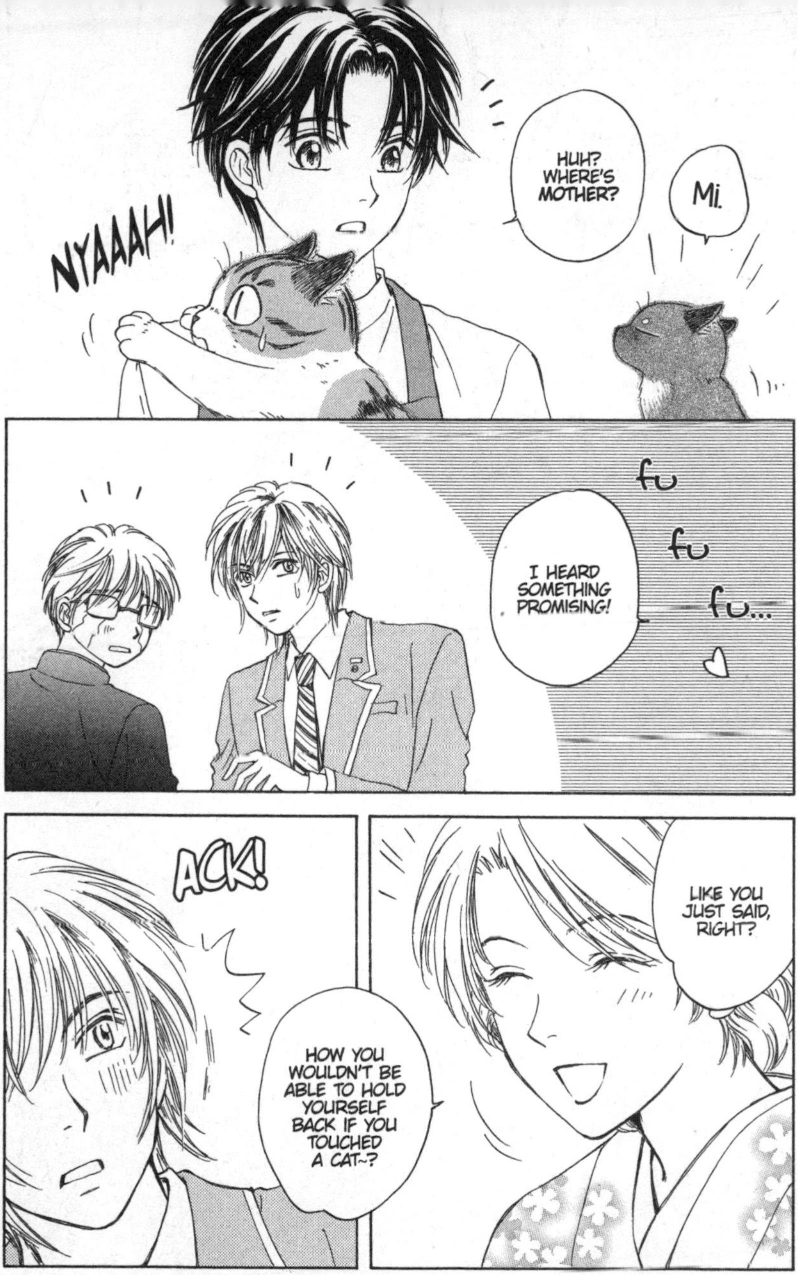
HUH? WHERE'S MOTHER?
Mi.
NYAAAH!
fu fu fu...
I HEARD SOMETHING PROMISING!
LIKE YOU JUST SAID, RIGHT?
HOW YOU WOULDN'T BE ABLE TO HOLD YOURSELF BACK IF YOU TOUCHED A CAT~?
ACK!

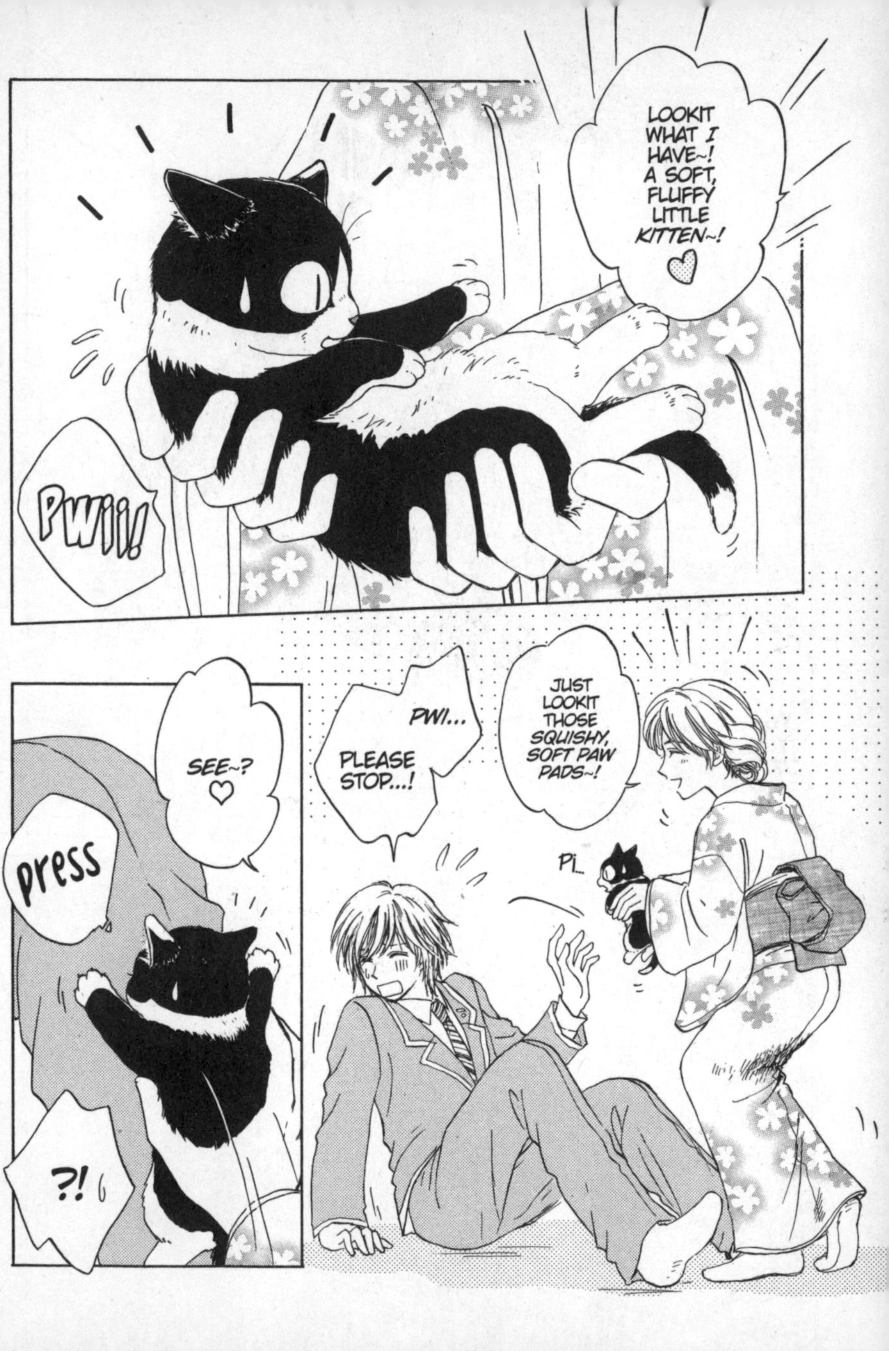
LOOKIT WHAT I HAVE~! A SOFT, FLUFFY LITTLE KITTEN~! ♡
Pwii!
JUST LOOKIT THOSE SQUISHY, SOFT PAW PADS~!
PWI... PLEASE STOP...!
Pi..
SEE~? ♡
press
?!

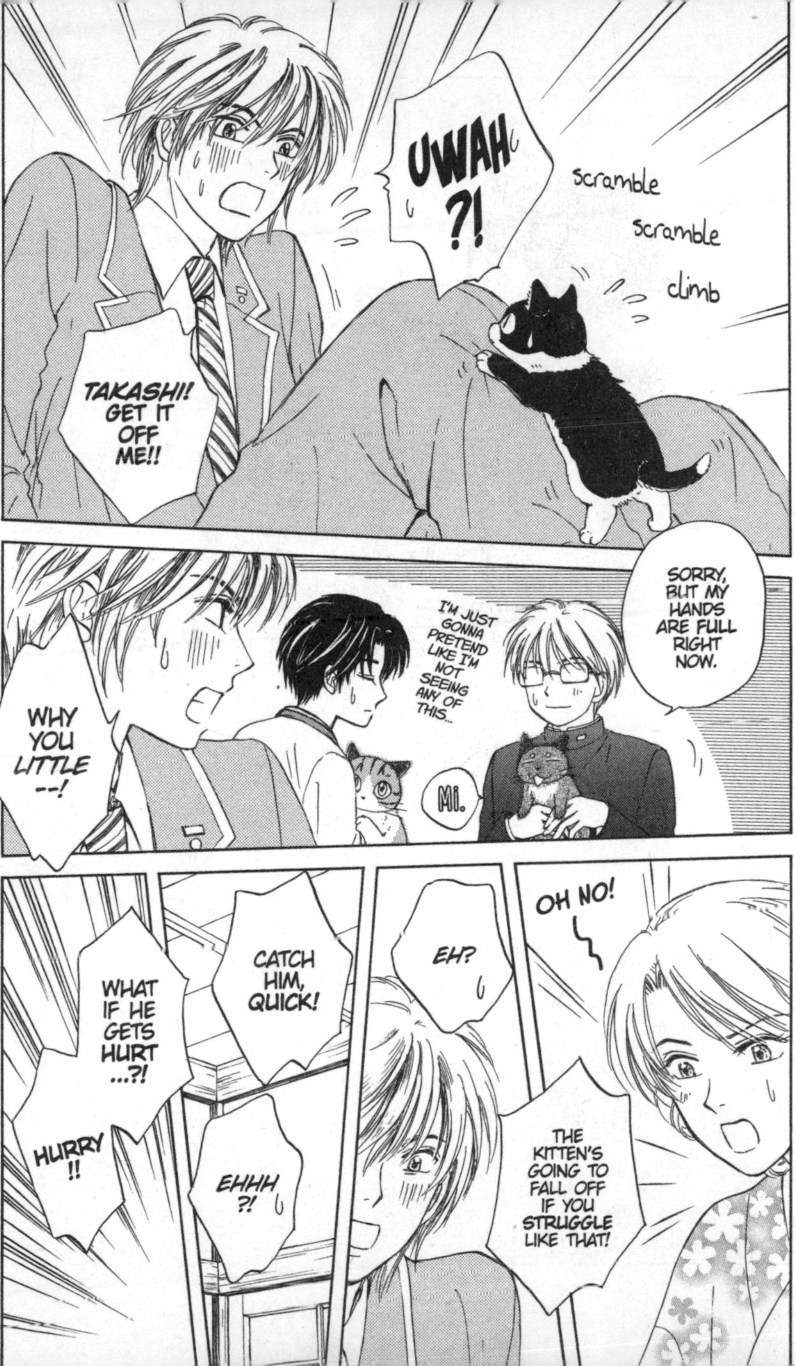
UWAH ?!
scramble
scramble
climb
TAKASHI! GET IT OFF ME!!
SORRY, BUT MY HANDS ARE FULL RIGHT NOW.
I'M JUST GONNA PRETEND LIKE I'M NOT SEEING ANY OF THIS...
Mi.
WHY YOU LITTLE --!
OH NO!
THE KITTEN'S GOING TO FALL OFF IF YOU STRUGGLE LIKE THAT!
EH?
EHHH ?!
CATCH HIM, QUICK!
WHAT IF HE GETS HURT ...?!
HURRY !!

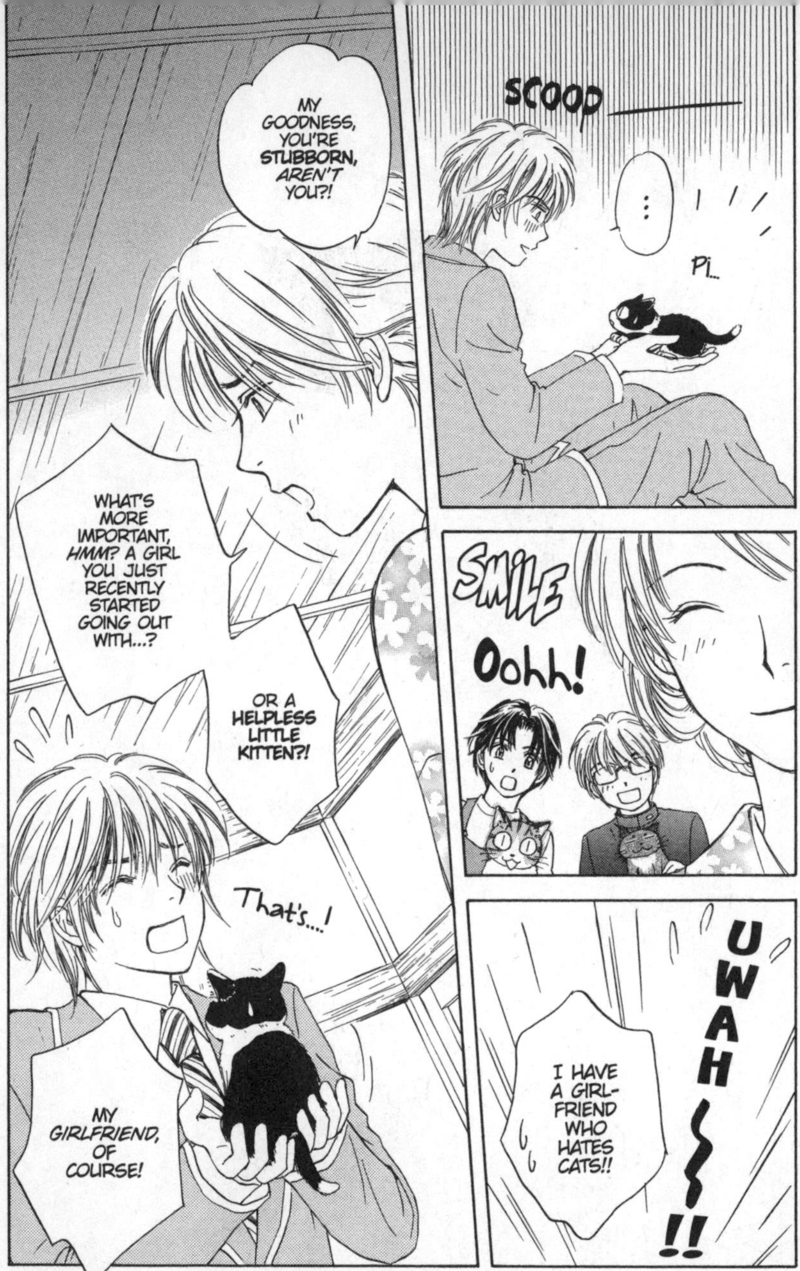
SCOOP
...
Pi...
SMILE
Oohh!
UWAH~!!
I HAVE A GIRL-FRIEND WHO HATES CATS!!
MY GOODNESS, YOU'RE STUBBORN, AREN'T YOU?!
WHAT'S MORE IMPORTANT, HMM? A GIRL YOU JUST RECENTLY STARTED GOING OUT WITH...?
OR A HELPLESS LITTLE KITTEN?!
That's...!
MY GIRLFRIEND, OF COURSE!

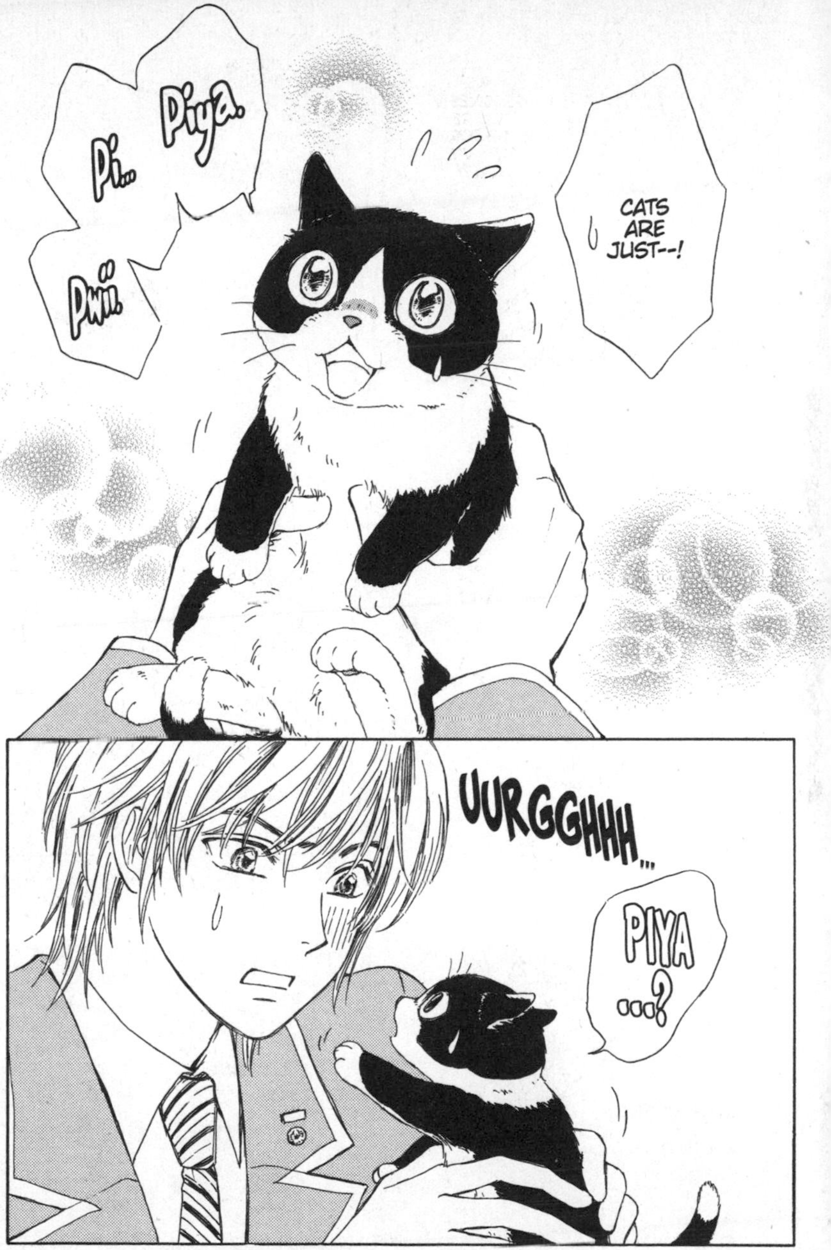
CATS ARE JUST--!
Pi... Piya.
Pwii.
UURGGHHH...
PIYA ...?

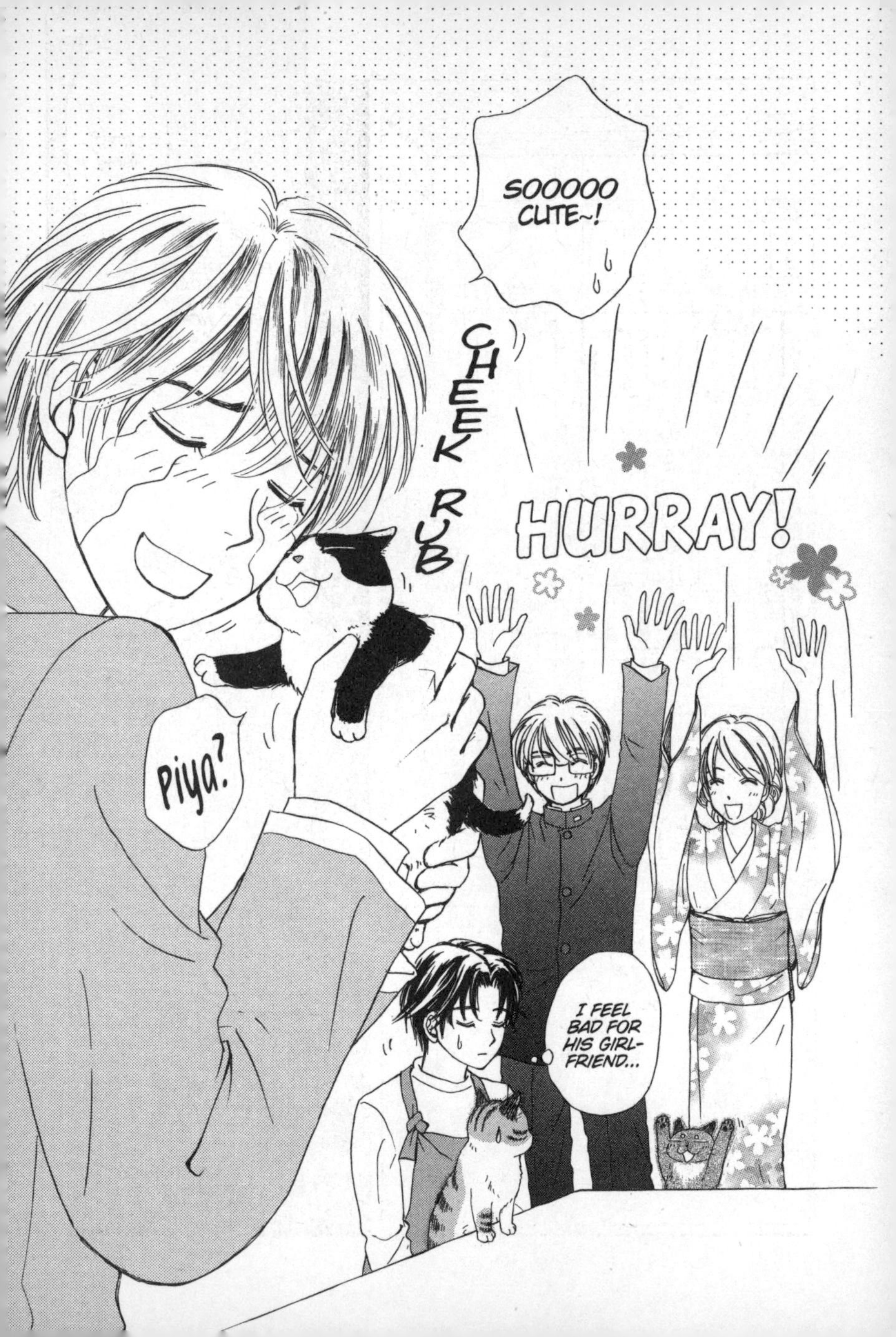
SOOOOO CUTE~!
HURRAY!
CHEEK RUB
Piya?
I FEEL BAD FOR HIS GIRL-FRIEND...

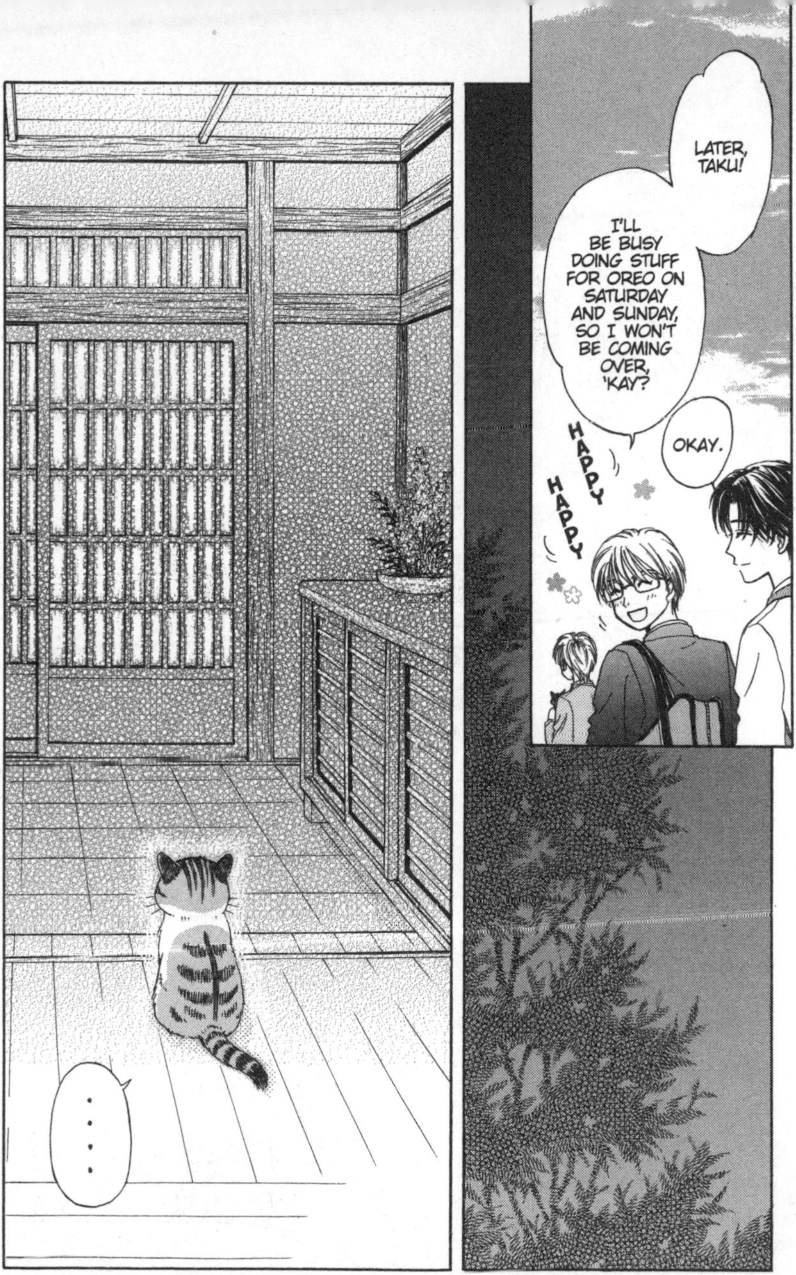
LATER, TAKU!
I'LL BE BUSY DOING STUFF FOR OREO ON SATURDAY AND SUNDAY, SO I WON'T BE COMING OVER, 'KAY?
HAPPY HAPPY
OKAY.
....

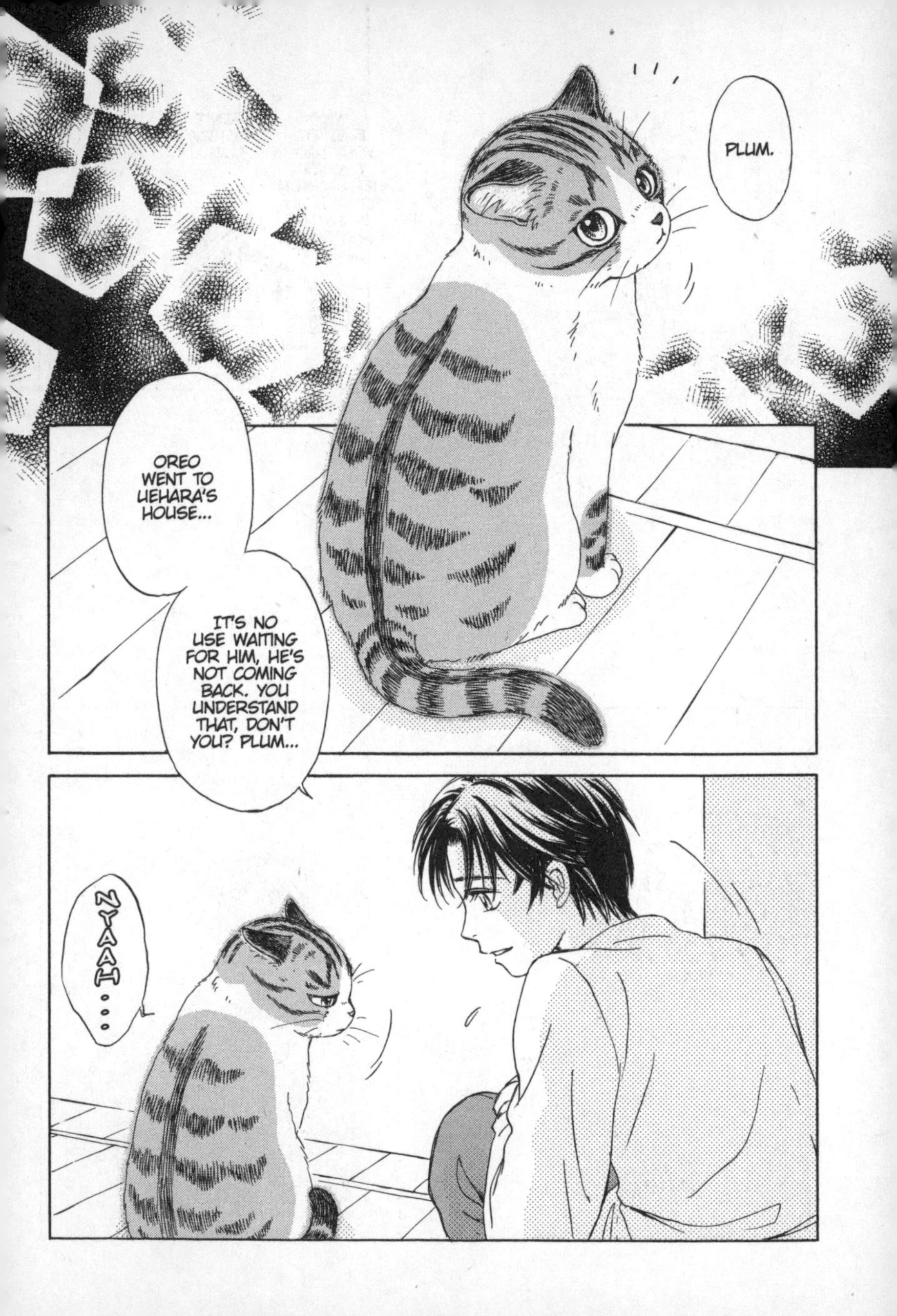
PLUM.
OREO WENT TO UEHARA'S HOUSE...
IT'S NO USE WAITING FOR HIM, HE'S NOT COMING BACK. YOU UNDERSTAND THAT, DON'T YOU? PLUM...
NYAAH...

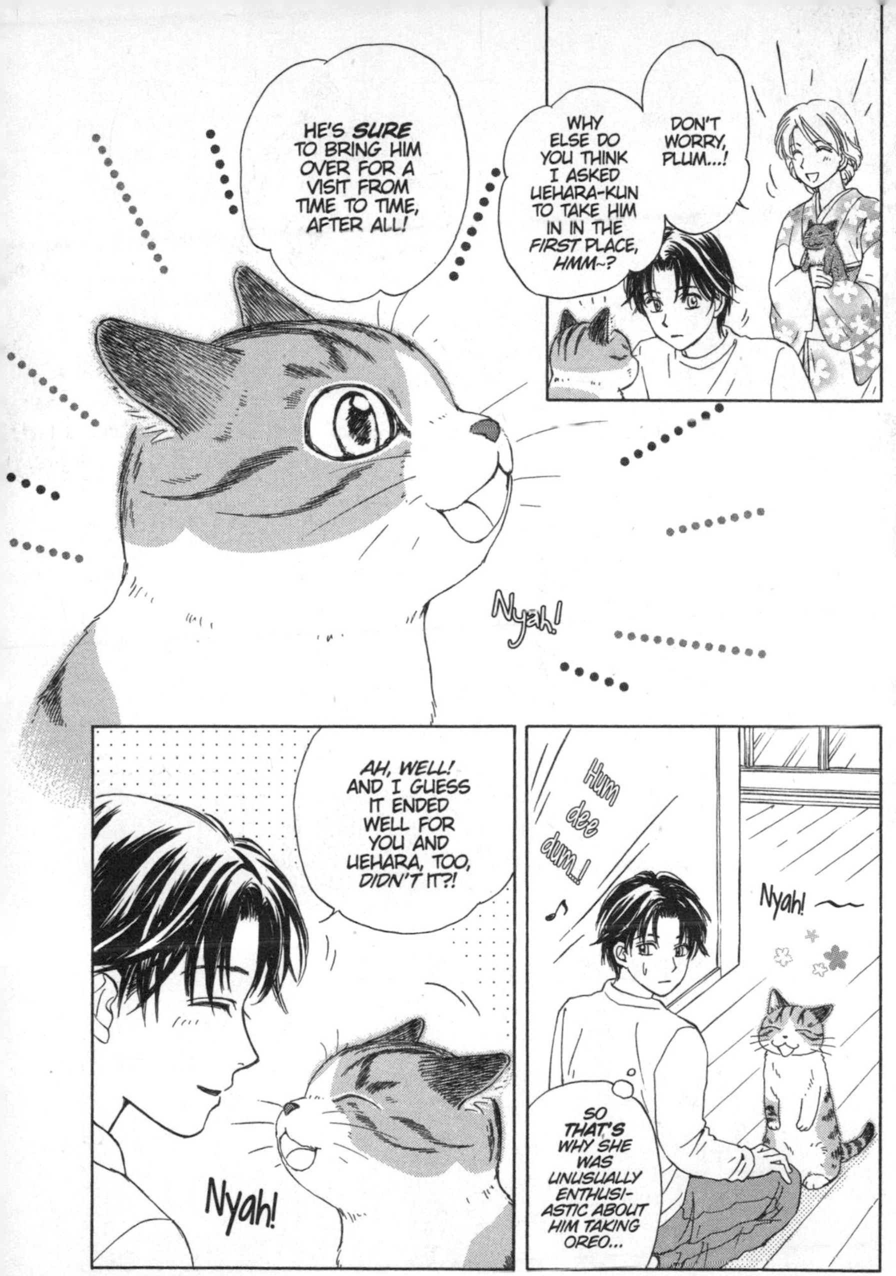
DON'T WORRY, PLUM...!
WHY ELSE DO YOU THINK I ASKED UEHARA-KUN TO TAKE HIM IN IN THE *FIRST* PLACE, HMM~?
HE'S ***SURE*** TO BRING HIM OVER FOR A VISIT FROM TIME TO TIME, AFTER ALL!
Nyah!
Hum dee dum...!
Nyah! ~
SO ***THAT'S*** WHY SHE WAS UNUSUALLY ENTHUSI-ASTIC ABOUT HIM TAKING OREO...
AH, WELL! AND I GUESS IT ENDED WELL FOR YOU AND UEHARA, TOO, *DIDN'T* IT?!
Nyah!

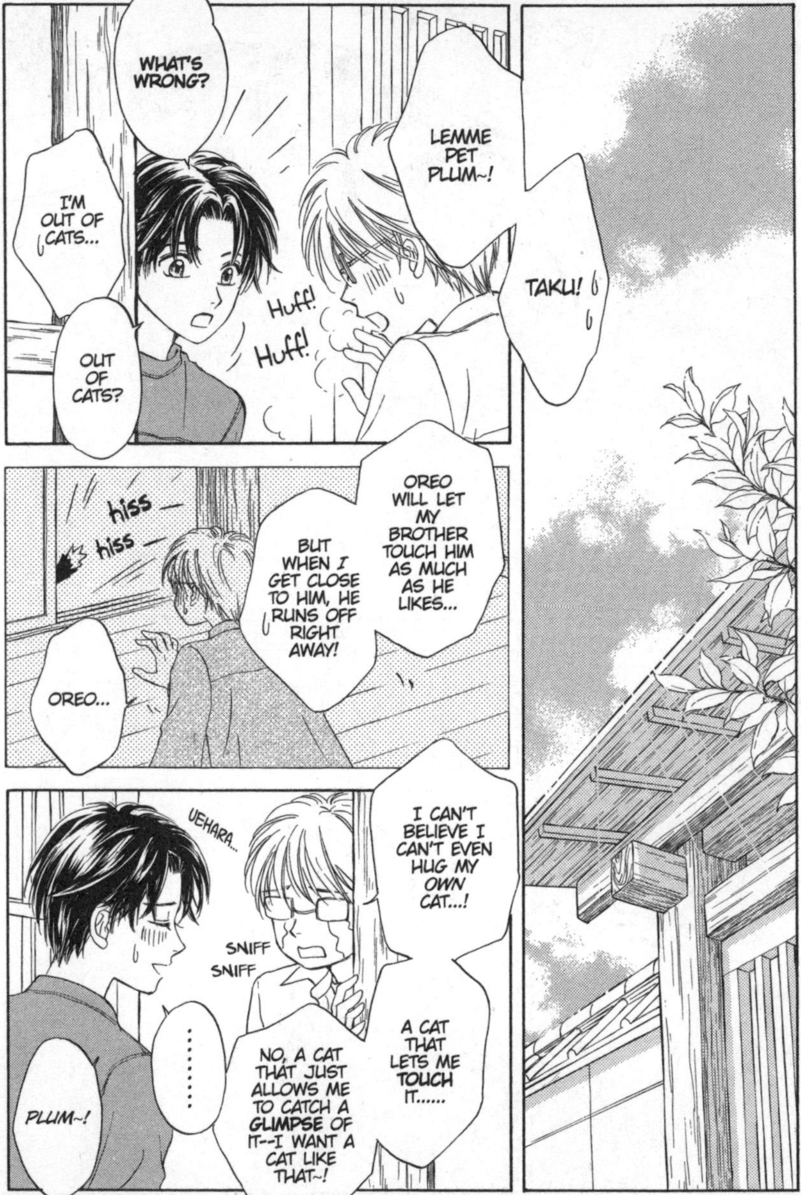
LEMME PET PLUM~!
TAKU!
WHAT'S WRONG?
Huff!
Huff!
I'M OUT OF CATS...
OUT OF CATS?
hiss
hiss
OREO WILL LET MY BROTHER TOUCH HIM AS MUCH AS HE LIKES...
BUT WHEN I GET CLOSE TO HIM, HE RUNS OFF RIGHT AWAY!
OREO...
UEHARA...
I CAN'T BELIEVE I CAN'T EVEN HUG MY OWN CAT...!
SNIFF
SNIFF
A CAT THAT LETS ME TOUCH IT......
NO, A CAT THAT JUST ALLOWS ME TO CATCH A GLIMPSE OF IT--I WANT A CAT LIKE THAT~!
......
PLUM~!

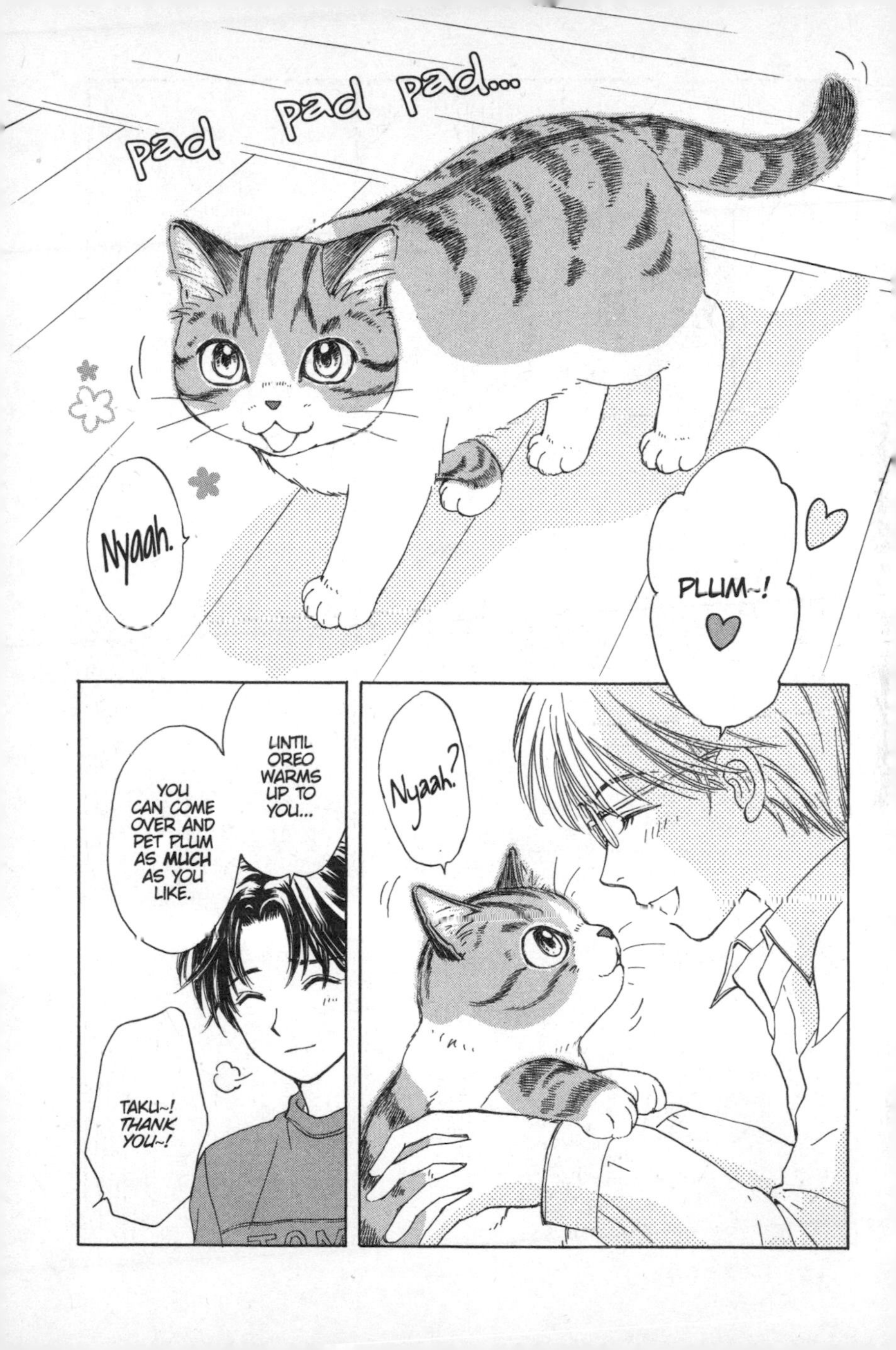
pad pad pad...
Nyaah.
PLUM~!
Nyaah?
UNTIL OREO WARMS UP TO YOU...
YOU CAN COME OVER AND PET PLUM AS MUCH AS YOU LIKE.
TAKU~! THANK YOU~!

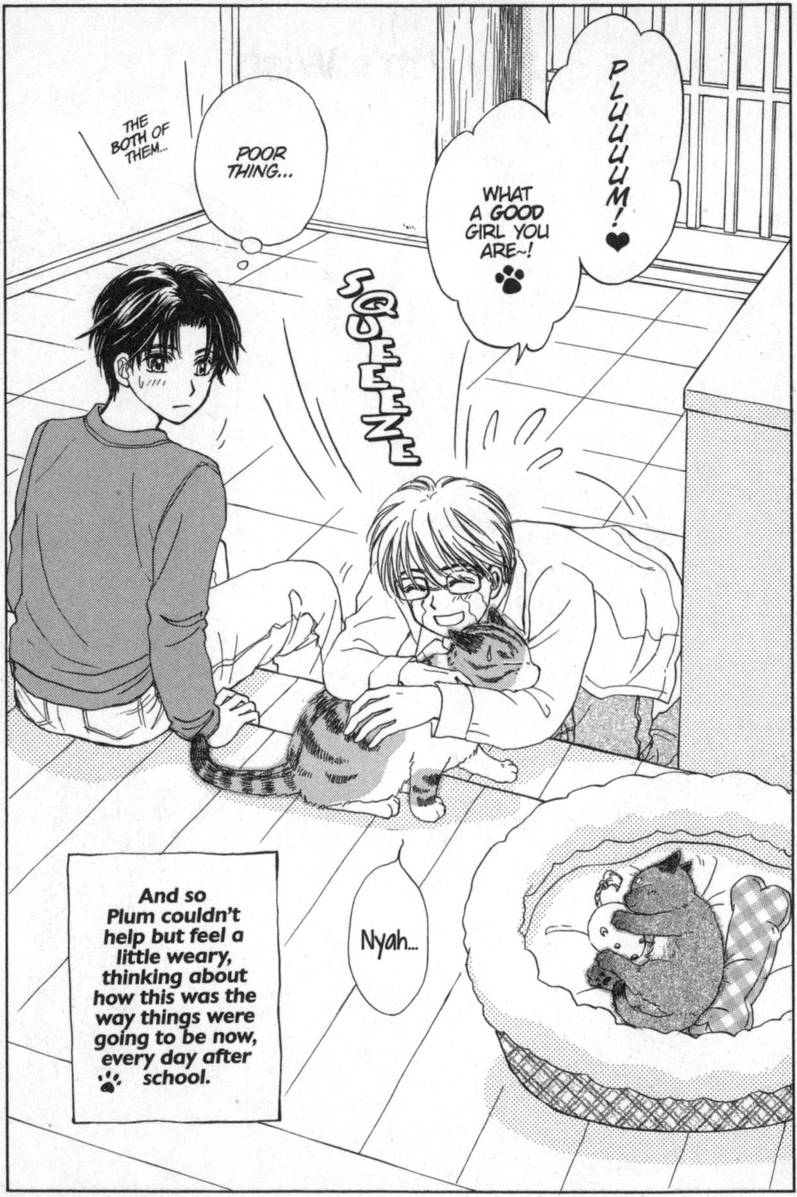
PLUUUUM! ❤
WHAT A GOOD GIRL YOU ARE~!
SQUEEZE
POOR THING...
THE BOTH OF THEM...
Nyah...
And so Plum couldn't help but feel a little weary, thinking about how this was the way things were going to be now, every day after school.

(15) The End

Short.11

July 7th's Wish

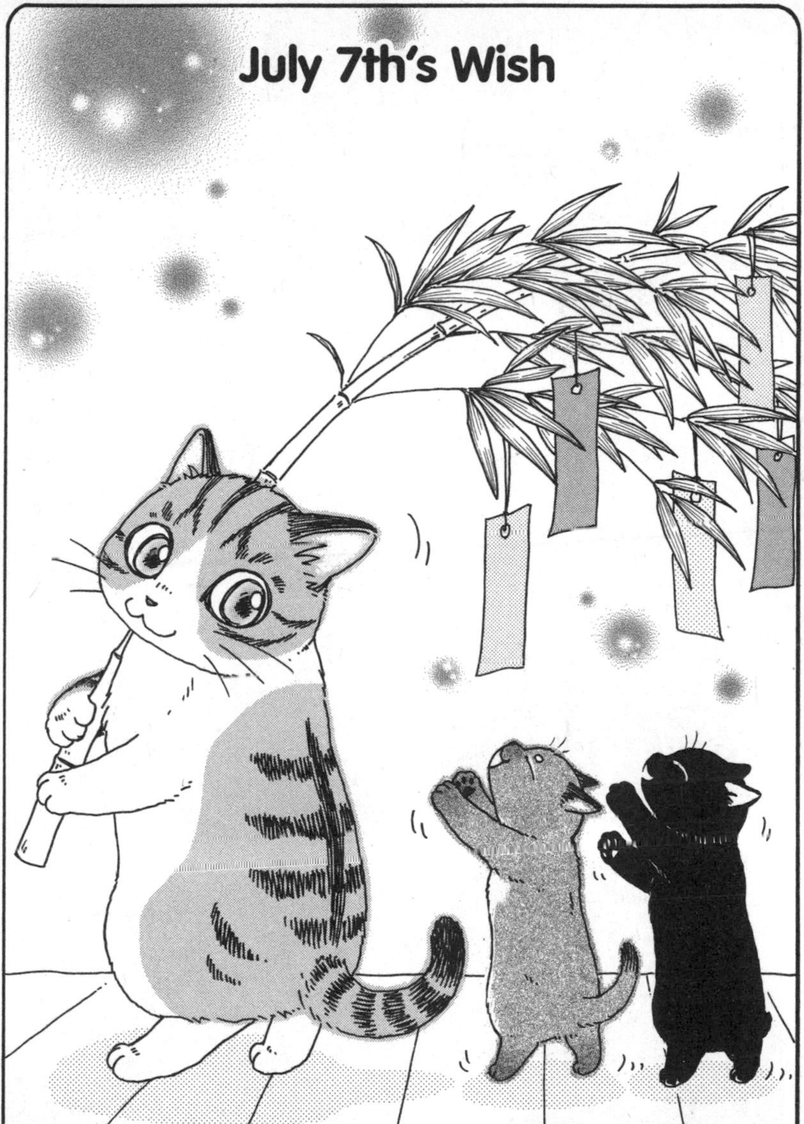

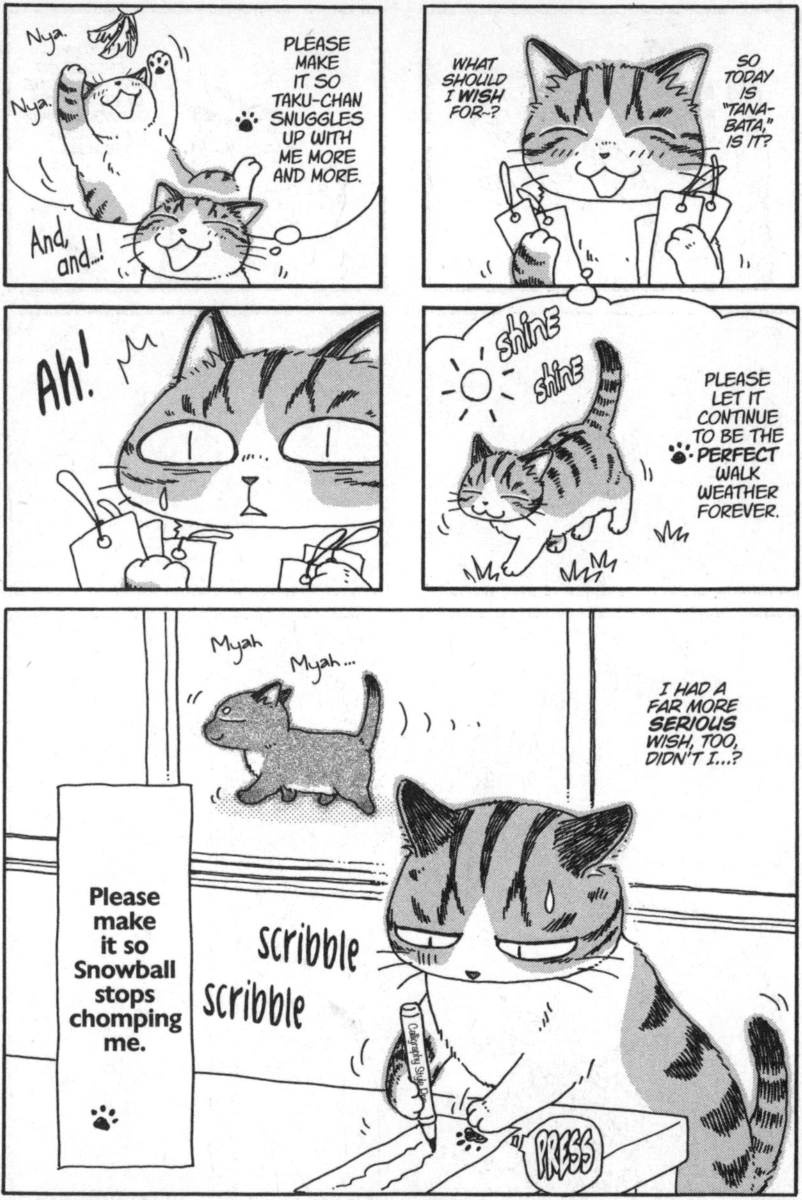
SO TODAY IS "TANA-BATA," IS IT?
WHAT SHOULD I WISH FOR~?
PLEASE MAKE IT SO TAKU-CHAN SNUGGLES UP WITH ME MORE AND MORE.
Nya.
Nya.
And, and...!
shine
shine
PLEASE LET IT CONTINUE TO BE THE PERFECT WALK WEATHER FOREVER.
Ah!
I HAD A FAR MORE SERIOUS WISH, TOO, DIDN'T I...?
Myah
Myah...
scribble
scribble
Please make it so Snowball stops chomping me.
PRESS

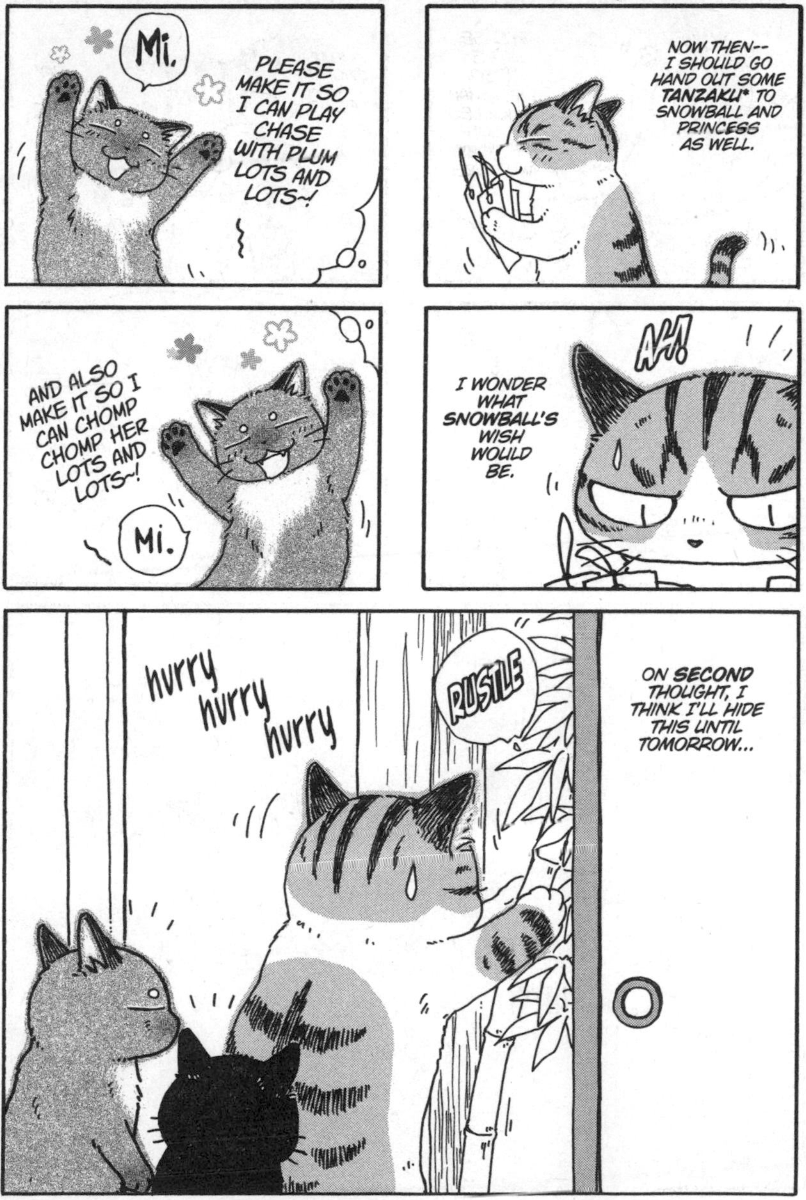
NOW THEN-- I SHOULD GO HAND OUT SOME TANZAKU* TO SNOWBALL AND PRINCESS AS WELL.
Mi.
PLEASE MAKE IT SO I CAN PLAY CHASE WITH PLUM LOTS AND LOTS~!
AH!
I WONDER WHAT SNOWBALL'S WISH WOULD BE.
AND ALSO MAKE IT SO I CAN CHOMP CHOMP HER LOTS AND LOTS~!
Mi.
ON SECOND THOUGHT, I THINK I'LL HIDE THIS UNTIL TOMORROW...
RUSTLE
hurry hurry hurry

*The strips of paper that wishes are written on during Tanabata. Traditional Japanese poems are also written on tanzaku.

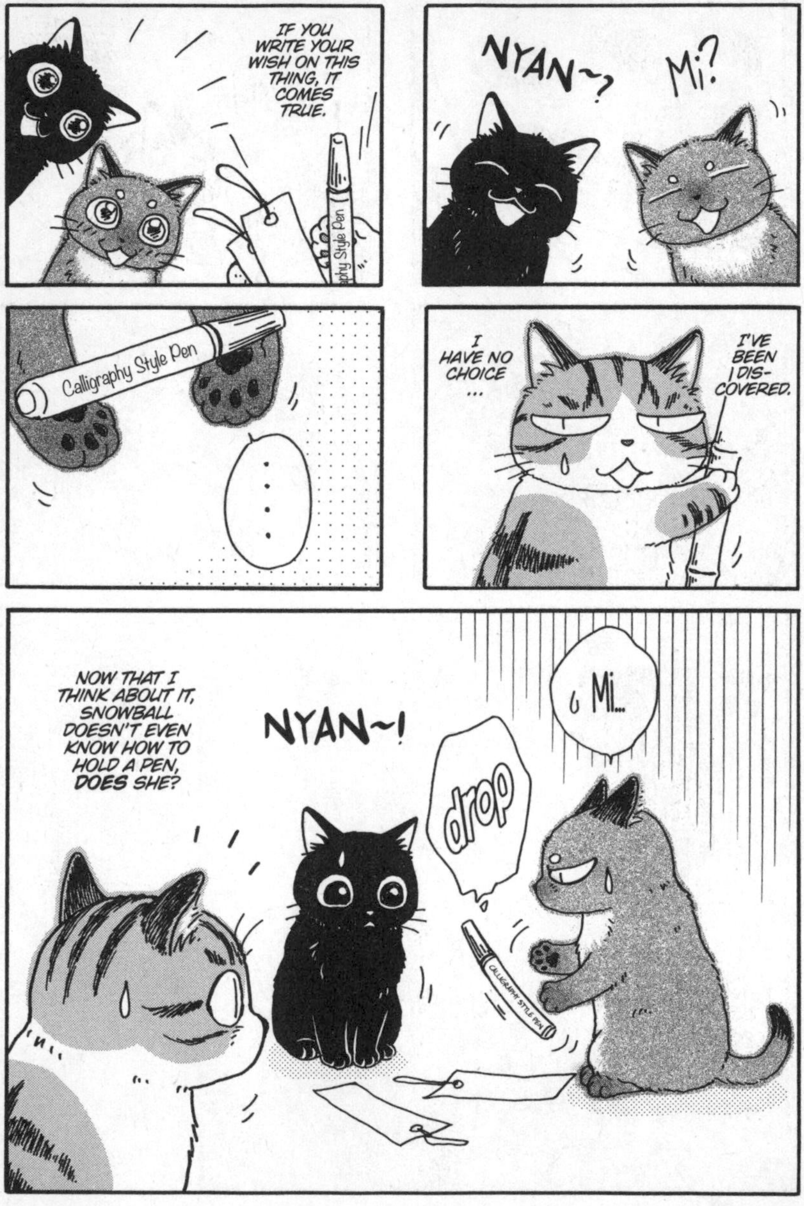
NYAN~?
Mi?
IF YOU WRITE YOUR WISH ON THIS THING, IT COMES TRUE.
...aphy Style Pen
I'VE BEEN DIS-COVERED.
I HAVE NO CHOICE ...
Calligraphy Style Pen
....
Mi...
drop
CALLIGRAPHY STYLE PEN
NYAN~!
NOW THAT I THINK ABOUT IT, SNOWBALL DOESN'T EVEN KNOW HOW TO HOLD A PEN, **DOES** SHE?

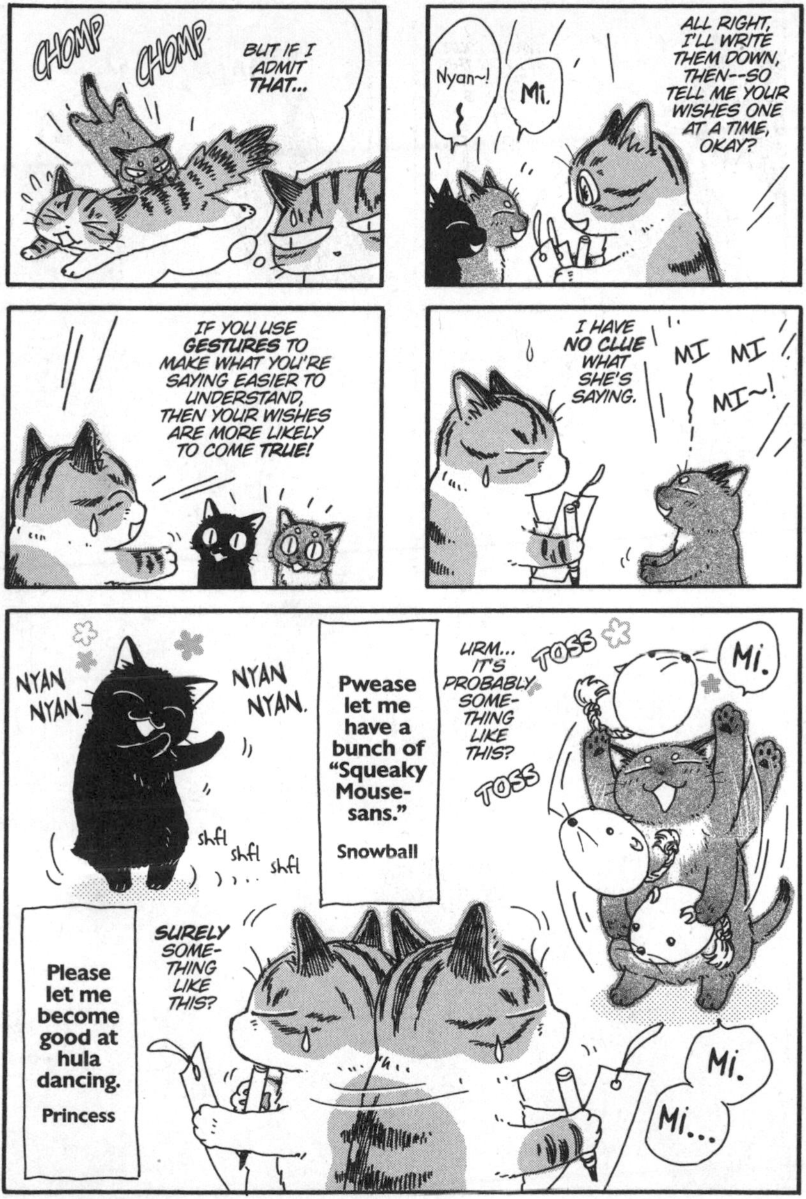
Nyan~!
Mi.
ALL RIGHT, I'LL WRITE THEM DOWN, THEN--SO TELL ME YOUR WISHES ONE AT A TIME, OKAY?
BUT IF I ADMIT THAT...
CHOMP
CHOMP
MI MI
MI~!
I HAVE NO CLUE WHAT SHE'S SAYING.
IF YOU USE GESTURES TO MAKE WHAT YOU'RE SAYING EASIER TO UNDERSTAND, THEN YOUR WISHES ARE MORE LIKELY TO COME TRUE!
Mi.
TOSS
URM... IT'S PROBABLY SOME-THING LIKE THIS?
TOSS
Pwease let me have a bunch of "Squeaky Mouse-sans." Snowball
NYAN NYAN.
NYAN NYAN.
shfl shfl shfl
Mi.
Mi...
SURELY SOME-THING LIKE THIS?
Please let me become good at hula dancing. Princess

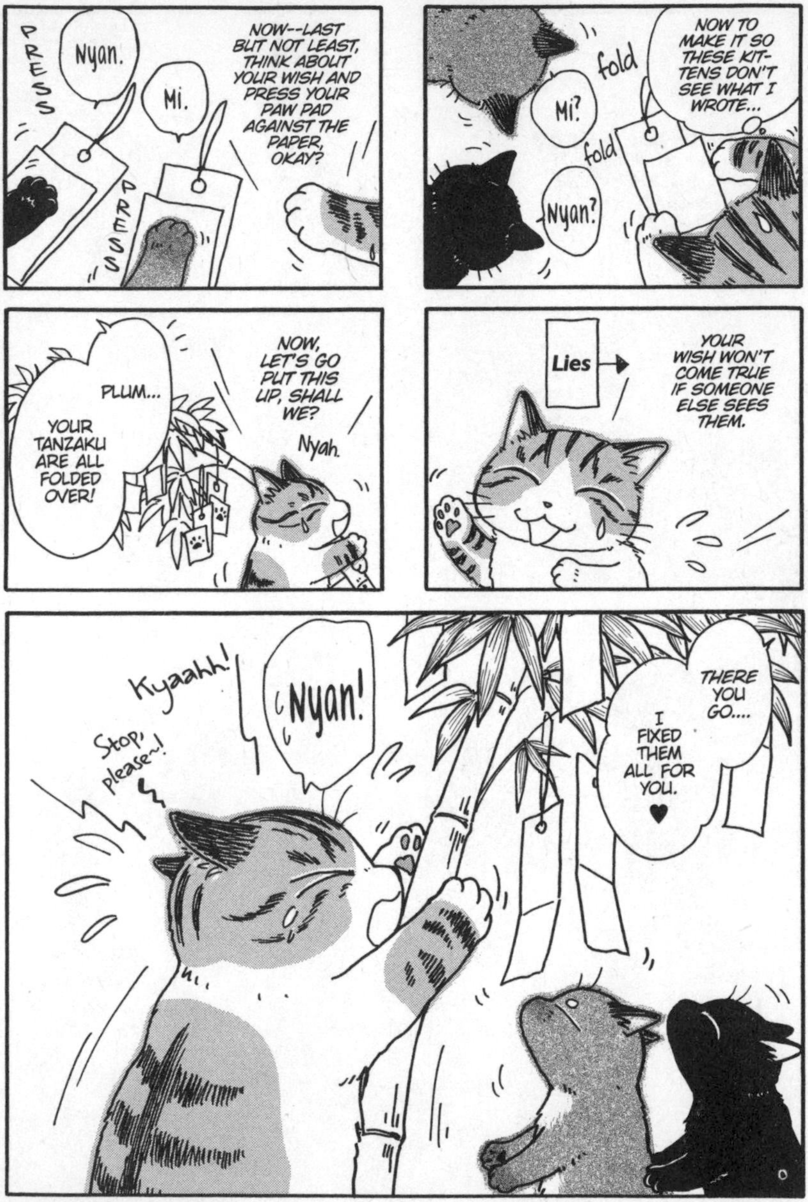
NOW TO MAKE IT SO THESE KIT-TENS DON'T SEE WHAT I WROTE...
fold
Mi?
fold
Nyan?
NOW--LAST BUT NOT LEAST, THINK ABOUT YOUR WISH AND PRESS YOUR PAW PAD AGAINST THE PAPER, OKAY?
Nyan.
PRESS
Mi.
PRESS
YOUR WISH WON'T COME TRUE IF SOMEONE ELSE SEES THEM.
Lies
NOW, LET'S GO PUT THIS UP, SHALL WE?
Nyah.
PLUM... YOUR TANZAKU ARE ALL FOLDED OVER!
THERE YOU GO.... I FIXED THEM ALL FOR YOU. ♥
Nyan!
Kyaahh!
Stop, please~!

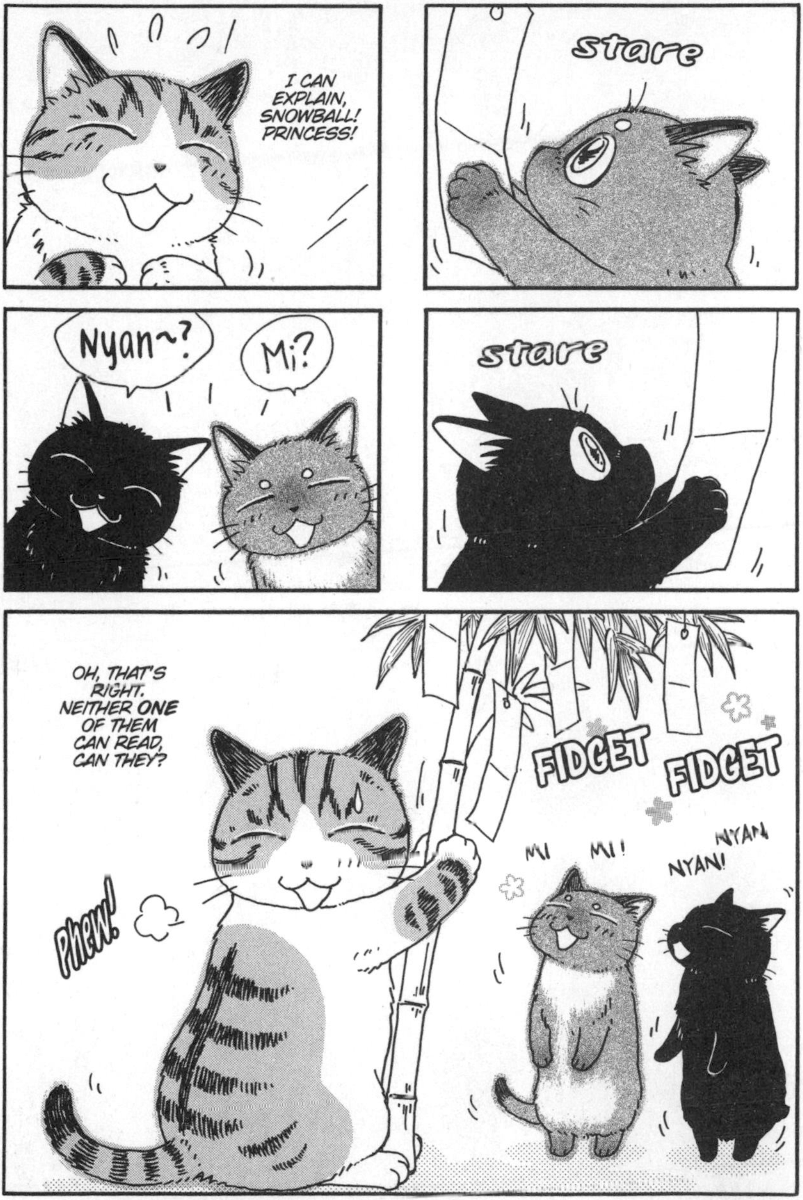
stare
I CAN EXPLAIN, SNOWBALL! PRINCESS!
stare
Mi?
Nyan~?
FIDGET FIDGET
NYAN NYAN!
MI MI!
OH, THAT'S RIGHT. NEITHER ONE OF THEM CAN READ, CAN THEY?
Phew!

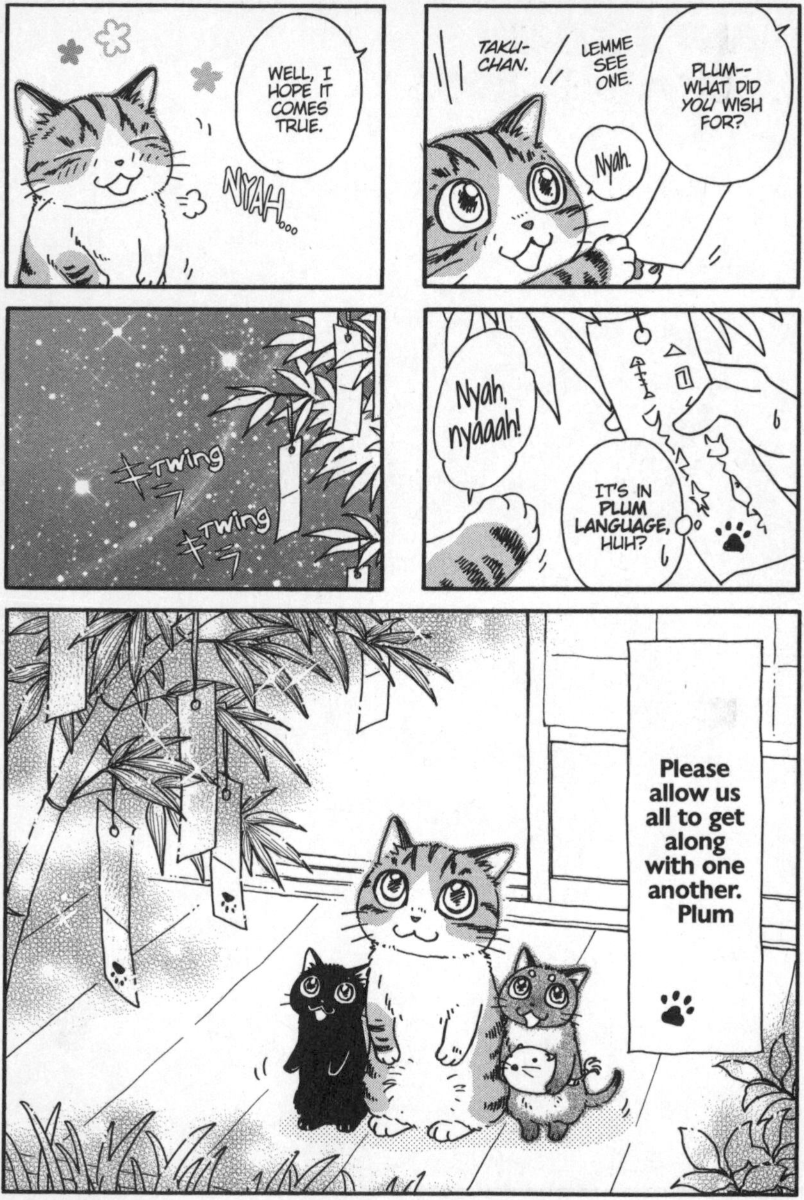
PLUM-- WHAT DID YOU WISH FOR?
LEMME SEE ONE.
TAKU-CHAN.
Nyah.
WELL, I HOPE IT COMES TRUE.
NYAH...
Nyah, nyaaah!
IT'S IN PLUM LANGUAGE, HUH?
TWING
TWING
Please allow us all to get along with one another. Plum

The End

CHAPTER 16

I WANT TO EAT DELICIOUS THINGS

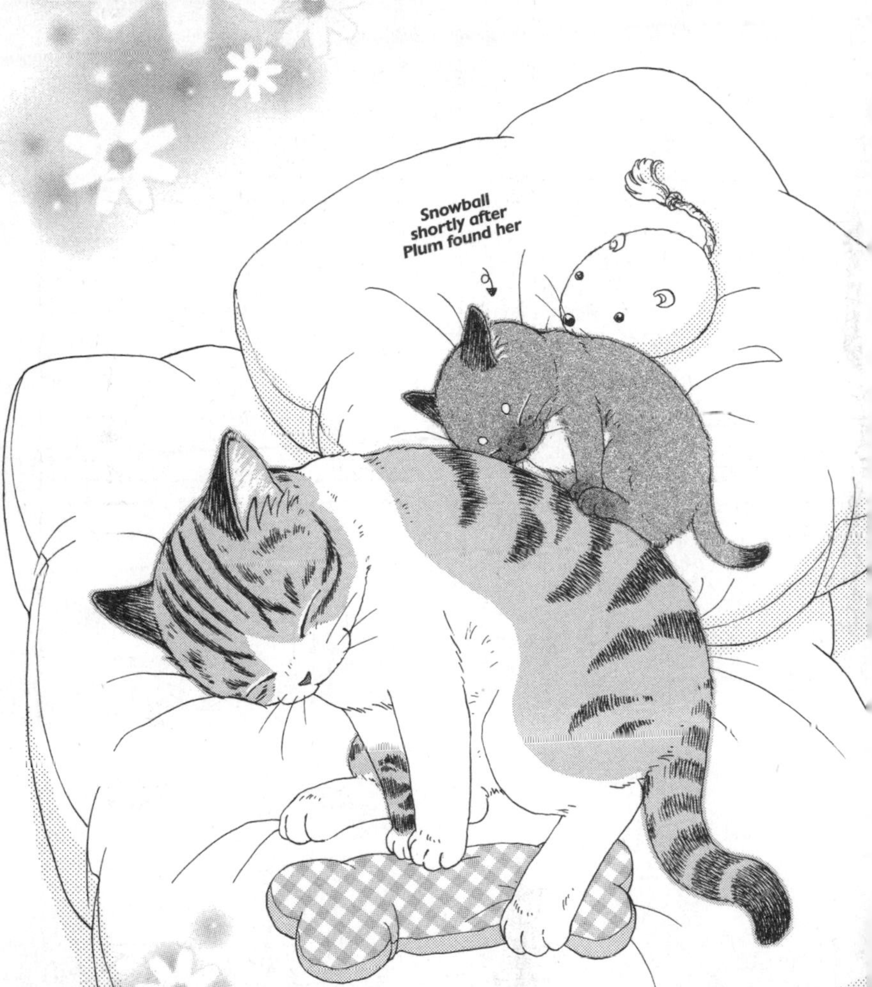
Snowball shortly after Plum found her

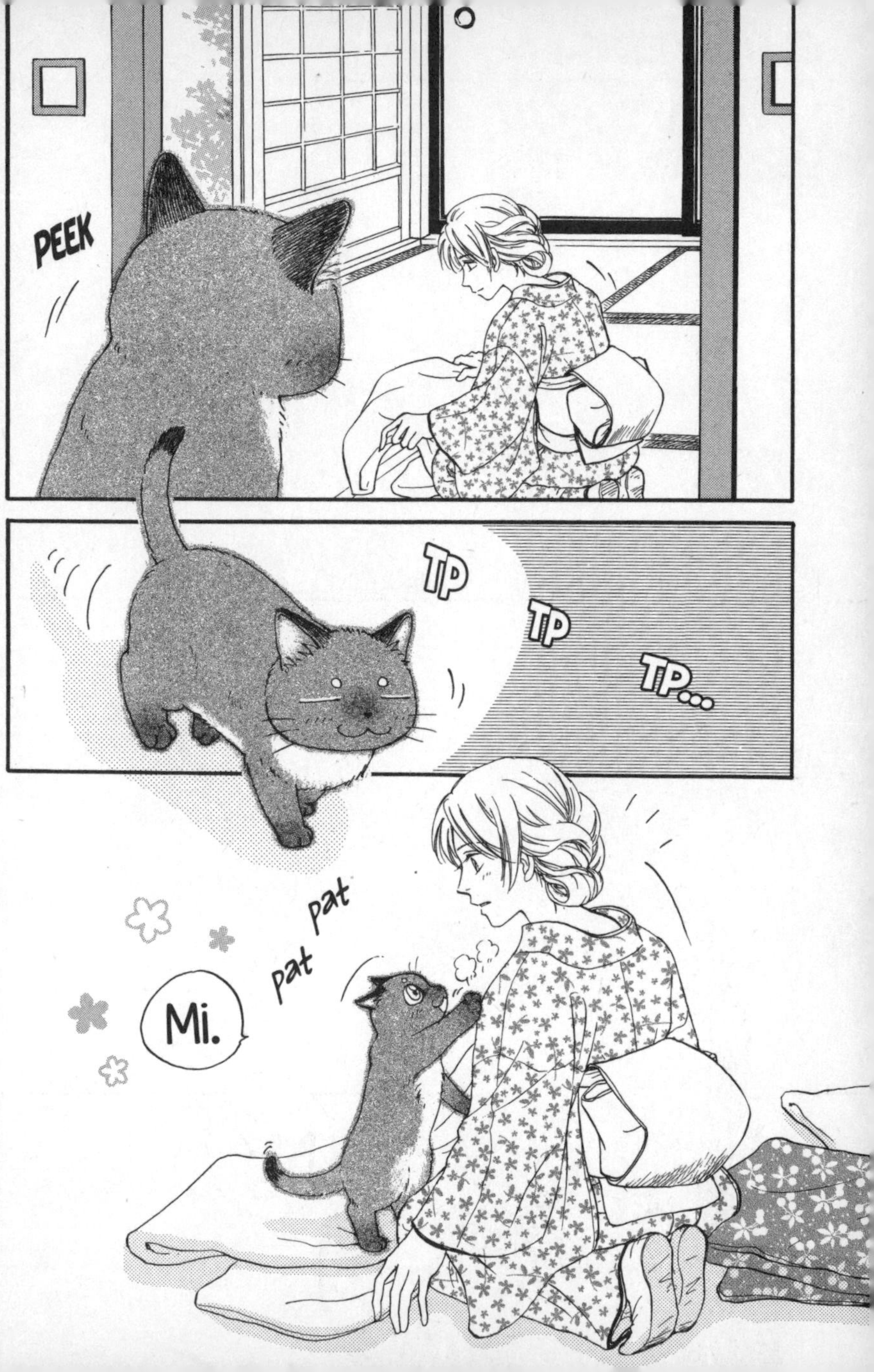
PEEK
TP
TP
TP...
pat
pat
Mi.

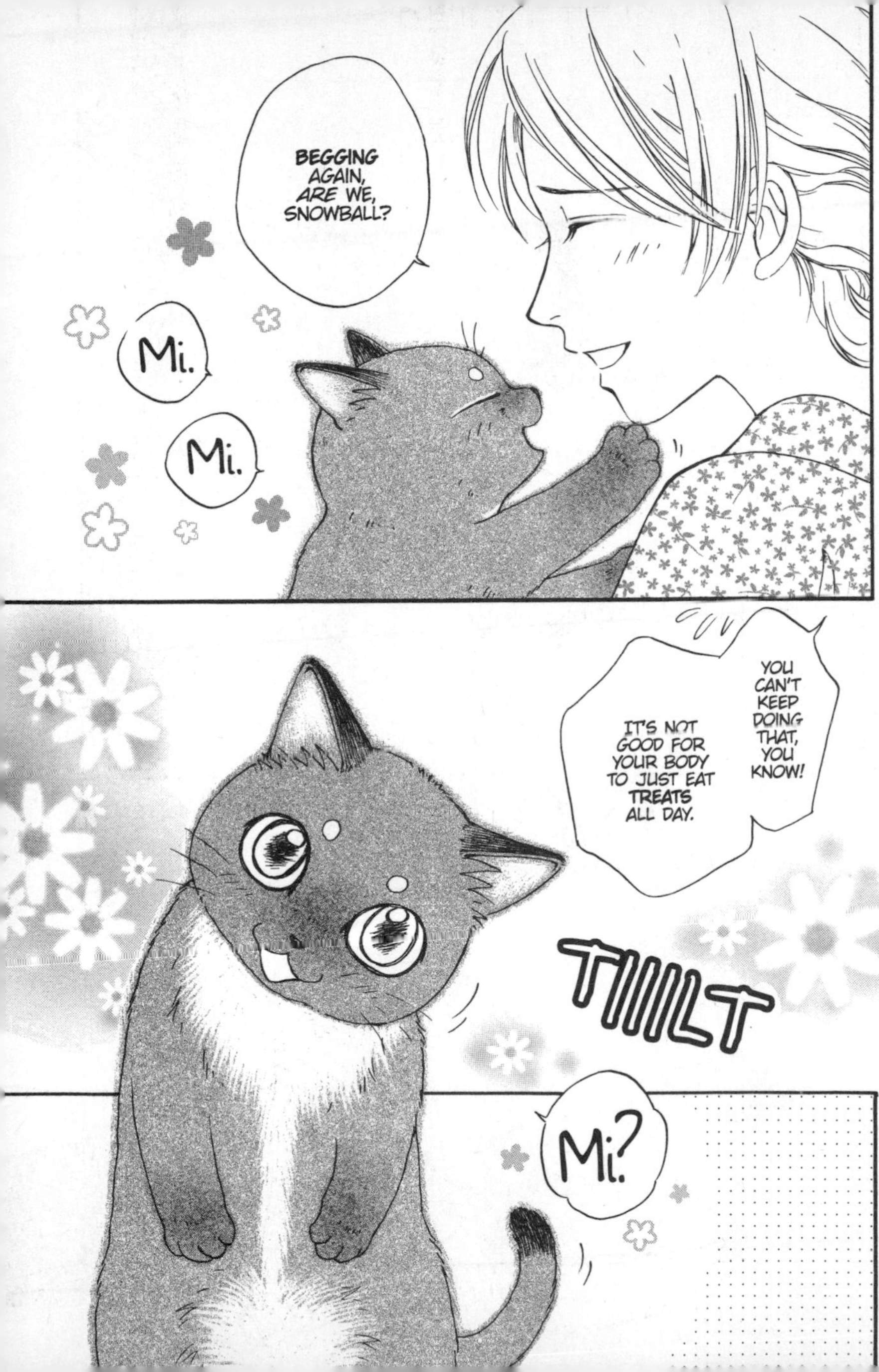
BEGGING AGAIN, ARE WE, SNOWBALL?
Mi.
Mi.
YOU CAN'T KEEP DOING THAT, YOU KNOW!
IT'S NOT GOOD FOR YOUR BODY TO JUST EAT TREATS ALL DAY.
TIILT
Mi?

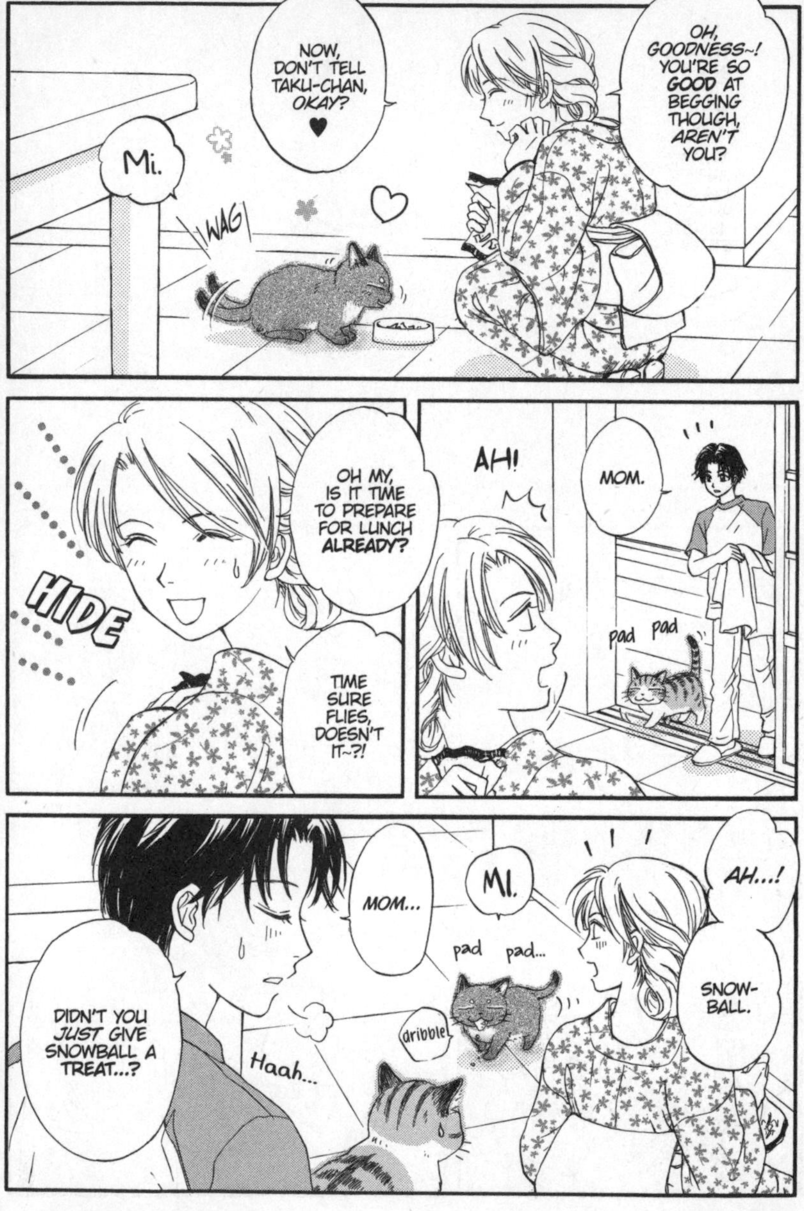
OH, GOODNESS~! YOU'RE SO GOOD AT BEGGING THOUGH, AREN'T YOU?
NOW, DON'T TELL TAKU-CHAN, OKAY? ♥
Mi.
WAG
MOM.
AH!
pad pad
OH MY, IS IT TIME TO PREPARE FOR LUNCH ALREADY?
TIME SURE FLIES, DOESN'T IT~?!
HIDE
AH...!
SNOW-BALL.
MI.
MOM...
pad pad...
dribble
Haah...
DIDN'T YOU JUST GIVE SNOWBALL A TREAT...?

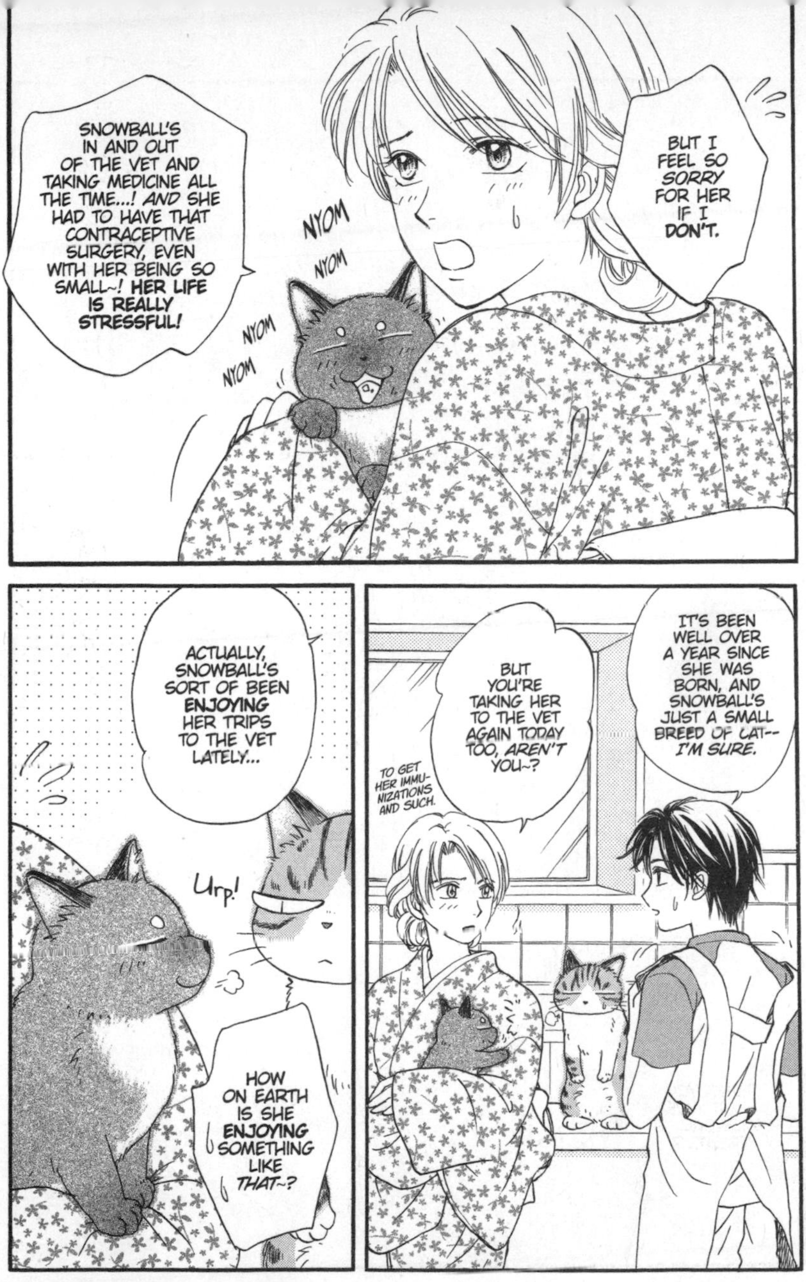
BUT I FEEL SO SORRY FOR HER IF I DON'T.
SNOWBALL'S IN AND OUT OF THE VET AND TAKING MEDICINE ALL THE TIME...! AND SHE HAD TO HAVE THAT CONTRACEPTIVE SURGERY, EVEN WITH HER BEING SO SMALL~! HER LIFE IS REALLY STRESSFUL!
NYOM
NYOM
NYOM
NYOM
IT'S BEEN WELL OVER A YEAR SINCE SHE WAS BORN, AND SNOWBALL'S JUST A SMALL BREED OF CAT-- I'M SURE.
BUT YOU'RE TAKING HER TO THE VET AGAIN TODAY TOO, AREN'T YOU~?
TO GET HER IMMUNIZATIONS AND SUCH.
ACTUALLY, SNOWBALL'S SORT OF BEEN ENJOYING HER TRIPS TO THE VET LATELY...
Urp!
HOW ON EARTH IS SHE ENJOYING SOMETHING LIKE THAT~?

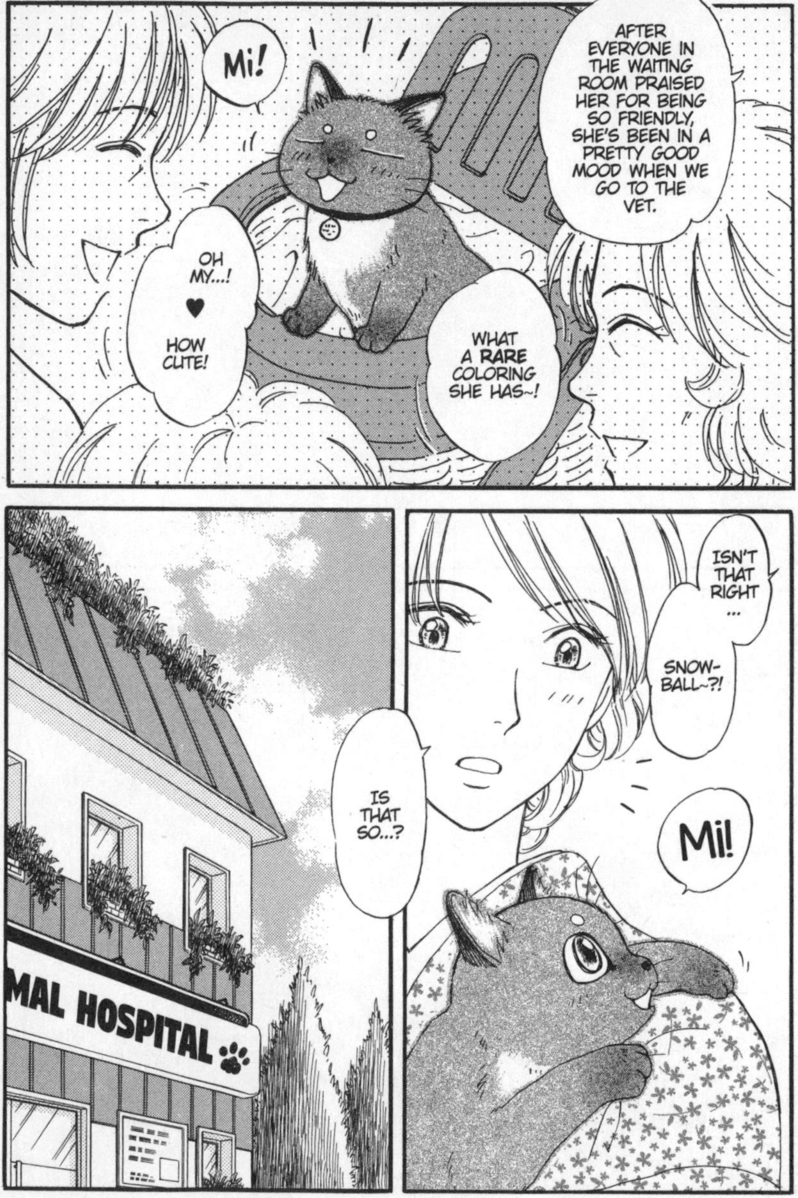
AFTER EVERYONE IN THE WAITING ROOM PRAISED HER FOR BEING SO FRIENDLY, SHE'S BEEN IN A PRETTY GOOD MOOD WHEN WE GO TO THE VET.
Mi!
WHAT A RARE COLORING SHE HAS~!
OH MY...! ♥ HOW CUTE!
ISN'T THAT RIGHT... SNOW-BALL~?!
Mi!
IS THAT SO...?
MAL HOSPITAL

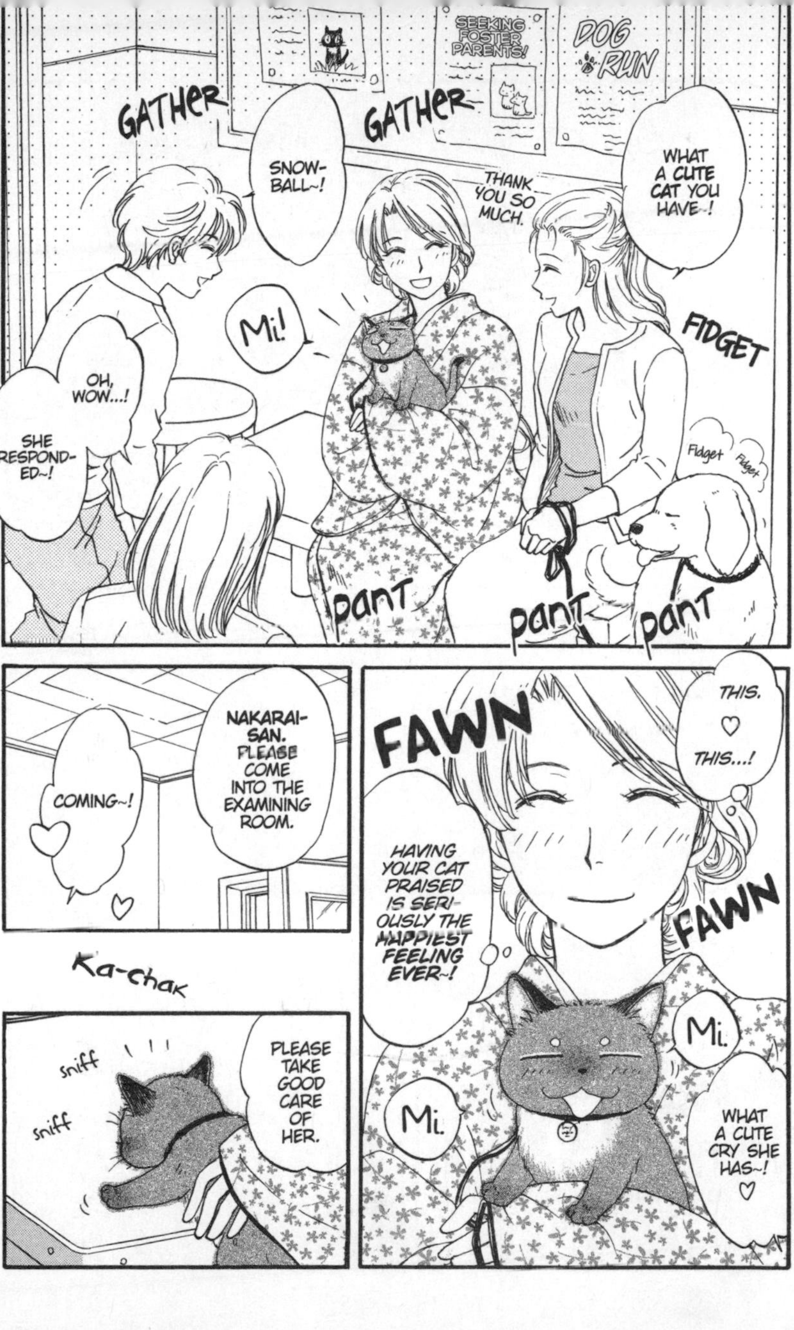
DOG RUN
SEEKING FOSTER PARENTS!
WHAT A CUTE CAT YOU HAVE~!
THANK YOU SO MUCH.
GATHER
SNOW-BALL~!
GATHER
FIDGET
Mi!
OH, WOW...!
SHE RESPOND-ED~!
Fidget Fidget
pant
pant
pant
THIS. ♡ THIS...!
FAWN
HAVING YOUR CAT PRAISED IS SERI-OUSLY THE HAPPIEST FEELING EVER~!
FAWN
Mi.
WHAT A CUTE CRY SHE HAS~! ♡
Mi.
NAKARAI-SAN. PLEASE COME INTO THE EXAMINING ROOM.
COMING~! ♡
♡
Ka-chak
PLEASE TAKE GOOD CARE OF HER.
sniff
sniff

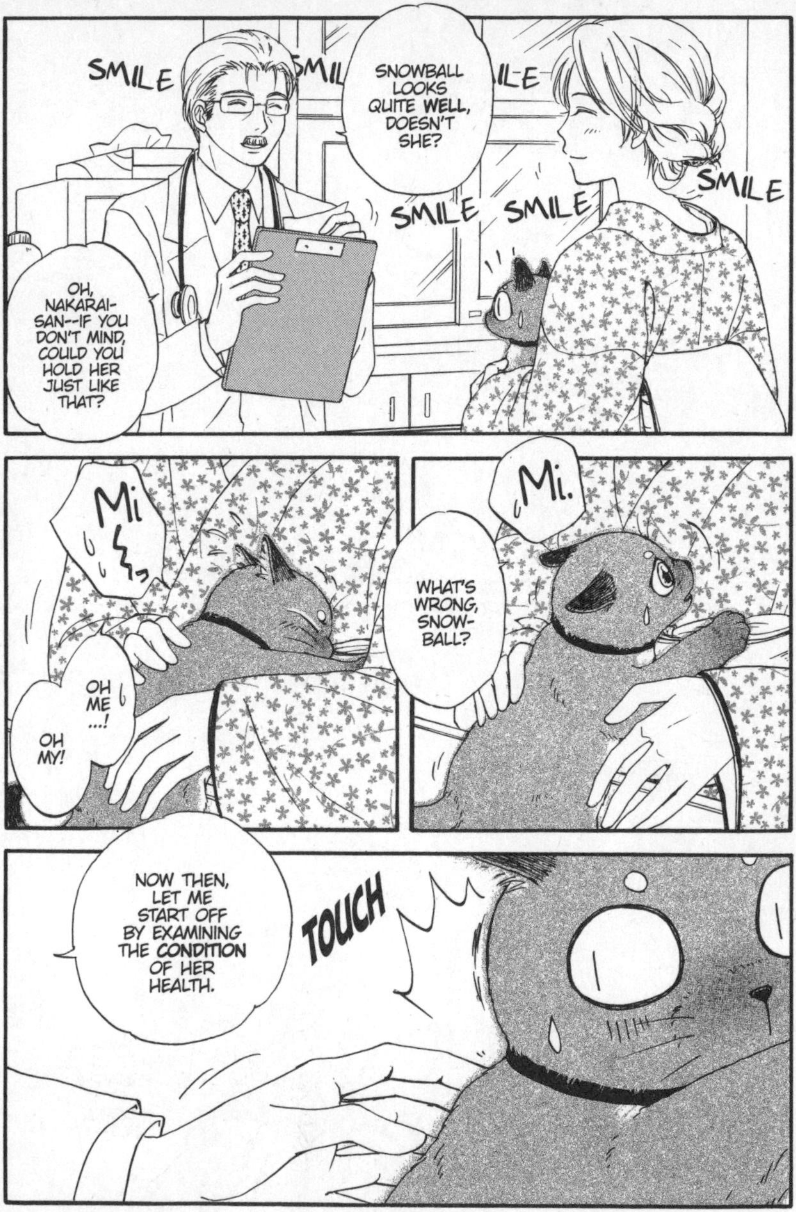
SNOWBALL LOOKS QUITE WELL, DOESN'T SHE?
SMILE
SMILE SMILE
SMILE
OH, NAKARAI-SAN--IF YOU DON'T MIND, COULD YOU HOLD HER JUST LIKE THAT?
Mi.
WHAT'S WRONG, SNOW-BALL?
Mi
OH ME ...!
OH MY!
NOW THEN, LET ME START OFF BY EXAMINING THE CONDITION OF HER HEALTH.
TOUCH

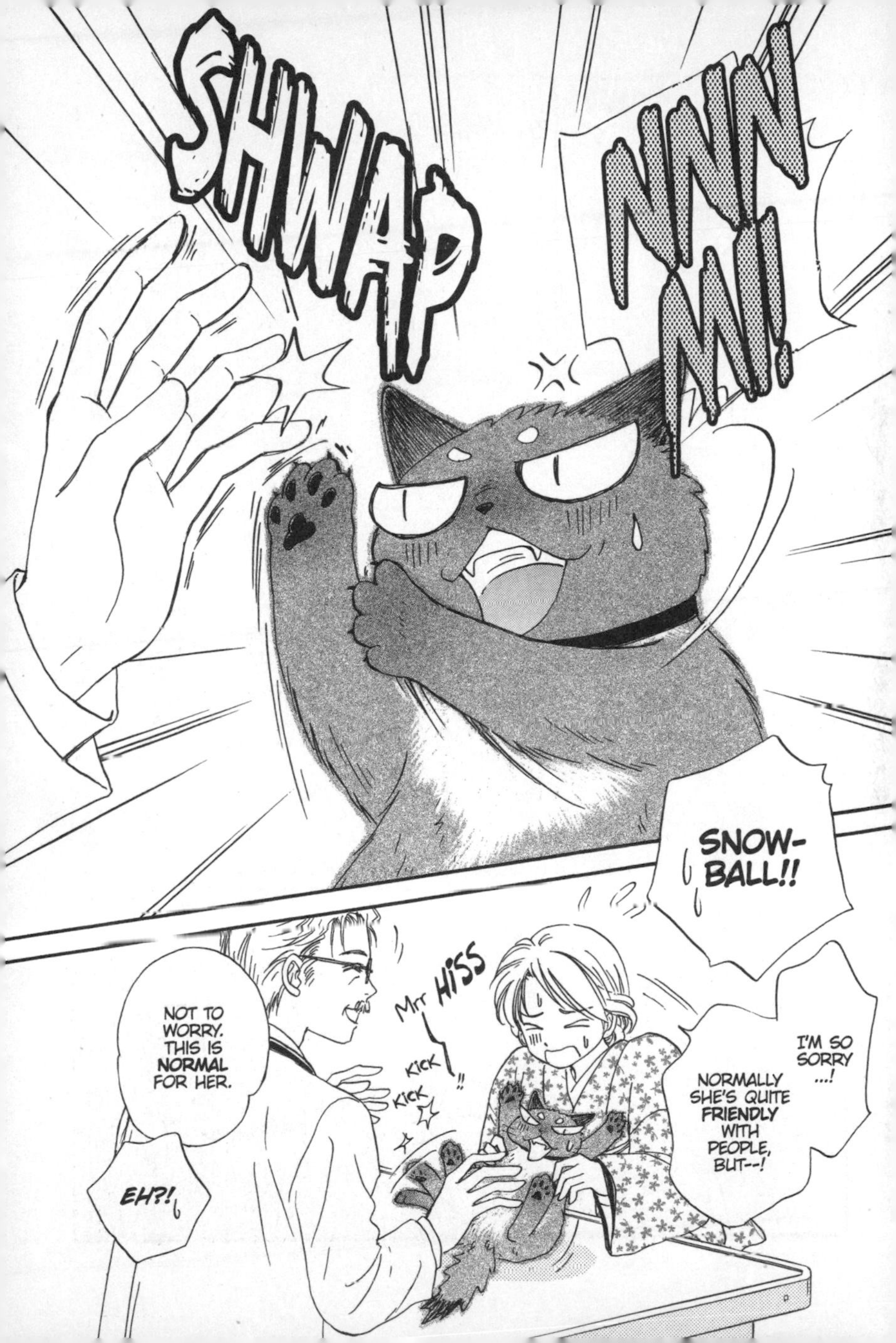

NNNN MM!!
SHWAP
SNOW-BALL!!
I'M SO SORRY ...!
NORMALLY SHE'S QUITE FRIENDLY WITH PEOPLE, BUT--!
Mrr HISS
KICK KICK !!
NOT TO WORRY. THIS IS NORMAL FOR HER.
EH?!

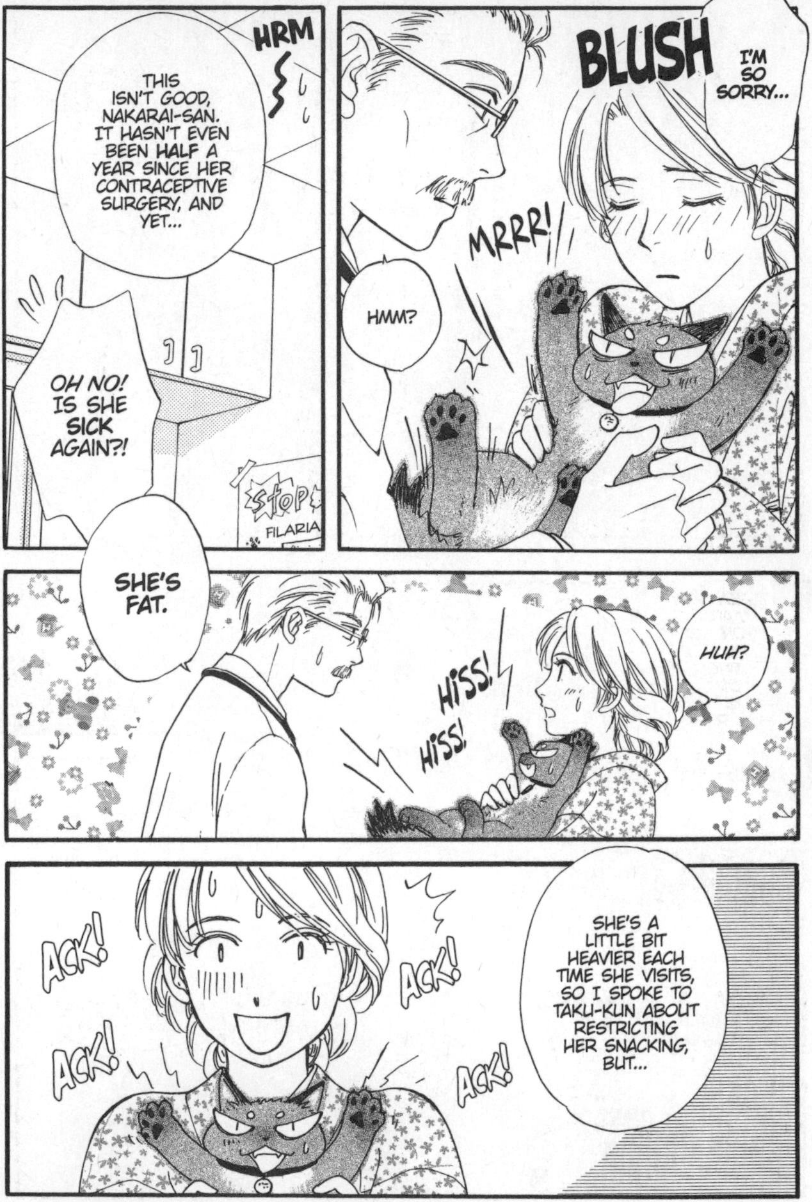
BLUSH
I'M SO SORRY...
MRRR!
HMM?
HRM
THIS ISN'T GOOD, NAKARAI-SAN. IT HASN'T EVEN BEEN HALF A YEAR SINCE HER CONTRACEPTIVE SURGERY, AND YET...
OH NO! IS SHE SICK AGAIN?!
STOP
FILARIA
SHE'S FAT.
HUH?
HISS!
HISS!
SHE'S A LITTLE BIT HEAVIER EACH TIME SHE VISITS, SO I SPOKE TO TAKU-KUN ABOUT RESTRICTING HER SNACKING, BUT...
ACK!
ACK!
ACK!
ACK!

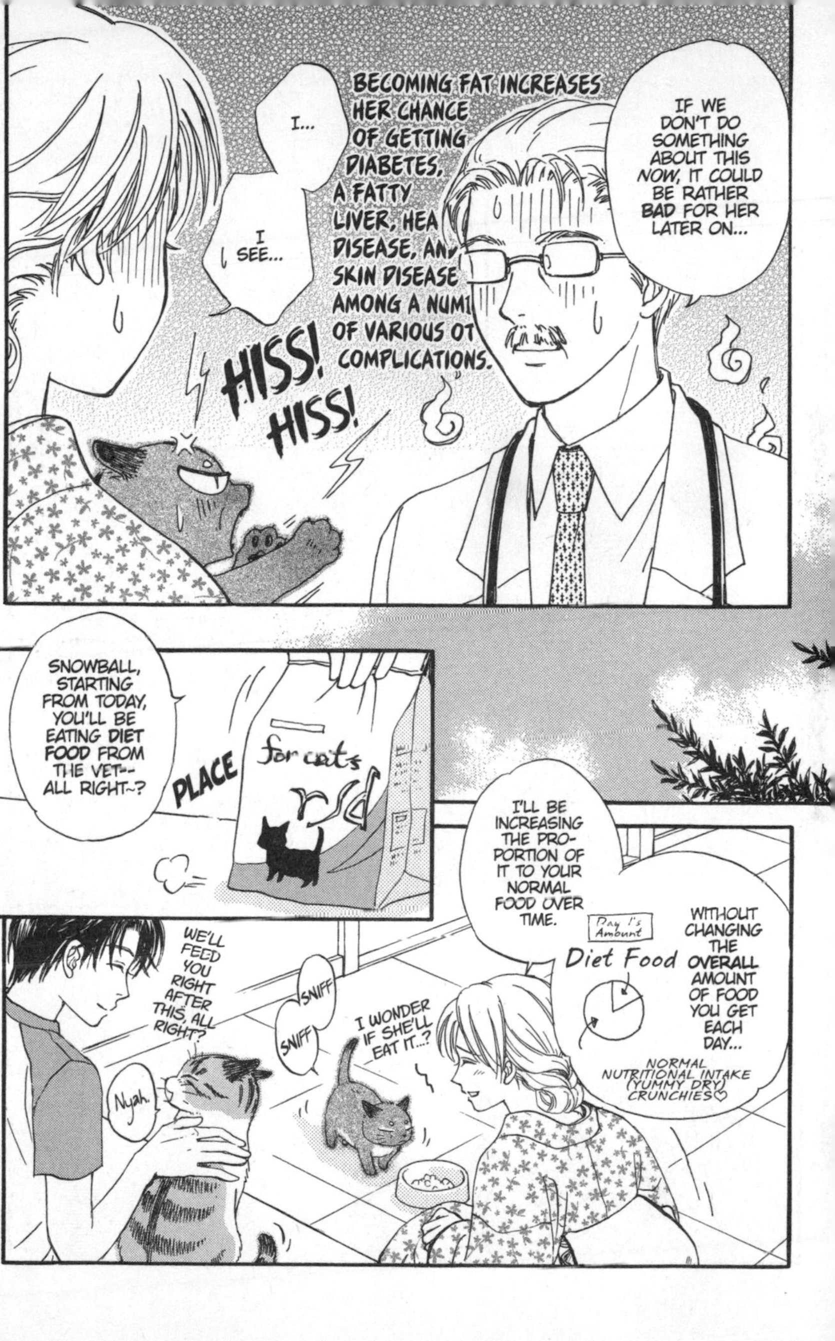
IF WE DON'T DO SOMETHING ABOUT THIS NOW, IT COULD BE RATHER BAD FOR HER LATER ON...
BECOMING FAT INCREASES HER CHANCE OF GETTING DIABETES, A FATTY LIVER, HEA DISEASE, AN SKIN DISEASE AMONG A NUM OF VARIOUS OT COMPLICATIONS.
I...
I SEE...
HISS! HISS!
SNOWBALL, STARTING FROM TODAY, YOU'LL BE EATING DIET FOOD FROM THE VET-- ALL RIGHT~?
for cats
PLACE
WITHOUT CHANGING THE OVERALL AMOUNT OF FOOD YOU GET EACH DAY...
I'LL BE INCREASING THE PROPORTION OF IT TO YOUR NORMAL FOOD OVER TIME.
Day 1's Amount
Diet Food
NORMAL NUTRITIONAL INTAKE (YUMMY DRY) CRUNCHIES♡
I WONDER IF SHE'LL EAT IT...?
SNIFF SNIFF
WE'LL FEED YOU RIGHT AFTER THIS, ALL RIGHT?
Nyah.

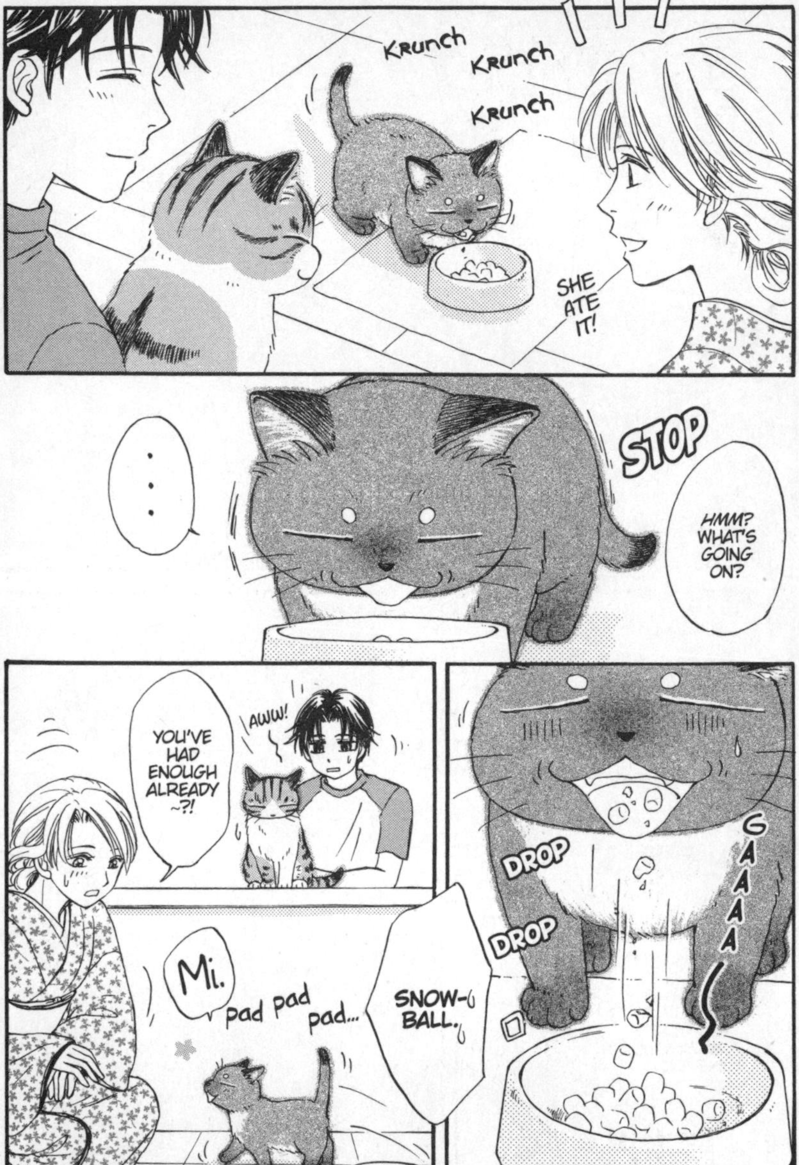
Krunch
Krunch
Krunch
SHE ATE IT!
STOP
HMM? WHAT'S GOING ON?
...
GAAAA~
DROP
DROP
AWW!
YOU'VE HAD ENOUGH ALREADY ~?!
SNOW-BALL.
pad pad pad...
Mi.

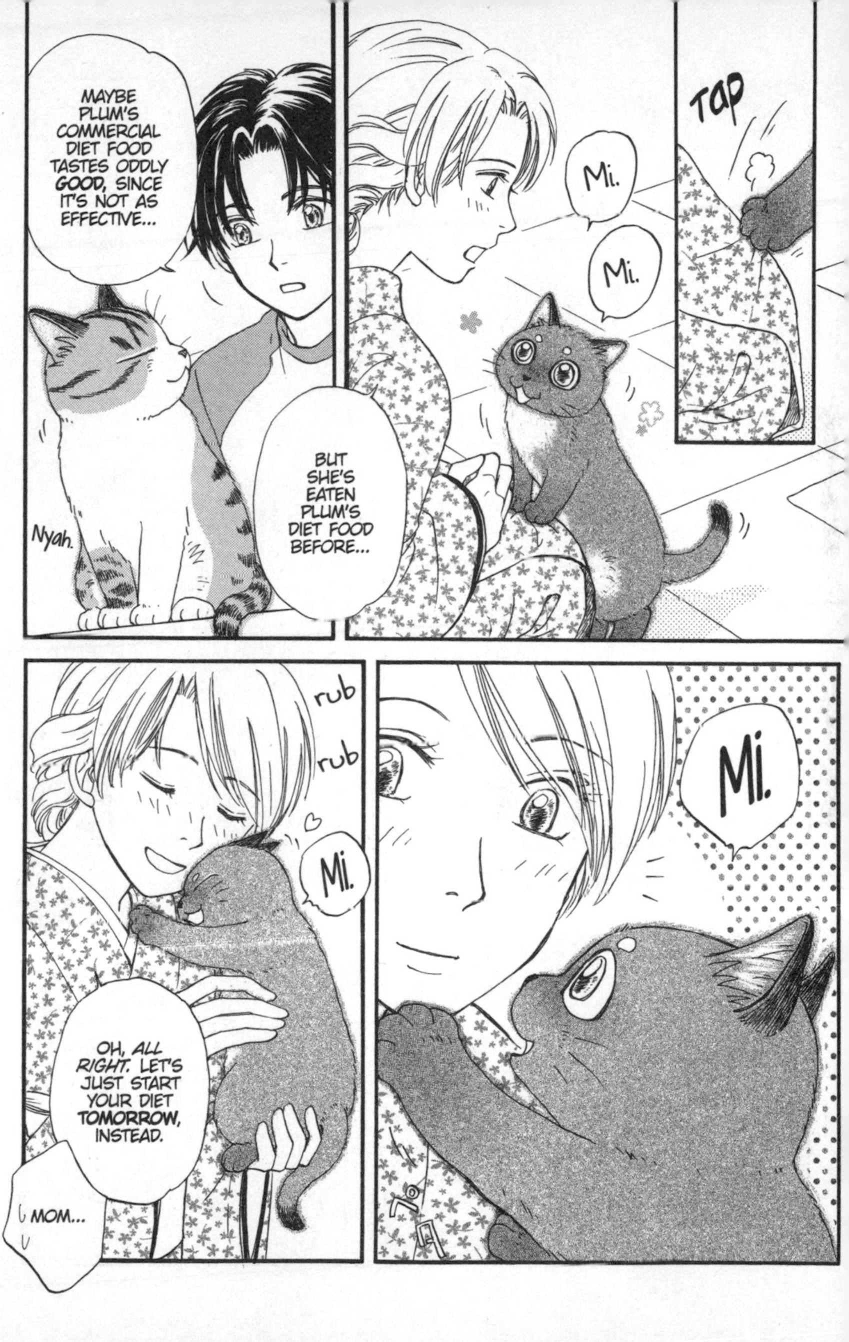
Tap
Mi.
Mi.
BUT SHE'S EATEN PLUM'S DIET FOOD BEFORE...
MAYBE PLUM'S COMMERCIAL DIET FOOD TASTES ODDLY GOOD, SINCE IT'S NOT AS EFFECTIVE...
Nyah.
Mi.
rub
rub
Mi.
OH, ALL RIGHT. LET'S JUST START YOUR DIET TOMORROW, INSTEAD.
MOM...

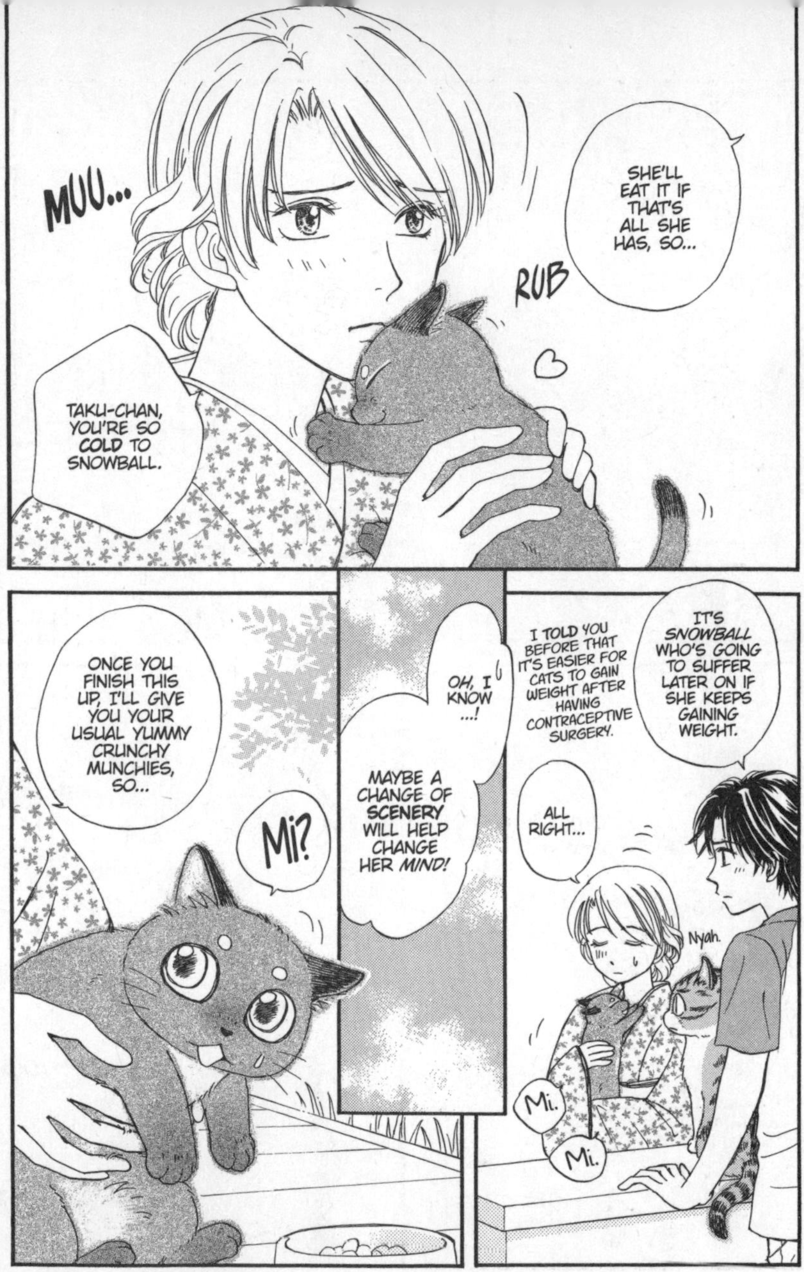
SHE'LL EAT IT IF THAT'S ALL SHE HAS, SO...
MUU...
RUB
TAKU-CHAN, YOU'RE SO COLD TO SNOWBALL.
IT'S SNOWBALL WHO'S GOING TO SUFFER LATER ON IF SHE KEEPS GAINING WEIGHT.
I TOLD YOU BEFORE THAT IT'S EASIER FOR CATS TO GAIN WEIGHT AFTER HAVING CONTRACEPTIVE SURGERY.
ALL RIGHT...
Nyah.
Mi.
Mi.
OH, I KNOW ...!
MAYBE A CHANGE OF SCENERY WILL HELP CHANGE HER MIND!
ONCE YOU FINISH THIS UP, I'LL GIVE YOU YOUR USUAL YUMMY CRUNCHY MUNCHIES, SO...
Mi?

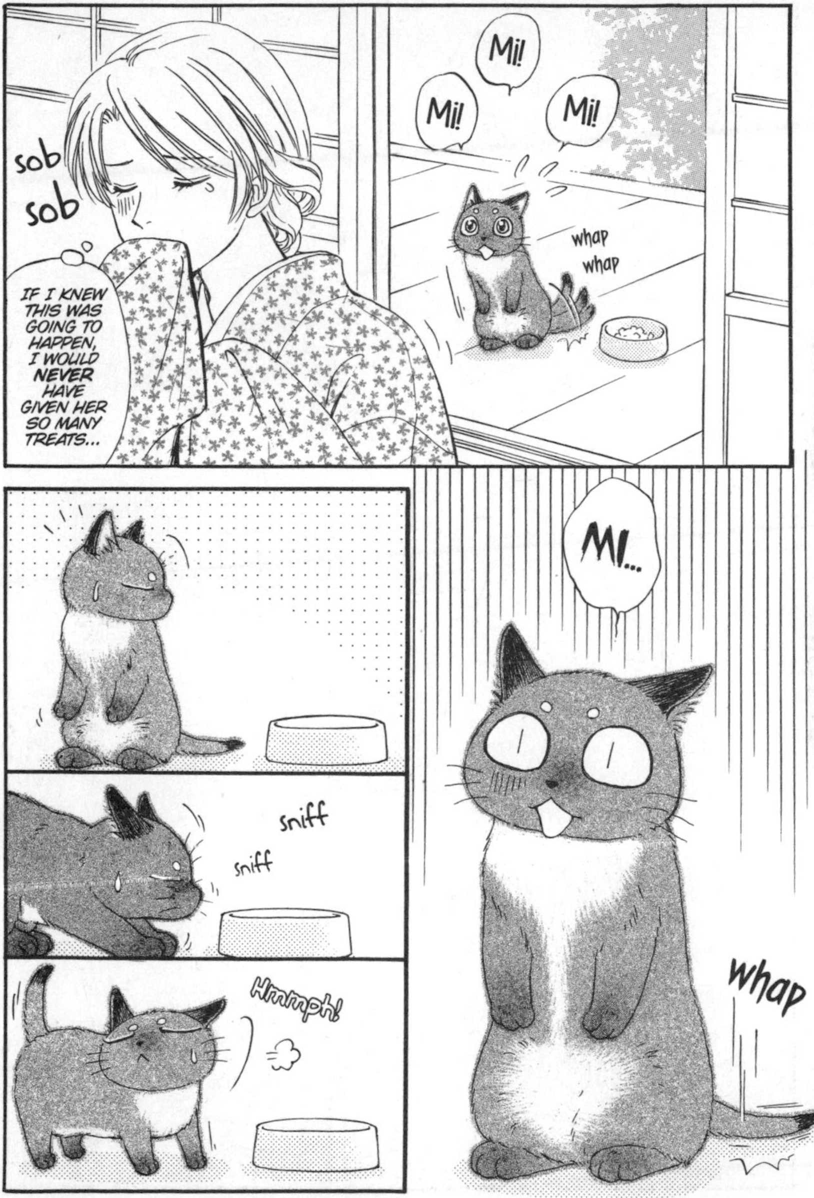
Mi!
Mi!
Mi!
whap
whap
sob
sob
IF I KNEW THIS WAS GOING TO HAPPEN, I WOULD NEVER HAVE GIVEN HER SO MANY TREATS...
MI...
whap
sniff
sniff
Hmmph!

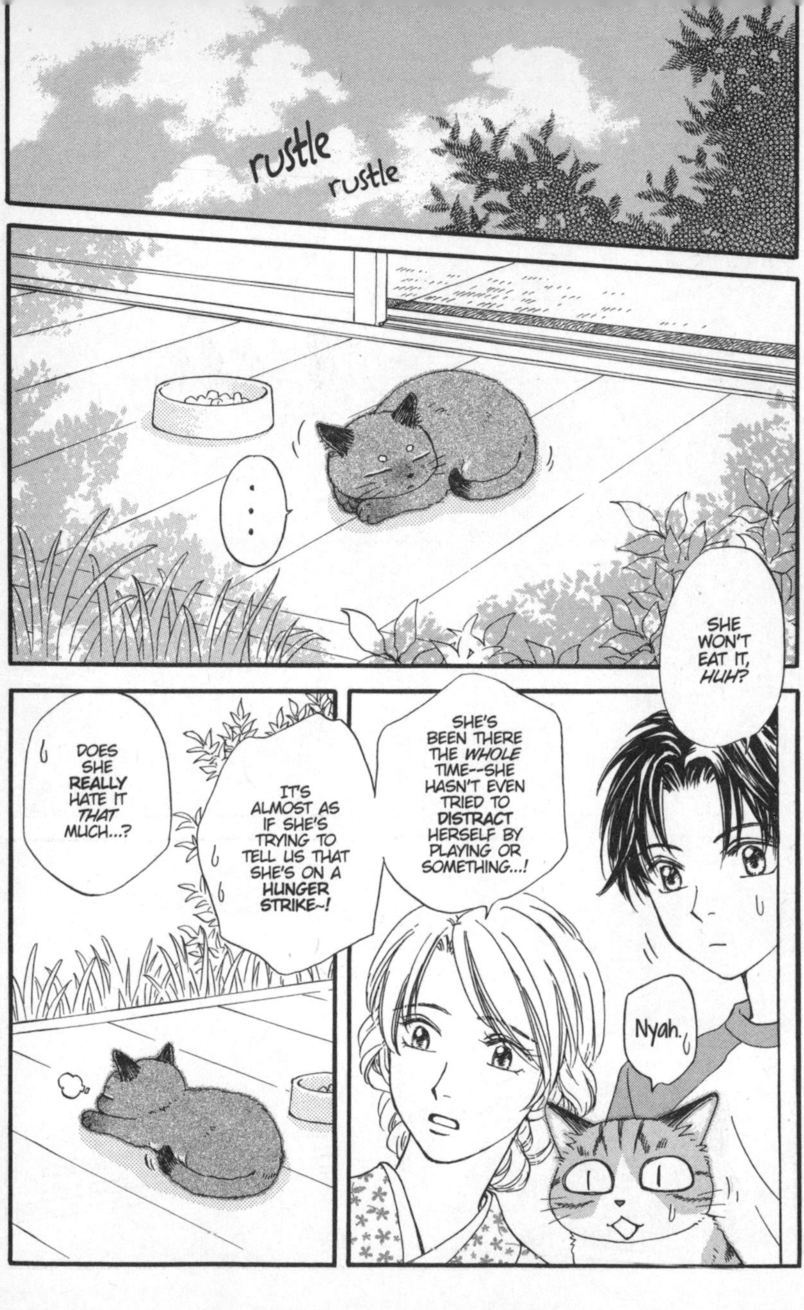
rustle
rustle
...
SHE WON'T EAT IT, *HUH?*
SHE'S BEEN THERE THE *WHOLE* TIME--SHE HASN'T EVEN TRIED TO **DISTRACT** HERSELF BY PLAYING OR SOMETHING...!
Nyah.
IT'S ALMOST AS IF SHE'S TRYING TO TELL US THAT SHE'S ON A **HUNGER STRIKE**~!
DOES SHE **REALLY** HATE IT *THAT* MUCH...?

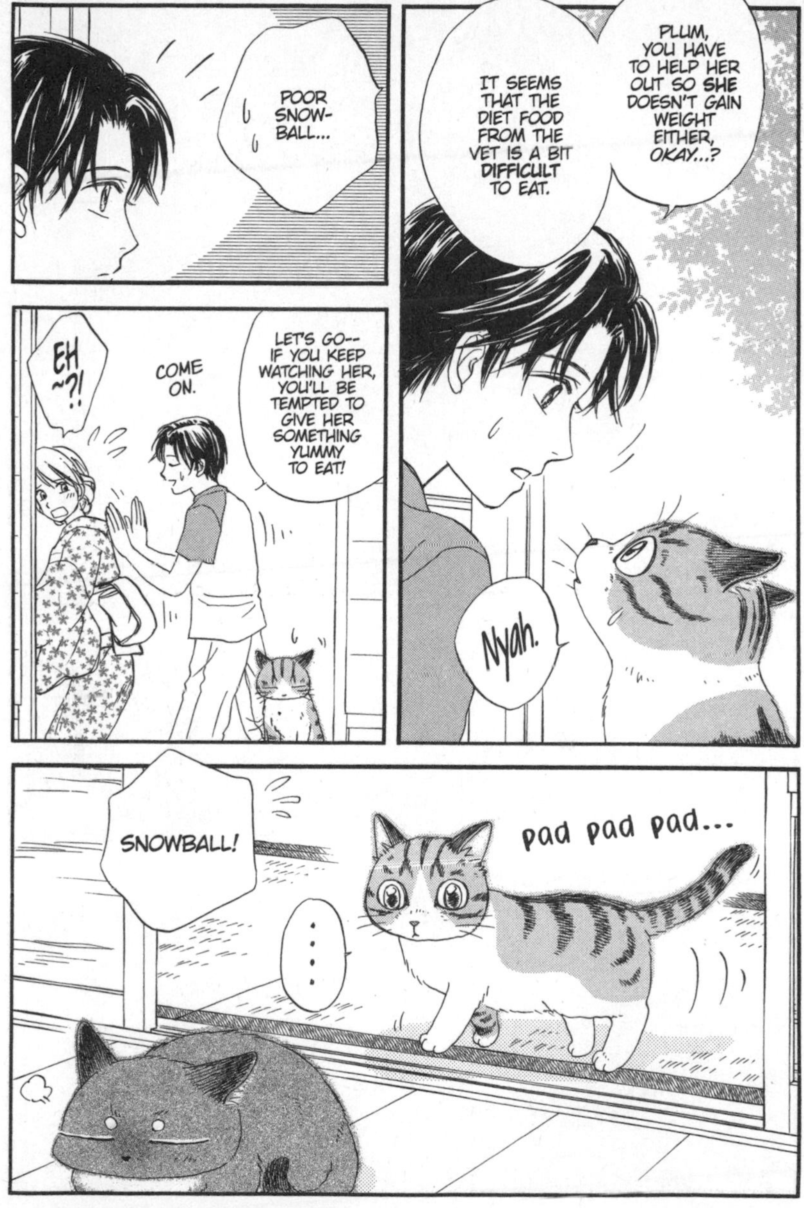
PLUM, YOU HAVE TO HELP HER OUT SO SHE DOESN'T GAIN WEIGHT EITHER, OKAY...?
IT SEEMS THAT THE DIET FOOD FROM THE VET IS A BIT DIFFICULT TO EAT.
Nyah.
POOR SNOW-BALL...
LET'S GO-- IF YOU KEEP WATCHING HER, YOU'LL BE TEMPTED TO GIVE HER SOMETHING YUMMY TO EAT!
COME ON.
EH ~?!
pad pad pad...
SNOWBALL!
....

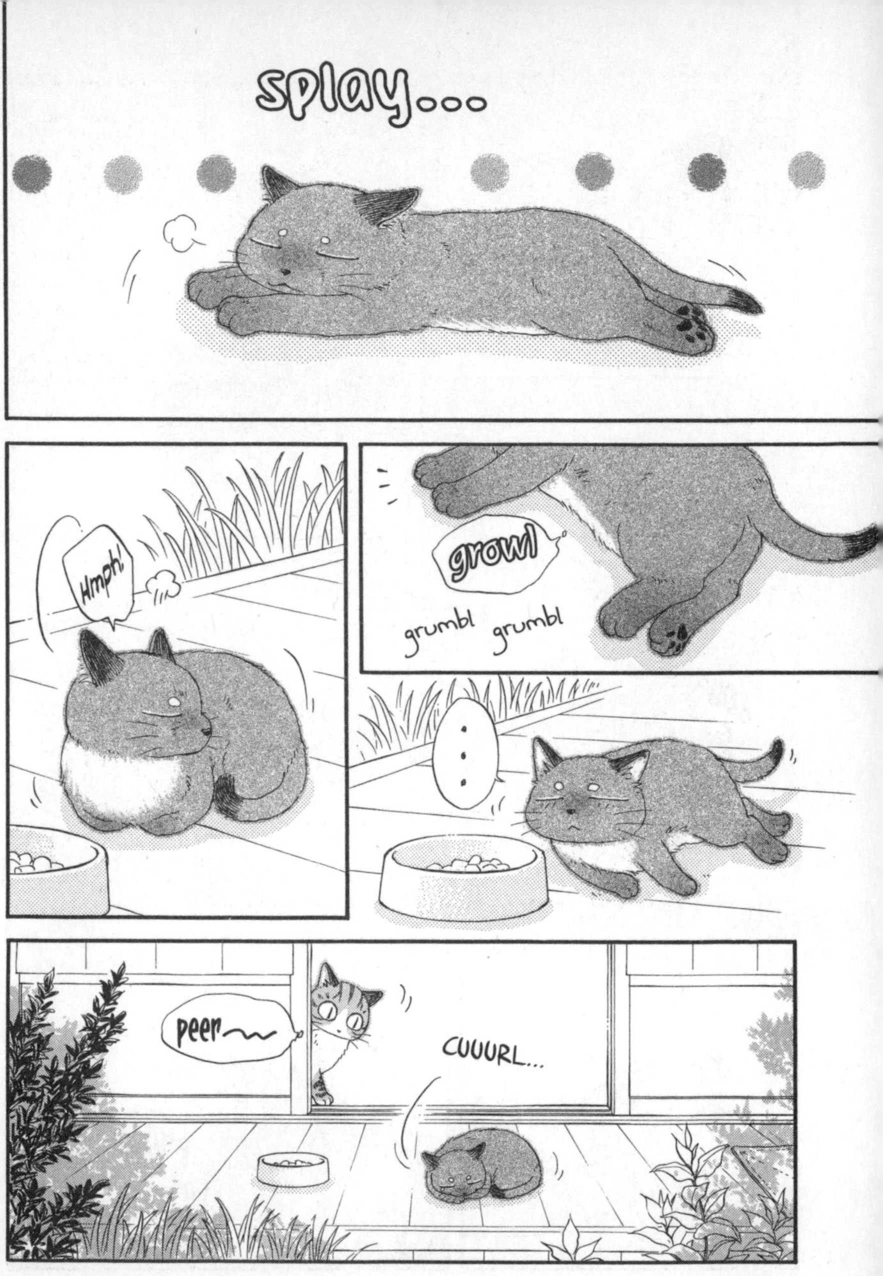
splay...
growl
grumbl grumbl
...
Hmph!
CUUURL...
peer~

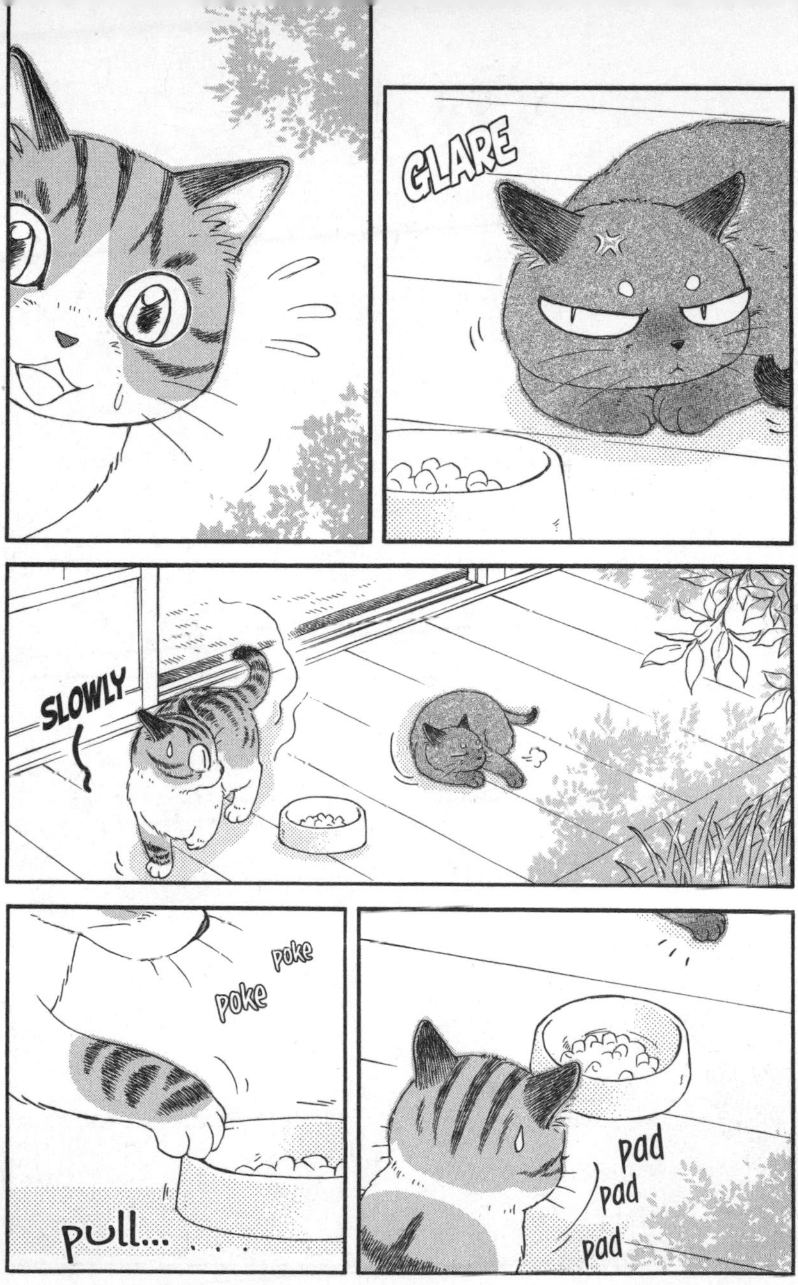
GLARE
SLOWLY
pad
pad
pad
poke
poke
pull... . . .

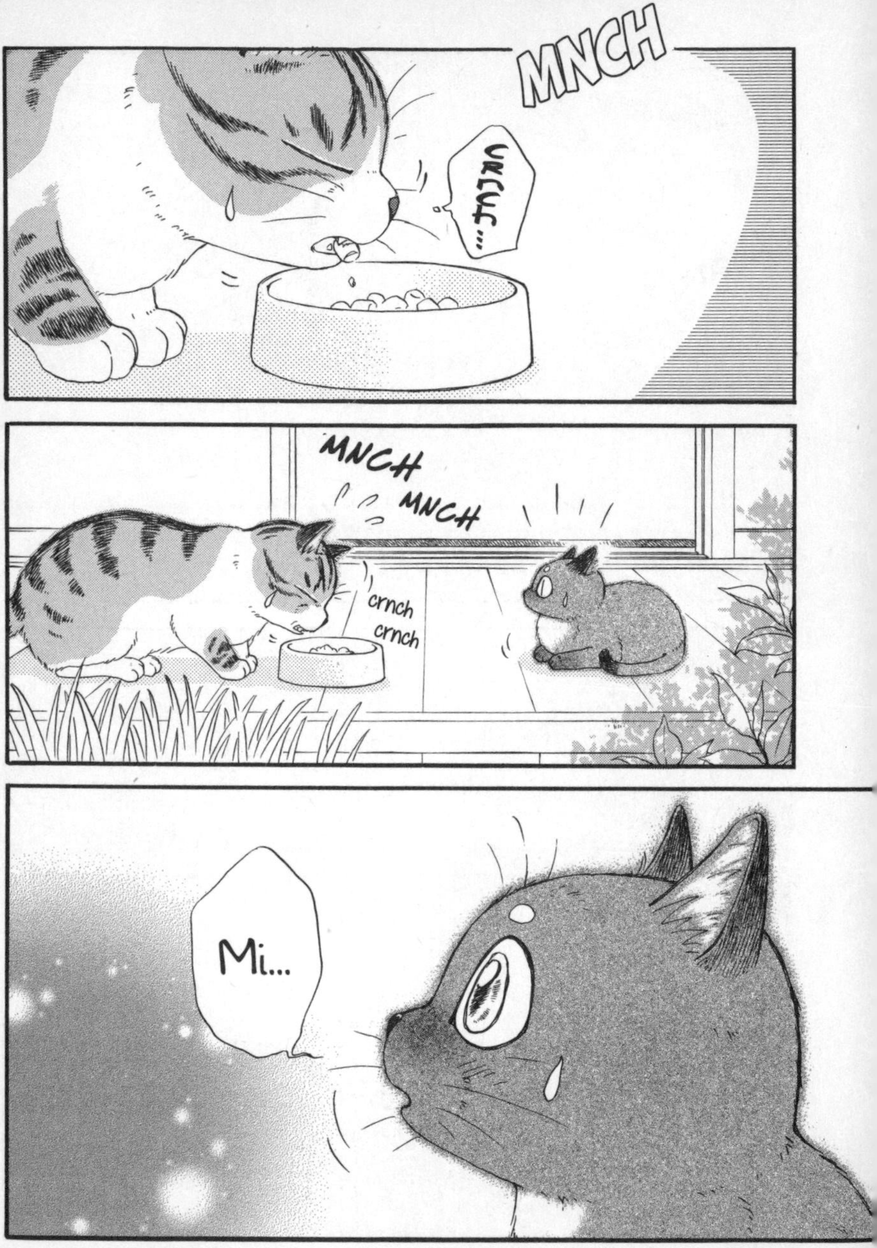
MNCH
URGGH...
MNCH
MNCH
crnch
crnch
Mi...

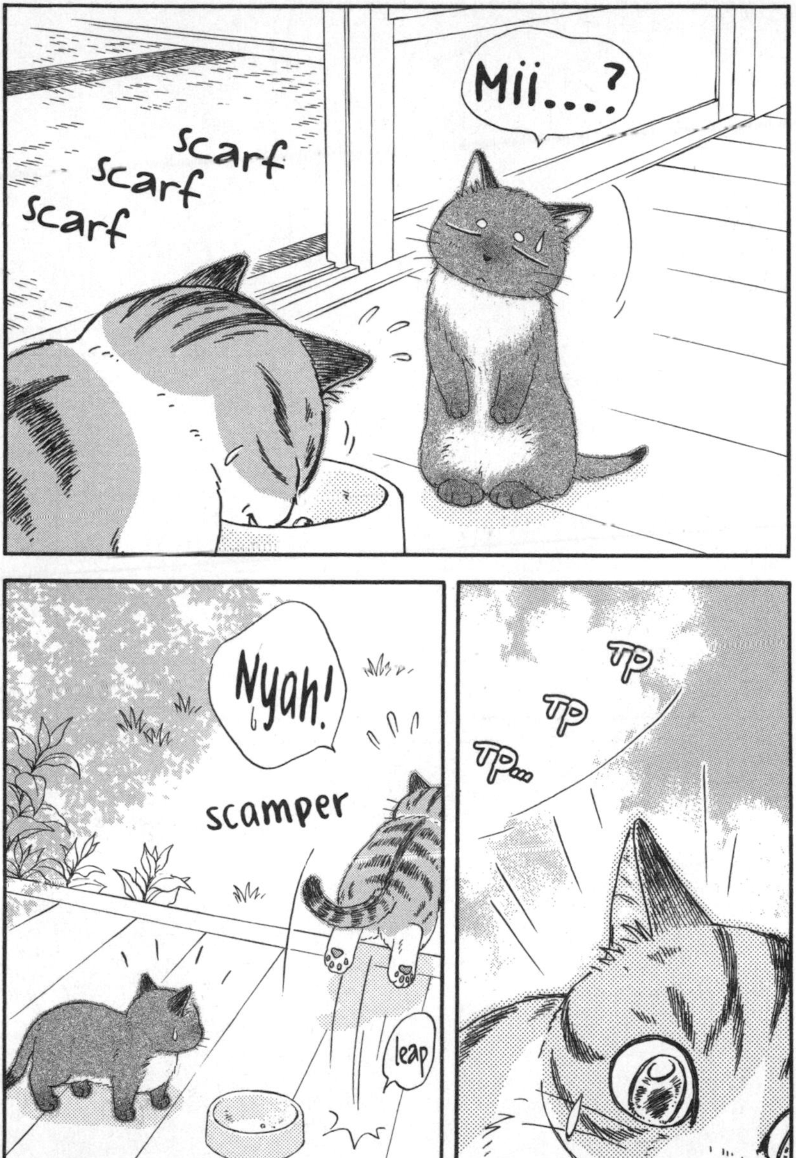
Mii...?
scarf
scarf
scarf
TP
TP
TP...
Nyah!
scamper
leap

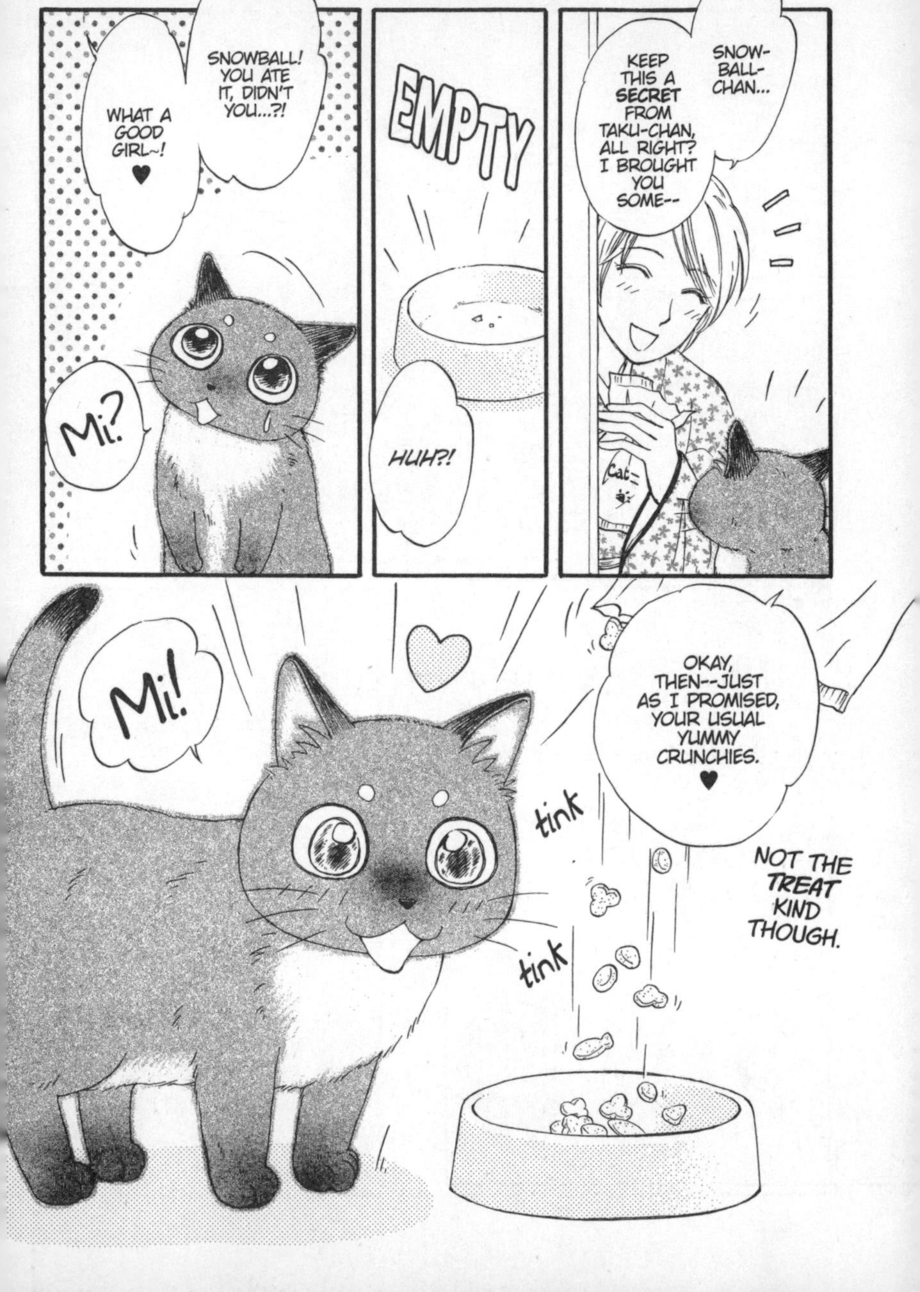
SNOW-BALL-CHAN...
KEEP THIS A SECRET FROM TAKU-CHAN, ALL RIGHT? I BROUGHT YOU SOME--
Cat
EMPTY
HUH?!
SNOWBALL! YOU ATE IT, DIDN'T YOU...?!
WHAT A GOOD GIRL~! ♥
Mi?
OKAY, THEN--JUST AS I PROMISED, YOUR USUAL YUMMY CRUNCHIES. ♥
NOT THE TREAT KIND THOUGH.
tink
tink
Mi!

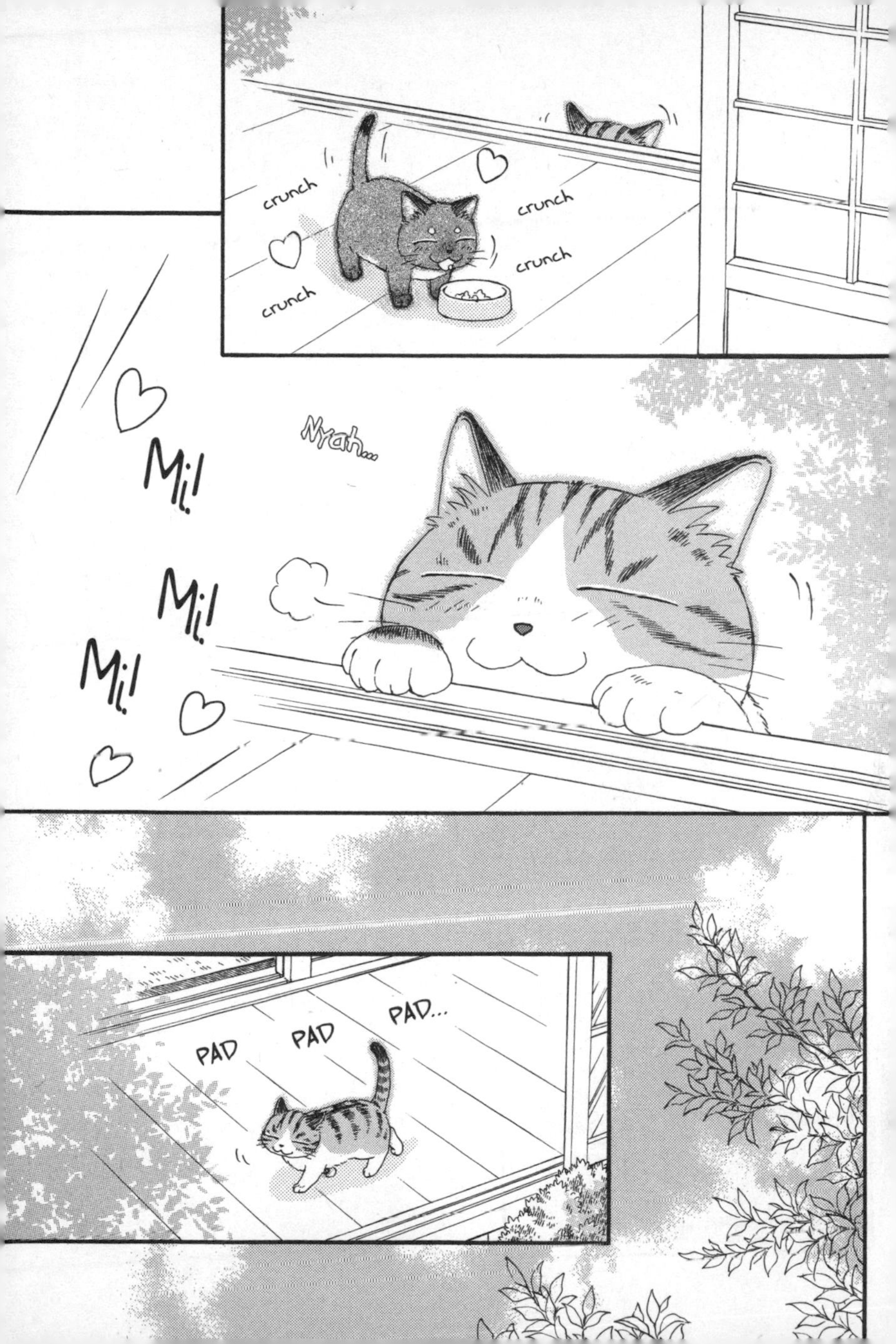
crunch
crunch
crunch
crunch
Nyah...
Mi!
Mi!
Mi!
PAD
PAD
PAD...

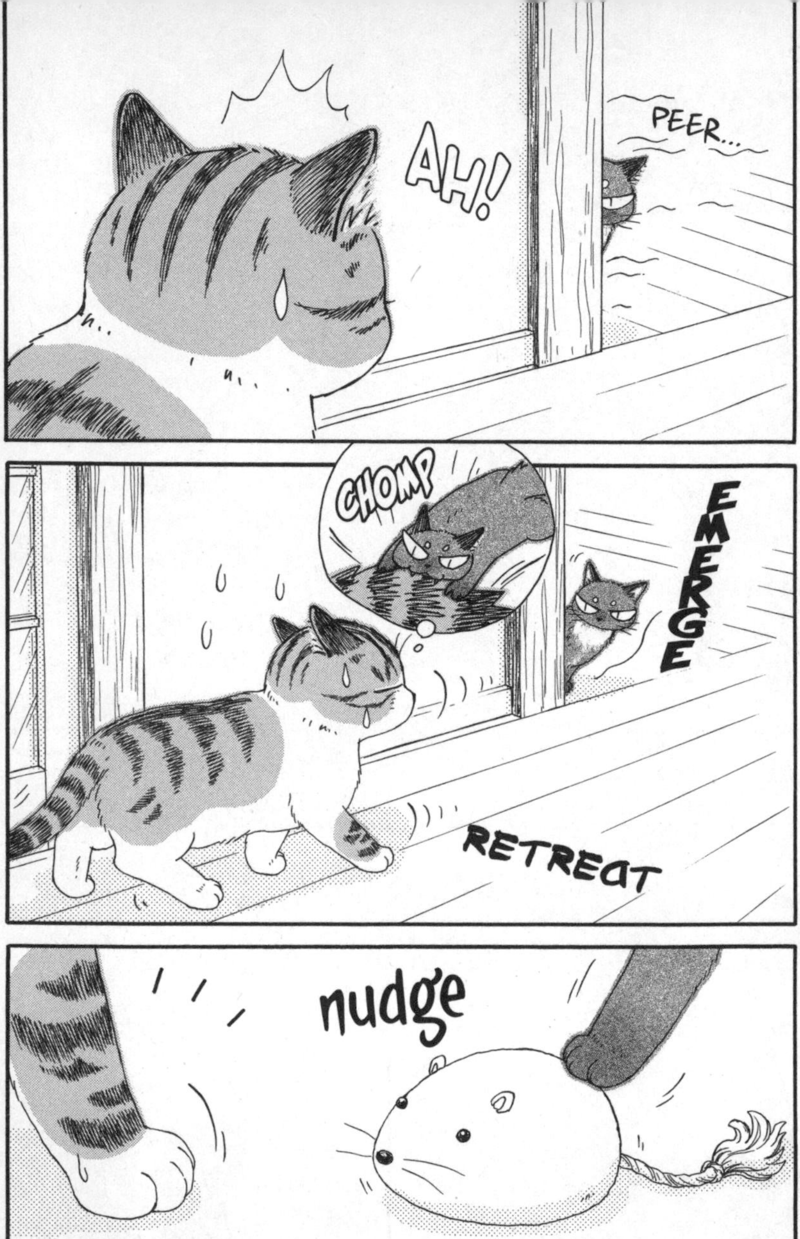
PEER...
AH!
EMERGE
CHOMP
RETREAT
nudge

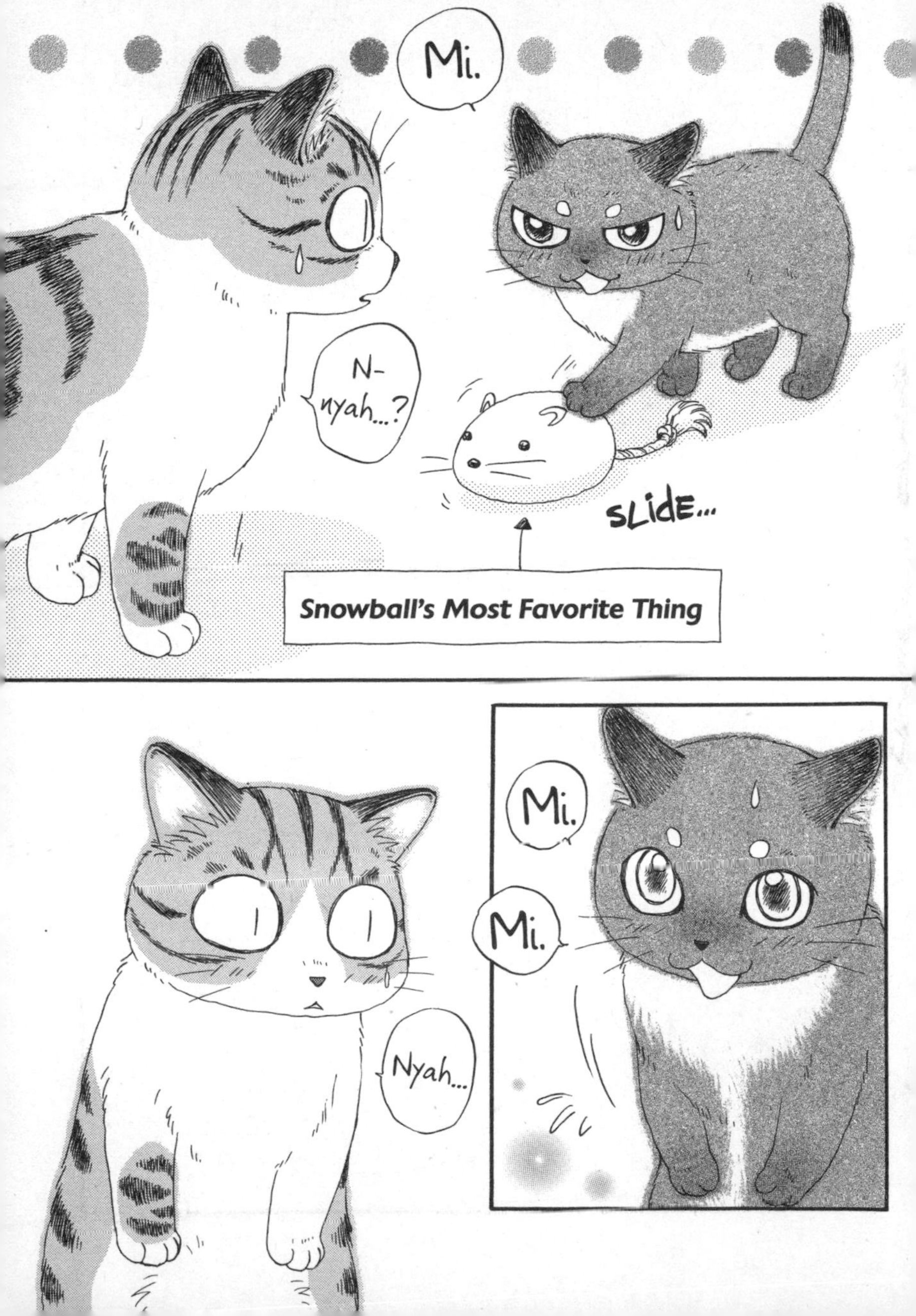
Mi.
N-nyah...?
SLIDE...
Snowball's Most Favorite Thing
Mi.
Mi.
Nyah...

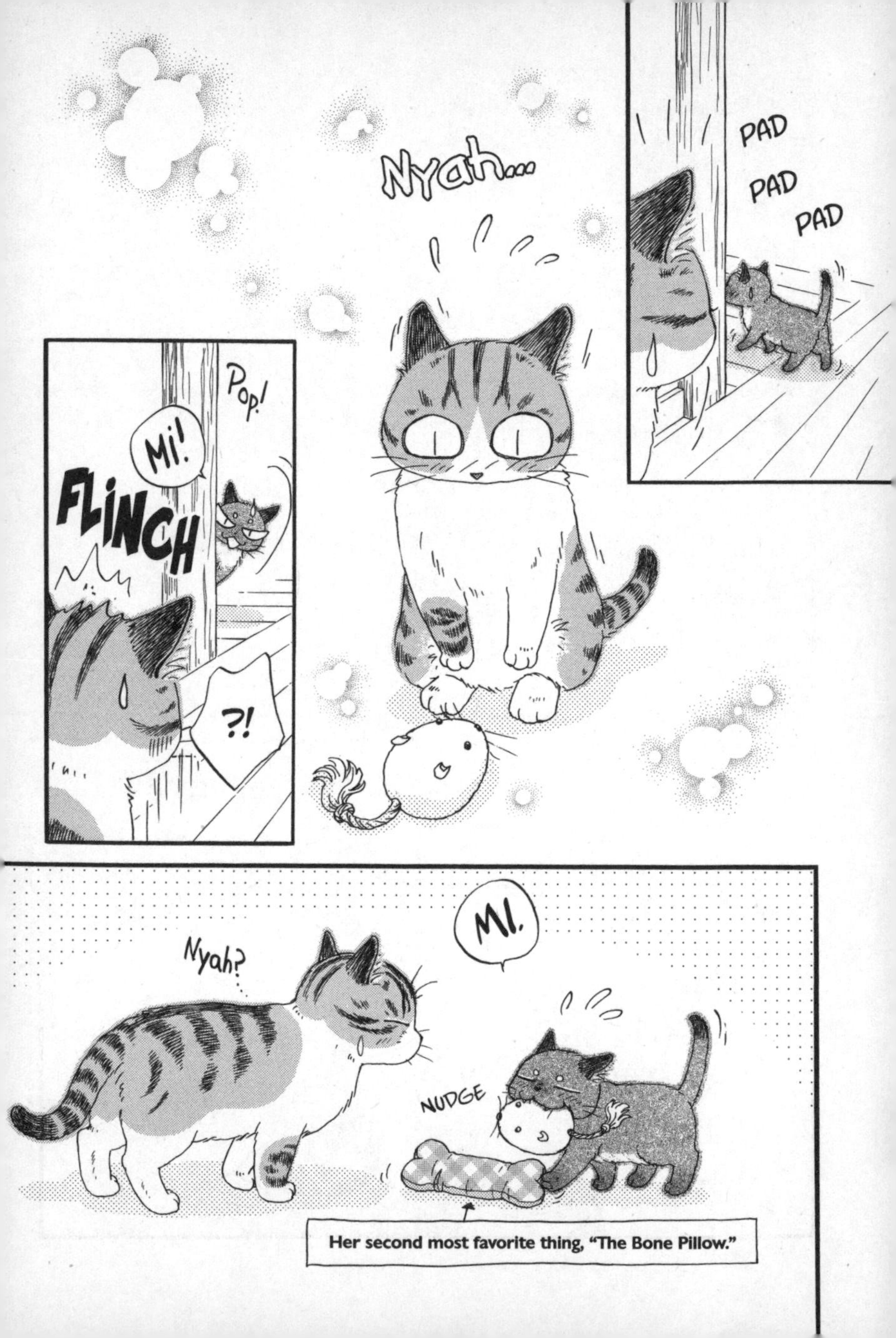
PAD
PAD
PAD
Nyah...
Pop!
Mi!
FLINCH
?!
MI.
Nyah?
NUDGE
Her second most favorite thing, "The Bone Pillow."

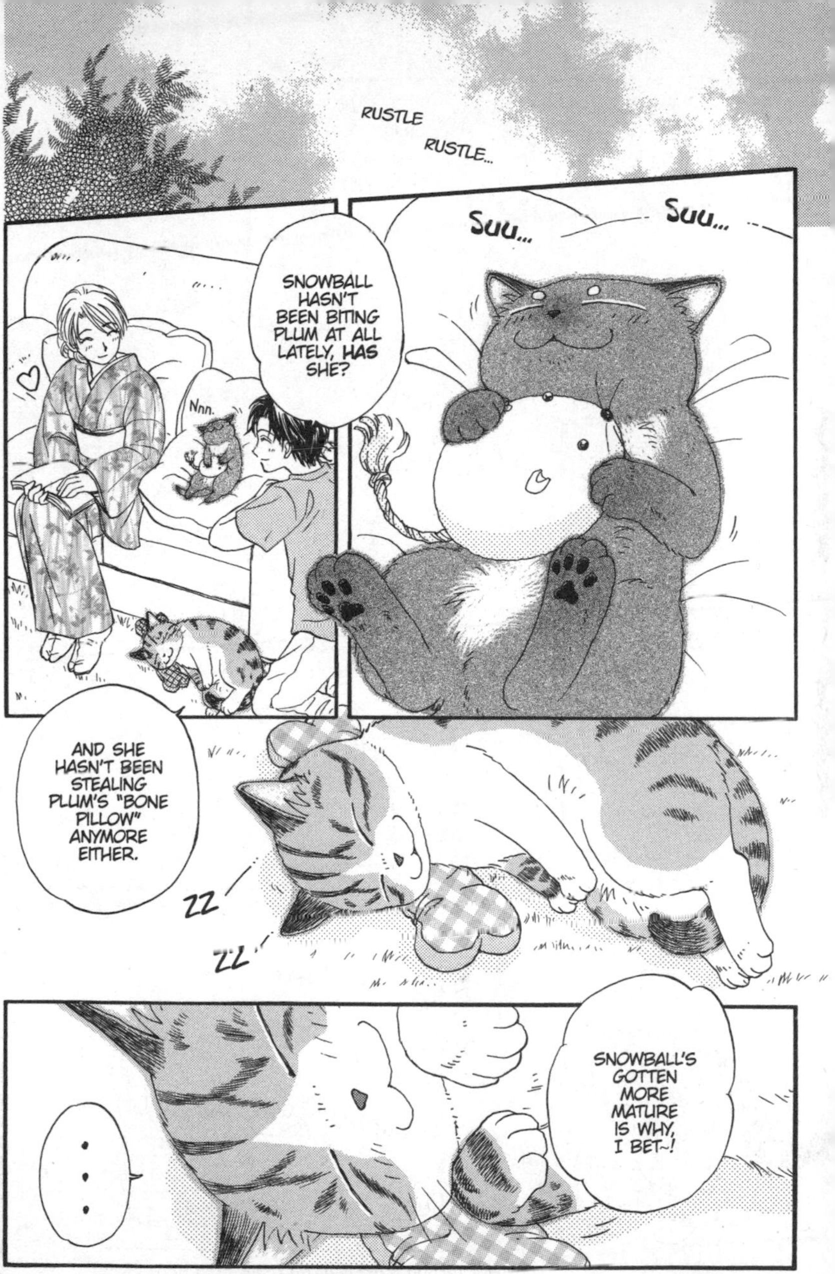
RUSTLE
RUSTLE...
Suu...
Suu...
SNOWBALL HASN'T BEEN BITING PLUM AT ALL LATELY, HAS SHE?
Nnn.
AND SHE HASN'T BEEN STEALING PLUM'S "BONE PILLOW" ANYMORE EITHER.
ZZ
ZZ
SNOWBALL'S GOTTEN MORE MATURE IS WHY, I BET~!
...

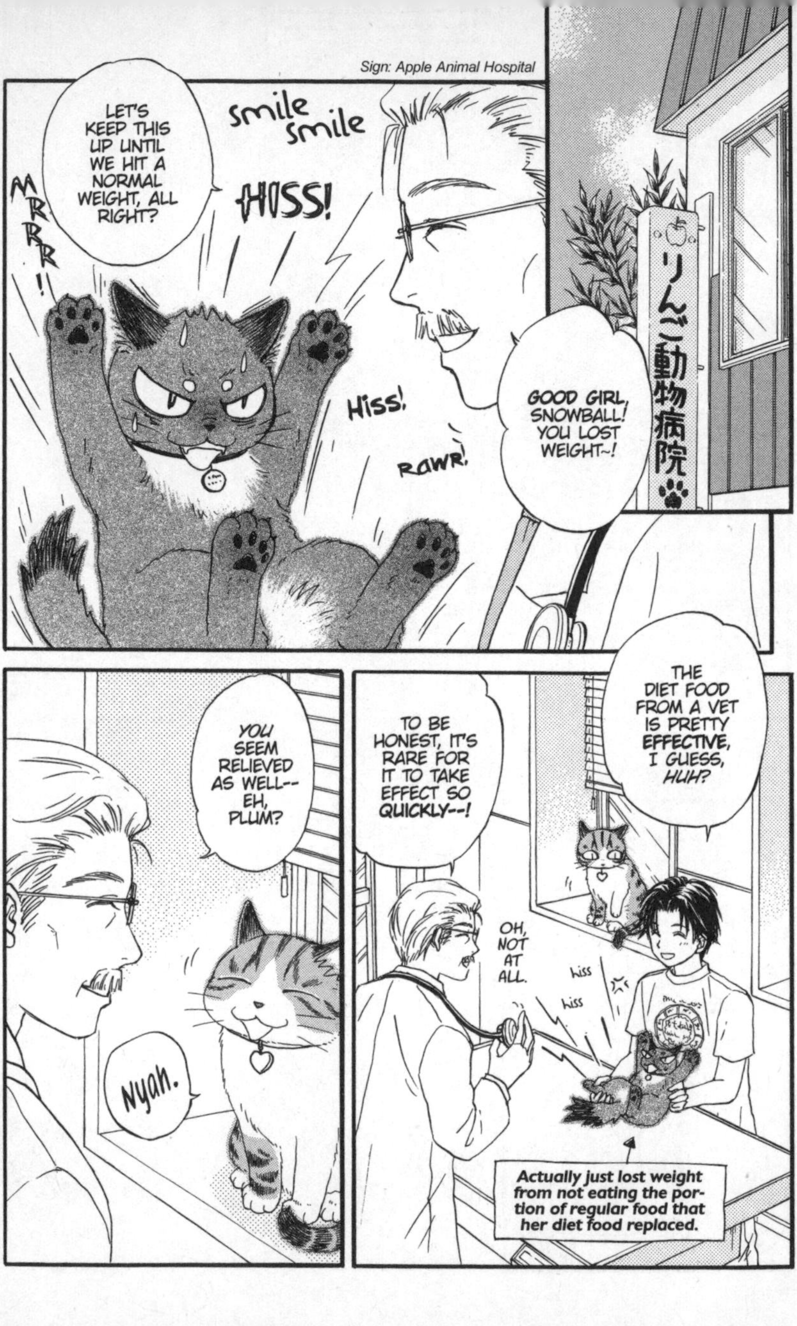
Sign: Apple Animal Hospital
りんご動物病院
GOOD GIRL, SNOWBALL! YOU LOST WEIGHT~!
RAWR!
Hiss!
HISS!
smile smile
LET'S KEEP THIS UP UNTIL WE HIT A NORMAL WEIGHT, ALL RIGHT?
MRRR!
THE DIET FOOD FROM A VET IS PRETTY EFFECTIVE, I GUESS, HUH?
TO BE HONEST, IT'S RARE FOR IT TO TAKE EFFECT SO QUICKLY--!
OH, NOT AT ALL.
hiss
hiss
Actually just lost weight from not eating the portion of regular food that her diet food replaced.
YOU SEEM RELIEVED AS WELL--EH, PLUM?
Nyah.

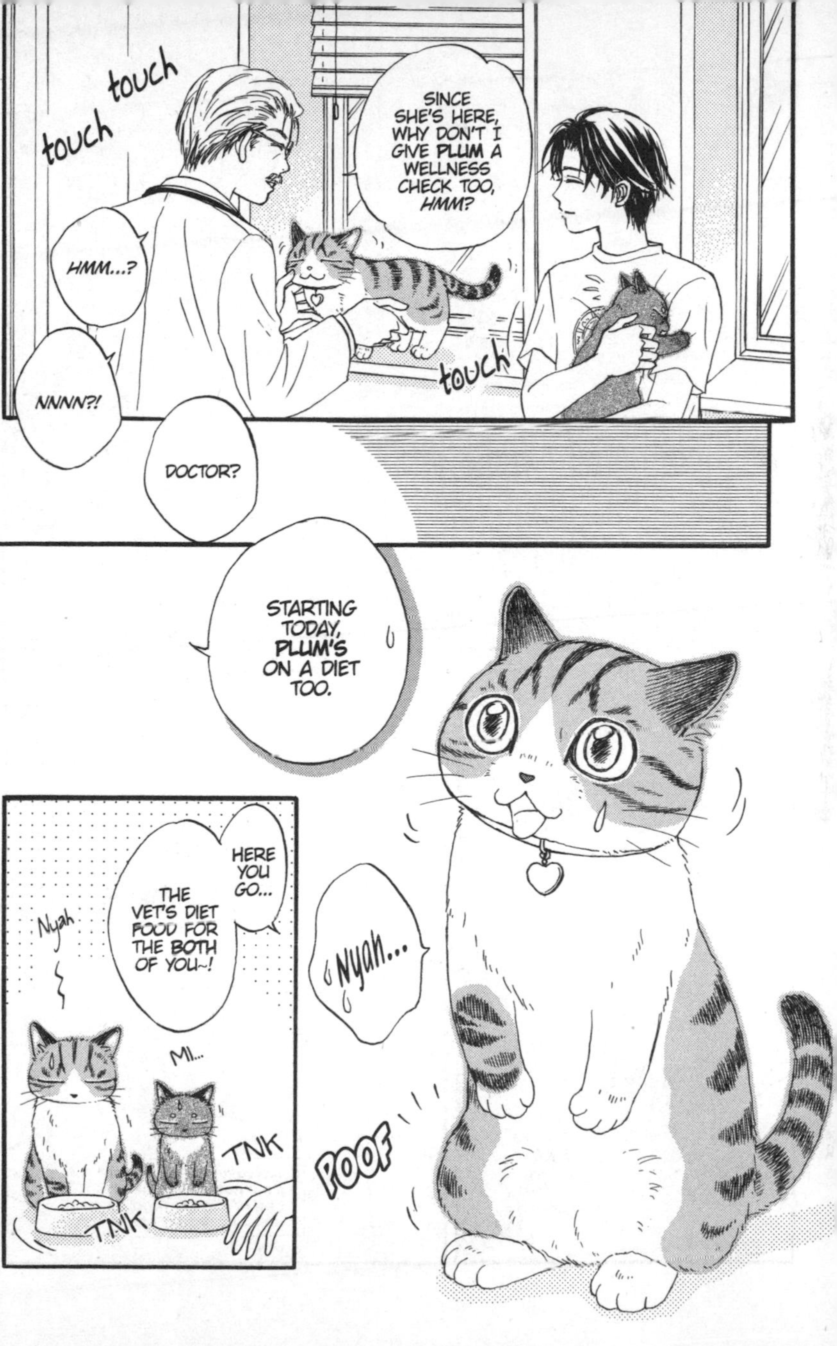
SINCE SHE'S HERE, WHY DON'T I GIVE PLUM A WELLNESS CHECK TOO, HMM?
touch
touch touch
HMM...?
NNNN?!
DOCTOR?
STARTING TODAY, PLUM'S ON A DIET TOO.
Nyah...
POOF
HERE YOU GO...
THE VET'S DIET FOOD FOR THE BOTH OF YOU~!
Nyah
MI...
TNK
TNK

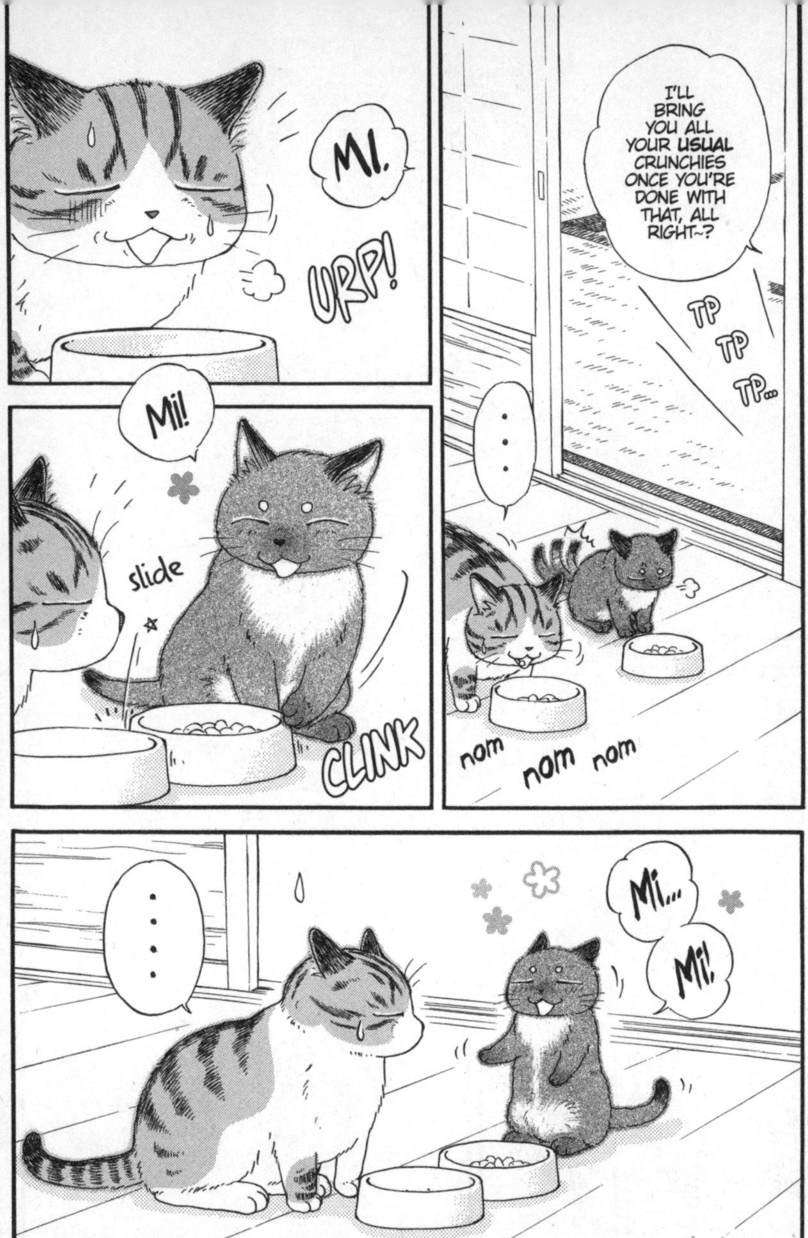
I'LL BRING YOU ALL YOUR USUAL CRUNCHIES ONCE YOU'RE DONE WITH THAT, ALL RIGHT~?
TP
TP
TP...
...
nom
nom nom
MI.
URP!
Mi!
slide
CLINK
Mi...
Mi!
....

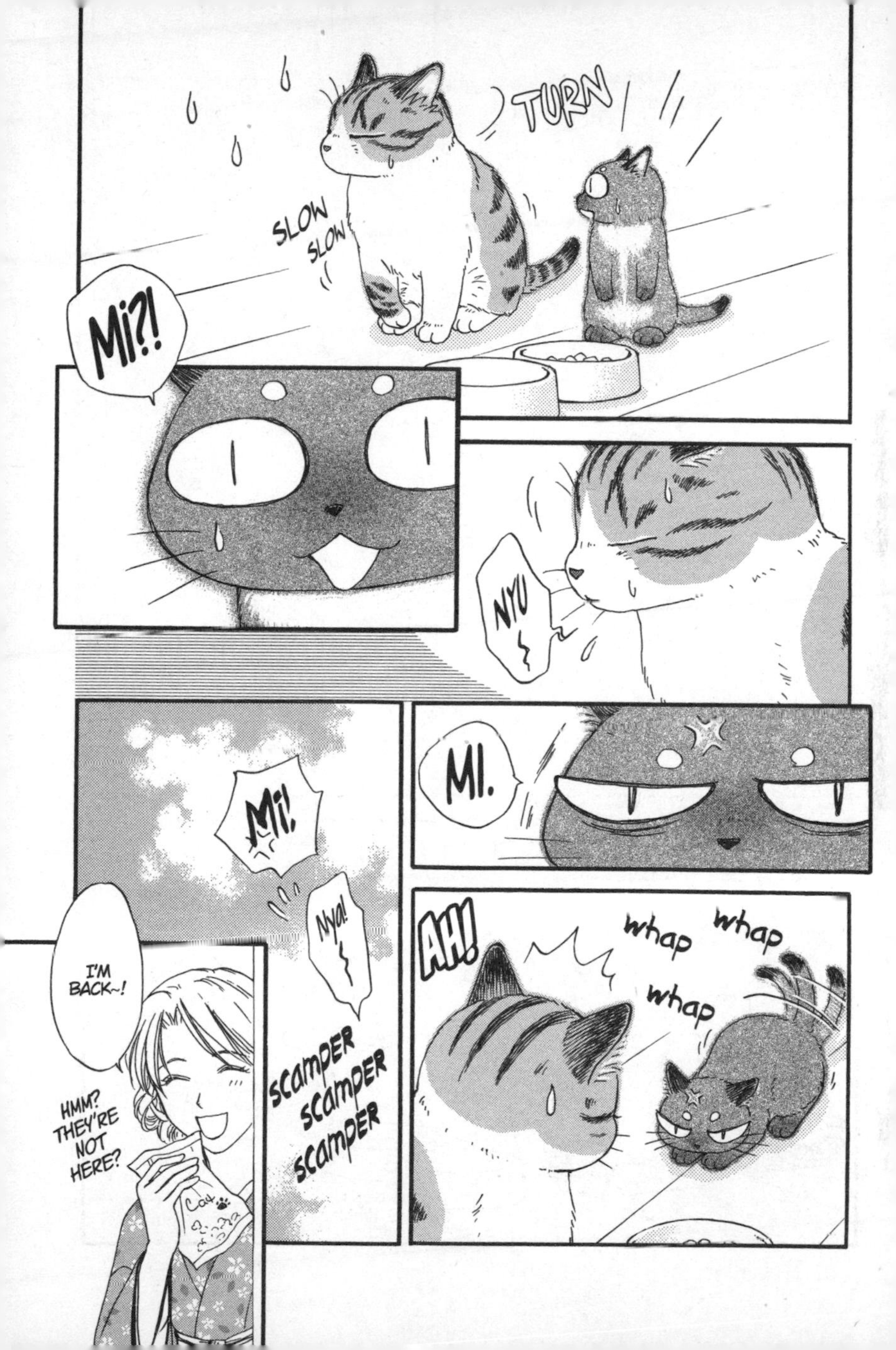
TURN
SLOW SLOW
NYU~
Mi?!
MI.
Mi!
Nya!~
AH!
whap whap whap
scamper scamper scamper scamper
I'M BACK~!
HMM? THEY'RE NOT HERE?

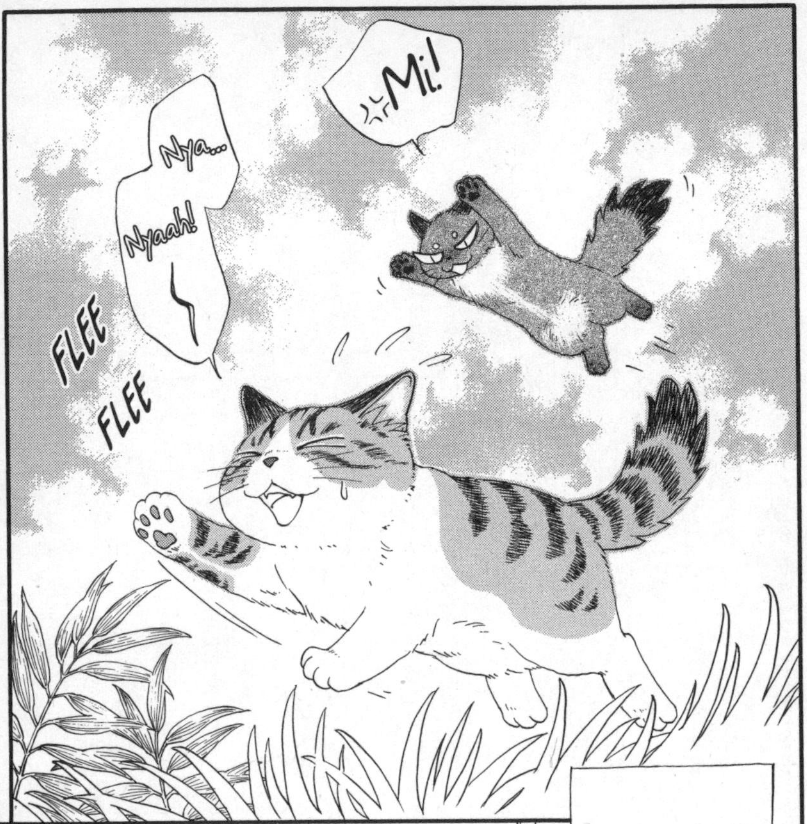
Mi!
Nya... Nyaah!
FLEE
FLEE

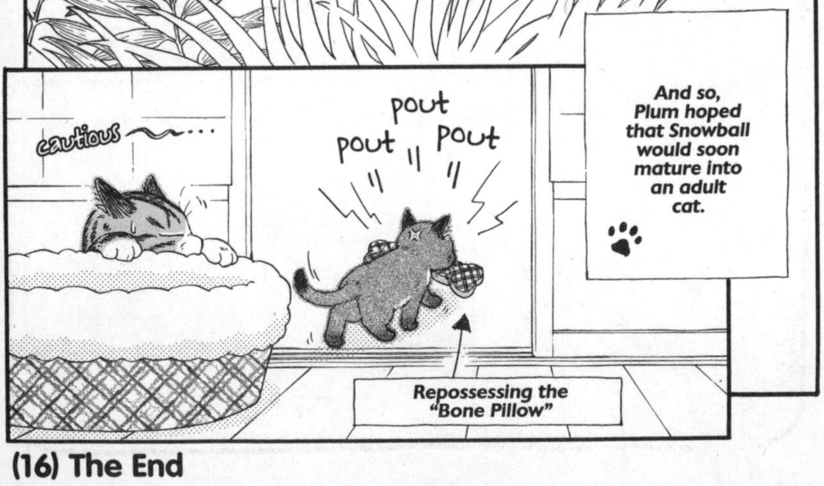
And so, Plum hoped that Snowball would soon mature into an adult cat.
pout pout pout
Repossessing the "Bone Pillow"
cautious...

(16) The End

Short.12

Cat Door

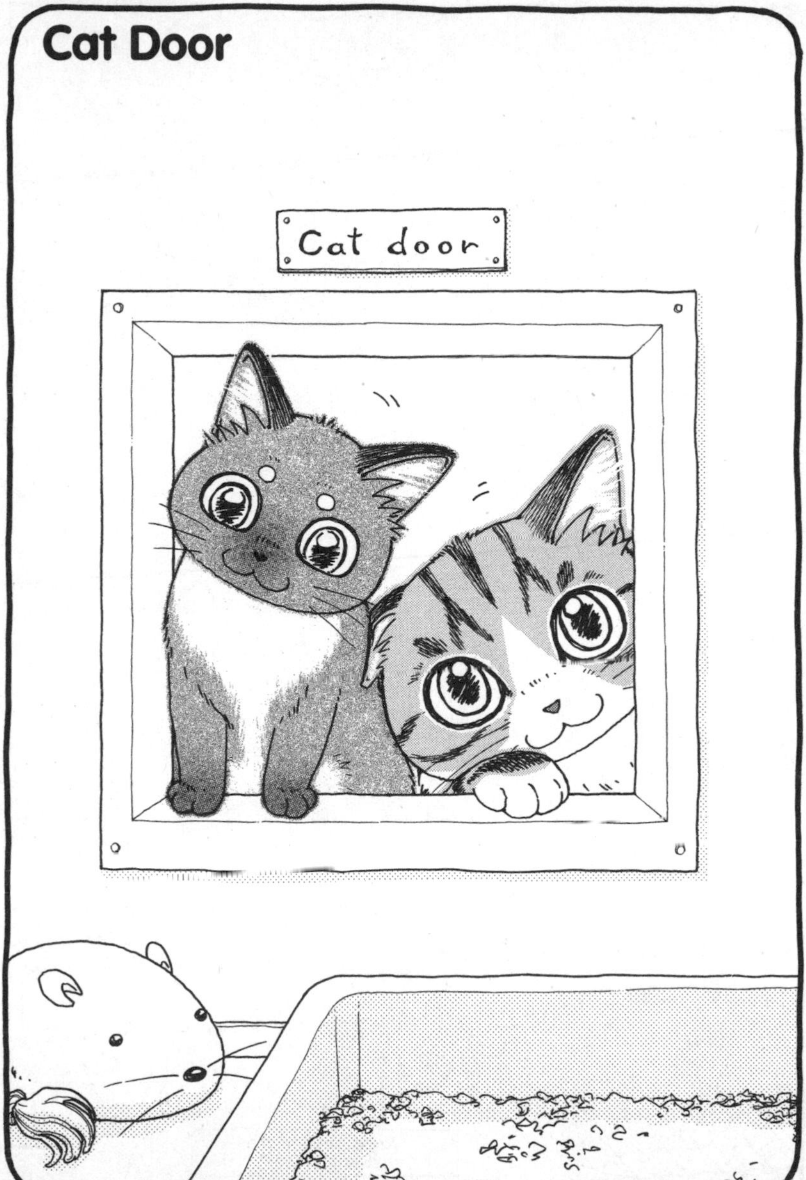
Cat door

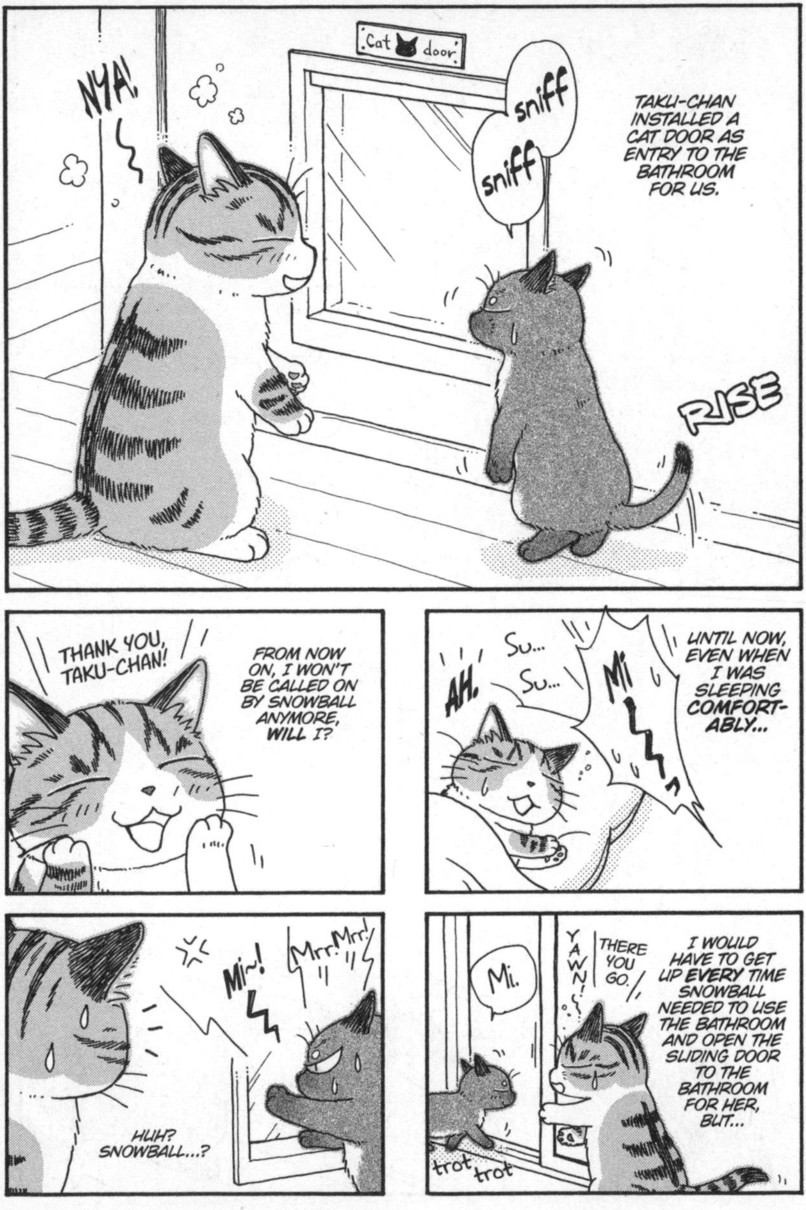
TAKU-CHAN INSTALLED A CAT DOOR AS ENTRY TO THE BATHROOM FOR US.
sniff sniff
Cat door
NYA!
RISE
UNTIL NOW, EVEN WHEN I WAS SLEEPING **COMFORT-ABLY...**
Mi~
Su... Su...
AH.
FROM NOW ON, I WON'T BE CALLED ON BY SNOWBALL ANYMORE, **WILL** I?
THANK YOU, TAKU-CHAN!
I WOULD HAVE TO GET UP **EVERY** TIME SNOWBALL NEEDED TO USE THE BATHROOM AND OPEN THE SLIDING DOOR TO THE BATHROOM FOR HER, BUT...
THERE YOU GO.
YAWN!
Mi.
trot trot
Mrr. Mrr!
Mi~!
HUH? SNOWBALL...?

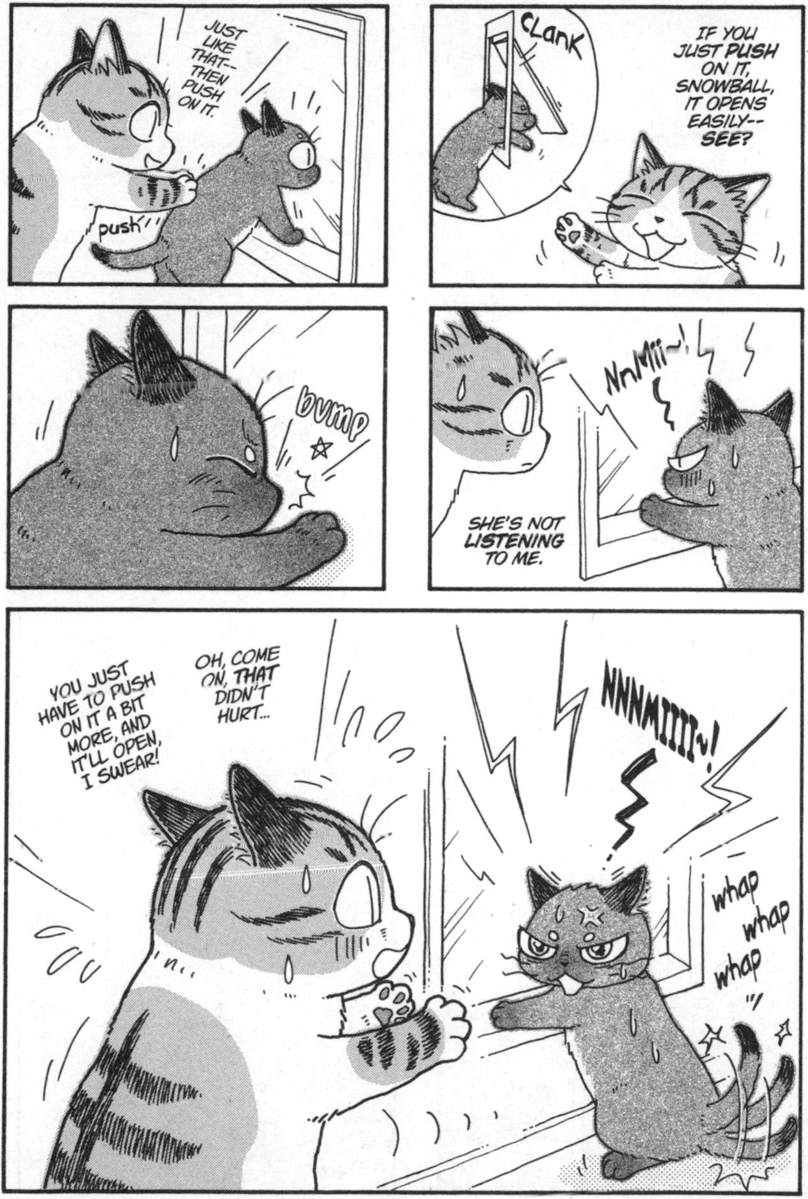
IF YOU JUST PUSH ON IT, SNOWBALL, IT OPENS EASILY-- SEE?
CLank
JUST LIKE THAT-- THEN PUSH ON IT.
push
NnMii~
SHE'S NOT LISTENING TO ME.
bump
NNNMIIII~!
whap whap whap
OH, COME ON, THAT DIDN'T HURT...
YOU JUST HAVE TO PUSH ON IT A BIT MORE, AND IT'LL OPEN, I SWEAR!

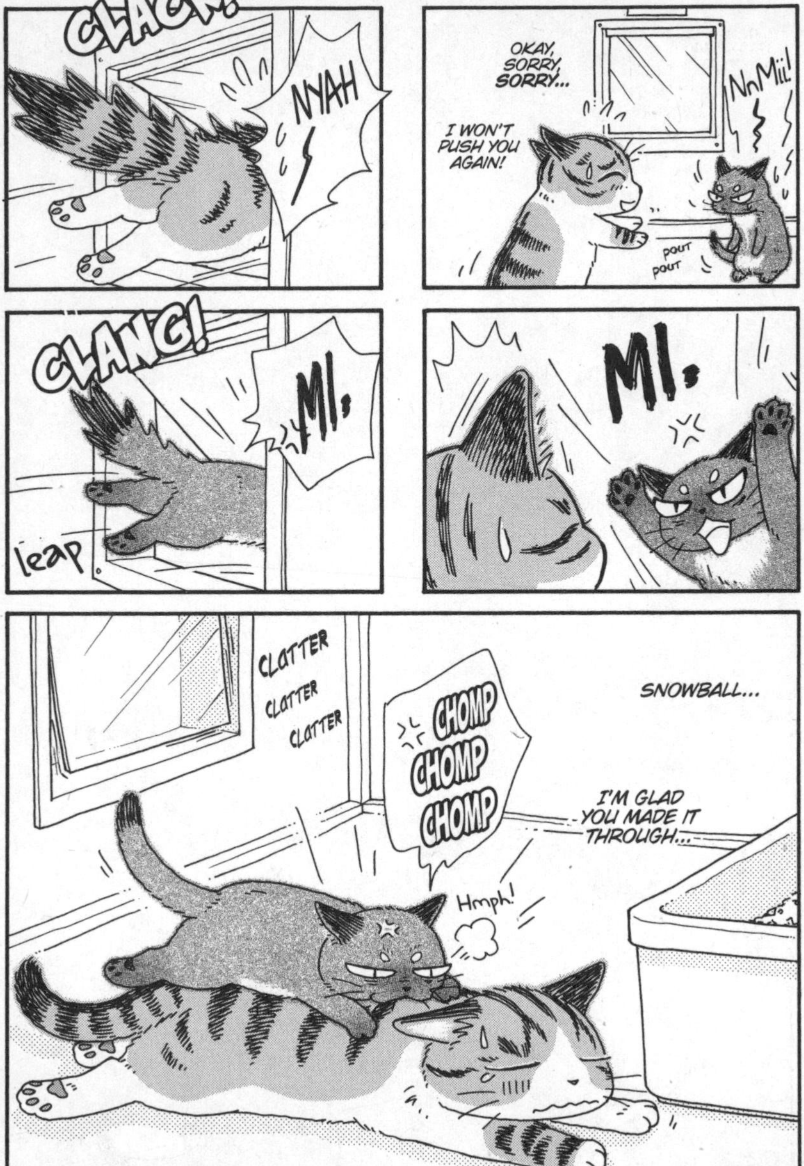
OKAY, SORRY, SORRY...
I WON'T PUSH YOU AGAIN!
NnMii!
pout pout
CLACK!
NYAH
MI.
CLANG!
MI.
leap
SNOWBALL...
I'M GLAD YOU MADE IT THROUGH...
CHOMP CHOMP CHOMP
Hmph!
CLATTER CLATTER CLATTER

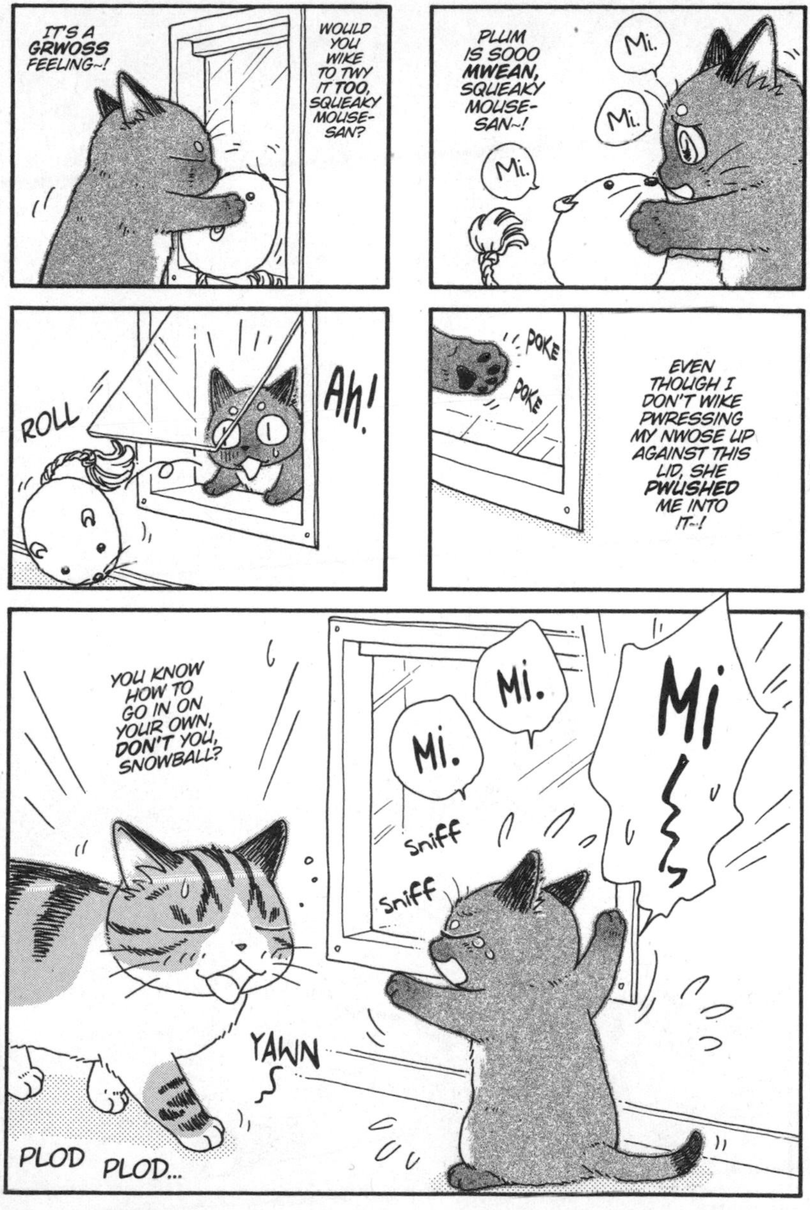
Mi.
Mi.
PLUM IS SOOO MWEAN, SQUEAKY MOUSE-SAN~!
Mi.
WOULD YOU WIKE TO TWY IT TOO, SQUEAKY MOUSE-SAN?
IT'S A GRWOSS FEELING~!
EVEN THOUGH I DON'T WIKE PWRESSING MY NWOSE UP AGAINST THIS LID, SHE PWUSHED ME INTO IT~!
POKE
POKE
Ah!
ROLL
Mi
Mi.
Mi.
YOU KNOW HOW TO GO IN ON YOUR OWN, DON'T YOU, SNOWBALL?
Sniff
Sniff
YAWN
PLOD PLOD...

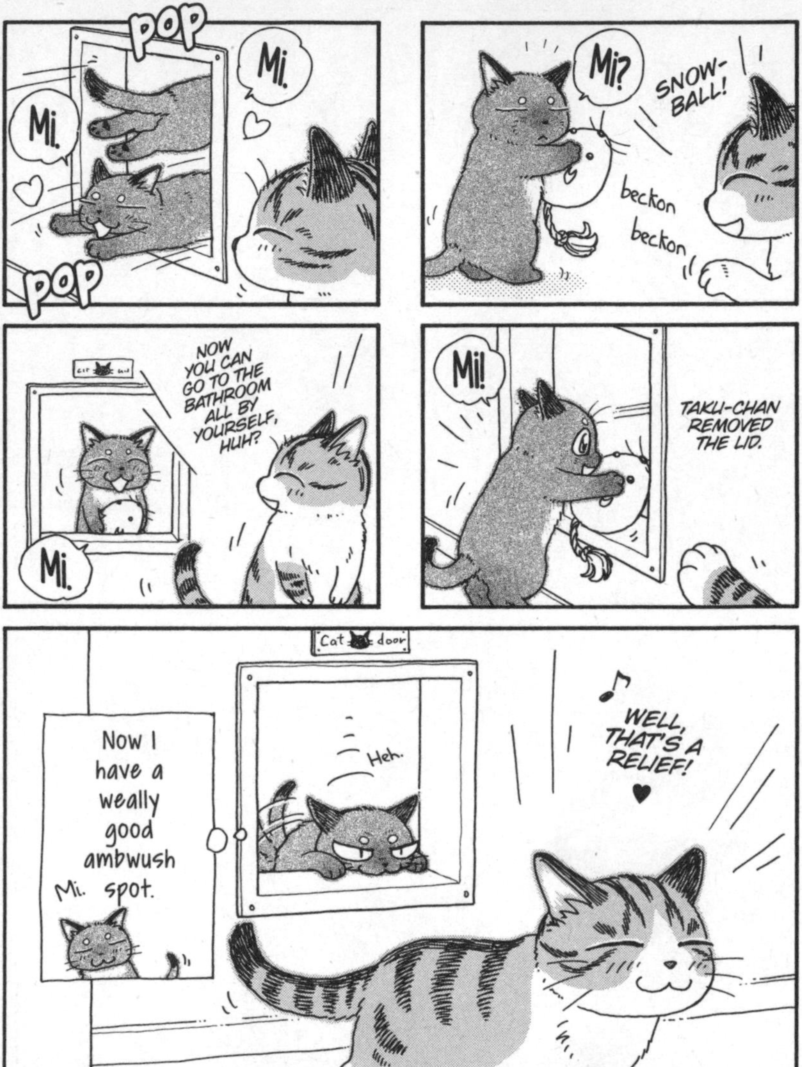
Mi?
SNOW-BALL!
beckon beckon
pop
Mi.
Mi.
pop
TAKU-CHAN REMOVED THE LID.
Mi!
NOW YOU CAN GO TO THE BATHROOM ALL BY YOURSELF, HUH?
Mi.
Cat door
WELL, THAT'S A RELIEF!
Heh.
Now I have a weally good ambwush spot.
Mi.
TROT TROT TROT

THE END

Short.13 Plum's Ecological Stance

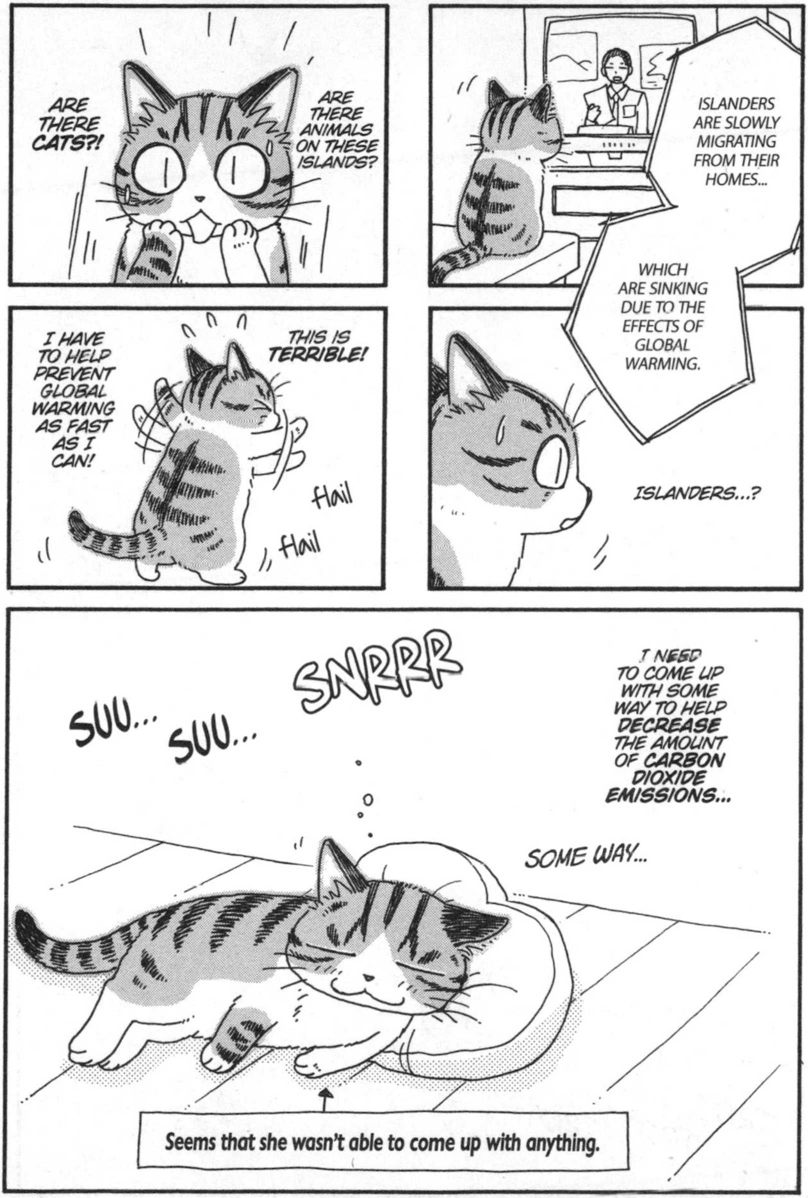
ISLANDERS ARE SLOWLY MIGRATING FROM THEIR HOMES...
WHICH ARE SINKING DUE TO THE EFFECTS OF GLOBAL WARMING.
ARE THERE ANIMALS ON THESE ISLANDS?
ARE THERE CATS?!
ISLANDERS...?
THIS IS TERRIBLE!
I HAVE TO HELP PREVENT GLOBAL WARMING AS FAST AS I CAN!
flail
flail
I NEED TO COME UP WITH SOME WAY TO HELP DECREASE THE AMOUNT OF CARBON DIOXIDE EMISSIONS...
SOME WAY...
SNRRR
SUU... SUU...
Seems that she wasn't able to come up with anything.

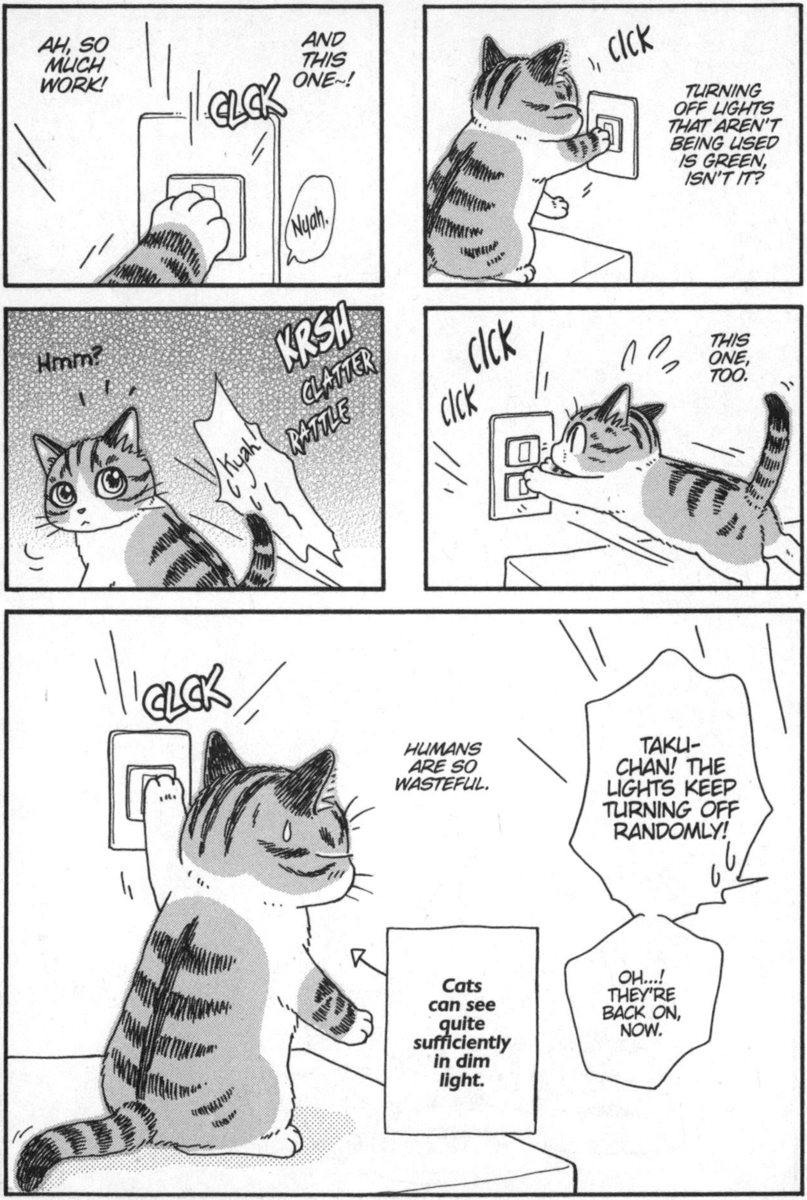
CLICK
TURNING OFF LIGHTS THAT AREN'T BEING USED IS GREEN, ISN'T IT?
AND THIS ONE~!
AH, SO MUCH WORK!
CLICK
Nyah.
THIS ONE, TOO.
CLICK
CLICK
KRSH
CLATTER
RATTLE
Hmm?
Kyah!
TAKU-CHAN! THE LIGHTS KEEP TURNING OFF RANDOMLY!
HUMANS ARE SO WASTEFUL.
CLICK
OH...! THEY'RE BACK ON, NOW.
Cats can see quite sufficiently in dim light.

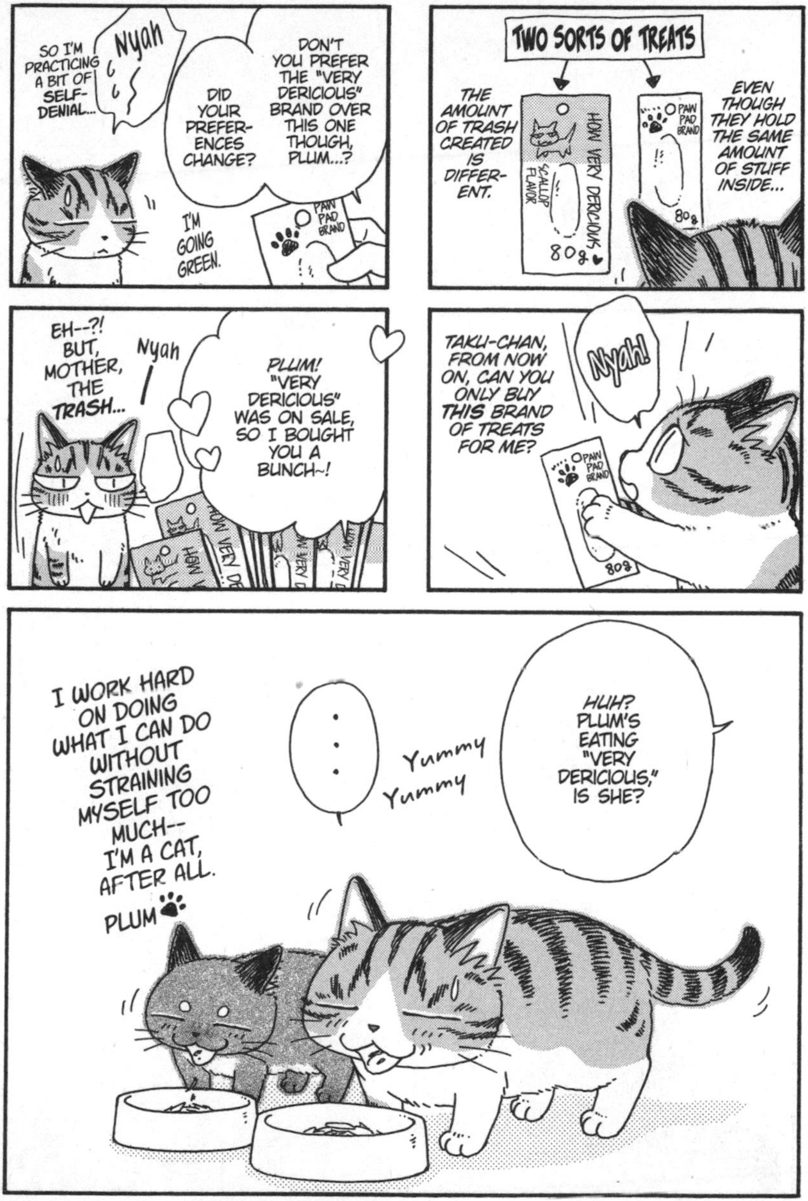
TWO SORTS OF TREATS
EVEN THOUGH THEY HOLD THE SAME AMOUNT OF STUFF INSIDE...
PAW PAD BRAND
80g
HOW VERY DERICIOUS
SCALLOP FLAVOR
80g
THE AMOUNT OF TRASH CREATED IS DIFFERENT.
DON'T YOU PREFER THE "VERY DERICIOUS" BRAND OVER THIS ONE THOUGH, PLUM...?
DID YOUR PREFERENCES CHANGE?
Nyah
SO I'M PRACTICING A BIT OF SELF-DENIAL...
PAW PAD BRAND
I'M GOING GREEN.
Nyah!
TAKU-CHAN, FROM NOW ON, CAN YOU ONLY BUY THIS BRAND OF TREATS FOR ME?
PAW PAD BRAND
80g
PLUM! "VERY DERICIOUS" WAS ON SALE, SO I BOUGHT YOU A BUNCH~!
Nyah
EH--?! BUT, MOTHER, THE TRASH...
HUH? PLUM'S EATING "VERY DERICIOUS," IS SHE?
Yummy Yummy
...
I WORK HARD ON DOING WHAT I CAN DO WITHOUT STRAINING MYSELF TOO MUCH-- I'M A CAT, AFTER ALL.
PLUM

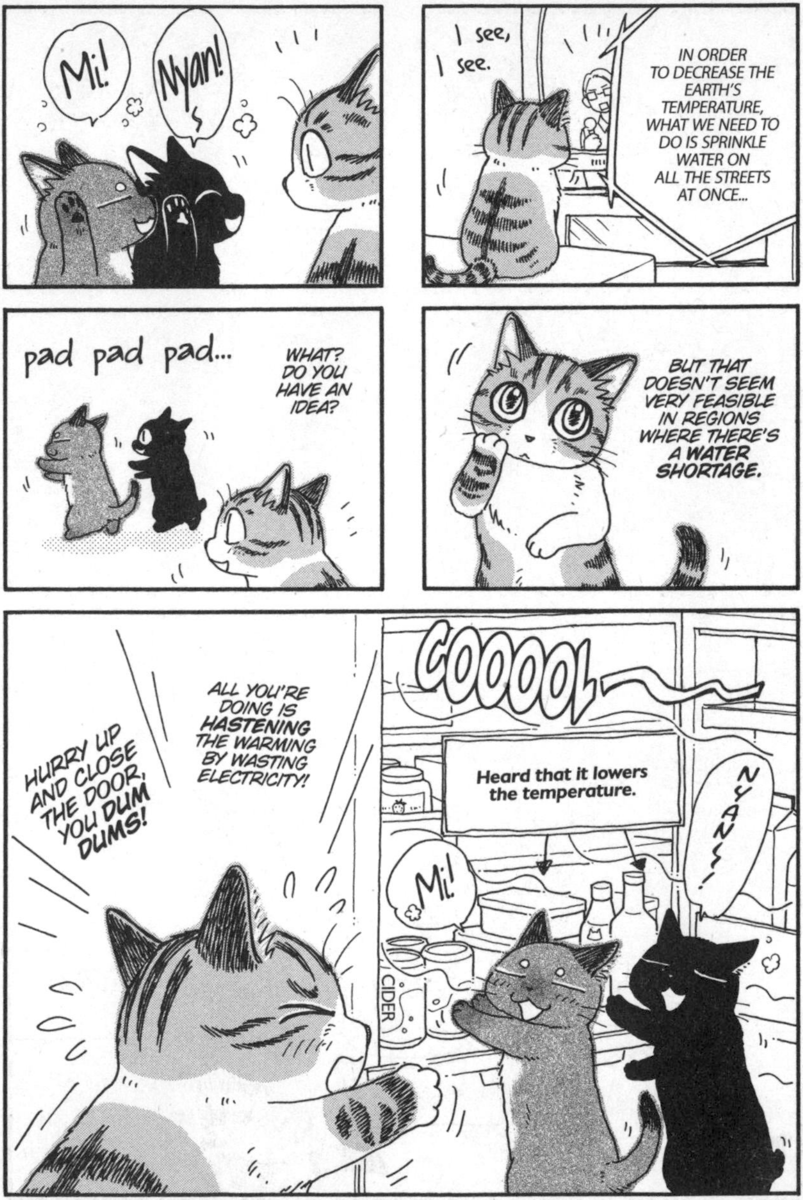
I see, I see.
IN ORDER TO DECREASE THE EARTH'S TEMPERATURE, WHAT WE NEED TO DO IS SPRINKLE WATER ON ALL THE STREETS AT ONCE...
Nyan!
Mi!
BUT THAT DOESN'T SEEM VERY FEASIBLE IN REGIONS WHERE THERE'S A WATER SHORTAGE.
WHAT? DO YOU HAVE AN IDEA?
pad pad pad...
COOOOL
Heard that it lowers the temperature.
NYAN!
Mi!
CIDER
ALL YOU'RE DOING IS HASTENING THE WARMING BY WASTING ELECTRICITY!
HURRY UP AND CLOSE THE DOOR, YOU DUM DUMS!

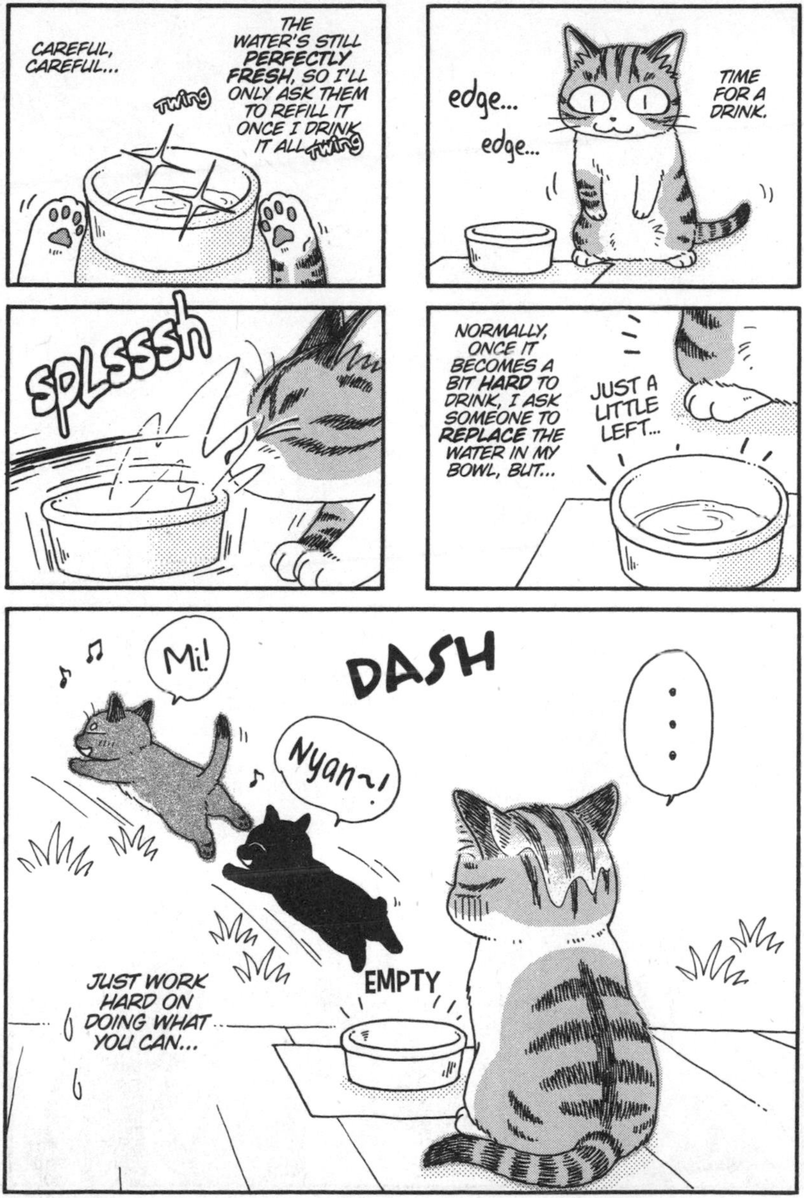
TIME FOR A DRINK.
edge...
edge...
THE WATER'S STILL **PERFECTLY FRESH**, SO I'LL ONLY ASK THEM TO REFILL IT ONCE I DRINK IT ALL
twing
CAREFUL, CAREFUL...
twing
JUST A LITTLE LEFT...
NORMALLY, ONCE IT BECOMES A BIT **HARD** TO DRINK, I ASK SOMEONE TO **REPLACE** THE WATER IN MY BOWL, BUT...
SPLSSSH
...
DASH
Nyan~!
Mi!
EMPTY
JUST WORK HARD ON DOING WHAT YOU CAN...

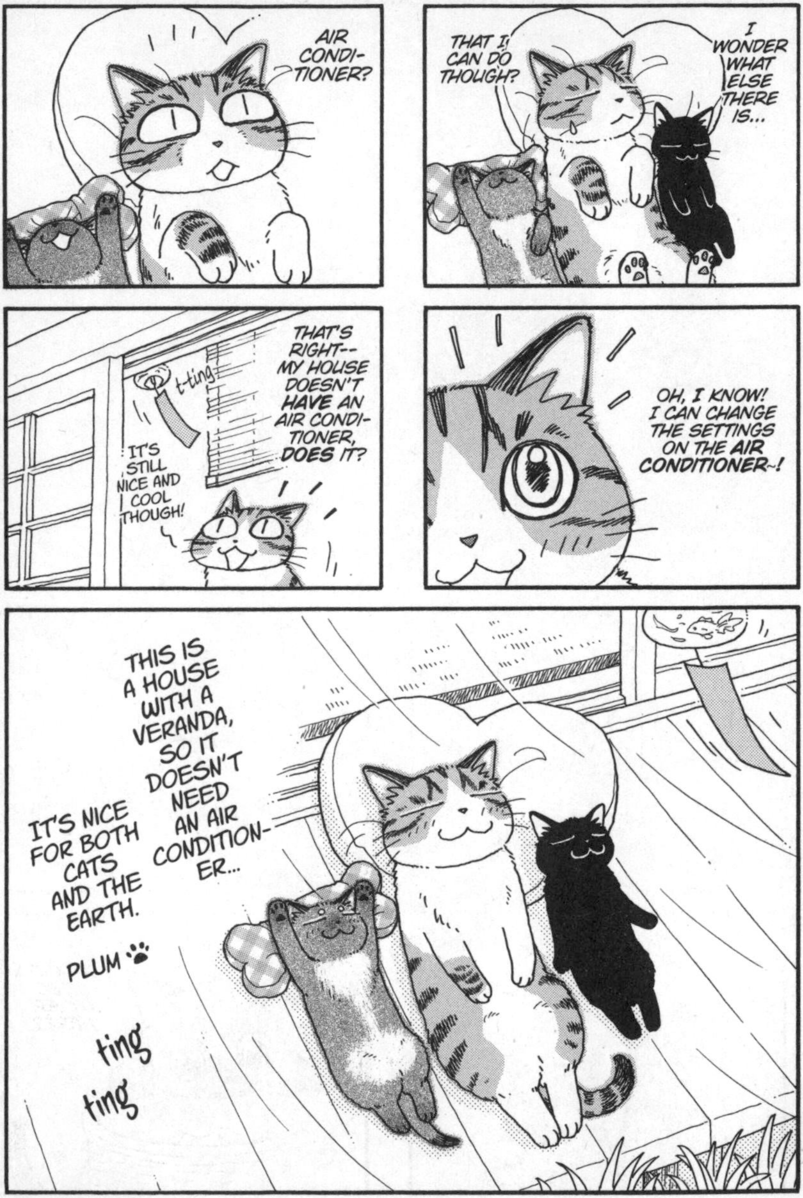
I WONDER WHAT ELSE THERE IS...
THAT I CAN DO THOUGH?
AIR CONDITIONER?
OH, I KNOW! I CAN CHANGE THE SETTINGS ON THE AIR CONDITIONER~!
THAT'S RIGHT-- MY HOUSE DOESN'T HAVE AN AIR CONDITIONER, DOES IT?
t-ting
IT'S STILL NICE AND COOL THOUGH!
THIS IS A HOUSE WITH A VERANDA, SO IT DOESN'T NEED AN AIR CONDITIONER...
IT'S NICE FOR BOTH CATS AND THE EARTH.
PLUM
ting
ting

The End

Short.14 The Kidnapping Incident of Squeaky Mouse-san

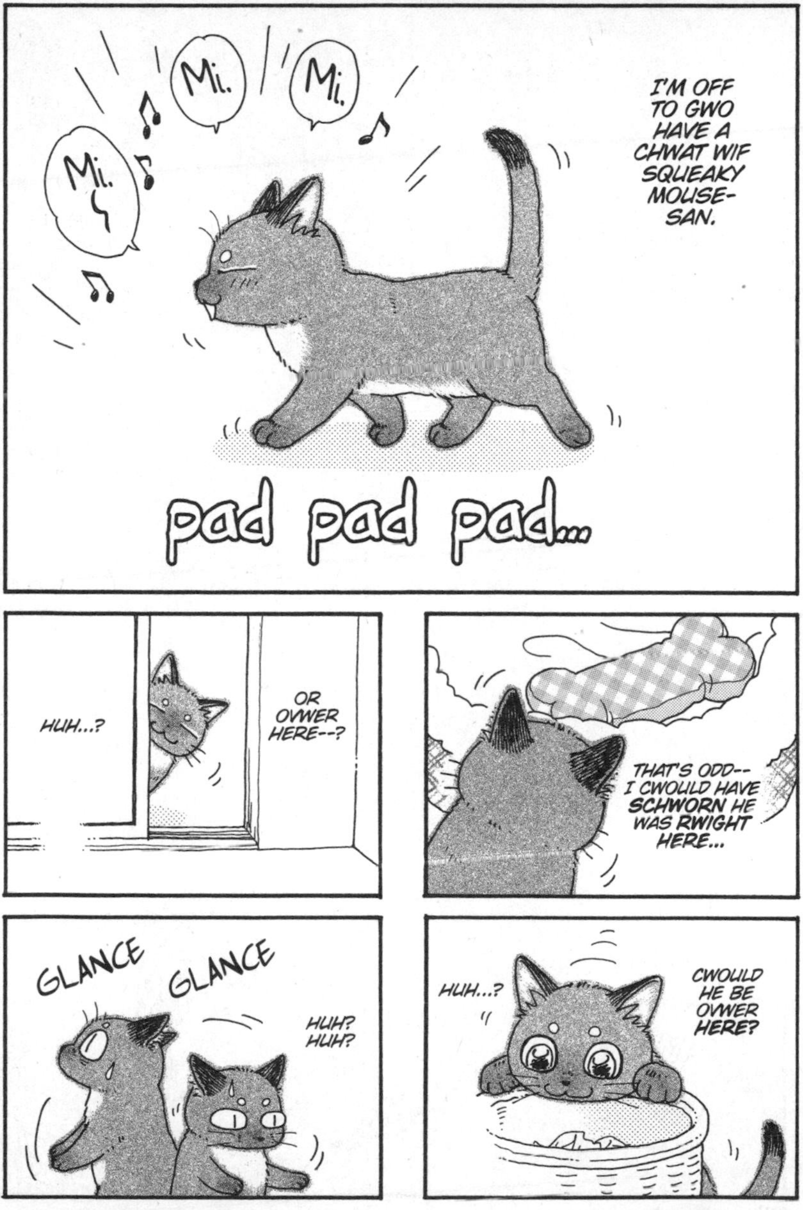
I'M OFF TO GWO HAVE A CHWAT WIF SQUEAKY MOUSE-SAN.
Mi.
Mi.
Mi.
pad pad pad...
THAT'S ODD-- I CWOULD HAVE SCHWORN HE WAS RWIGHT HERE...
OR OVWER HERE--?
HUH...?
CWOULD HE BE OVWER HERE?
HUH...?
HUH? HUH?
GLANCE
GLANCE

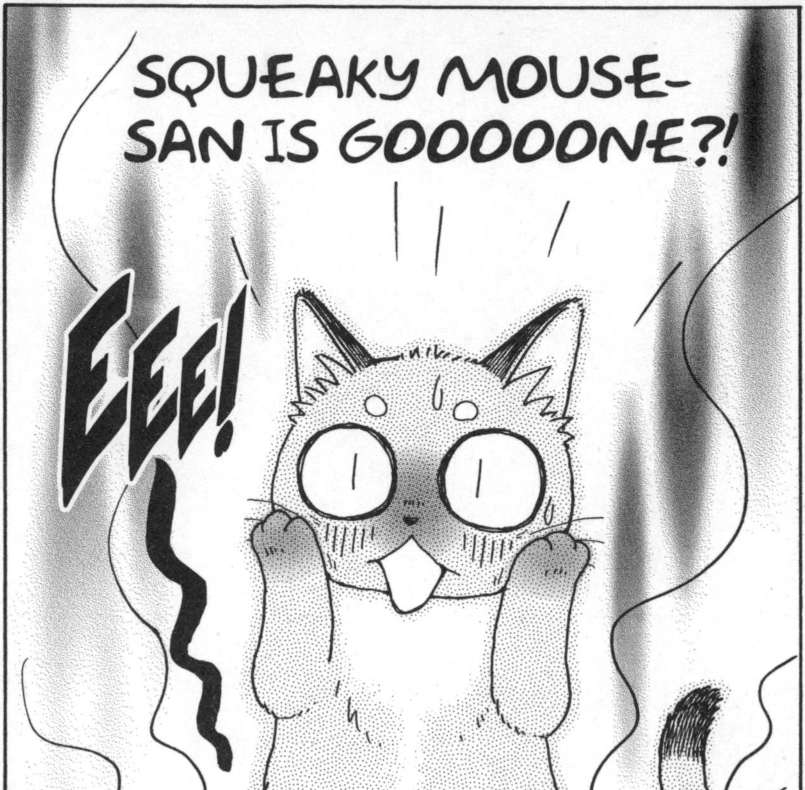
SQUEAKY MOUSE-SAN IS GOOOOONE?!
EEE!
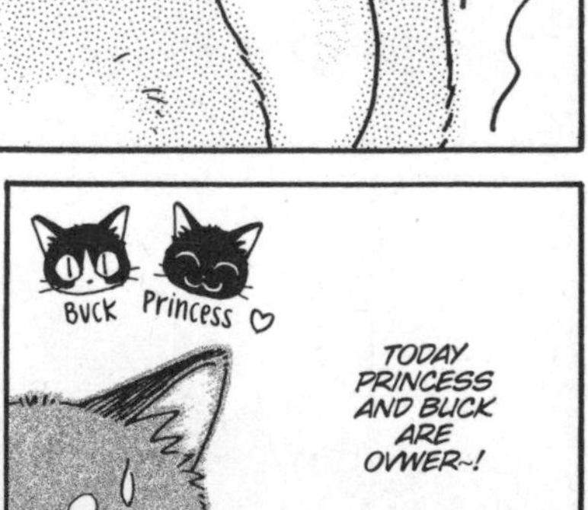
Buck
Princess ♡
TODAY PRINCESS AND BUCK ARE OVWER~!
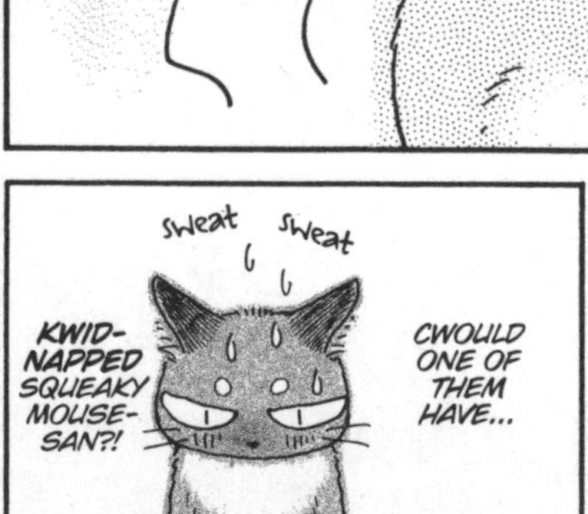
sweat sweat
CWOULD ONE OF THEM HAVE...
KWID-NAPPED SQUEAKY MOUSE-SAN?!

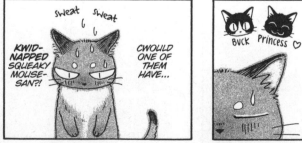

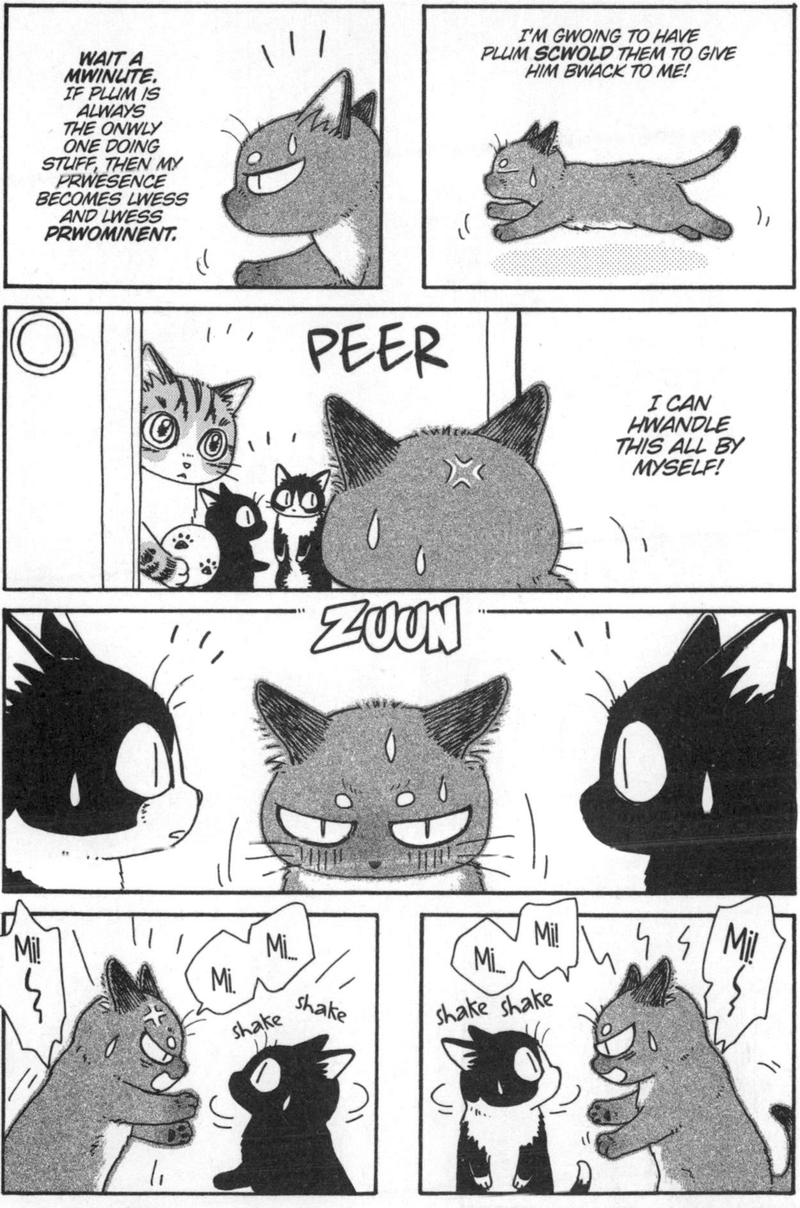
I'M GWOING TO HAVE PLUM SCWOLD THEM TO GIVE HIM BWACK TO ME!
WAIT A MWINUTE. IF PLUM IS ALWAYS THE ONWLY ONE DOING STUFF, THEN MY PRWESENCE BECOMES LWESS AND LWESS PRWOMINENT.
I CAN HWANDLE THIS ALL BY MYSELF!
PEER
ZUUN
Mi!
Mi!
Mi...
shake shake
Mi...
Mi.
shake
shake
Mi!

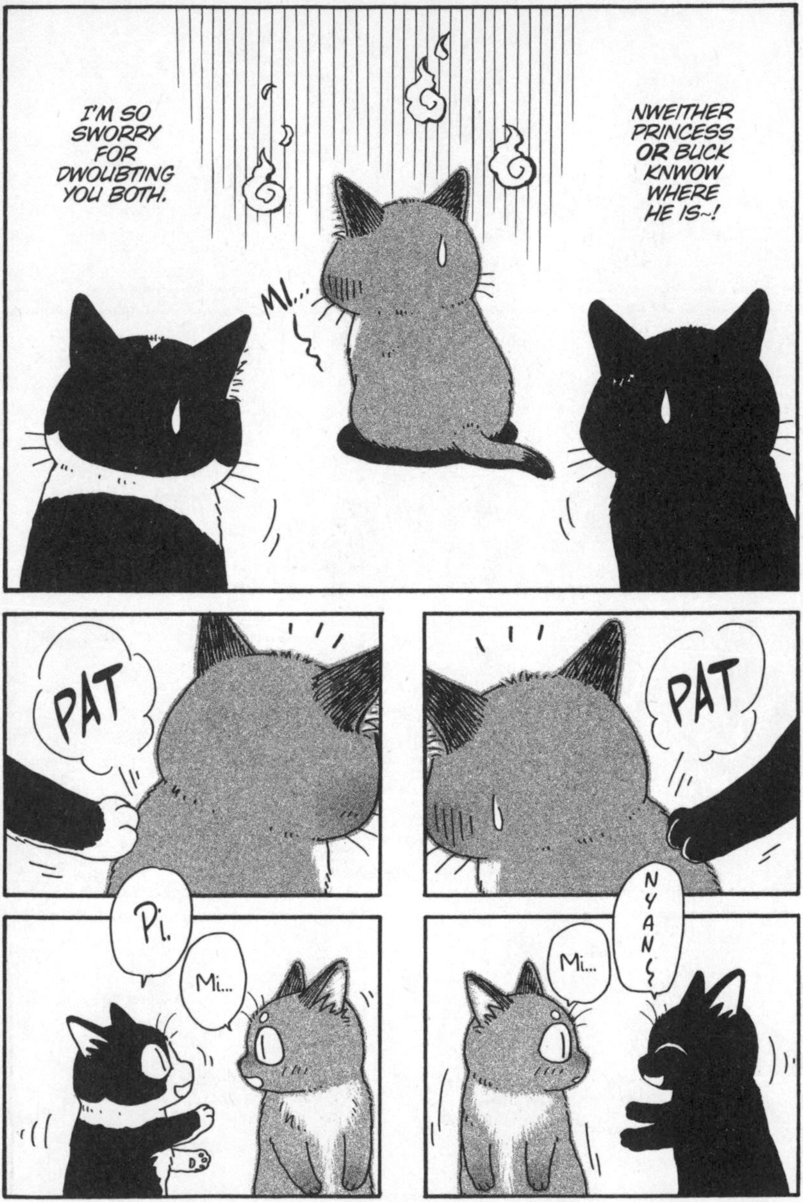
NWEITHER PRINCESS OR BUCK KNWOW WHERE HE IS~!
I'M SO SWORRY FOR DWOUBTING YOU BOTH.
MI...
PAT
PAT
NYAN
Mi...
Pi.
Mi...

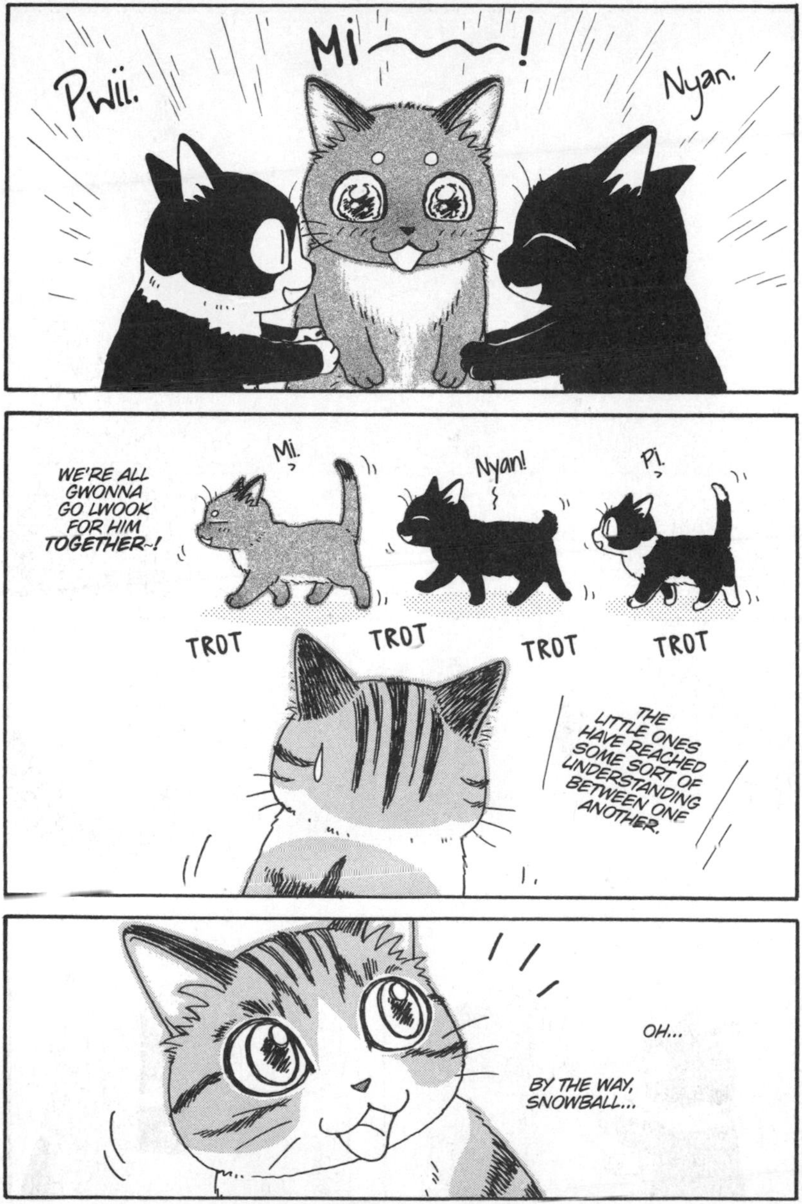
Nyan.
Mi~~~!
Pwii.
Pi!
Nyan!
Mi.
WE'RE ALL GWONNA GO LWOOK FOR HIM TOGETHER~!
TROT
TROT
TROT
TROT
THE LITTLE ONES HAVE REACHED SOME SORT OF UNDERSTANDING BETWEEN ONE ANOTHER.
OH...
BY THE WAY, SNOWBALL...

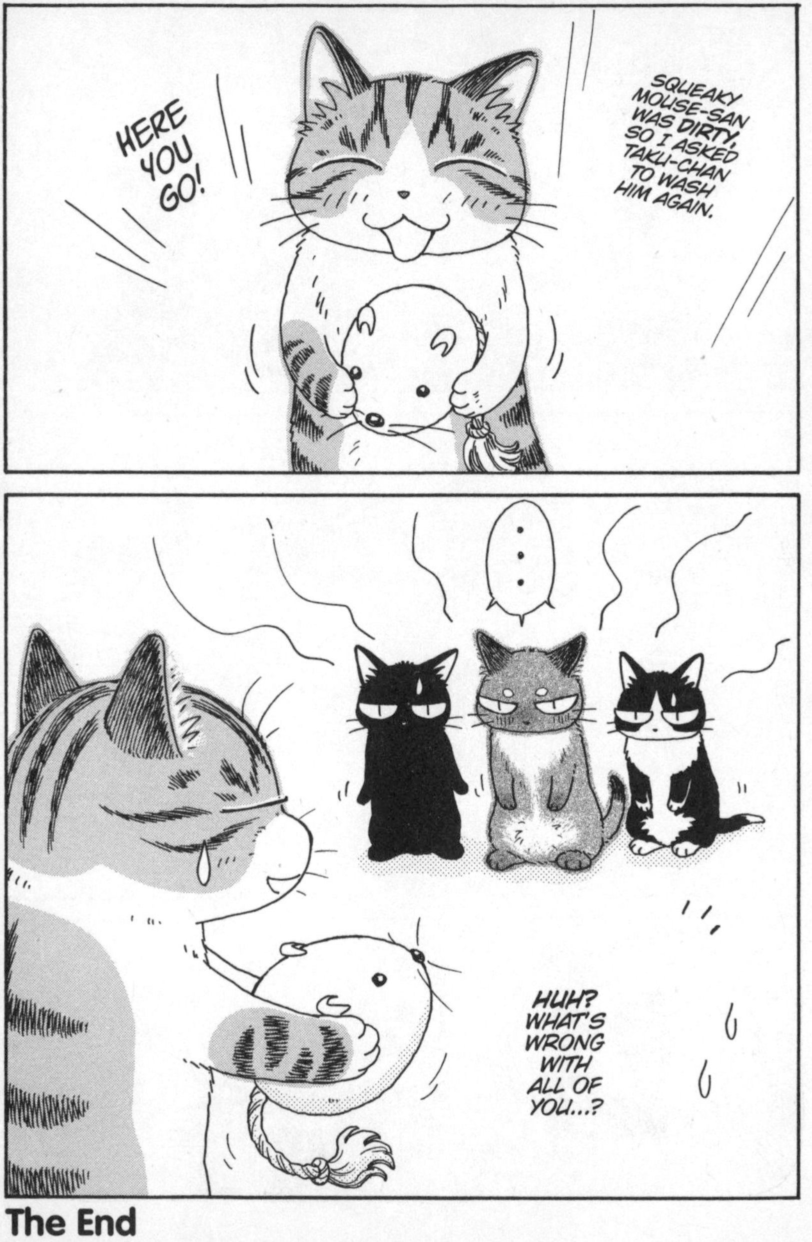
SQUEAKY MOUSE-SAN WAS DIRTY, SO I ASKED TAKU-CHAN TO WASH HIM AGAIN.
HERE YOU GO!
...
HUH? WHAT'S WRONG WITH ALL OF YOU...?

The End

Chapter 17
Plum Makes a Request of Mother

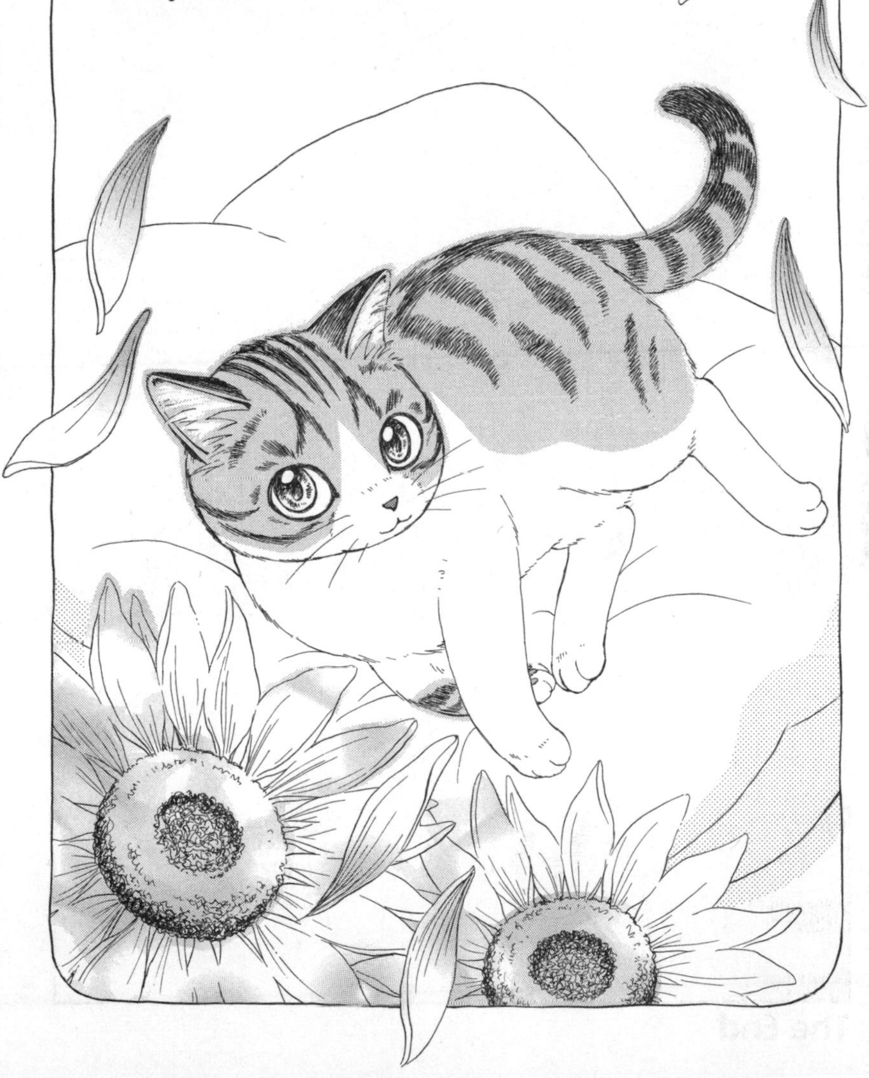

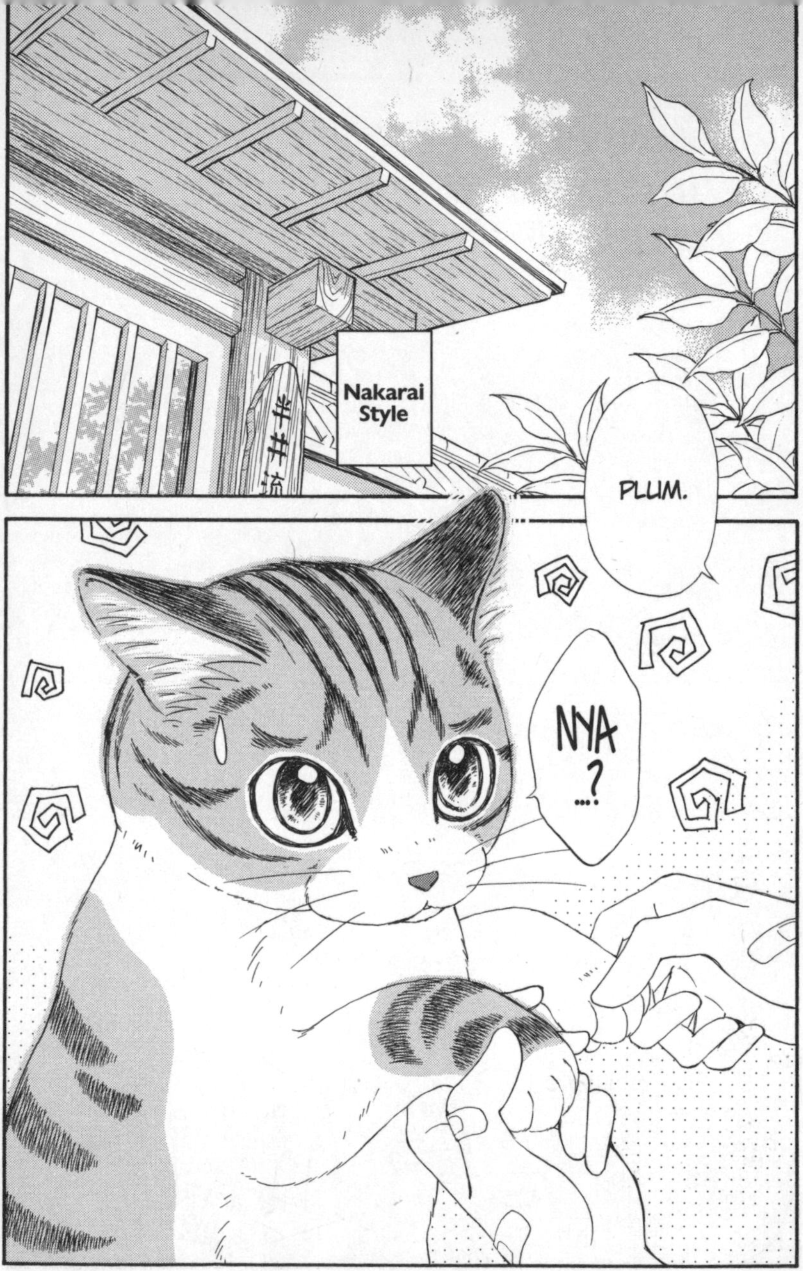
半井流
Nakarai Style
PLUM.
NYA ...?

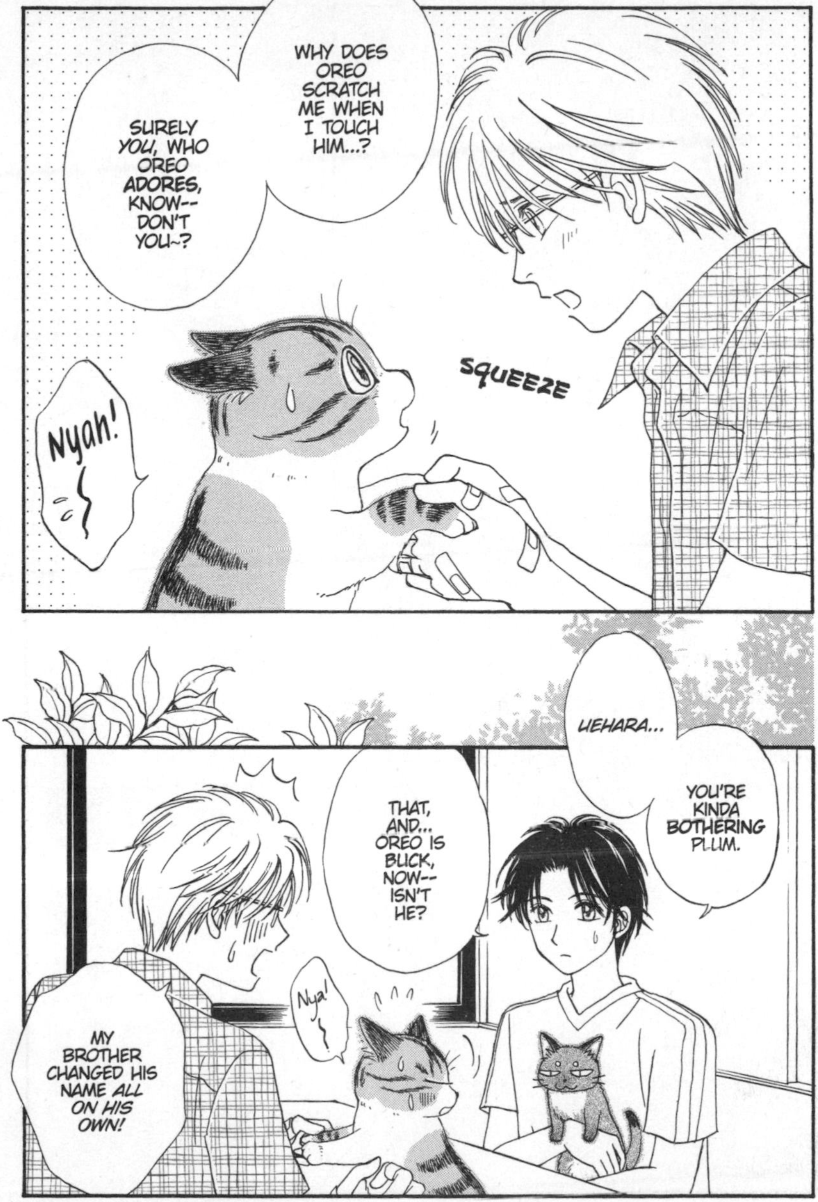
WHY DOES OREO SCRATCH ME WHEN I TOUCH HIM...?
SURELY *YOU*, WHO OREO ADORES, KNOW--DON'T YOU~?
SQUEEZE
Nyah!
UEHARA...
YOU'RE KINDA BOTHERING PLUM.
THAT, AND... OREO IS BLICK, NOW--ISN'T HE?
Nya!
MY BROTHER CHANGED HIS NAME *ALL* ON HIS OWN!

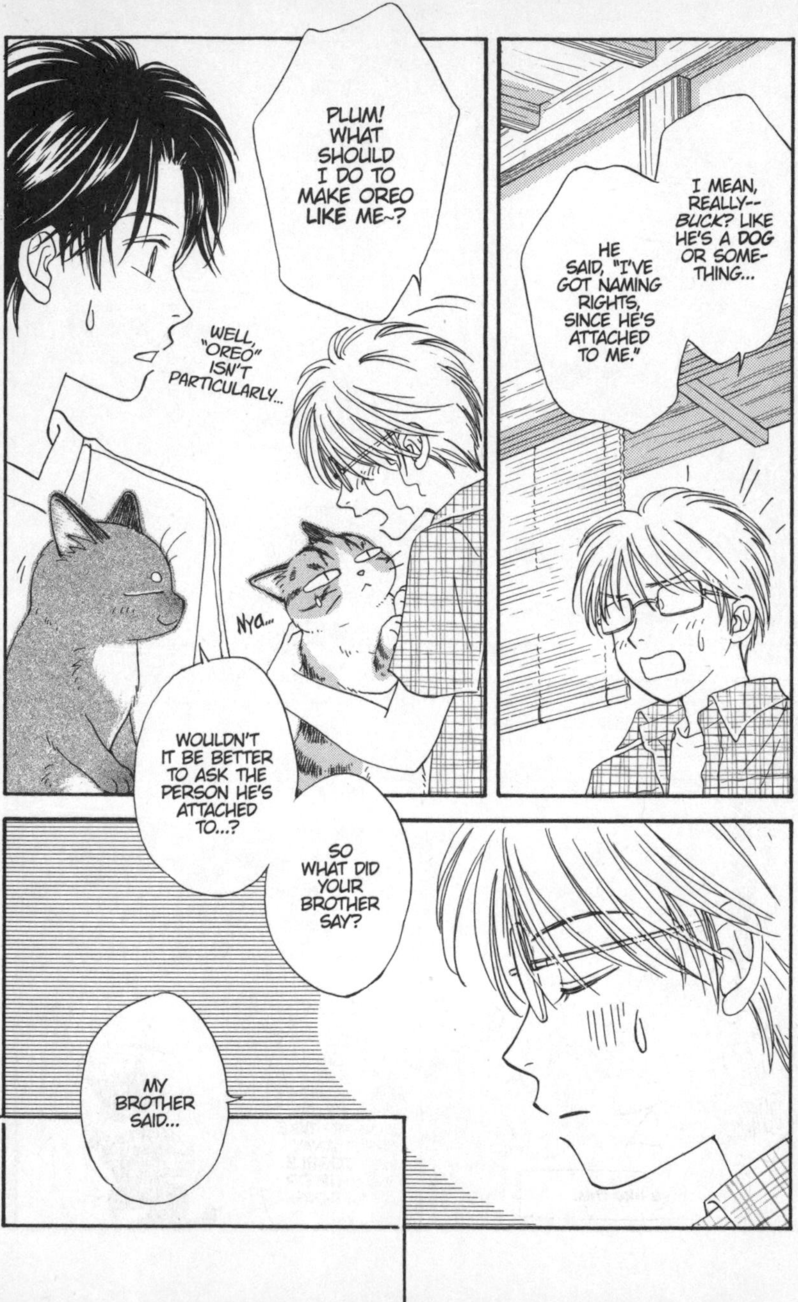
I MEAN, REALLY-- *BUCK*? LIKE HE'S A DOG OR SOME-THING...
HE SAID, "I'VE GOT NAMING RIGHTS, SINCE HE'S ATTACHED TO ME."
PLUM! WHAT SHOULD I DO TO MAKE OREO LIKE ME~?
WELL, "OREO" ISN'T PARTICULARLY...
Nya...
WOULDN'T IT BE BETTER TO ASK THE PERSON HE'S ATTACHED TO...?
SO WHAT DID YOUR BROTHER SAY?
MY BROTHER SAID...

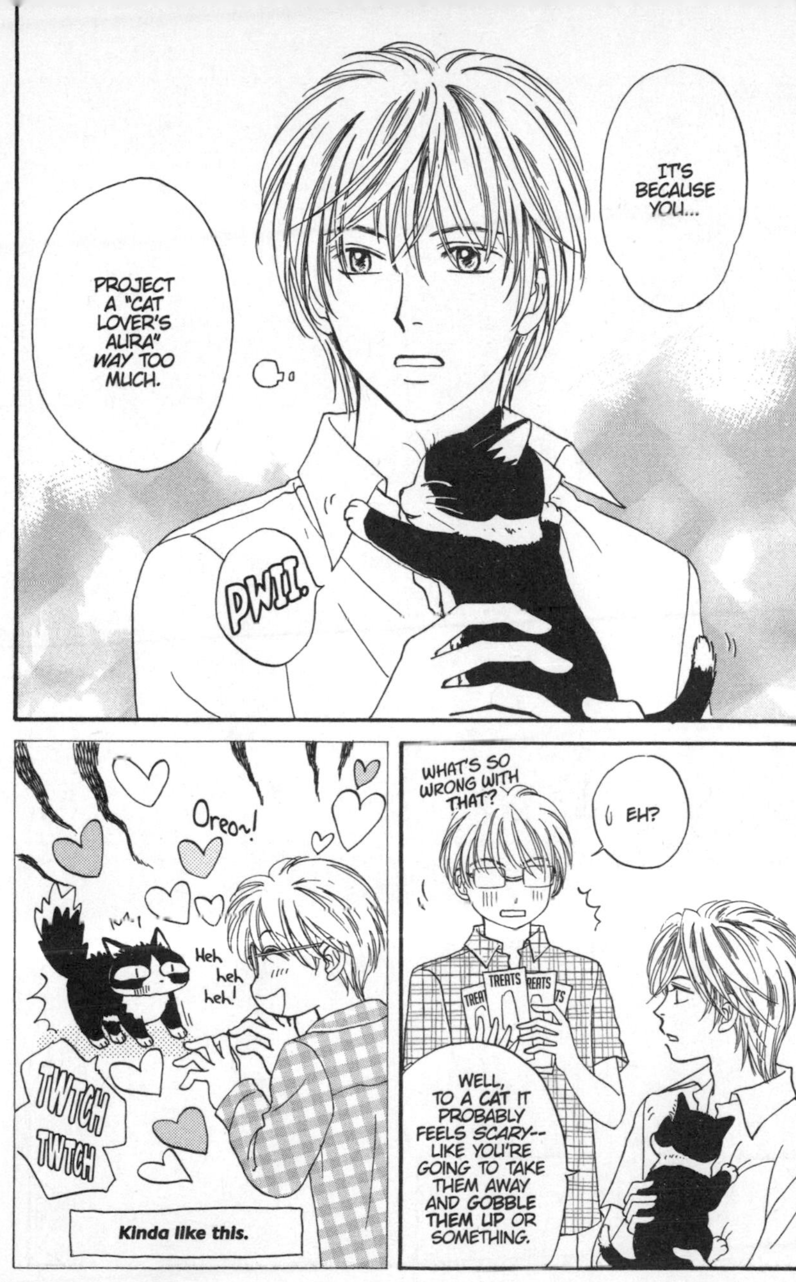
IT'S BECAUSE YOU...
PROJECT A "CAT LOVER'S AURA" WAY TOO MUCH.
PWII.
WHAT'S SO WRONG WITH THAT?
EH?
TREATS
WELL, TO A CAT IT PROBABLY FEELS SCARY-- LIKE YOU'RE GOING TO TAKE THEM AWAY AND GOBBLE THEM UP OR SOMETHING.
Oreo~!
Heh heh heh!
TWTCH TWTCH
Kinda like this.

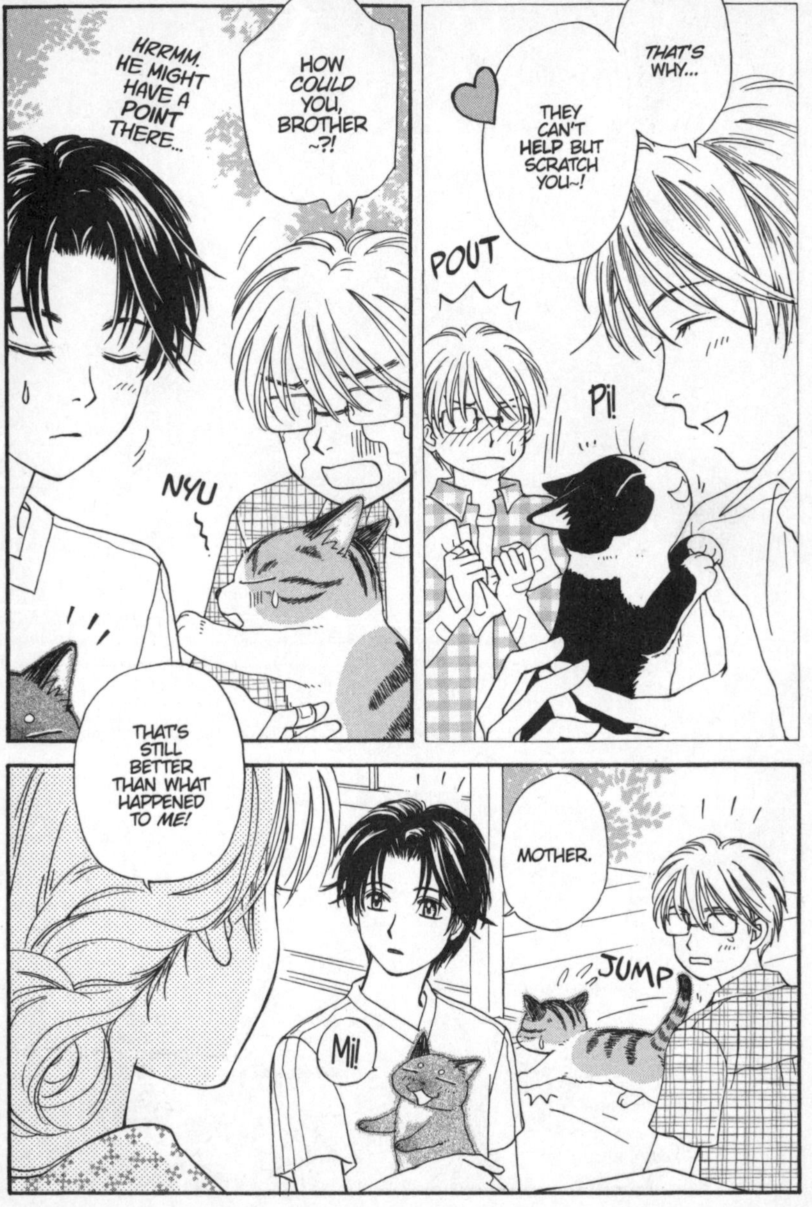
THAT'S WHY...
THEY CAN'T HELP BUT SCRATCH YOU~!
POUT
Pi!
HOW COULD YOU, BROTHER ~?!
HRRMM. HE MIGHT HAVE A POINT THERE...
NYU
THAT'S STILL BETTER THAN WHAT HAPPENED TO ME!
MOTHER.
JUMP
Mi!

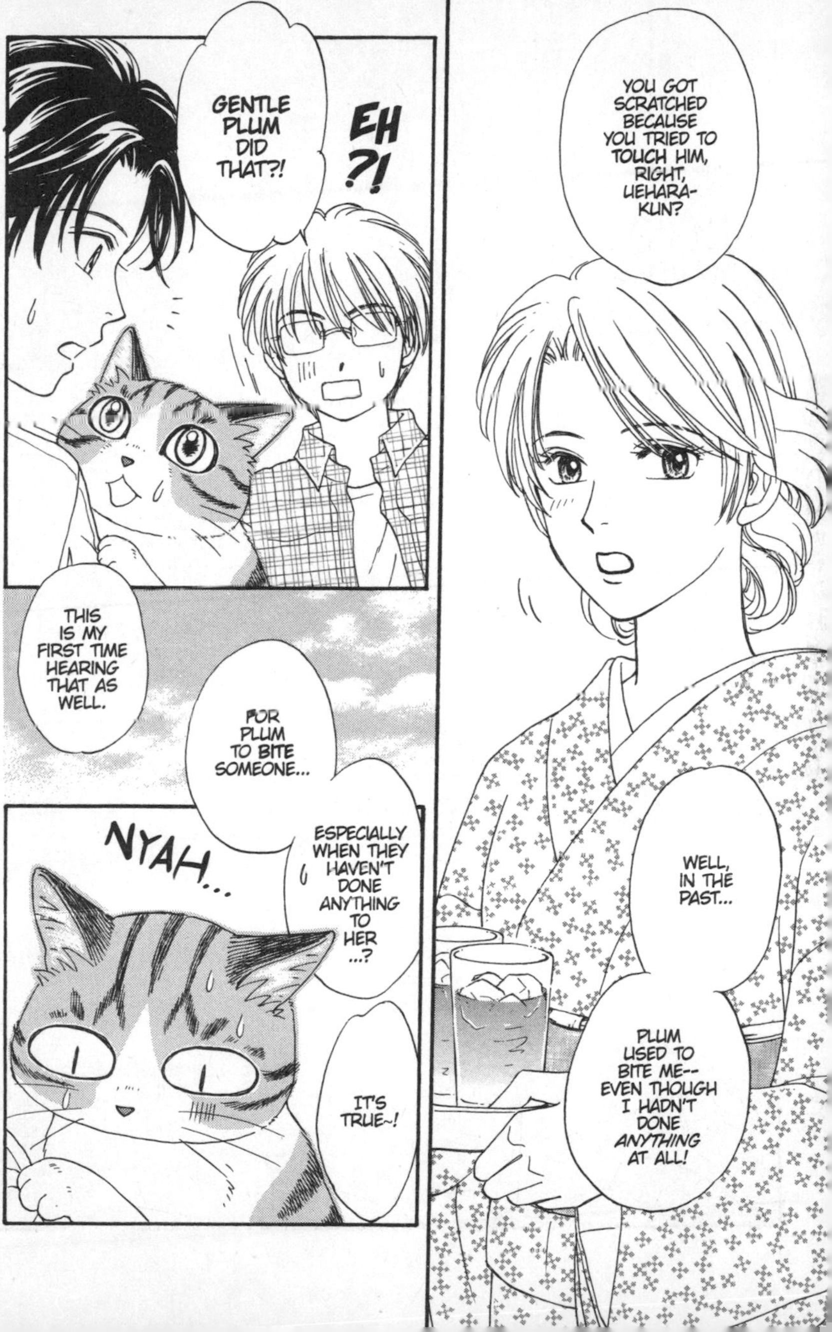
YOU GOT SCRATCHED BECAUSE YOU TRIED TO TOUCH HIM, RIGHT, UEHARA-KUN?
WELL, IN THE PAST...
PLUM USED TO BITE ME-- EVEN THOUGH I HADN'T DONE *ANYTHING* AT ALL!
GENTLE PLUM DID THAT?!
EH ?!
THIS IS MY FIRST TIME HEARING THAT AS WELL.
FOR PLUM TO BITE SOMEONE...
ESPECIALLY WHEN THEY HAVEN'T DONE ANYTHING TO HER ...?
NYAH...
IT'S TRUE~!

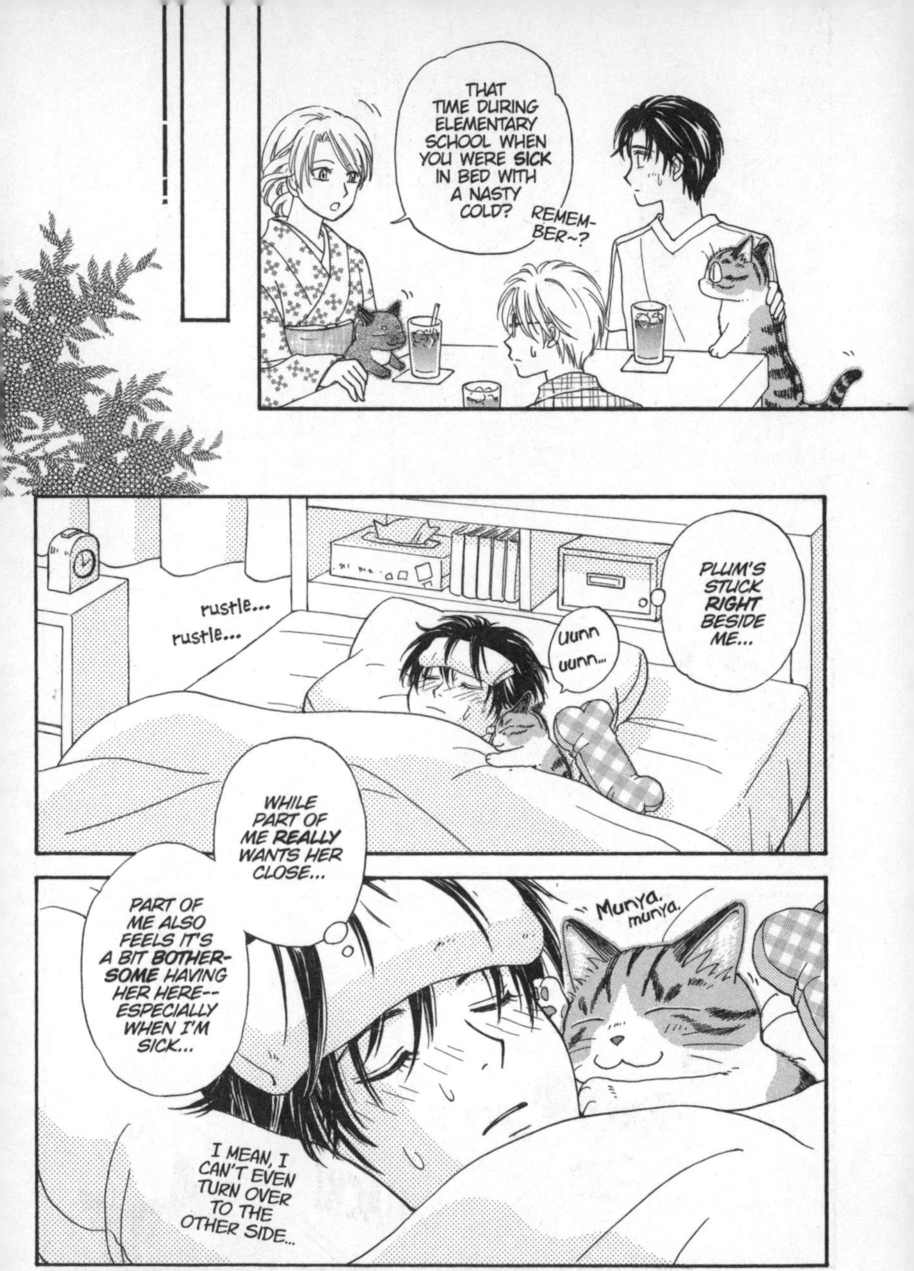
THAT TIME DURING ELEMENTARY SCHOOL WHEN YOU WERE SICK IN BED WITH A NASTY COLD?
REMEM-BER~?
PLUM'S STUCK RIGHT BESIDE ME...
uunn uunn...
rustle... rustle...
Munya. munya.
WHILE PART OF ME REALLY WANTS HER CLOSE...
PART OF ME ALSO FEELS IT'S A BIT BOTHER-SOME HAVING HER HERE-- ESPECIALLY WHEN I'M SICK...
I MEAN, I CAN'T EVEN TURN OVER TO THE OTHER SIDE...

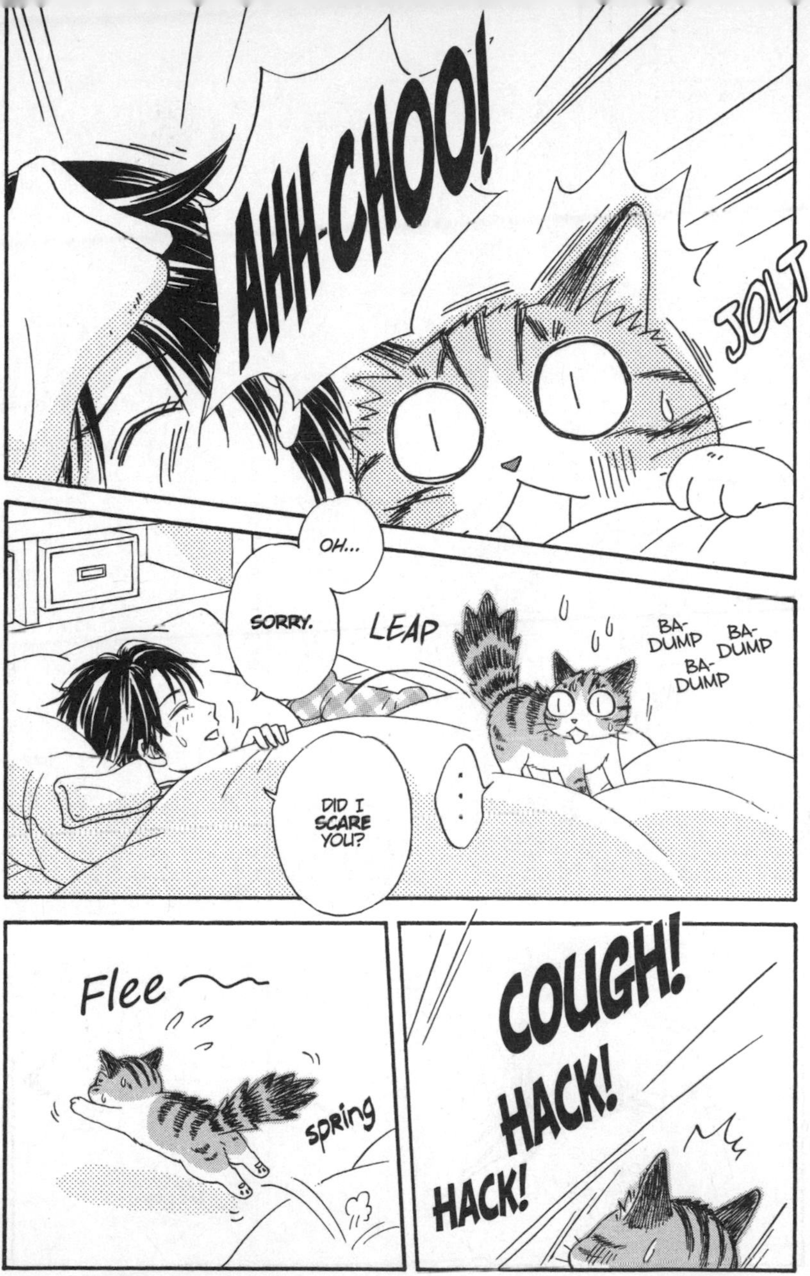
AHH-CHOO!
JOLT
OH...
SORRY.
LEAP
BA-DUMP BA-DUMP BA-DUMP
...
DID I SCARE YOU?
COUGH!
HACK!
HACK!
Flee
spring

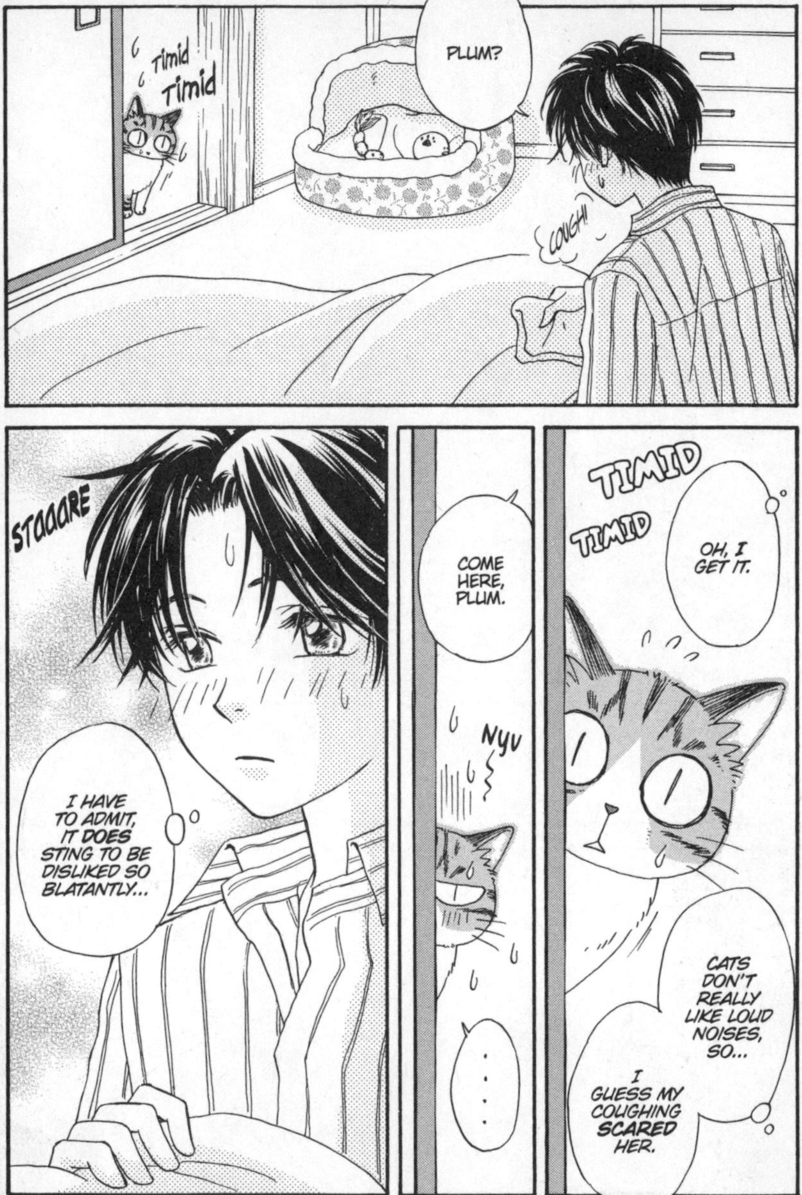
PLUM?
COUGH!
Timid
Timid
TIMID
TIMID
OH, I GET IT.
CATS DON'T REALLY LIKE LOUD NOISES, SO...
I GUESS MY COUGHING SCARED HER.
COME HERE, PLUM.
Nyu
...
STAAARE
I HAVE TO ADMIT, IT DOES STING TO BE DISLIKED SO BLATANTLY...

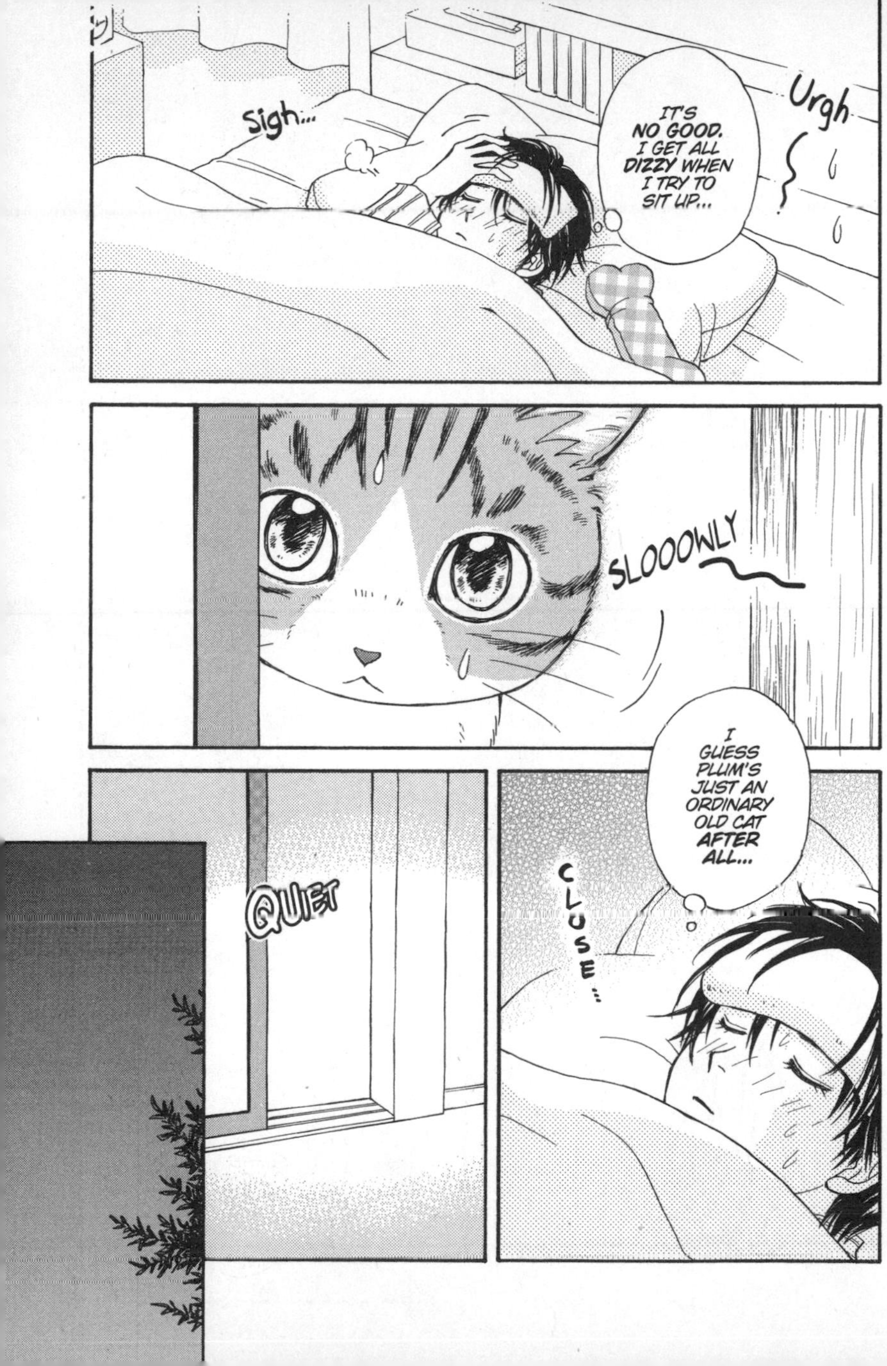
Urgh
IT'S NO GOOD. I GET ALL DIZZY WHEN I TRY TO SIT UP...
Sigh...
SLOOOWLY
I GUESS PLUM'S JUST AN ORDINARY OLD CAT AFTER ALL...
CLOSE...
QUIET

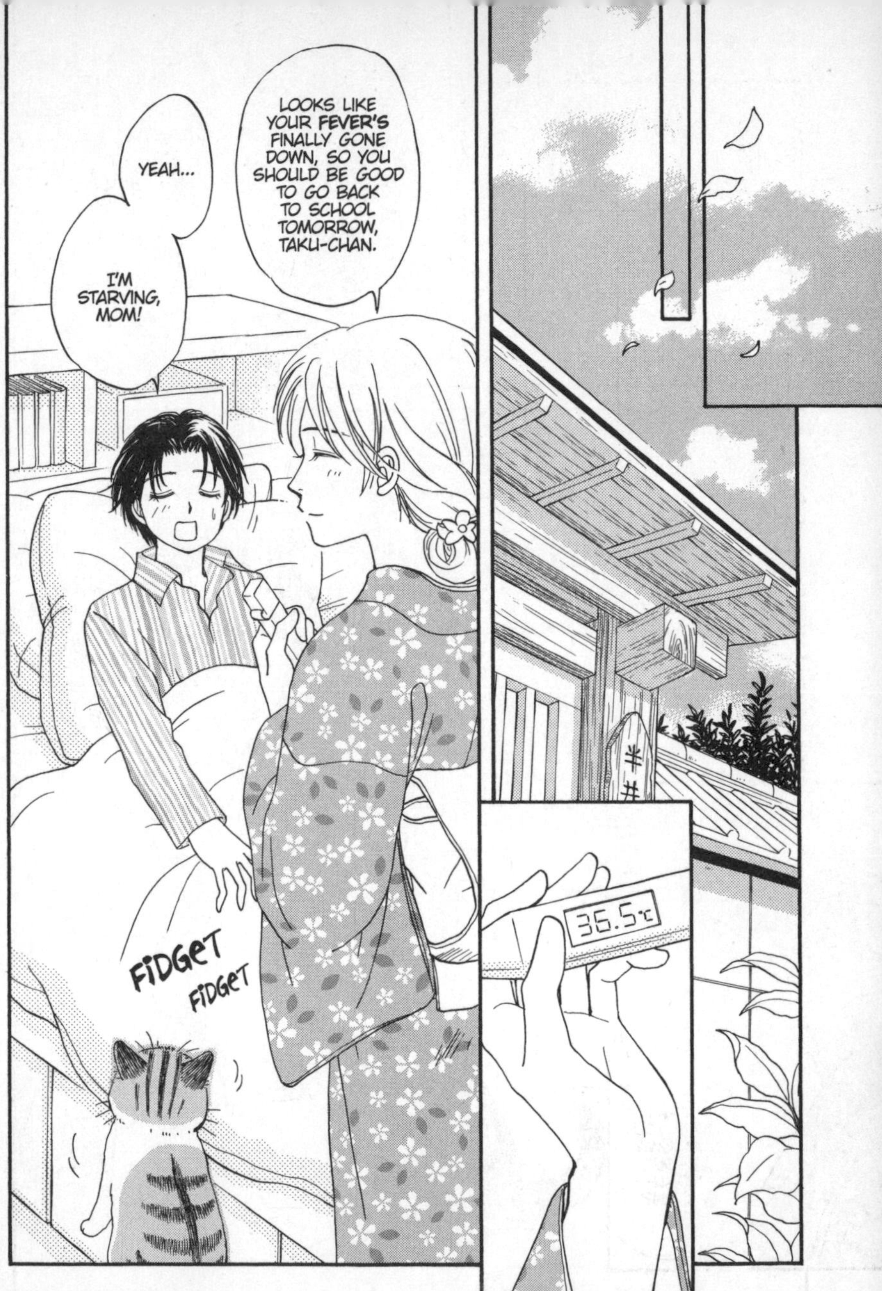
半井
36.5°c
LOOKS LIKE YOUR **FEVER'S** FINALLY GONE DOWN, SO YOU SHOULD BE GOOD TO GO BACK TO SCHOOL TOMORROW, TAKU-CHAN.
YEAH...
I'M STARVING, MOM!
FIDGET FIDGET

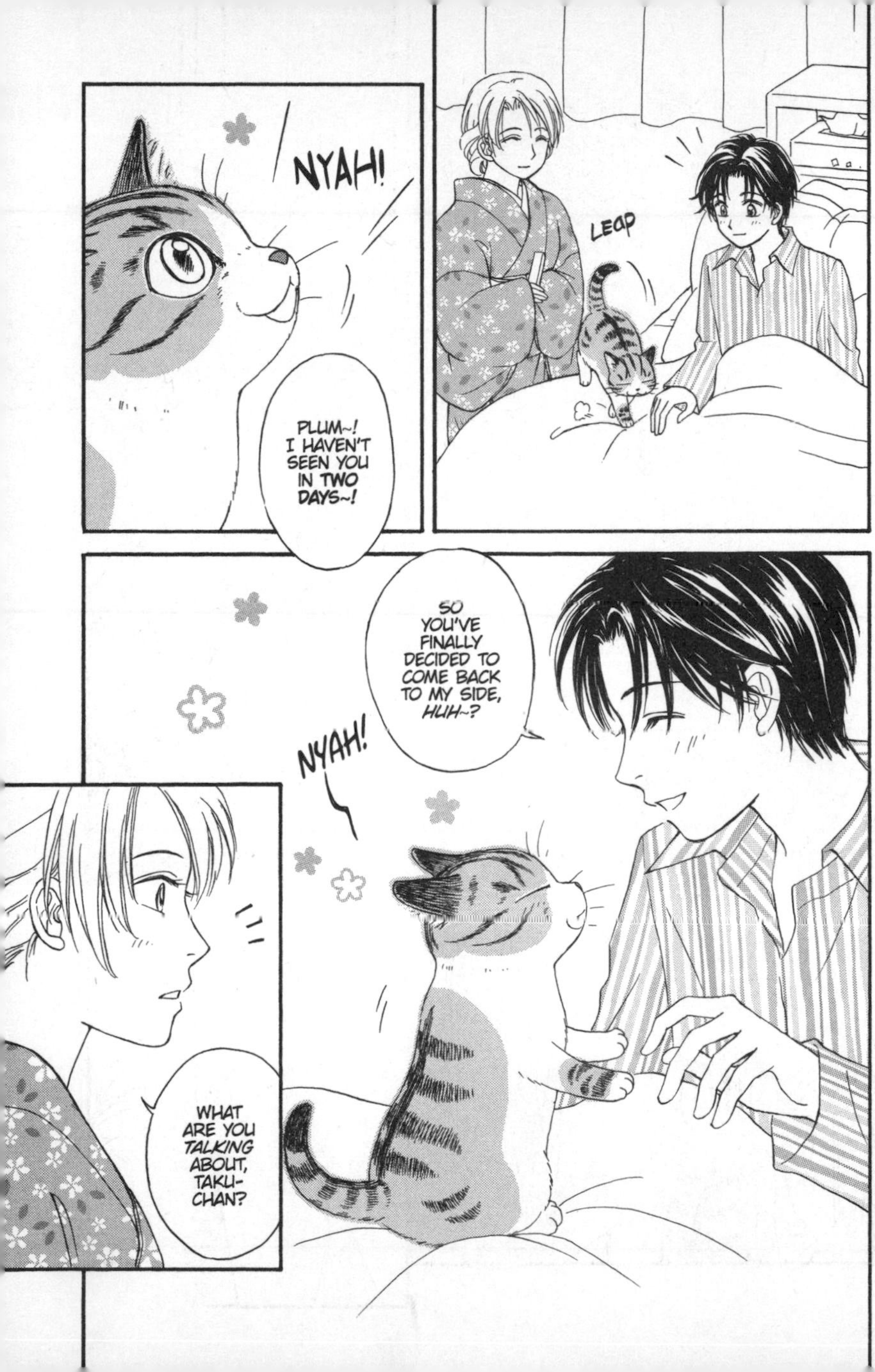
LEAP
NYAH!
PLUM~! I HAVEN'T SEEN YOU IN TWO DAYS~!
SO YOU'VE FINALLY DECIDED TO COME BACK TO MY SIDE, *HUH~?*
NYAH!
WHAT ARE YOU *TALKING* ABOUT, TAKU-CHAN?

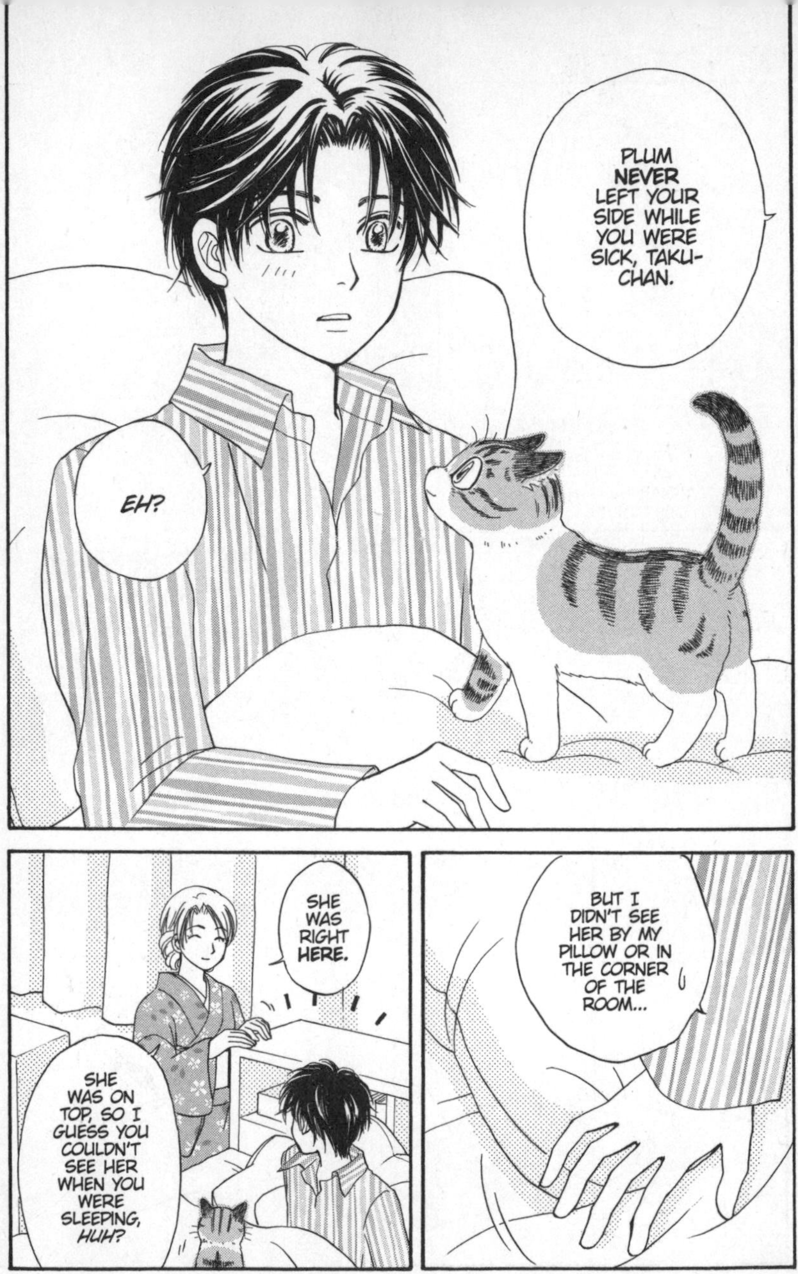
PLUM NEVER LEFT YOUR SIDE WHILE YOU WERE SICK, TAKU-CHAN.
EH?
BUT I DIDN'T SEE HER BY MY PILLOW OR IN THE CORNER OF THE ROOM...
SHE WAS RIGHT HERE.
SHE WAS ON TOP, SO I GUESS YOU COULDN'T SEE HER WHEN YOU WERE SLEEPING, HUH?

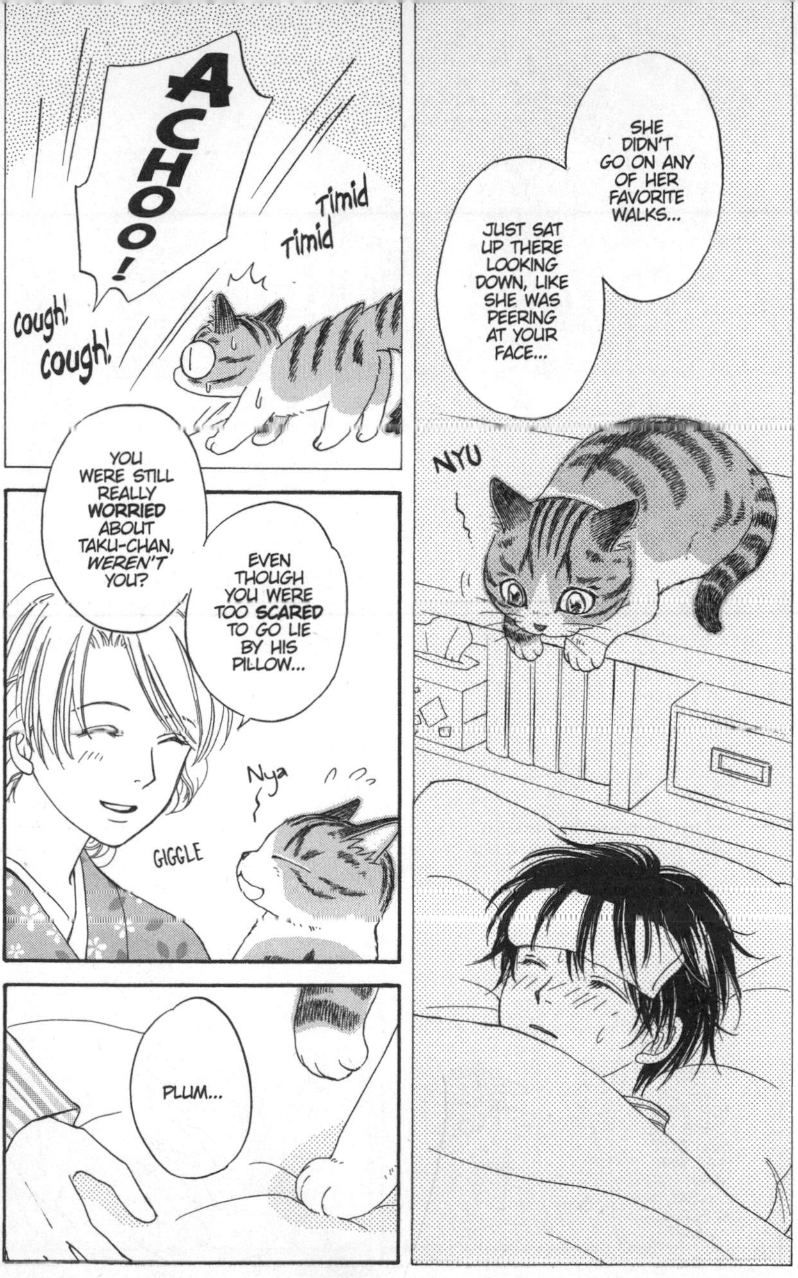

SHE DIDN'T GO ON ANY OF HER FAVORITE WALKS...
JUST SAT UP THERE LOOKING DOWN, LIKE SHE WAS PEERING AT YOUR FACE...
NYU
ACHOO!
Timid Timid
cough! cough!
YOU WERE STILL REALLY **WORRIED** ABOUT TAKU-CHAN, *WEREN'T* YOU?
EVEN THOUGH YOU WERE TOO **SCARED** TO GO LIE BY HIS PILLOW...
Nya
GIGGLE
PLUM...

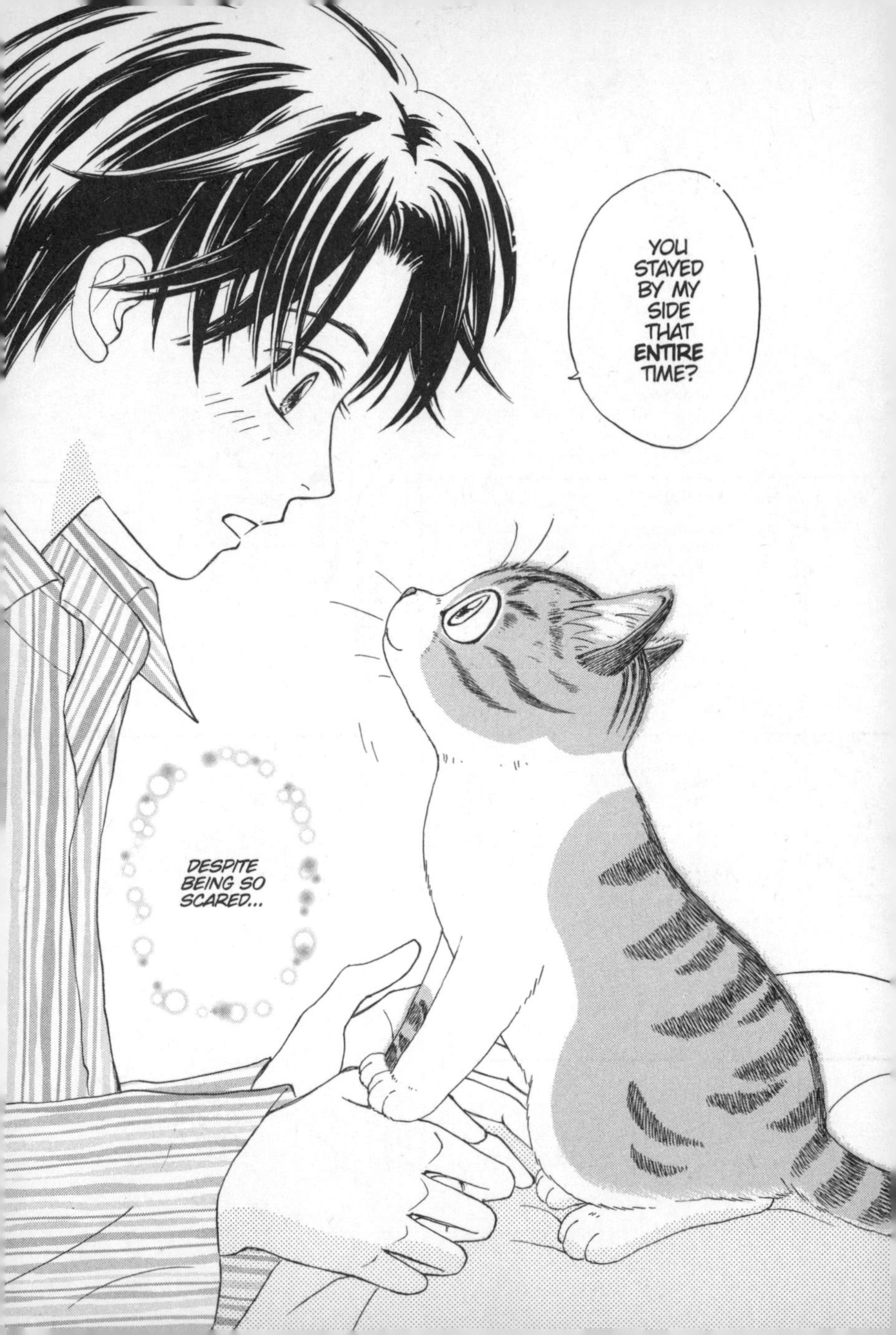
YOU STAYED BY MY SIDE THAT ENTIRE TIME?
DESPITE BEING SO SCARED...

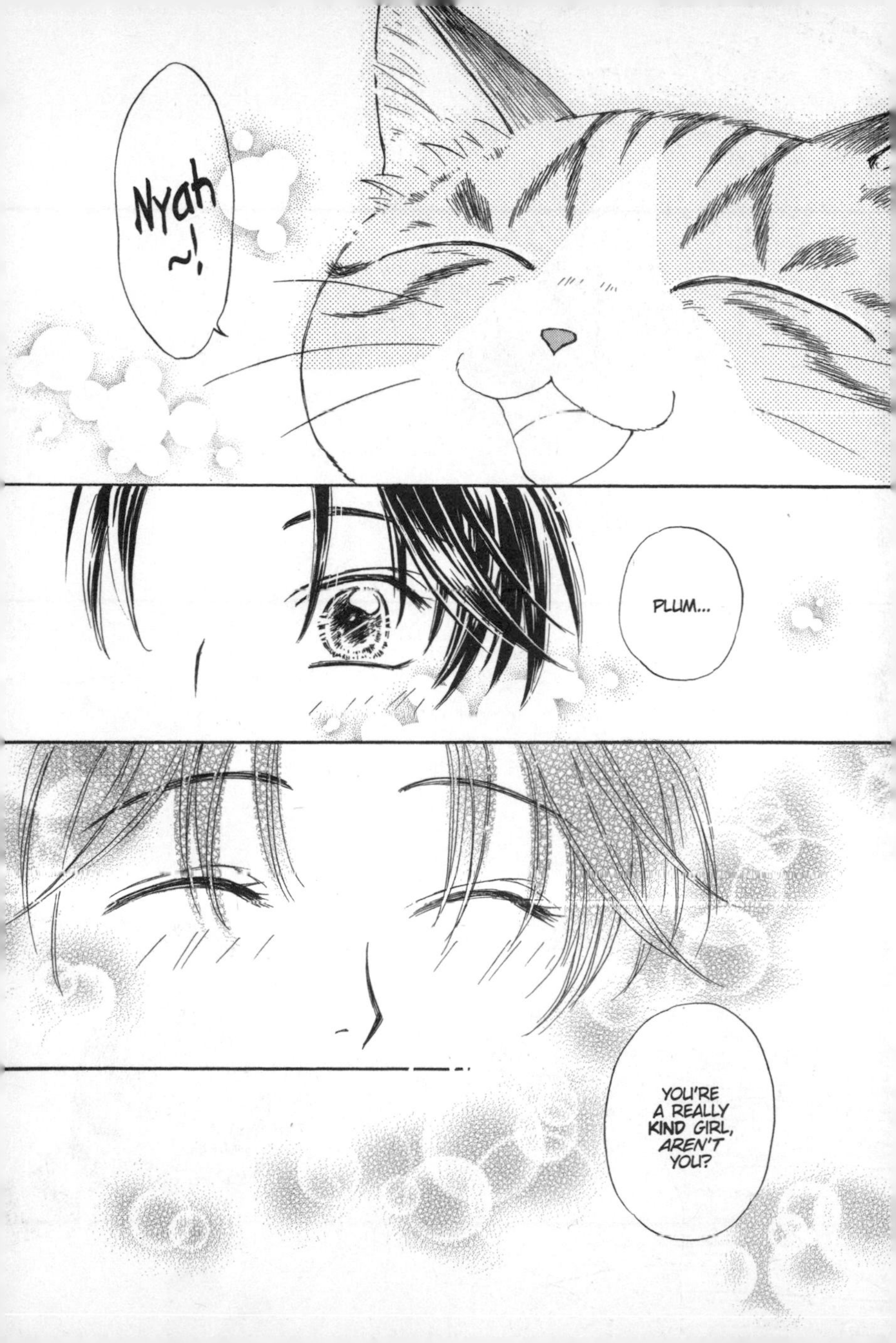
Nyah ~!
PLUM...
YOU'RE A REALLY KIND GIRL, AREN'T YOU?

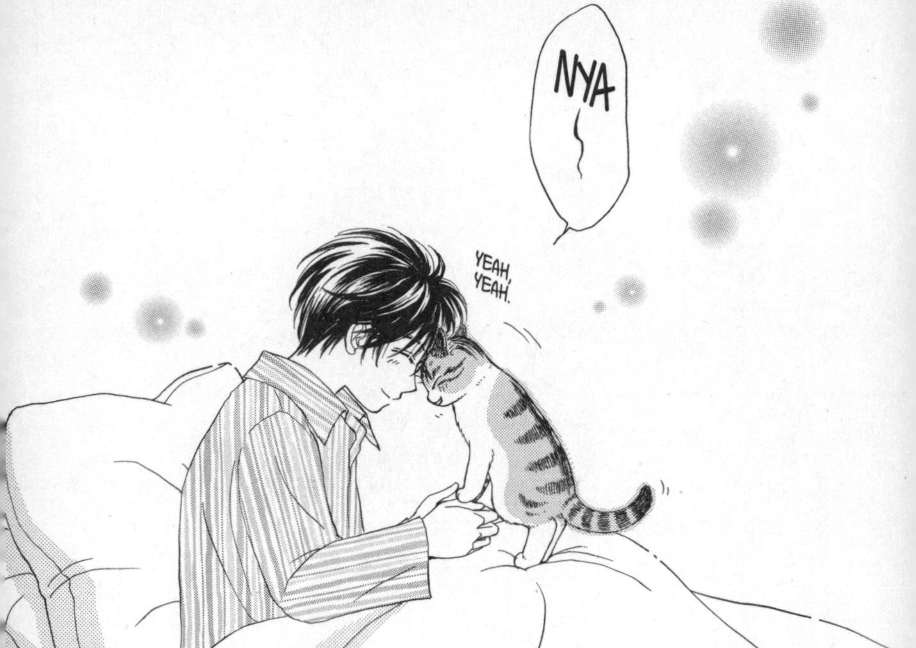
NYA
YEAH, YEAH.
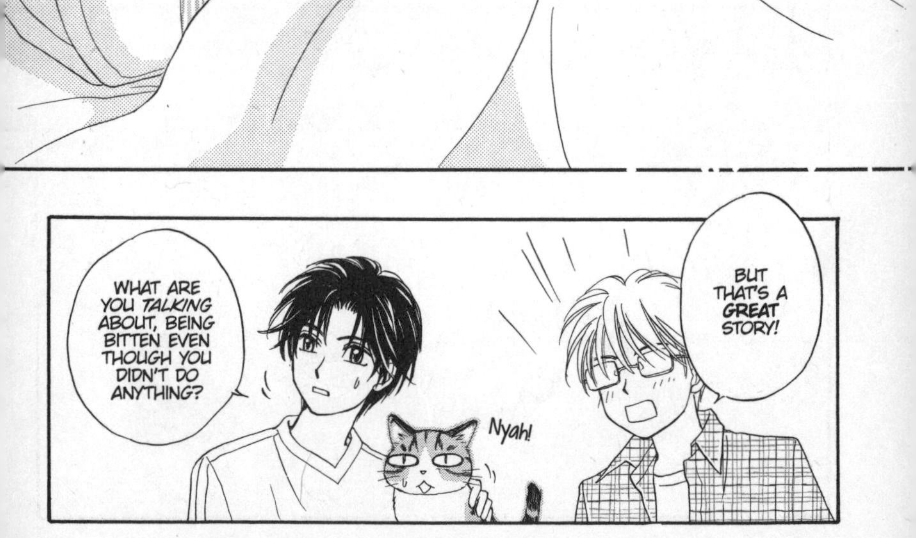
BUT THAT'S A GREAT STORY!
WHAT ARE YOU *TALKING* ABOUT, BEING BITTEN EVEN THOUGH YOU DIDN'T DO ANYTHING?
Nyah!

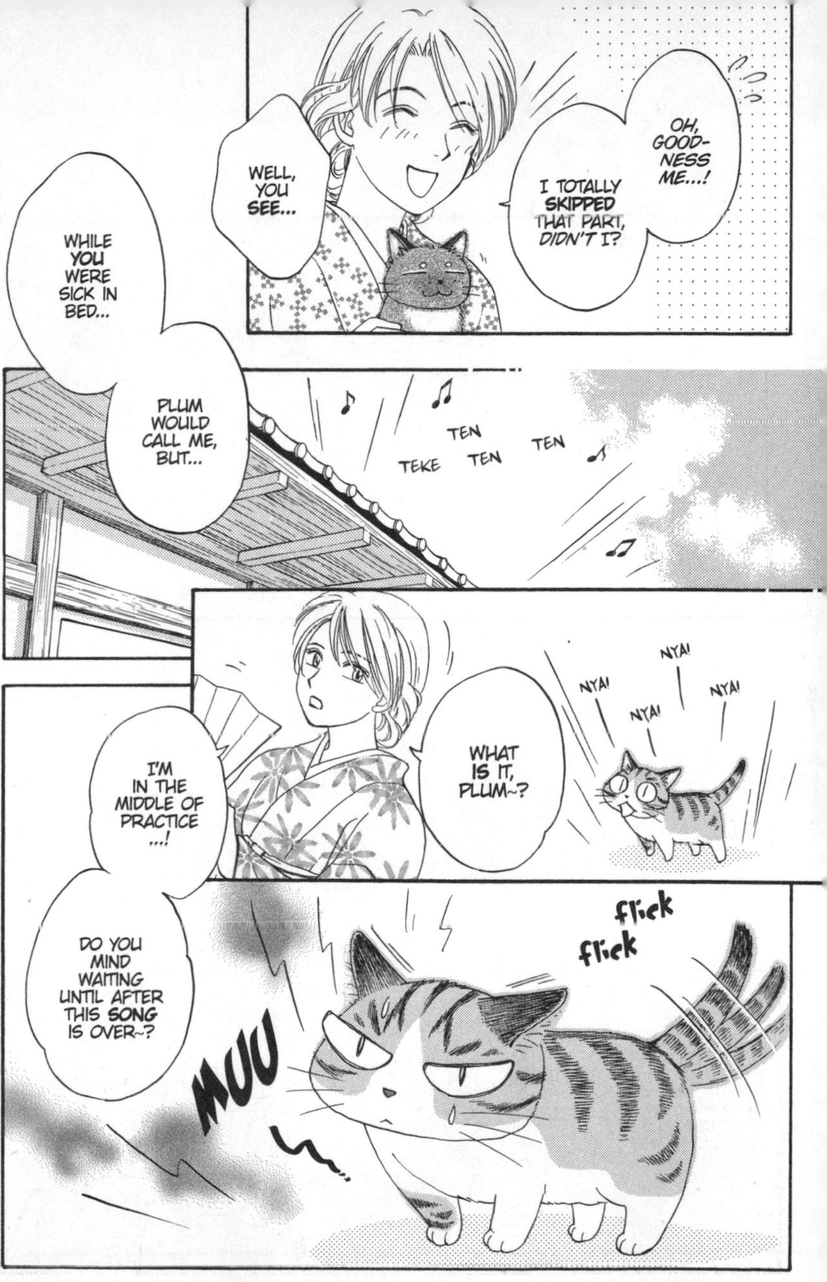
OH, GOODNESS ME...!
I TOTALLY SKIPPED THAT PART, DIDN'T I?
WELL, YOU SEE...
WHILE YOU WERE SICK IN BED...
PLUM WOULD CALL ME, BUT...
TEN TEKE TEN TEN
NYA! NYA! NYA! NYA!
WHAT IS IT, PLUM~?
I'M IN THE MIDDLE OF PRACTICE ...!
DO YOU MIND WAITING UNTIL AFTER THIS SONG IS OVER~?
flick flick
MUU

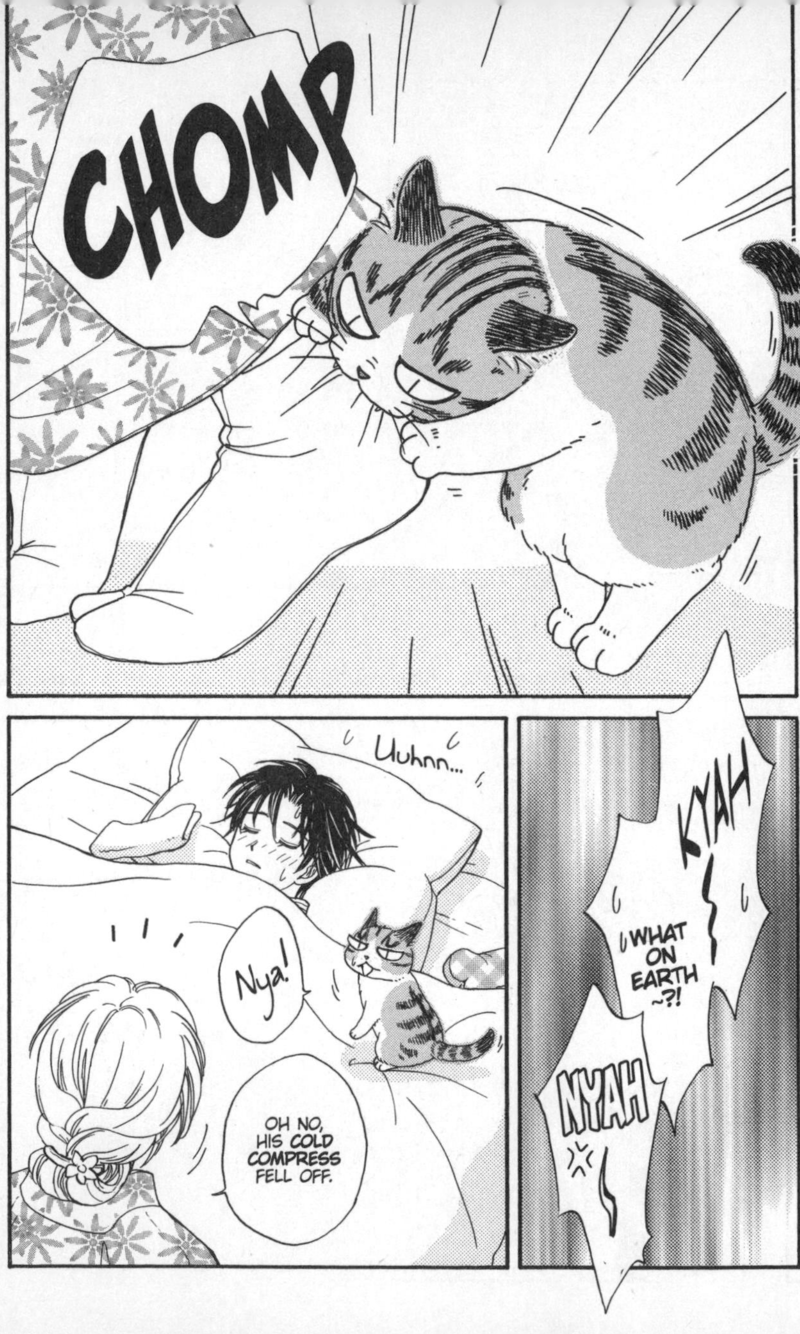
CHOMP
KYAH~
WHAT ON EARTH ~?!
NYAH~
Uuhnn...
Nya!
OH NO, HIS COLD COMPRESS FELL OFF.

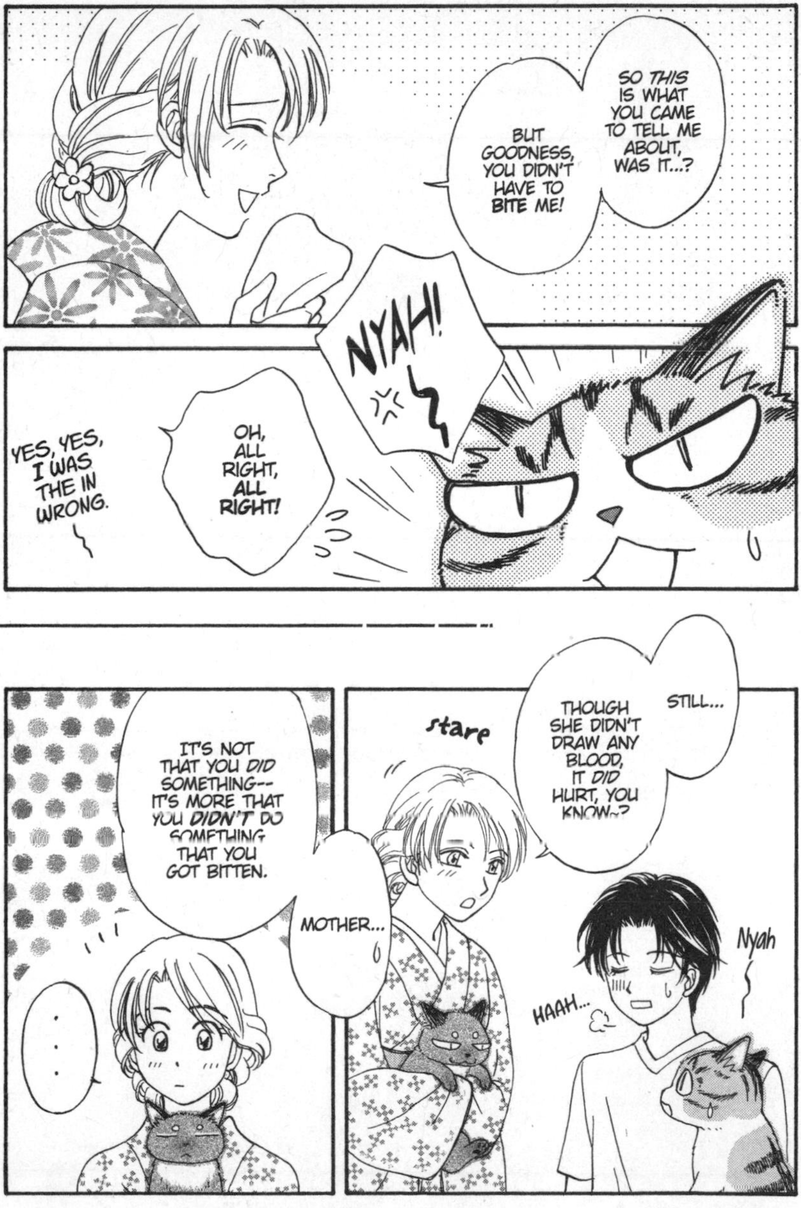
SO THIS IS WHAT YOU CAME TO TELL ME ABOUT, WAS IT...?
BUT GOODNESS, YOU DIDN'T HAVE TO BITE ME!
NYAH!
OH, ALL RIGHT, ALL RIGHT!
YES, YES, I WAS THE IN WRONG.
STILL...
THOUGH SHE DIDN'T DRAW ANY BLOOD, IT DID HURT, YOU KNOW...?
stare
Nyah
HAAH...
MOTHER...
IT'S NOT THAT YOU DID SOMETHING-- IT'S MORE THAT YOU DIDN'T DO SOMETHING THAT YOU GOT BITTEN.
...

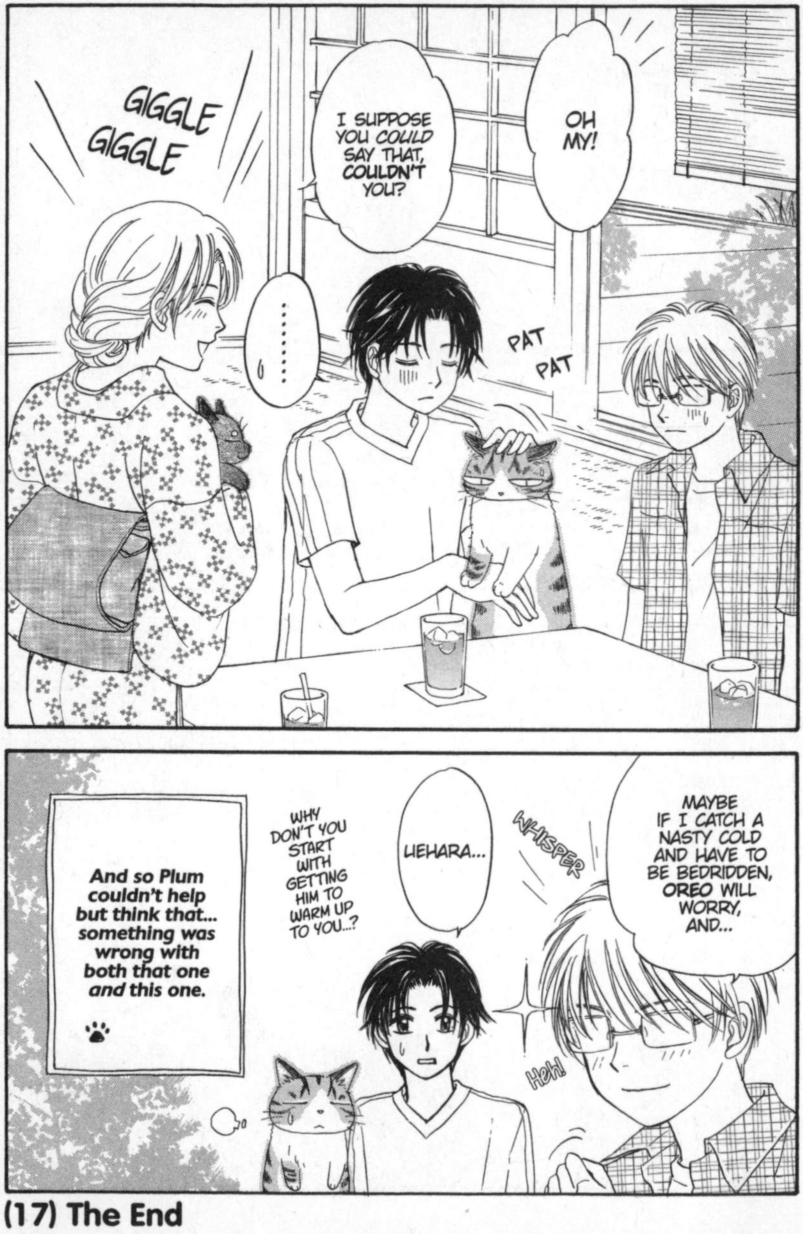
OH MY!
I SUPPOSE YOU COULD SAY THAT, COULDN'T YOU?
GIGGLE GIGGLE
PAT PAT
......
MAYBE IF I CATCH A NASTY COLD AND HAVE TO BE BEDRIDDEN, OREO WILL WORRY, AND...
WHISPER
UEHARA...
WHY DON'T YOU START WITH GETTING HIM TO WARM UP TO YOU...?
And so Plum couldn't help but think that... something was wrong with both that one and this one.
Heh!

(17) The End

Chapter 18
Snowball and Princess

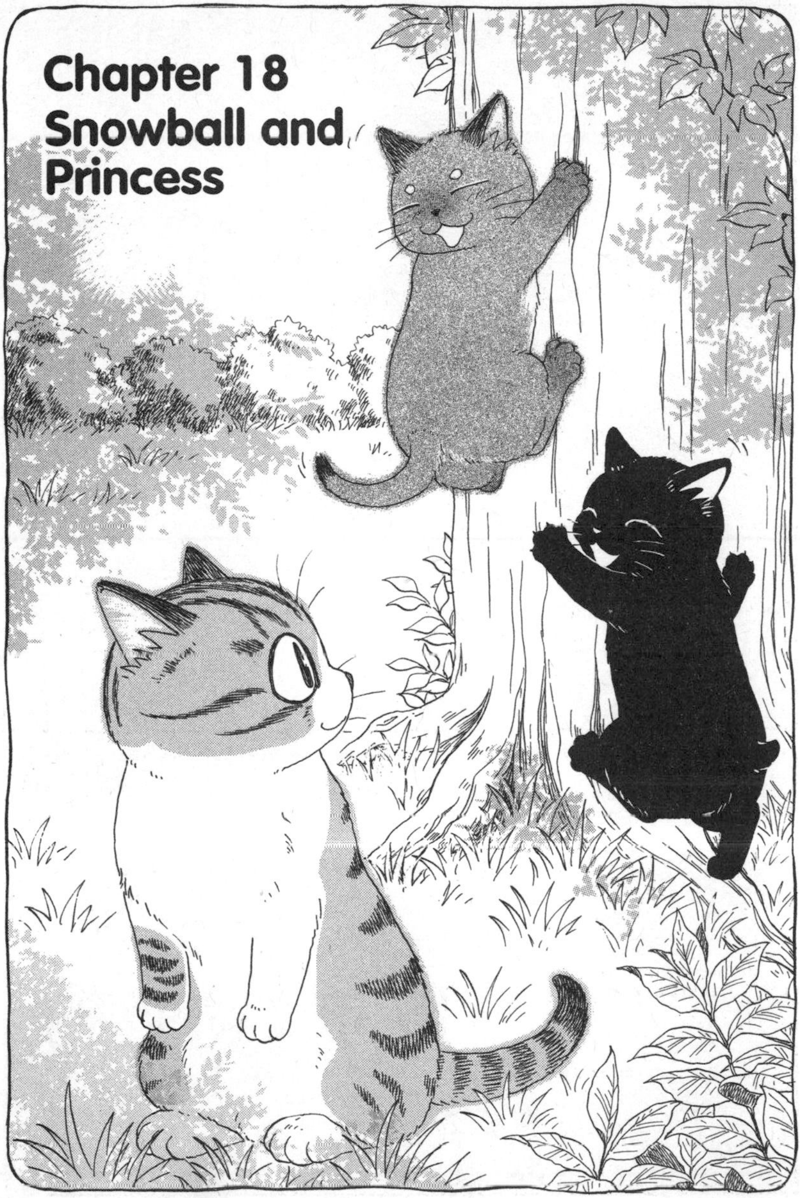

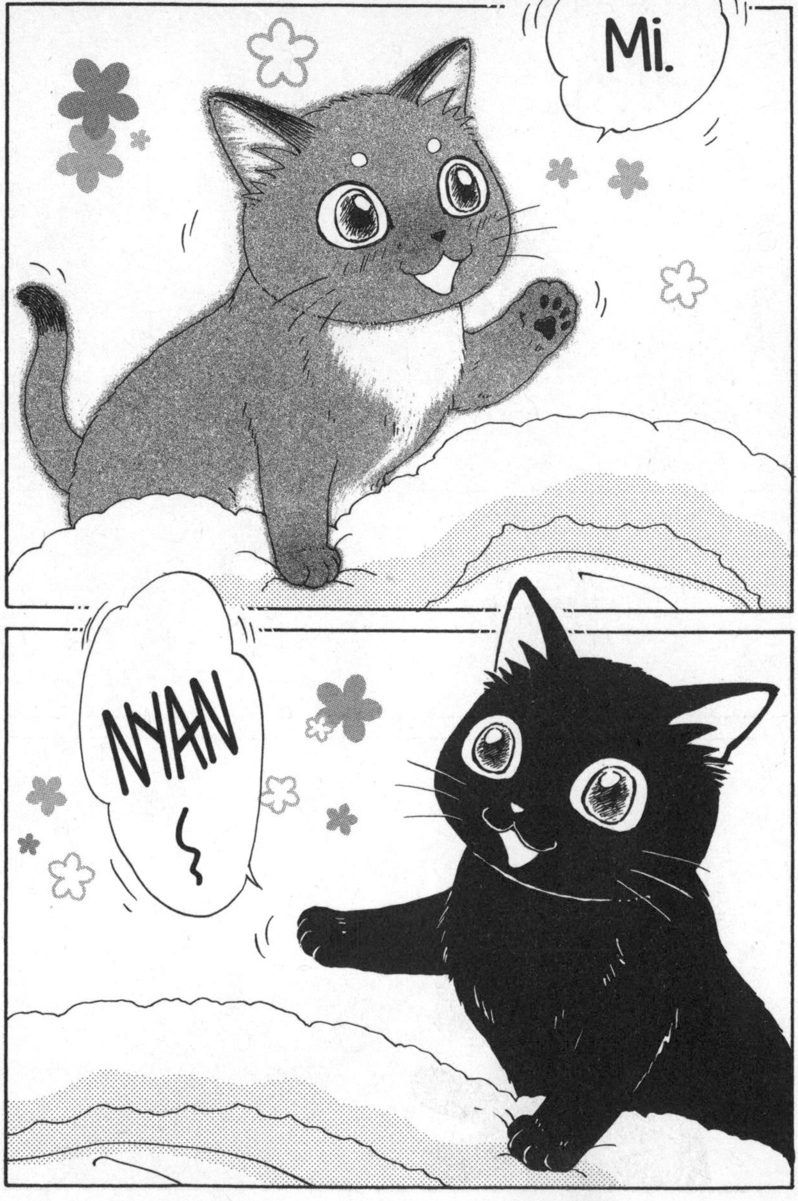
Mi.
NYAN

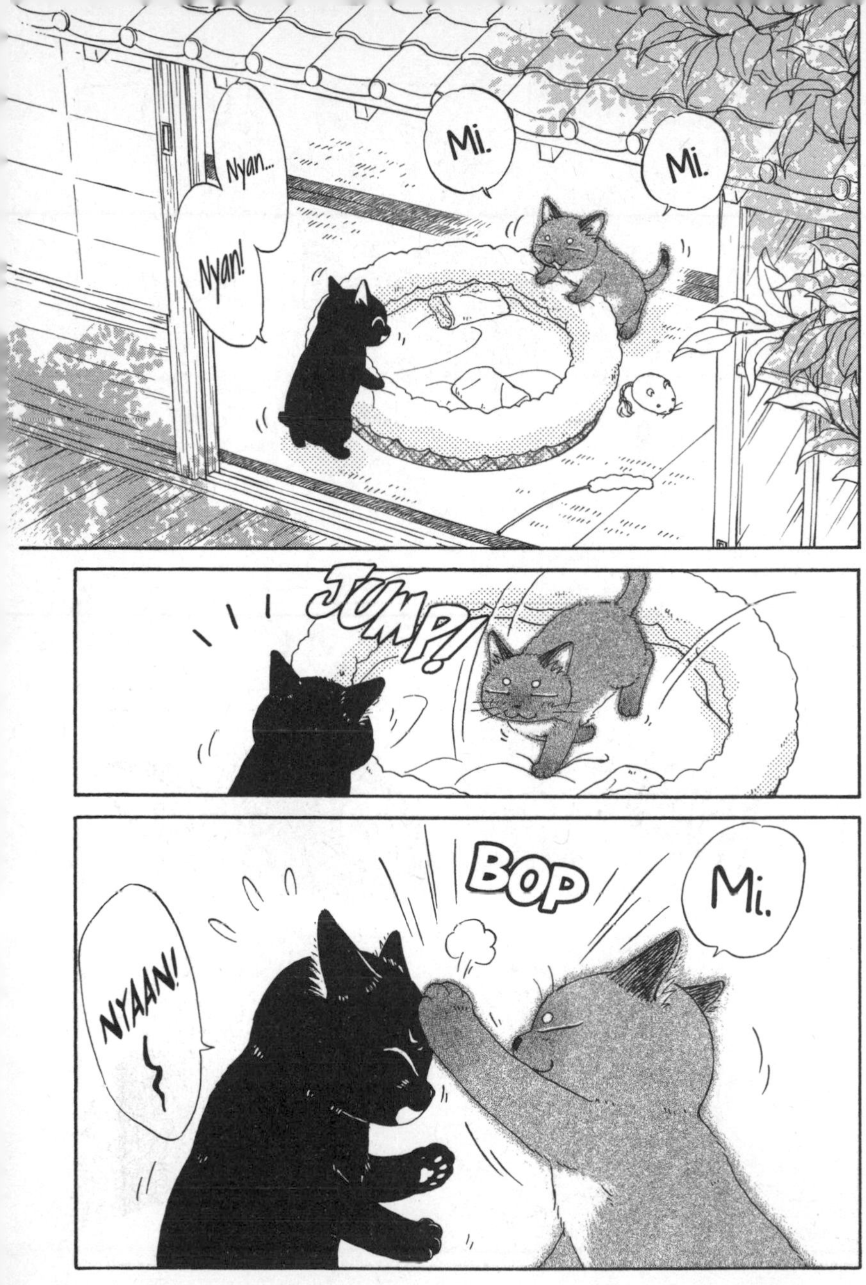
Mi.
Mi.
Nyan...
Nyan!
JUMP!
Mi.
BOP
NYAAN!

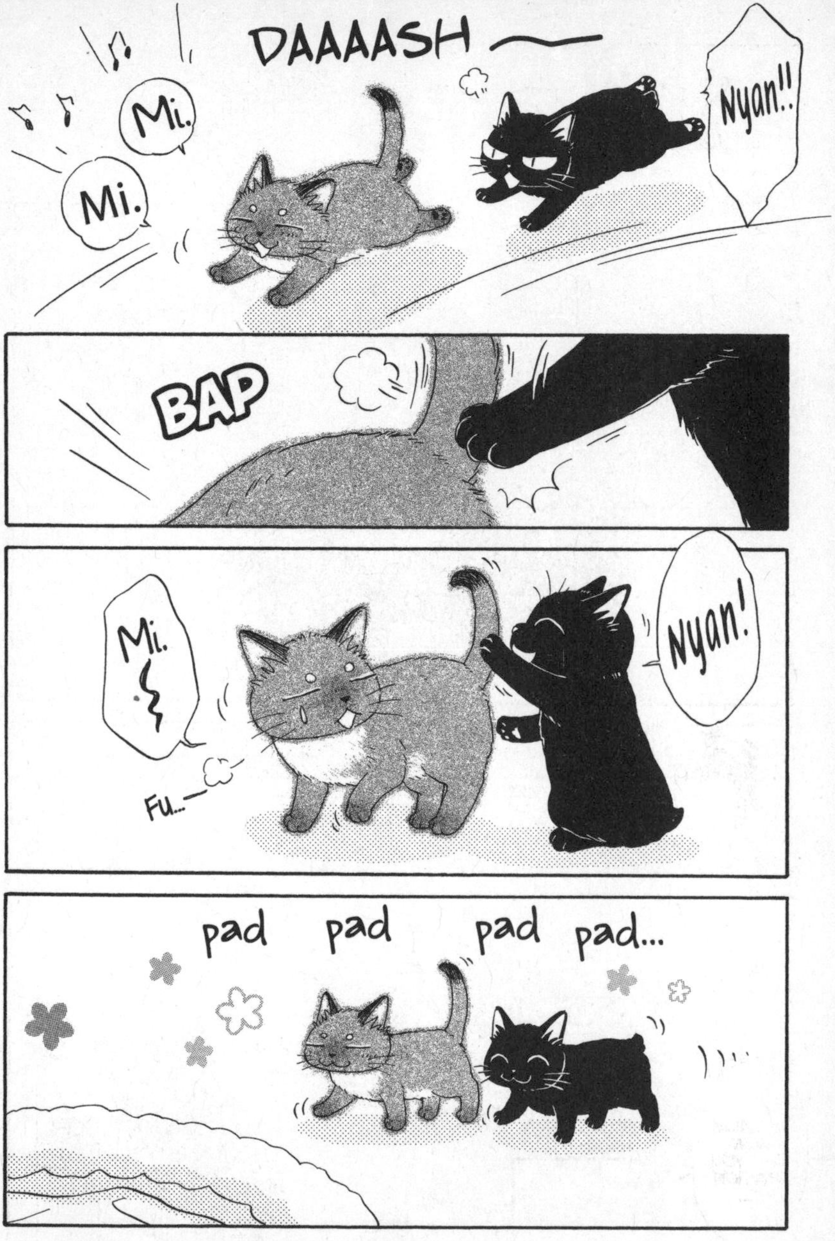
Nyan!!
DAAAASH
Mi.
Mi.
BAP
Nyan!
Mi.
Fu...
pad pad pad pad...

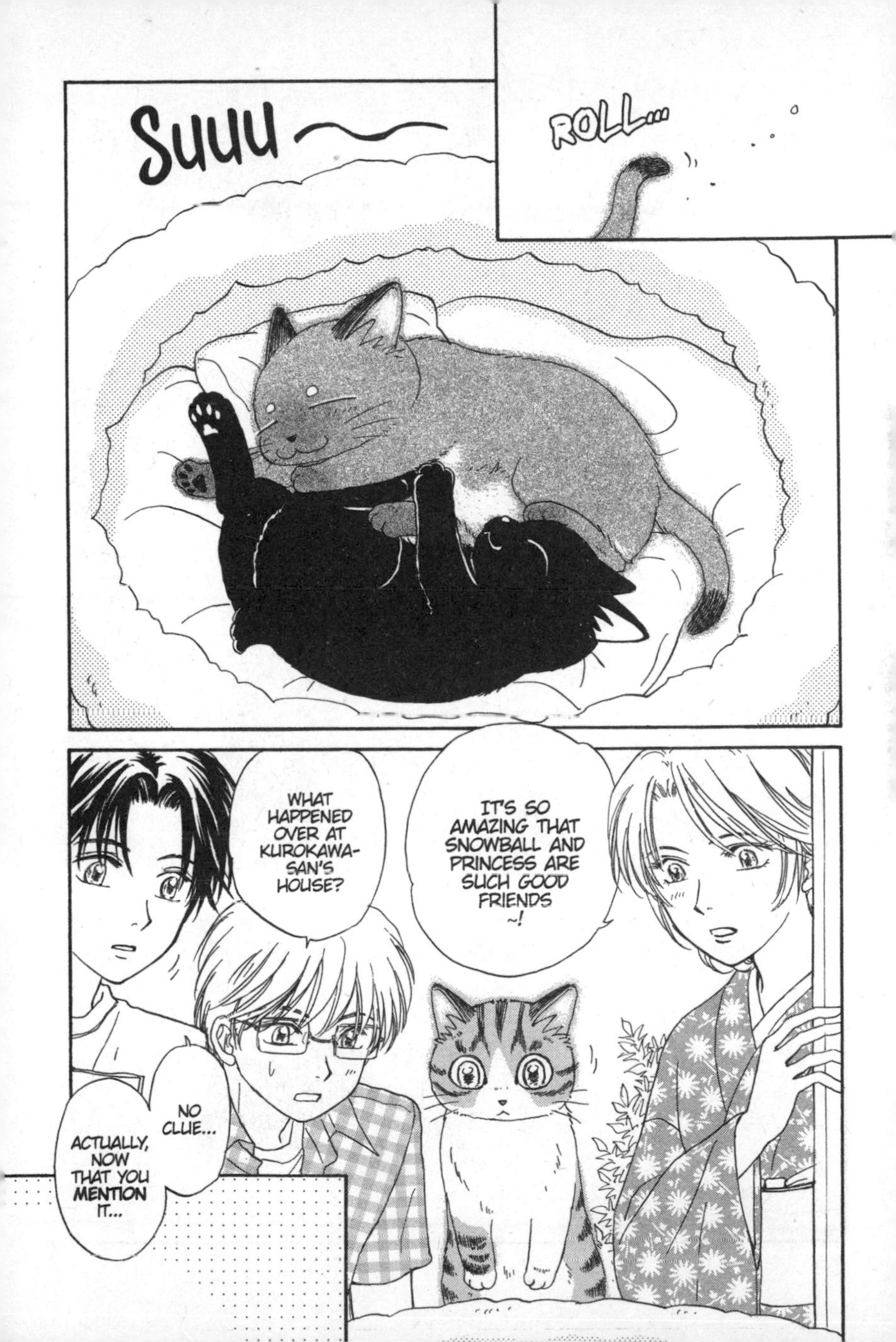
ROLL...
Suuu~~
IT'S SO AMAZING THAT SNOWBALL AND PRINCESS ARE SUCH GOOD FRIENDS ~!
WHAT HAPPENED OVER AT KUROKAWA-SAN'S HOUSE?
NO CLUE...
ACTUALLY, NOW THAT YOU MENTION IT...

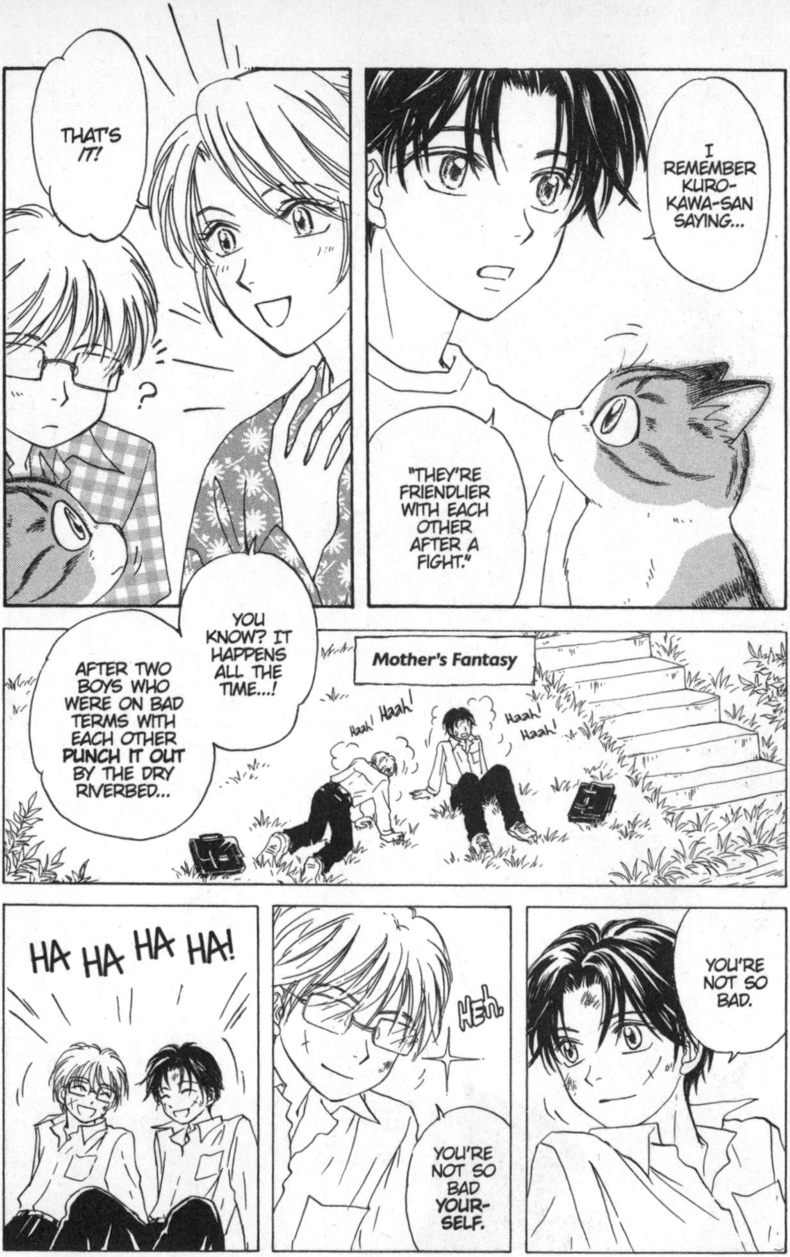
I REMEMBER KURO-KAWA-SAN SAYING...
"THEY'RE FRIENDLIER WITH EACH OTHER AFTER A FIGHT."
THAT'S IT!
YOU KNOW? IT HAPPENS ALL THE TIME...!
AFTER TWO BOYS WHO WERE ON BAD TERMS WITH EACH OTHER PUNCH IT OUT BY THE DRY RIVERBED...
Mother's Fantasy
Haah! Haah!
Haah! Haah!
YOU'RE NOT SO BAD.
HEH.
YOU'RE NOT SO BAD YOURSELF.
HA HA HA HA!

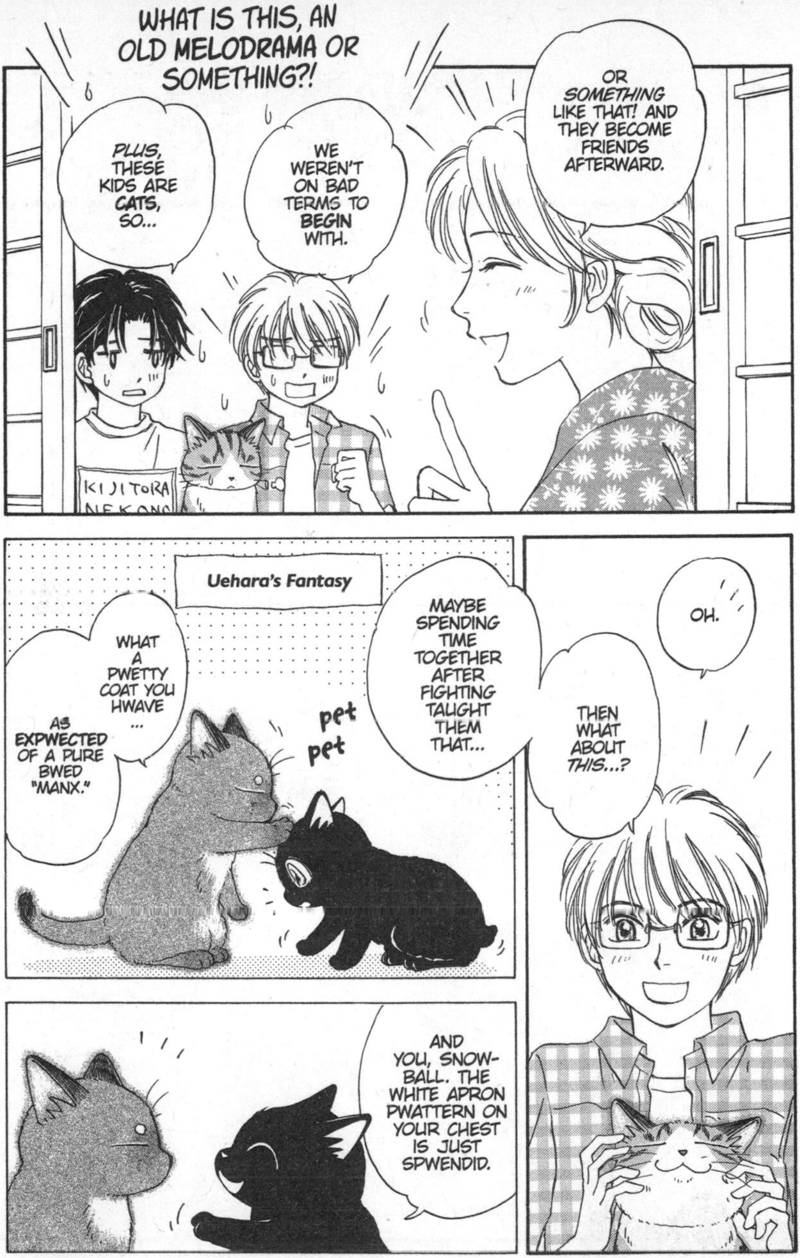
OR *SOMETHING* LIKE THAT! AND THEY BECOME FRIENDS AFTERWARD.
WE WEREN'T ON BAD TERMS TO **BEGIN** WITH.
PLUS, THESE KIDS ARE **CATS**, SO...
WHAT IS THIS, AN OLD MELODRAMA OR SOMETHING?!
KIJITORA NEKONO
MAYBE SPENDING TIME TOGETHER AFTER FIGHTING TAUGHT THEM THAT...
OH.
THEN WHAT ABOUT *THIS*...?
Uehara's Fantasy
WHAT A PWETTY COAT YOU HWAVE ...
AS EXPWECTED OF A PURE BWED "MANX."
pet pet
AND YOU, SNOW-BALL. THE WHITE APRON PWATTERN ON YOUR CHEST IS JUST SPWENDID.

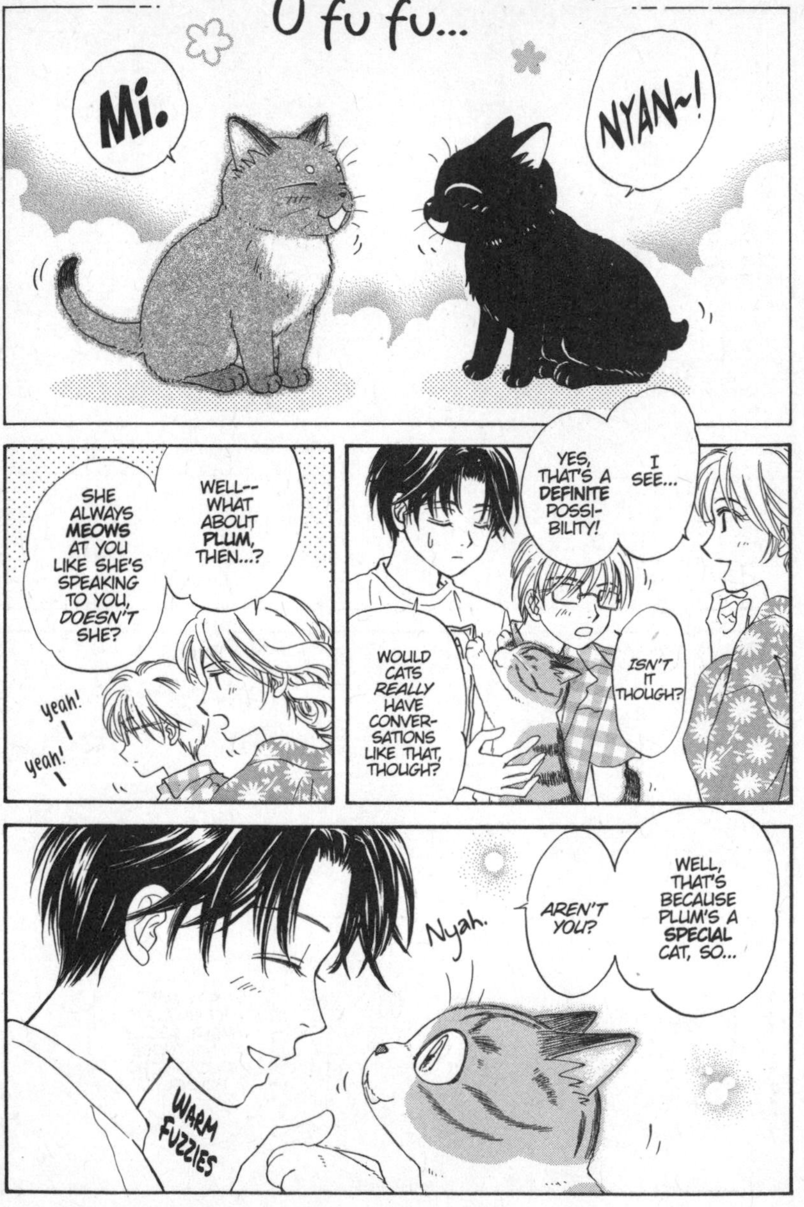
U fu fu...
NYAN~!
Mi.
I SEE...
YES, THAT'S A DEFINITE POSSIBILITY!
ISN'T IT THOUGH?
WOULD CATS REALLY HAVE CONVERSATIONS LIKE THAT, THOUGH?
WELL-- WHAT ABOUT PLUM, THEN...?
SHE ALWAYS MEOWS AT YOU LIKE SHE'S SPEAKING TO YOU, DOESN'T SHE?
yeah!
yeah!
WELL, THAT'S BECAUSE PLUM'S A SPECIAL CAT, SO...
AREN'T YOU?
Nyah.
WARM FUZZIES

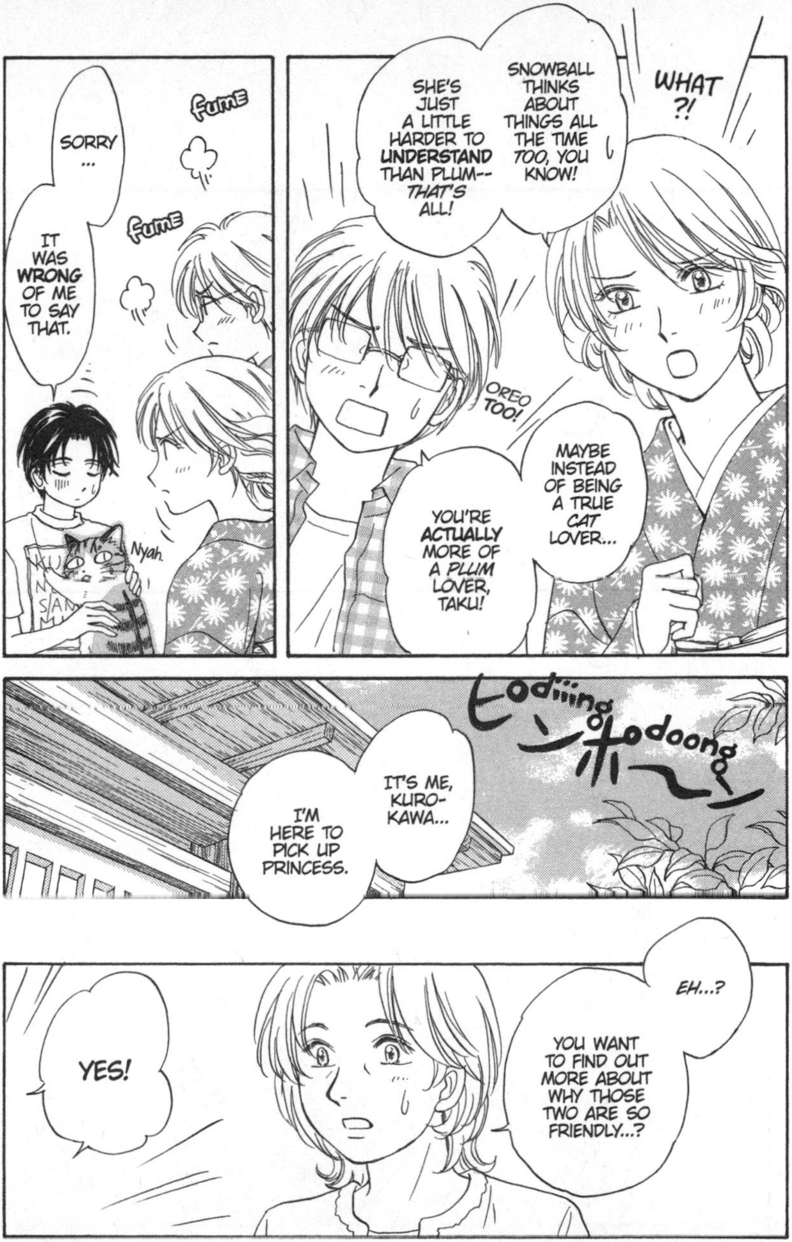
WHAT ?!
SNOWBALL THINKS ABOUT THINGS ALL THE TIME TOO, YOU KNOW!
SHE'S JUST A LITTLE HARDER TO UNDERSTAND THAN PLUM-- THAT'S ALL!
OREO TOO!
MAYBE INSTEAD OF BEING A TRUE CAT LOVER...
YOU'RE ACTUALLY MORE OF A PLUM LOVER, TAKU!
fume
fume
SORRY ...
IT WAS WRONG OF ME TO SAY THAT.
Nyah.
diiing
doong
IT'S ME, KURO-KAWA...
I'M HERE TO PICK UP PRINCESS.
EH...?
YOU WANT TO FIND OUT MORE ABOUT WHY THOSE TWO ARE SO FRIENDLY...?
YES!

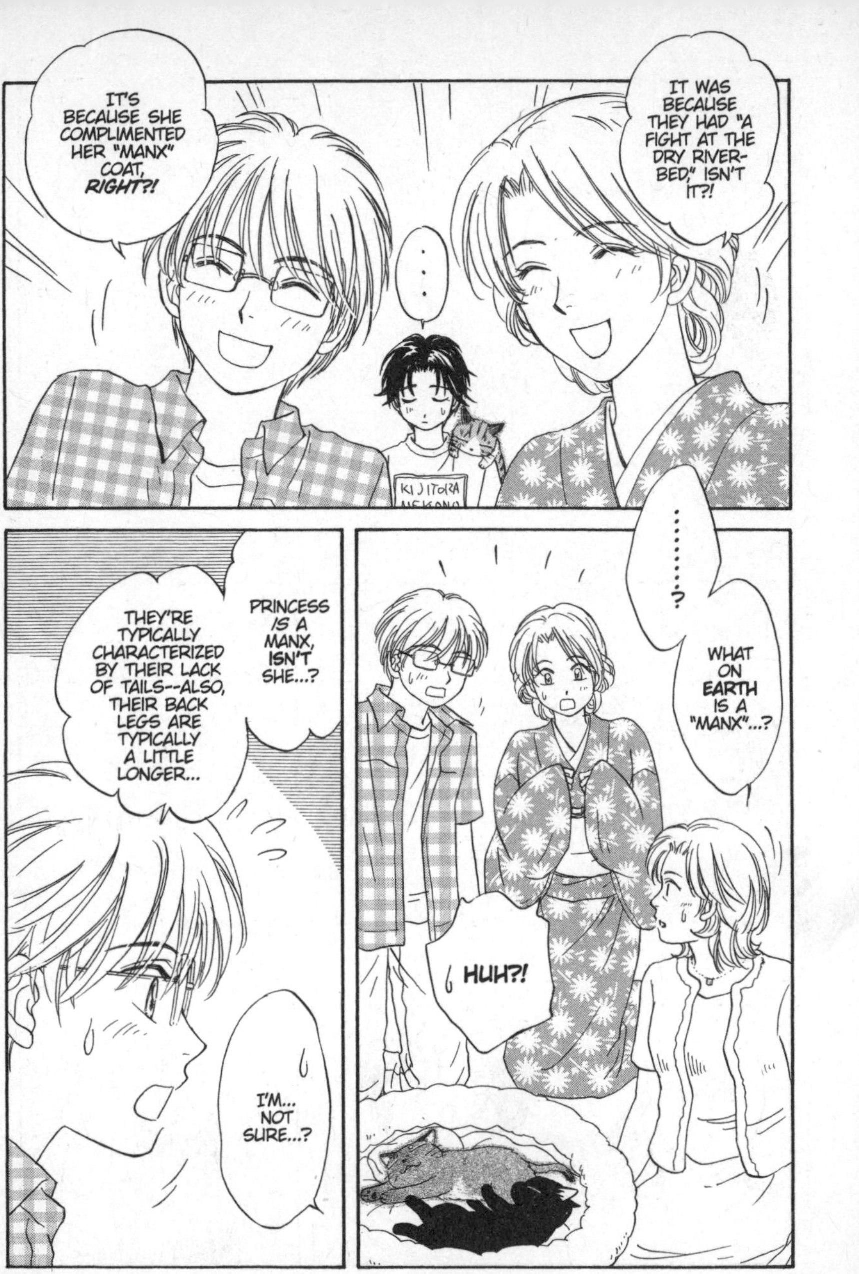
IT WAS BECAUSE THEY HAD "A FIGHT AT THE DRY RIVER-BED," ISN'T IT?!
...
IT'S BECAUSE SHE COMPLIMENTED HER "MANX" COAT, ***RIGHT?!***
......?
WHAT ON EARTH IS A "MANX"...?
HUH?!
PRINCESS IS A MANX, ISN'T SHE...?
THEY'RE TYPICALLY CHARACTERIZED BY THEIR LACK OF TAILS--ALSO, THEIR BACK LEGS ARE TYPICALLY A LITTLE LONGER...
I'M... NOT SURE...?

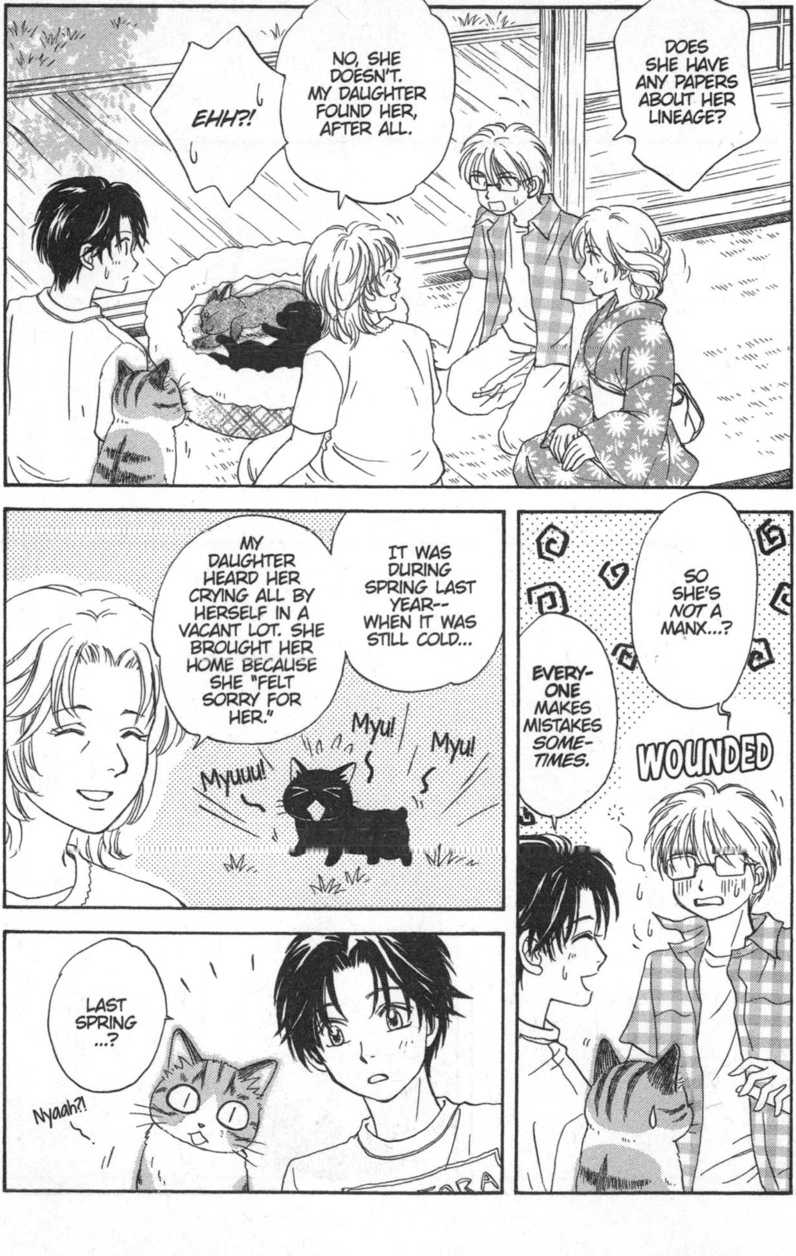
DOES SHE HAVE ANY PAPERS ABOUT HER LINEAGE?
NO, SHE DOESN'T. MY DAUGHTER FOUND HER, AFTER ALL.
EHH?!
SO SHE'S *NOT A* MANX...?
EVERY-ONE MAKES MISTAKES *SOME-TIMES.*
WOUNDED
IT WAS DURING SPRING LAST YEAR-- WHEN IT WAS STILL COLD...
MY DAUGHTER HEARD HER CRYING ALL BY HERSELF IN A VACANT LOT. SHE BROUGHT HER HOME BECAUSE SHE "FELT SORRY FOR HER."
Myu!
Myu!
Myuuu!
LAST SPRING ...?
Nyaah?!

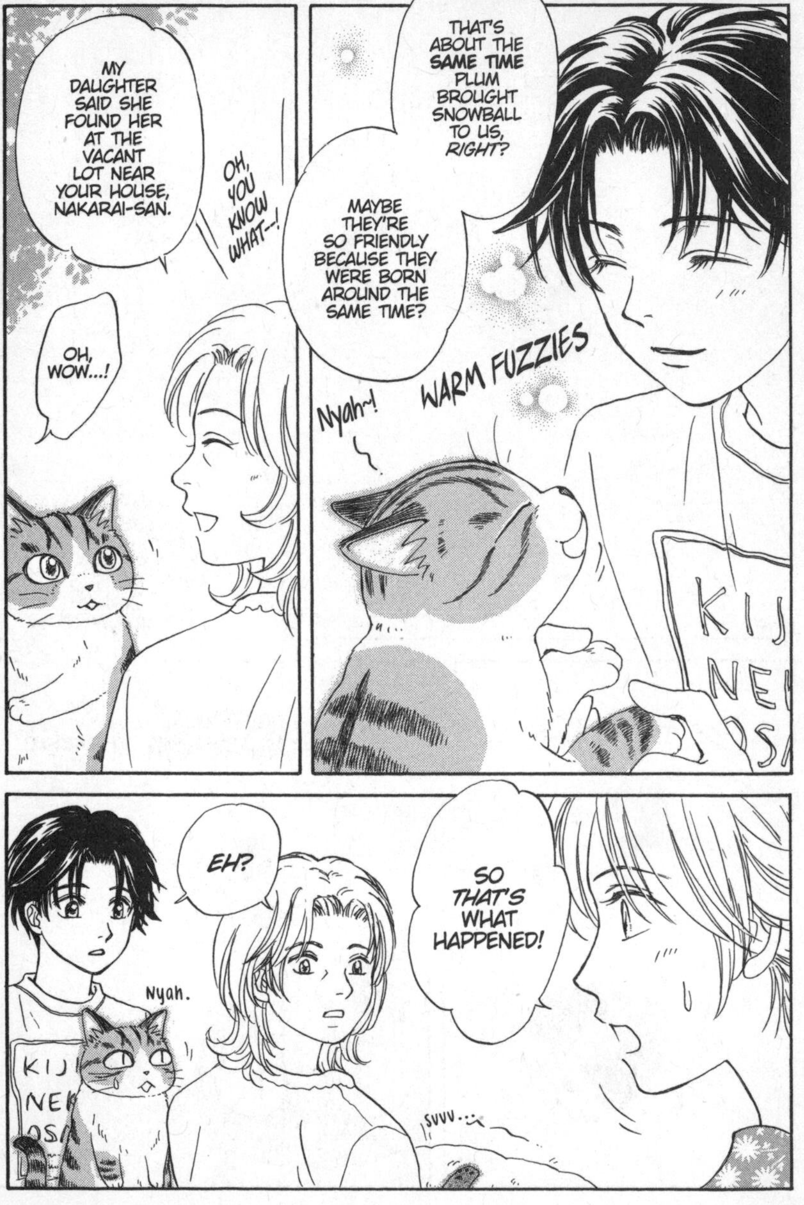
THAT'S ABOUT THE SAME TIME PLUM BROUGHT SNOWBALL TO US, *RIGHT?*
MAYBE THEY'RE SO FRIENDLY BECAUSE THEY WERE BORN AROUND THE SAME TIME?
WARM FUZZIES
Nyah~!
MY DAUGHTER SAID SHE FOUND HER AT THE VACANT LOT NEAR YOUR HOUSE, NAKARAI-SAN.
OH, YOU KNOW WHAT--!
OH, WOW...!
SO *THAT'S* WHAT HAPPENED!
EH?
Nyah.
SVVV...

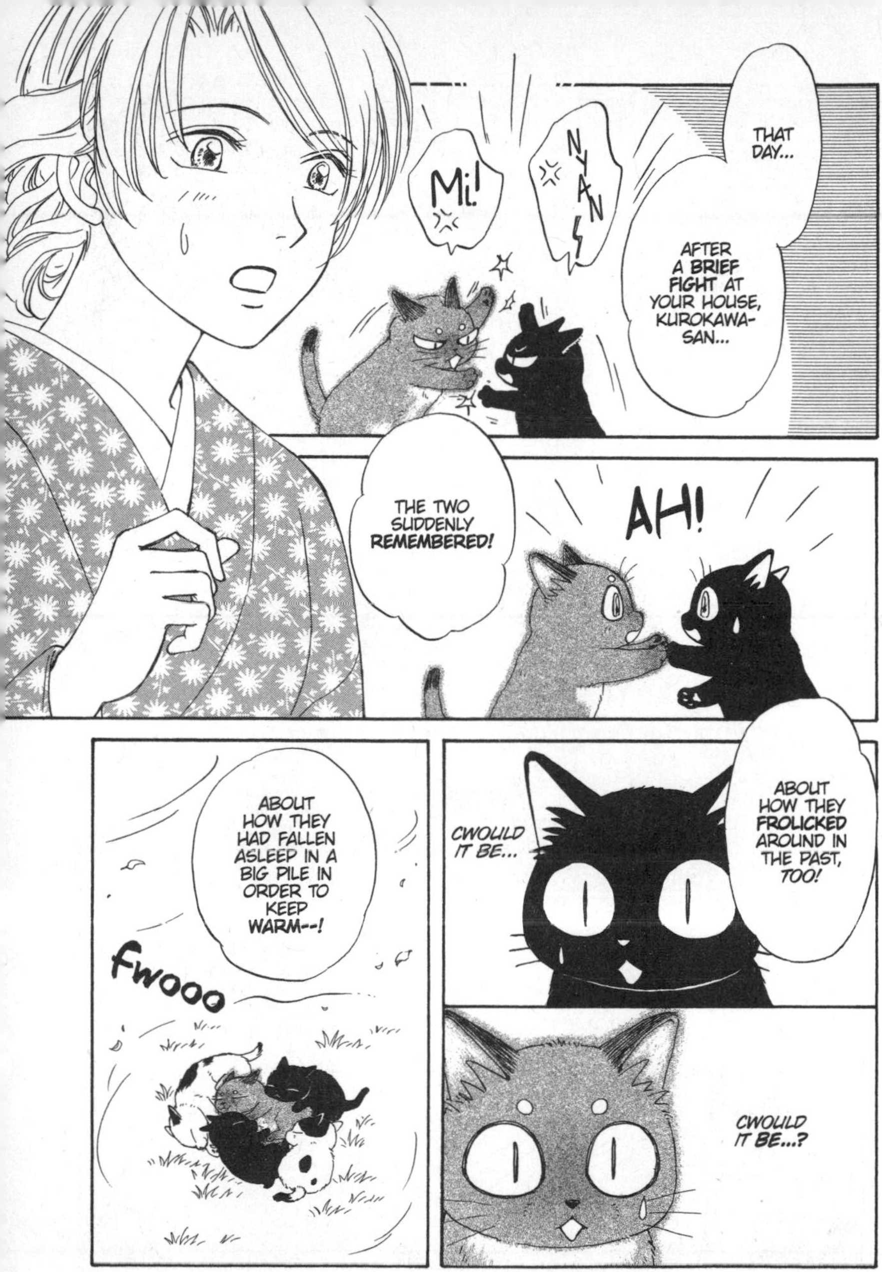
THAT DAY...
AFTER A BRIEF FIGHT AT YOUR HOUSE, KUROKAWA-SAN...
NYAN
Mi!
THE TWO SUDDENLY REMEMBERED!
AH!
ABOUT HOW THEY FROLICKED AROUND IN THE PAST, TOO!
CWOULD IT BE...
CWOULD IT BE...?
ABOUT HOW THEY HAD FALLEN ASLEEP IN A BIG PILE IN ORDER TO KEEP WARM--!
fwooo

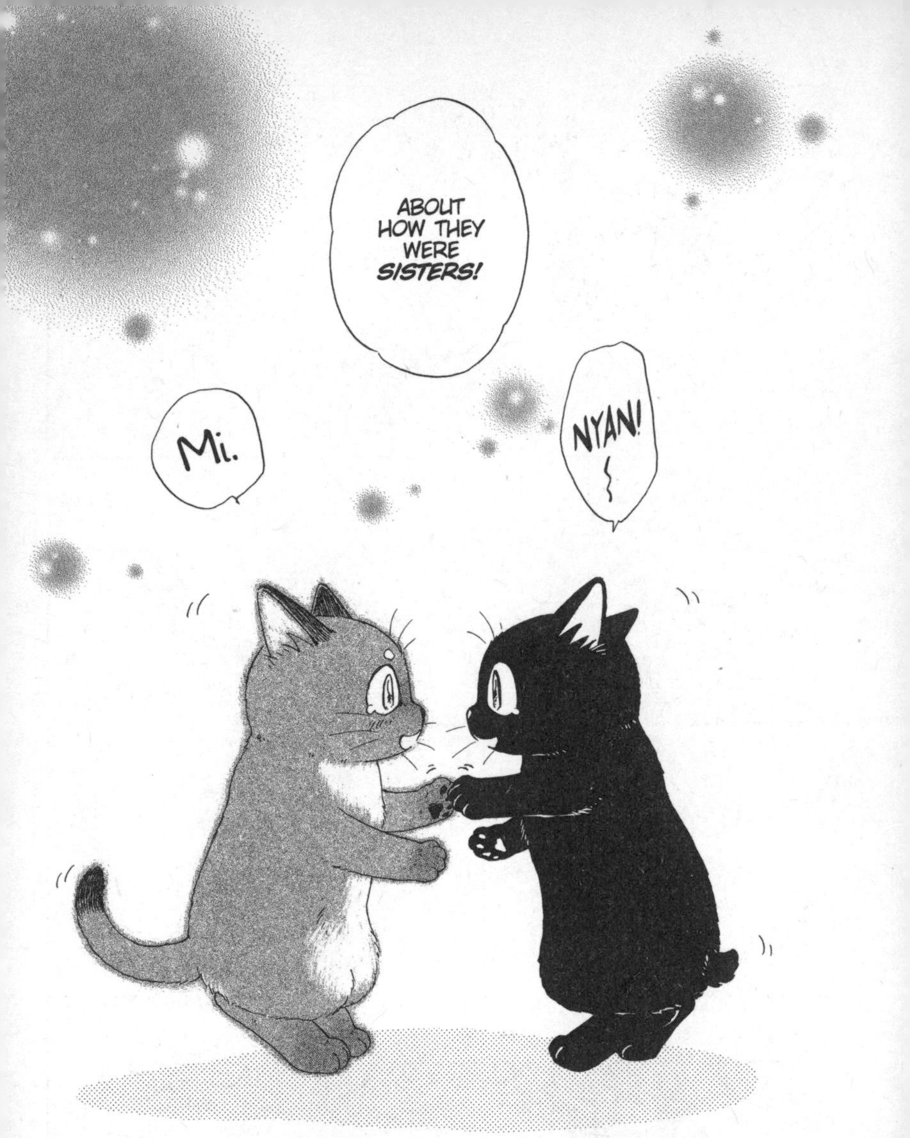
ABOUT HOW THEY WERE SISTERS!
NYAN!
Mi.

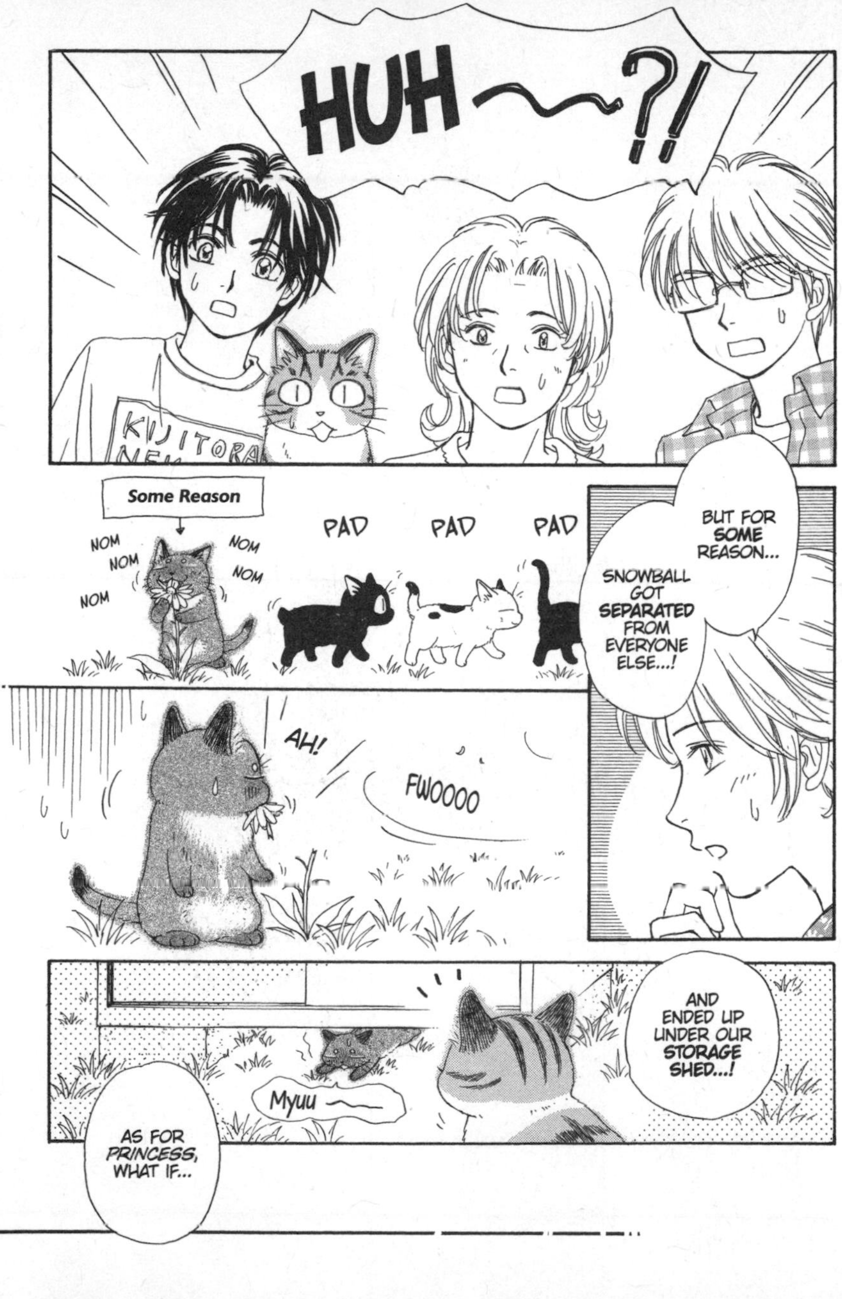
HUH~~?!
BUT FOR SOME REASON...
SNOWBALL GOT SEPARATED FROM EVERYONE ELSE...!
PAD
PAD
PAD
NOM
NOM
NOM
NOM
NOM
Some Reason
AH!
FWOOOO
AND ENDED UP UNDER OUR STORAGE SHED...!
Myuu~
AS FOR PRINCESS, WHAT IF...

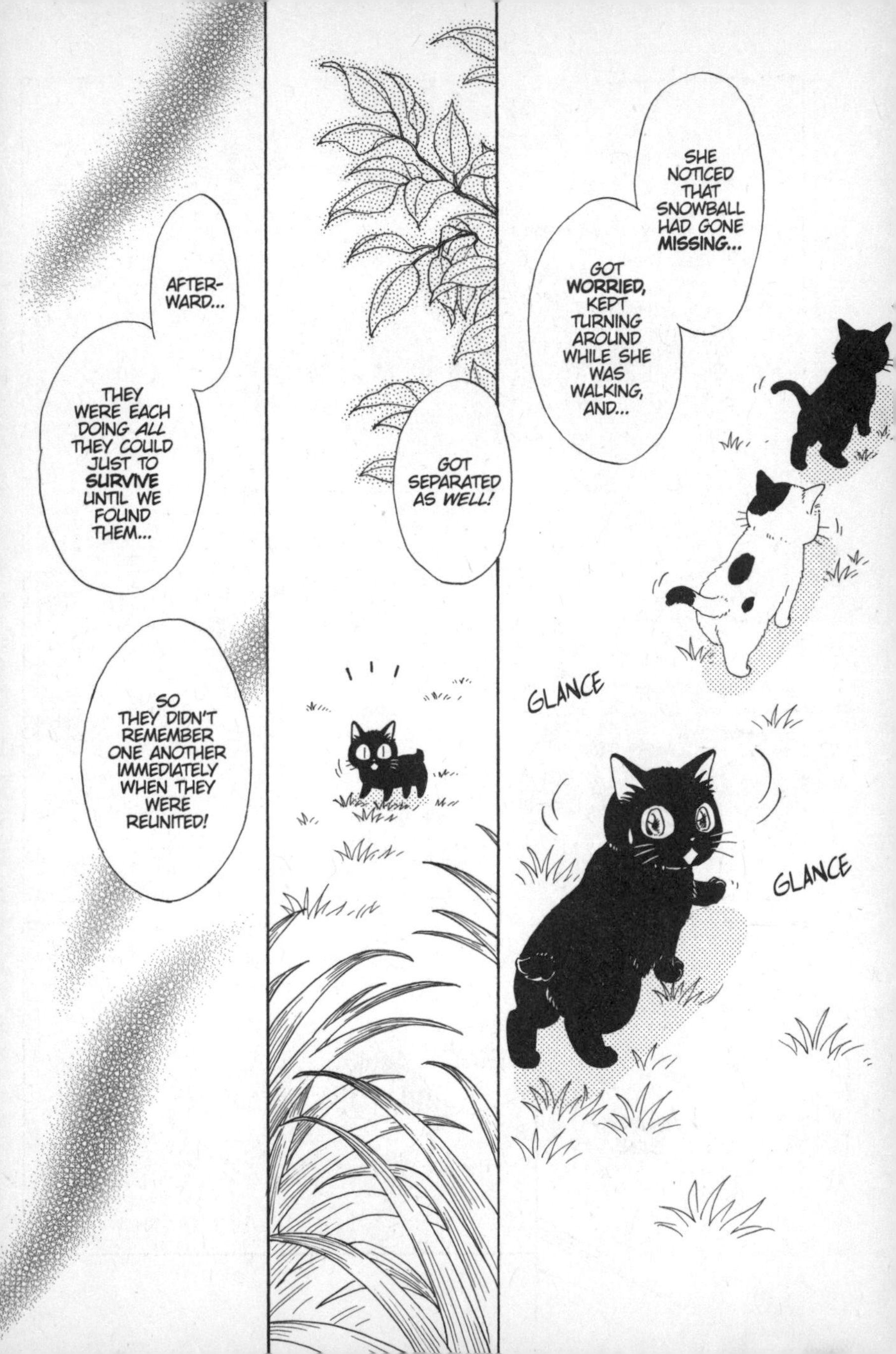
SHE NOTICED THAT SNOWBALL HAD GONE MISSING...
GOT WORRIED, KEPT TURNING AROUND WHILE SHE WAS WALKING, AND...
GLANCE
GLANCE
GOT SEPARATED AS WELL!
AFTER-WARD...
THEY WERE EACH DOING ALL THEY COULD JUST TO SURVIVE UNTIL WE FOUND THEM...
SO THEY DIDN'T REMEMBER ONE ANOTHER IMMEDIATELY WHEN THEY WERE REUNITED!

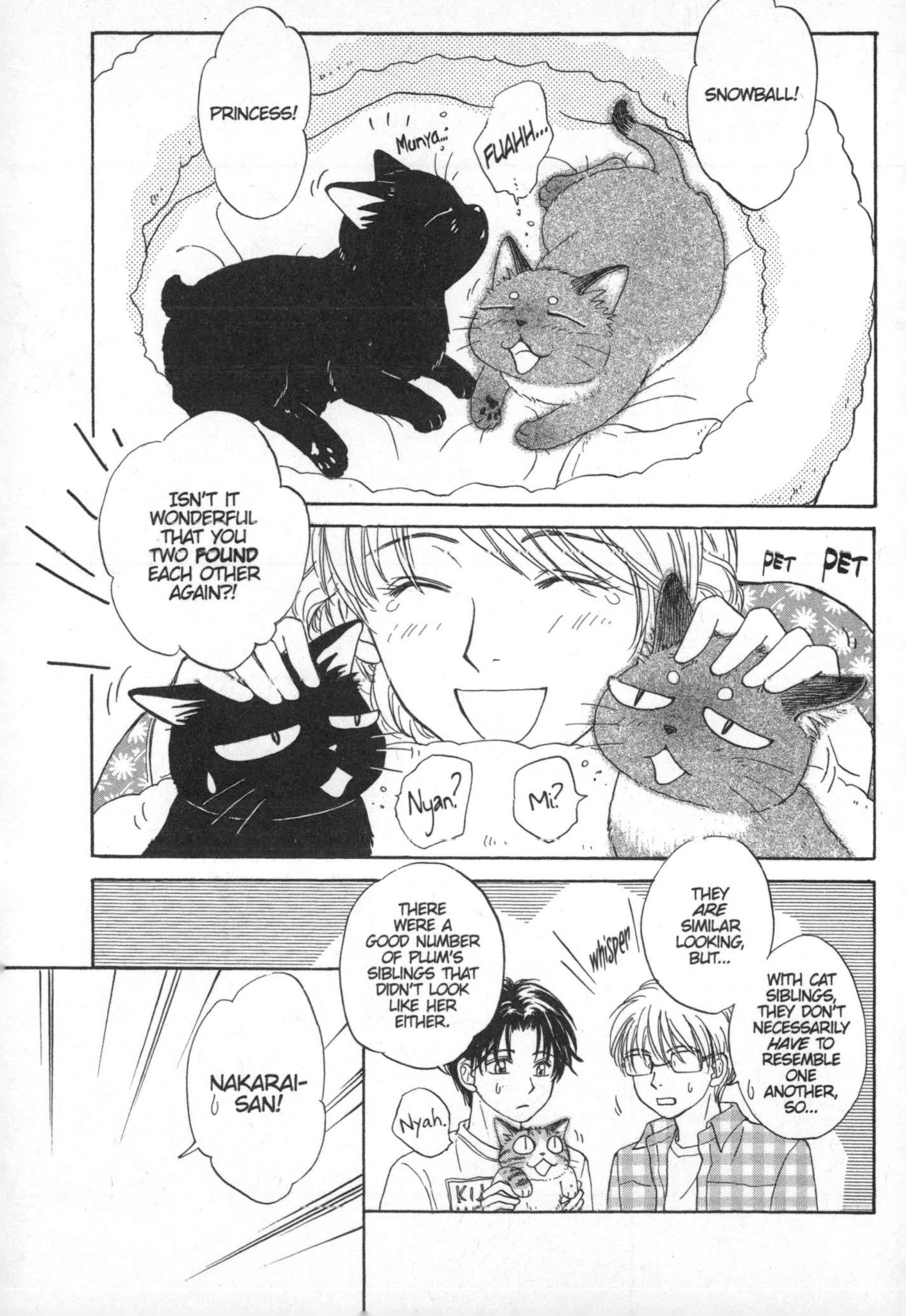
SNOWBALL!
FUAHH...
Munya...
PRINCESS!
PET PET
Mi?
Nyan?
ISN'T IT WONDERFUL THAT YOU TWO FOUND EACH OTHER AGAIN?!
THEY ARE SIMILAR LOOKING, BUT...
WITH CAT SIBLINGS, THEY DON'T NECESSARILY HAVE TO RESEMBLE ONE ANOTHER, SO...
whisper
THERE WERE A GOOD NUMBER OF PLUM'S SIBLINGS THAT DIDN'T LOOK LIKE HER EITHER.
Nyah.
NAKARAI-SAN!

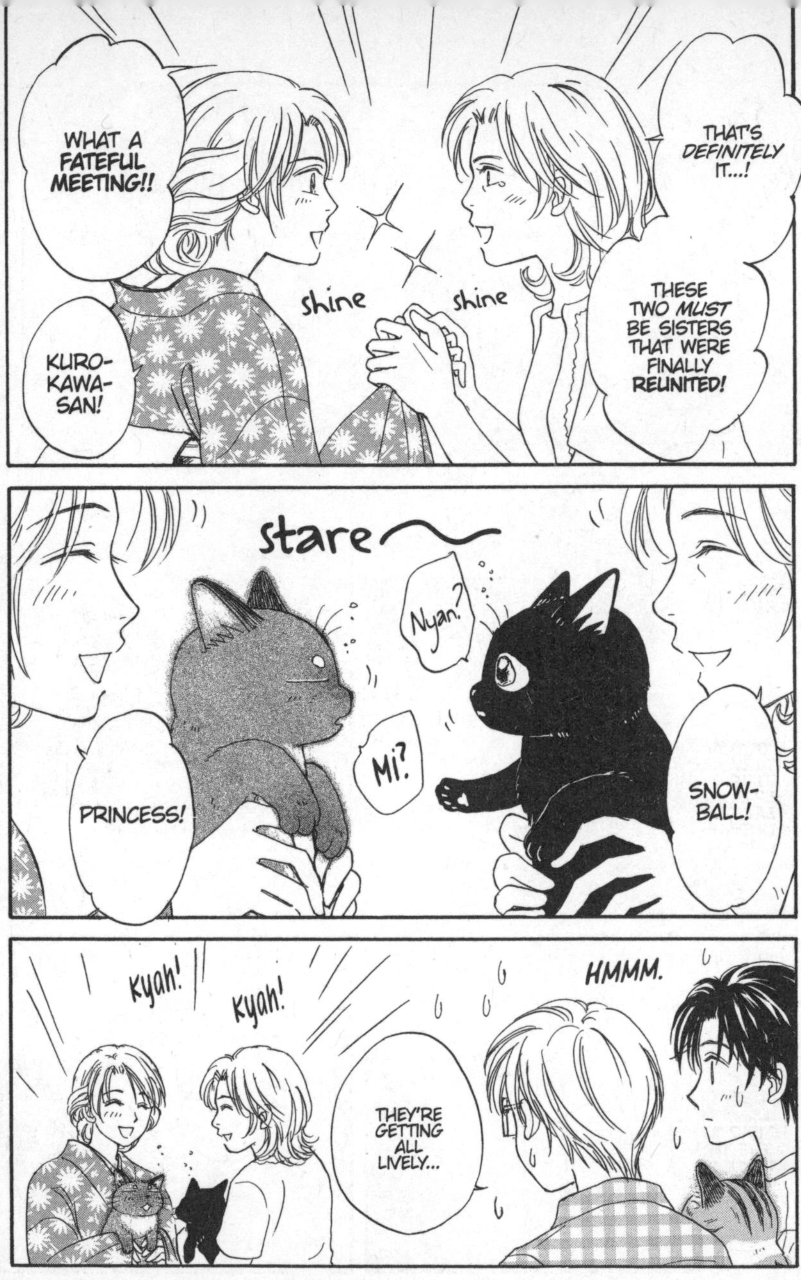
THAT'S DEFINITELY IT...!
WHAT A FATEFUL MEETING!!
shine
shine
THESE TWO MUST BE SISTERS THAT WERE FINALLY REUNITED!
KURO-KAWA-SAN!
stare~
Nyan?
SNOW-BALL!
Mi?
PRINCESS!
HMMM.
THEY'RE GETTING ALL LIVELY...
Kyah!
Kyah!

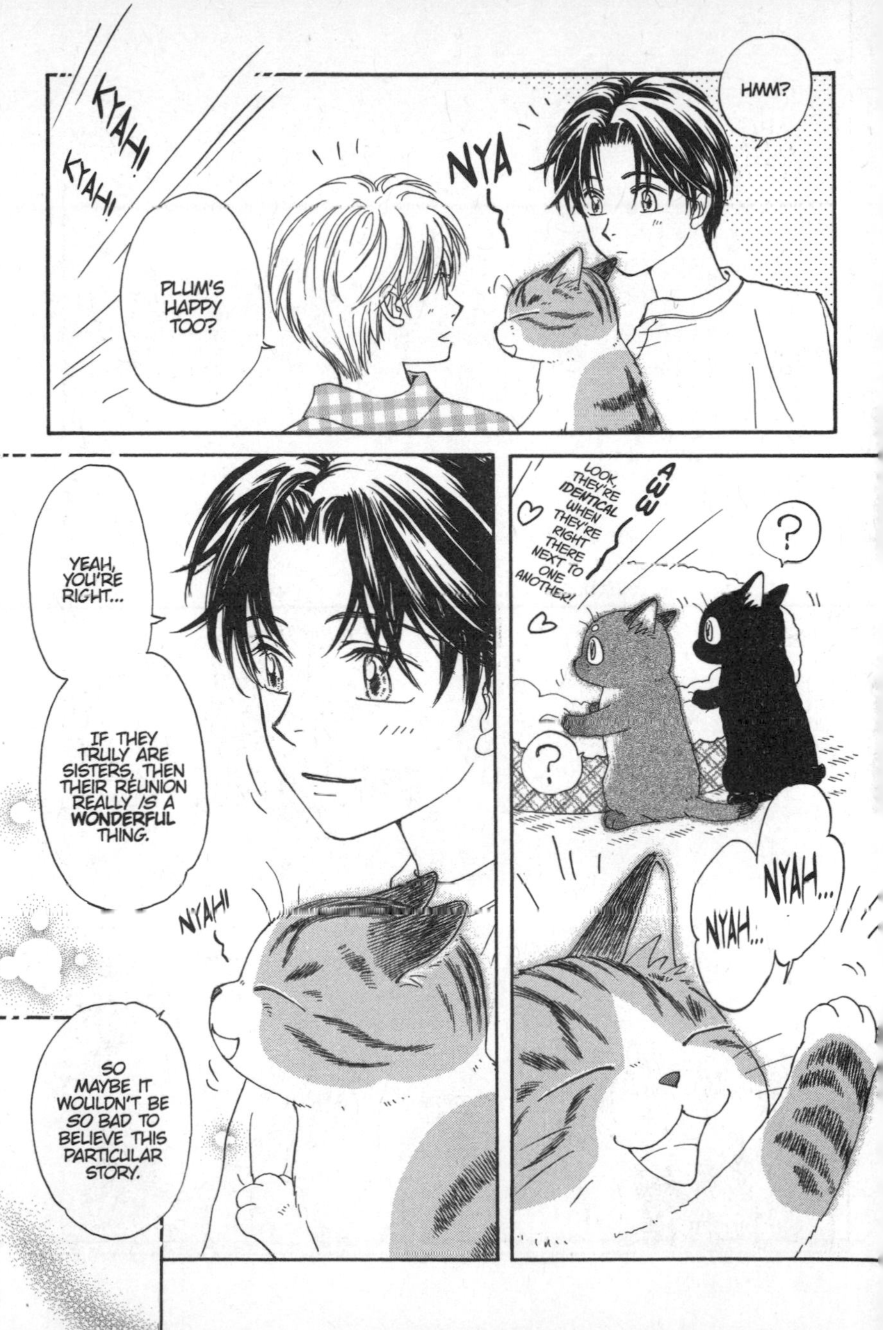
HMM?
NYA~
KYAH! KYAH!
PLUM'S HAPPY TOO?
AWW~
LOOK, THEY'RE IDENTICAL WHEN THEY'RE RIGHT THERE NEXT TO ONE ANOTHER!
?
?
NYAH... NYAH...
YEAH, YOU'RE RIGHT...
IF THEY TRULY ARE SISTERS, THEN THEIR REUNION REALLY IS A WONDERFUL THING.
NYAH!~
SO MAYBE IT WOULDN'T BE SO BAD TO BELIEVE THIS PARTICULAR STORY.

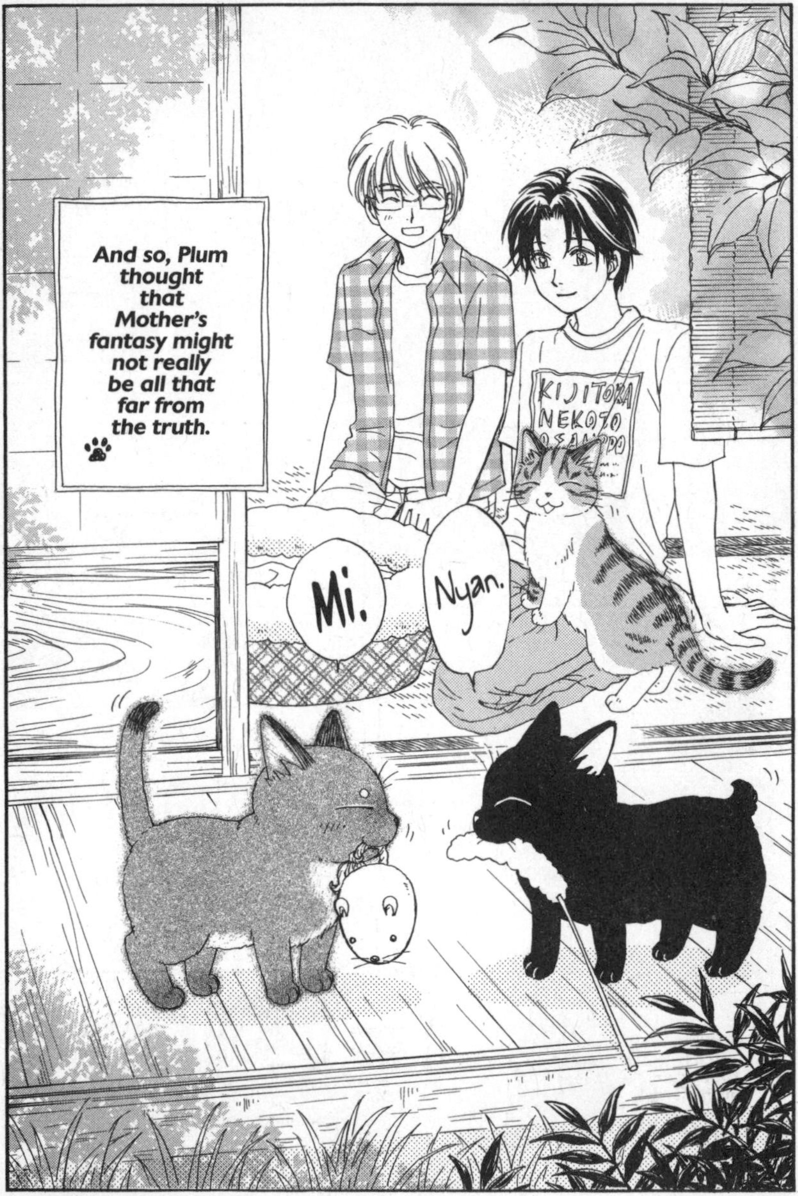
And so, Plum thought that Mother's fantasy might not really be all that far from the truth.
KIJITORA
NEKOTO
Nyan.
Mi.

(18) The End

♡ Stories About My Cats: Part 1 ♡

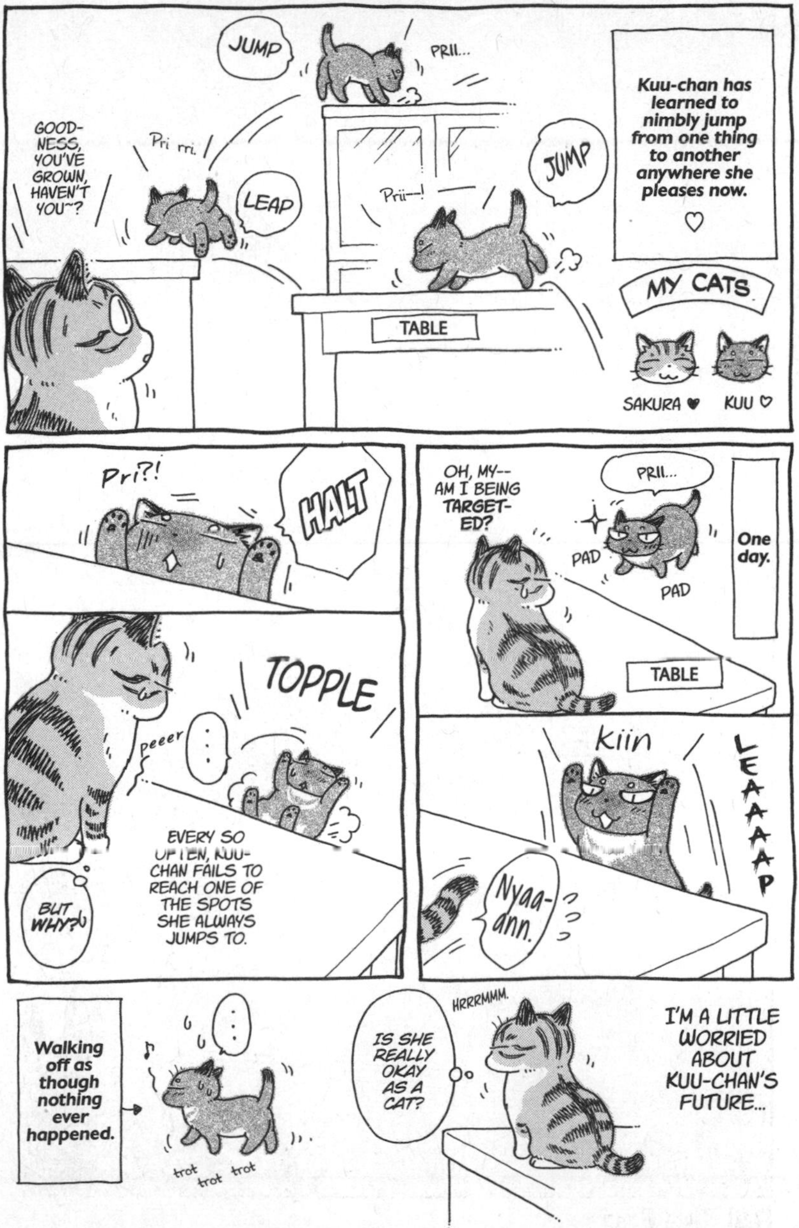

Kuu-chan has learned to nimbly jump from one thing to another anywhere she pleases now. ♡
MY CATS
SAKURA ♥
KUU ♡
JUMP
Prii--!
TABLE
PRII...
JUMP
LEAP
Pri rri.
GOOD-NESS, YOU'VE GROWN, HAVEN'T YOU~?
One day.
PRII...
PAD
PAD
OH, MY-- AM I BEING TARGET-ED?
TABLE
LEAAAAAP
kiin
Nyaa-ann.
HALT
Pri?!
TOPPLE
...
peeer
EVERY SO OFTEN, KUU-CHAN FAILS TO REACH ONE OF THE SPOTS SHE ALWAYS JUMPS TO.
BUT WHY?!
I'M A LITTLE WORRIED ABOUT KUU-CHAN'S FUTURE...
HRRRMMM.
IS SHE REALLY OKAY AS A CAT?
...
♪
trot trot trot
Walking off as though nothing ever happened.

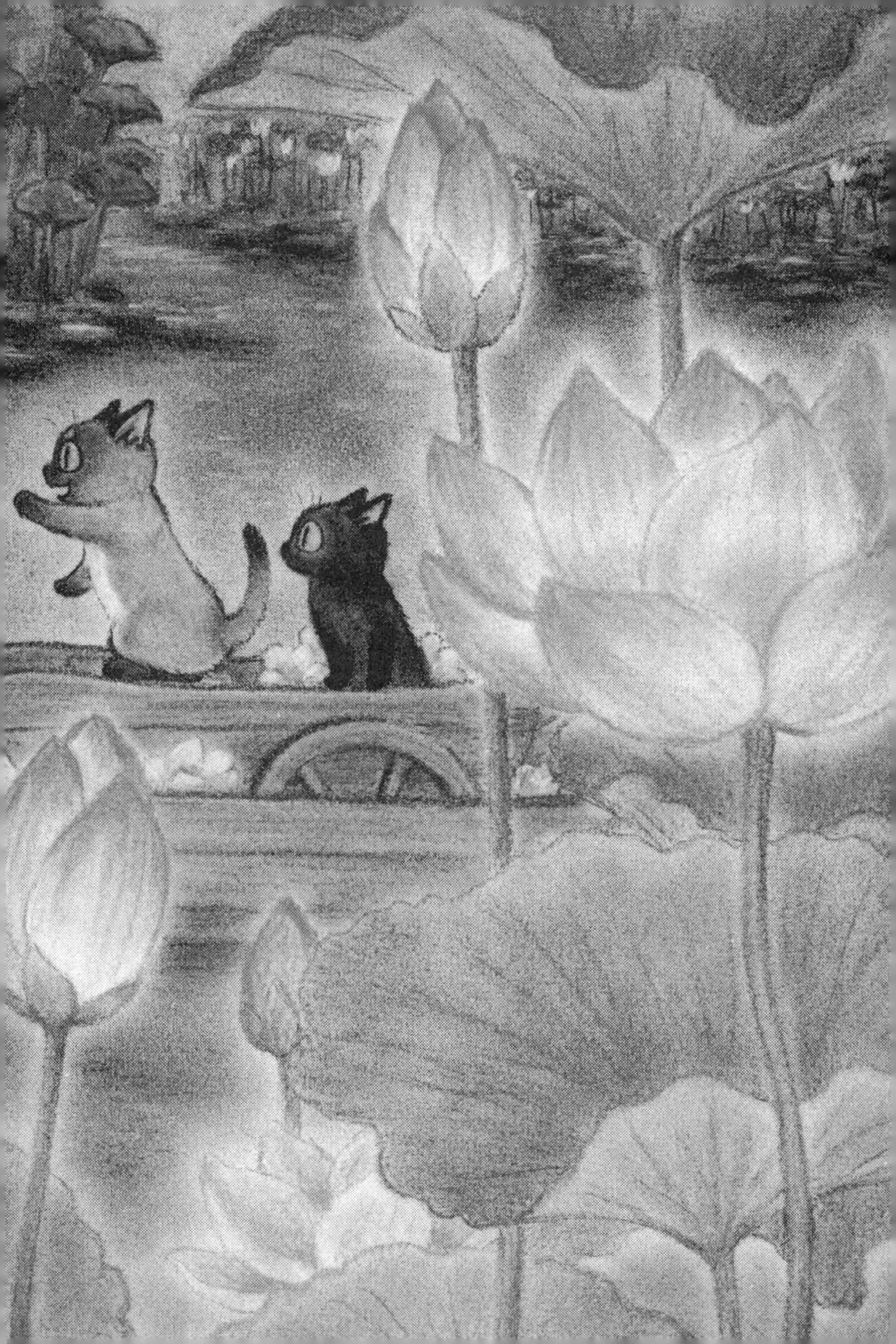

CHAPTER 15
A Short While

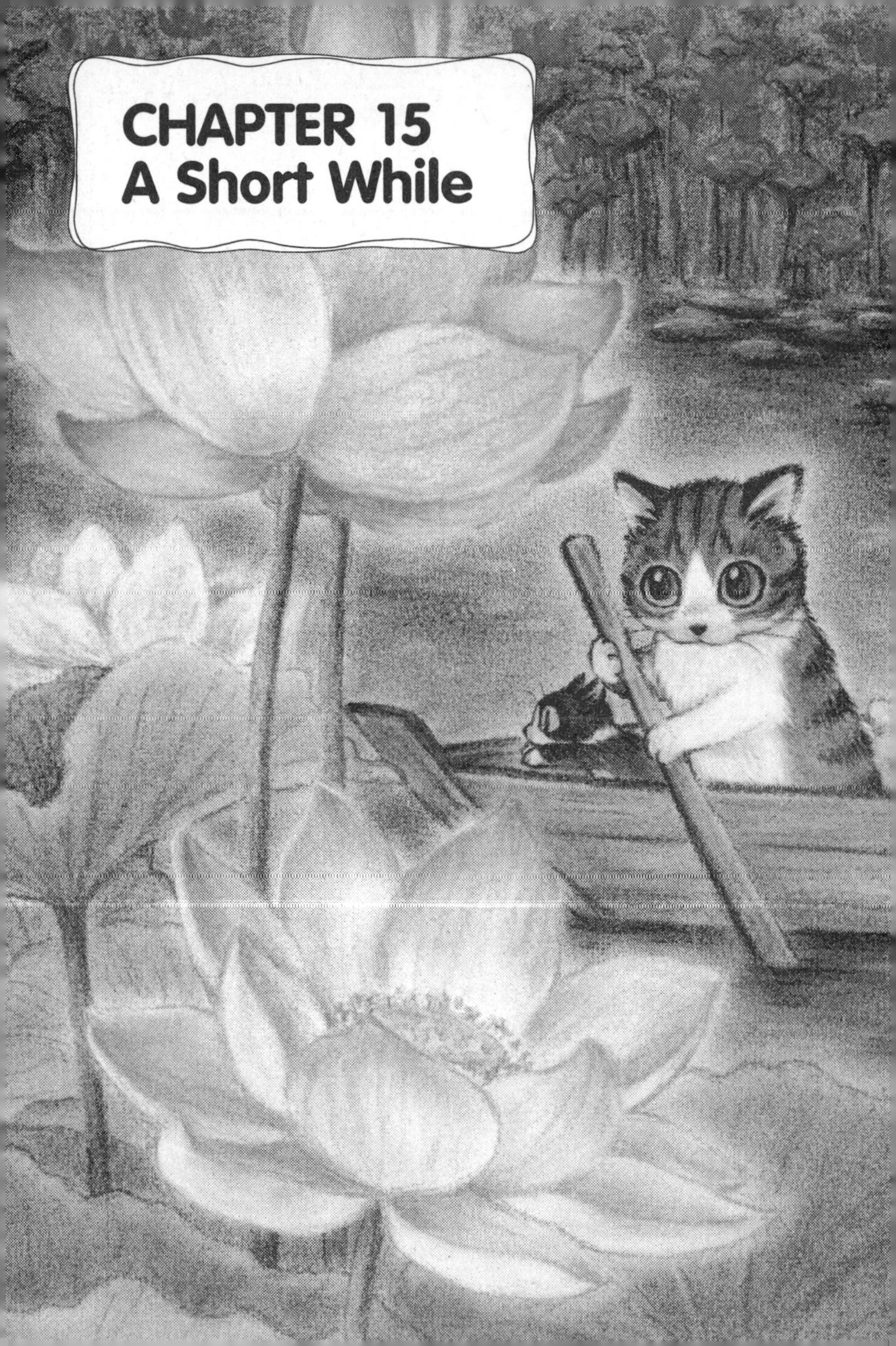

♡ Stories About My Cats: Part 2 ♡

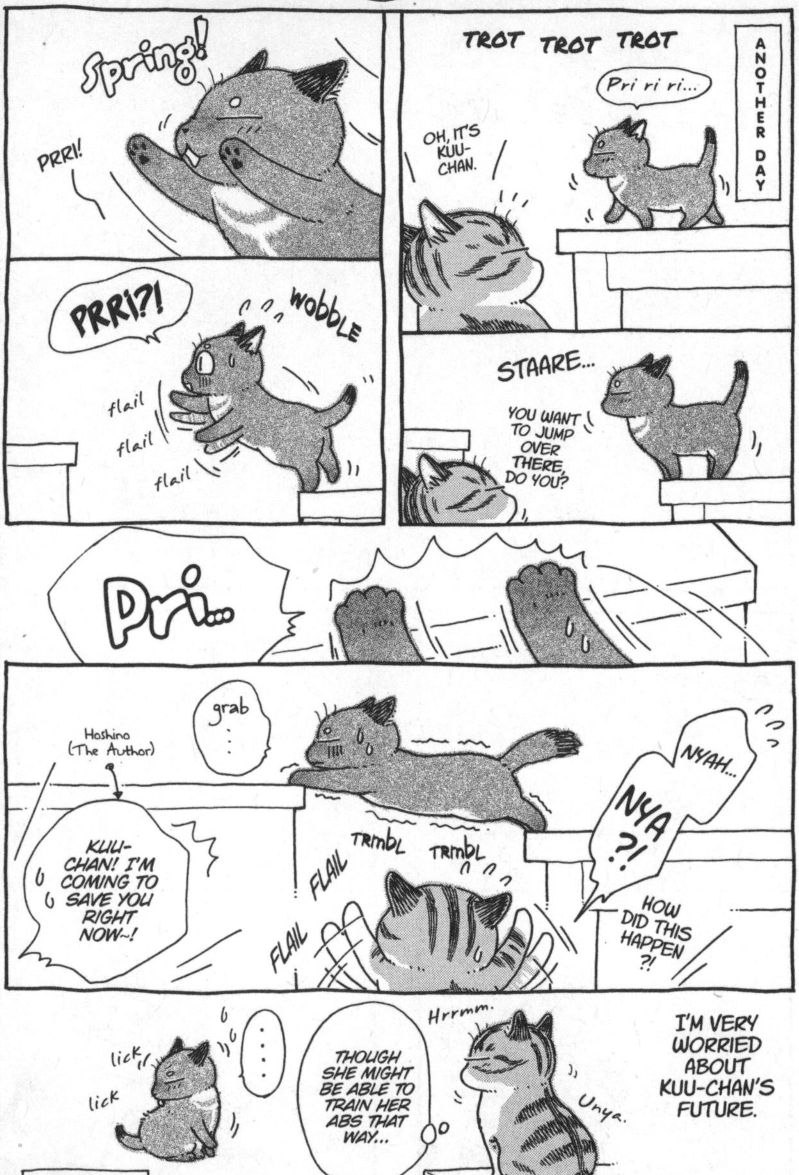

ANOTHER DAY
TROT TROT TROT
Pri ri ri...
OH, IT'S KUU-CHAN.
Spring!
PRRI!
STAARE...
YOU WANT TO JUMP OVER THERE, DO YOU?
PRRI?!
WOBBLE
flail
flail
flail
Pri...
NYAH...
NYA ?!
grab
Hoshino (The Author)
HOW DID THIS HAPPEN ?!
TRMBL TRMBL
FLAIL
FLAIL
KUU-CHAN! I'M COMING TO SAVE YOU RIGHT NOW~!
I'M VERY WORRIED ABOUT KUU-CHAN'S FUTURE.
Hrrmm.
Unya.
THOUGH SHE MIGHT BE ABLE TO TRAIN HER ABS THAT WAY...
...
lick
lick
The End

Short.15 A Short While

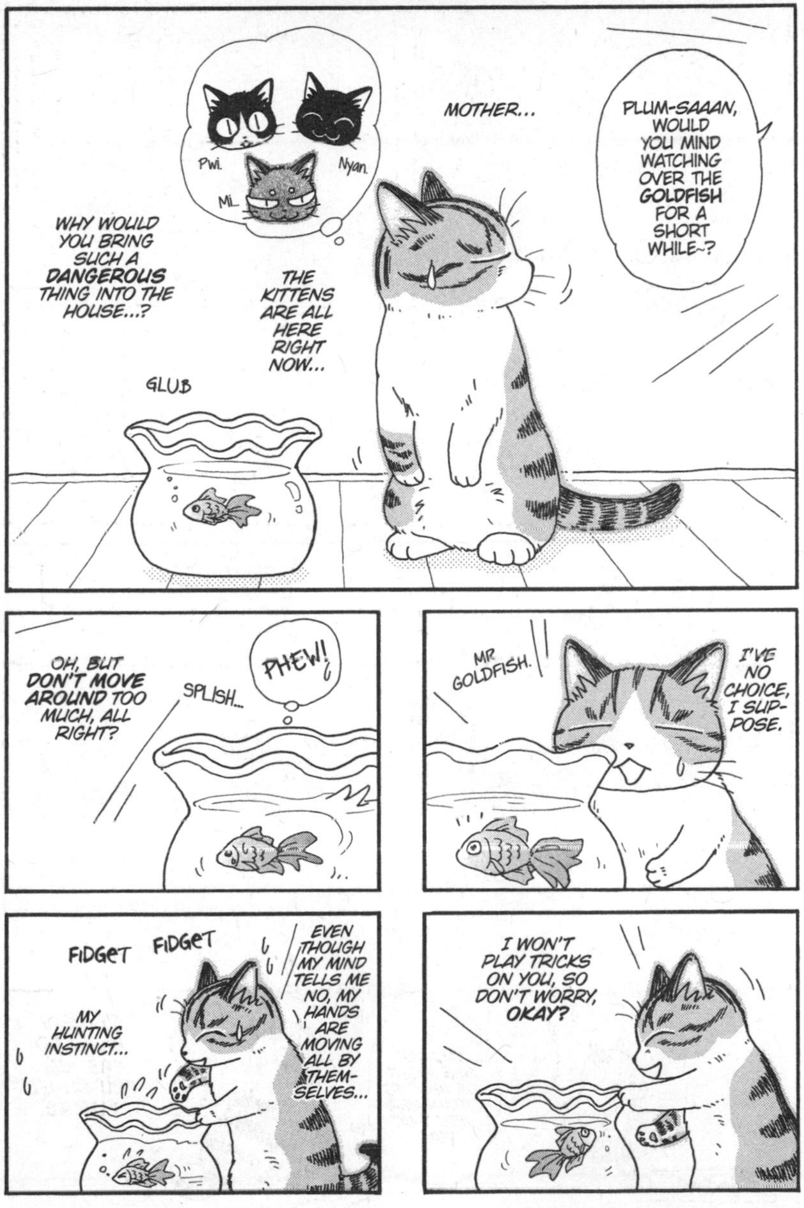
PLUM-SAAAN, WOULD YOU MIND WATCHING OVER THE GOLDFISH FOR A SHORT WHILE~?
MOTHER...
Nyan.
Pwi.
Mi...
THE KITTENS ARE ALL HERE RIGHT NOW...
WHY WOULD YOU BRING SUCH A DANGEROUS THING INTO THE HOUSE...?
GLUB
I'VE NO CHOICE, I SUP-POSE.
MR GOLDFISH.
PHEW!
SPLISH...
OH, BUT DON'T MOVE AROUND TOO MUCH, ALL RIGHT?
I WON'T PLAY TRICKS ON YOU, SO DON'T WORRY, OKAY?
EVEN THOUGH MY MIND TELLS ME NO, MY HANDS ARE MOVING ALL BY THEM-SELVES...
FIDGET FIDGET
MY HUNTING INSTINCT...

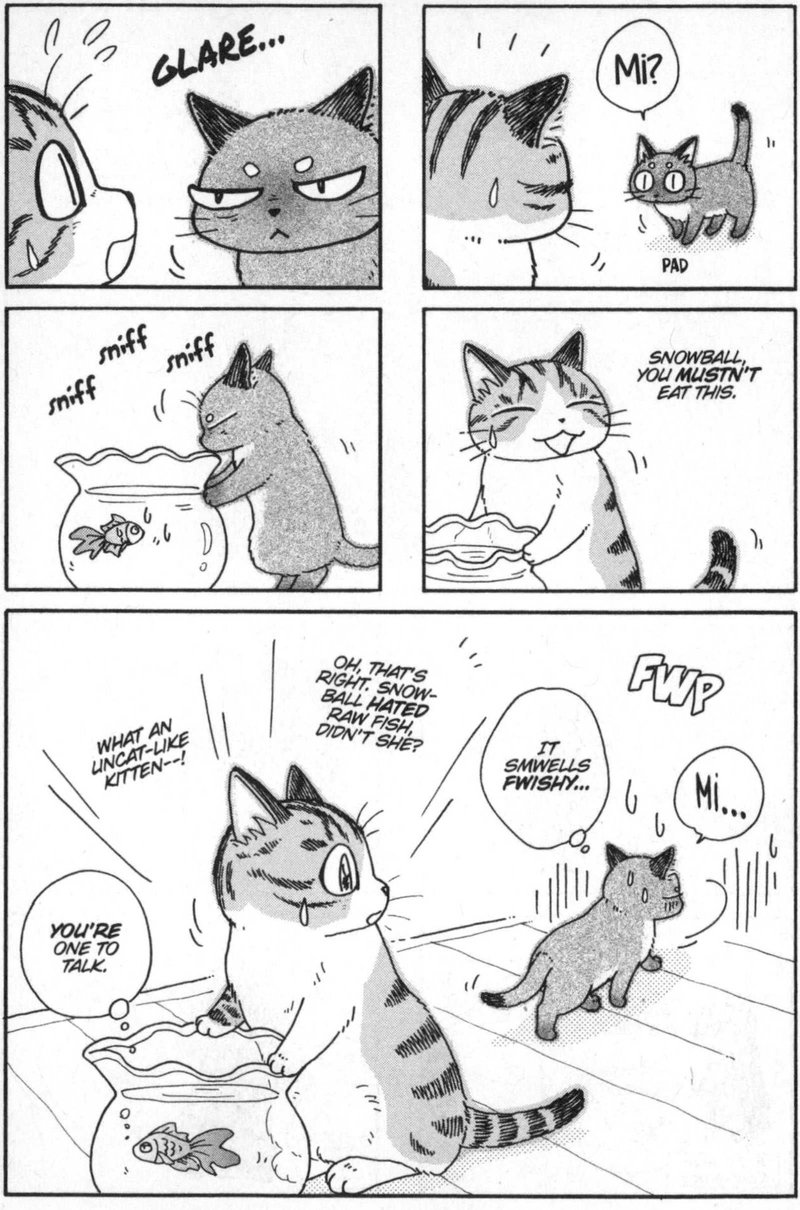
Mi?
PAD
GLARE...
SNOWBALL, YOU MUSTN'T EAT THIS.
sniff
sniff
sniff
FWP
Mi...
IT SMWELLS FWISHY...
OH, THAT'S RIGHT. SNOW-BALL HATED RAW FISH, DIDN'T SHE?
WHAT AN UNCAT-LIKE KITTEN--!
YOU'RE ONE TO TALK.

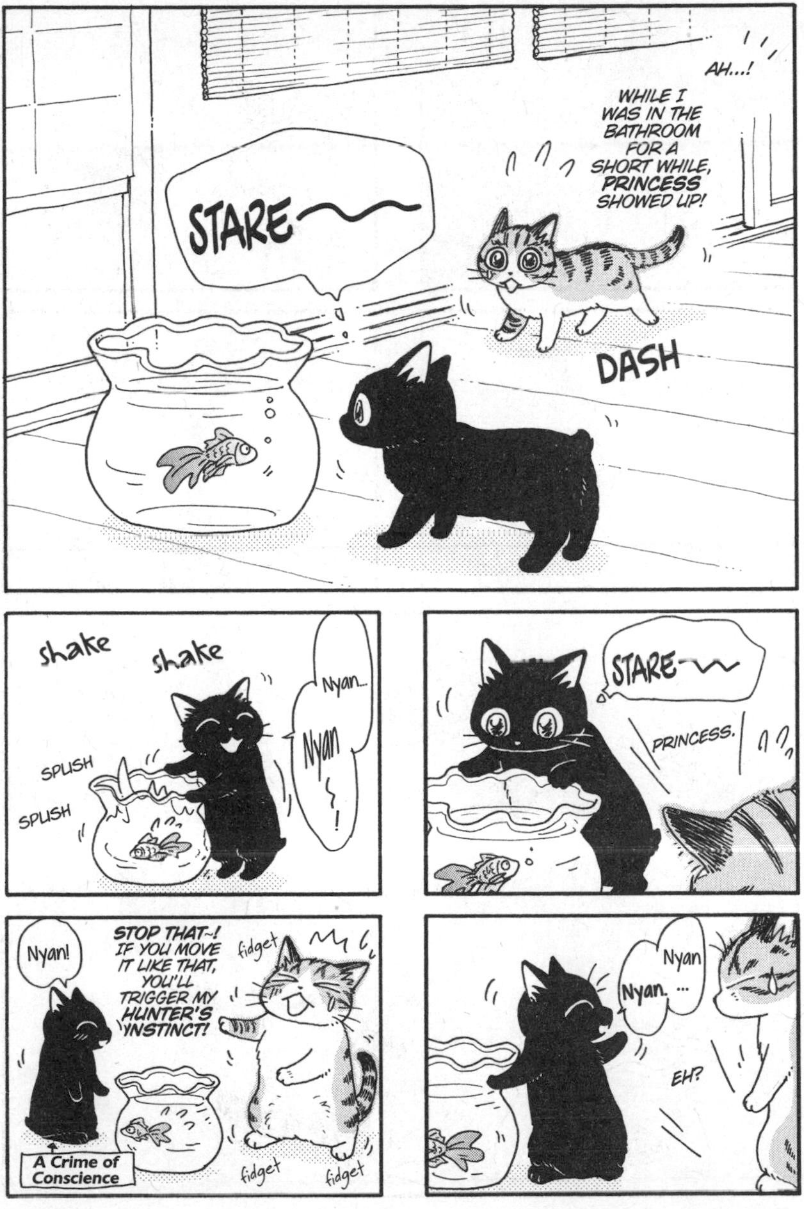
AH...!
WHILE I WAS IN THE BATHROOM FOR A SHORT WHILE, PRINCESS SHOWED UP!
DASH
STARE~~
STARE~
PRINCESS.
shake
shake
Nyan...
Nyan
SPLISH
SPLISH
Nyan
Nyan. ...
EH?
Nyan!
STOP THAT~! IF YOU MOVE IT LIKE THAT, YOU'LL TRIGGER MY HUNTER'S YNSTINCT!
fidget
fidget
fidget
A Crime of Conscience

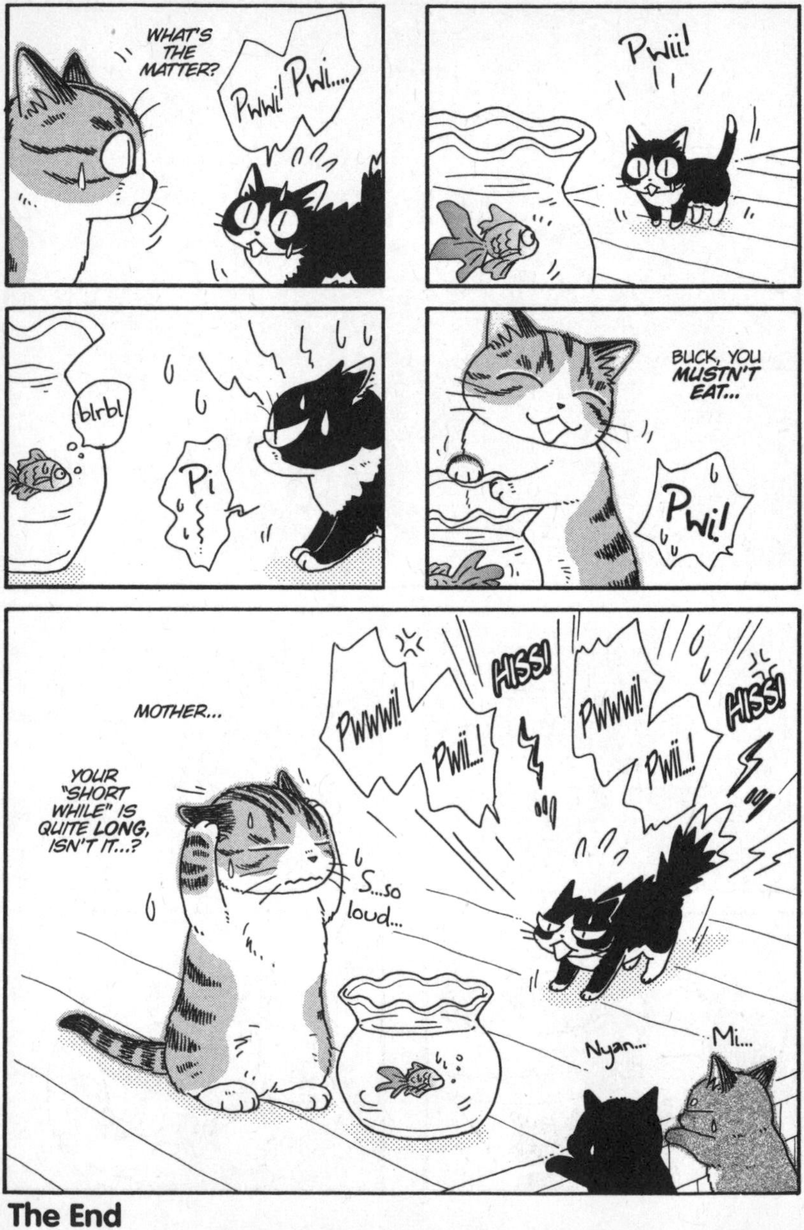
Pwii!
Pwwi! Pwi....
WHAT'S THE MATTER?
BUCK, YOU MUSTN'T EAT...
Pwi!
blrbl
Pi
HISS!
PWWWI!
PWII...!
HISS!
PWWWI!
PWII...!
MOTHER...
YOUR "SHORT WHILE" IS QUITE LONG, ISN'T IT...?
S...so loud...
Mi...
Nyan...

The End

Short.16 Plum and the Kittens

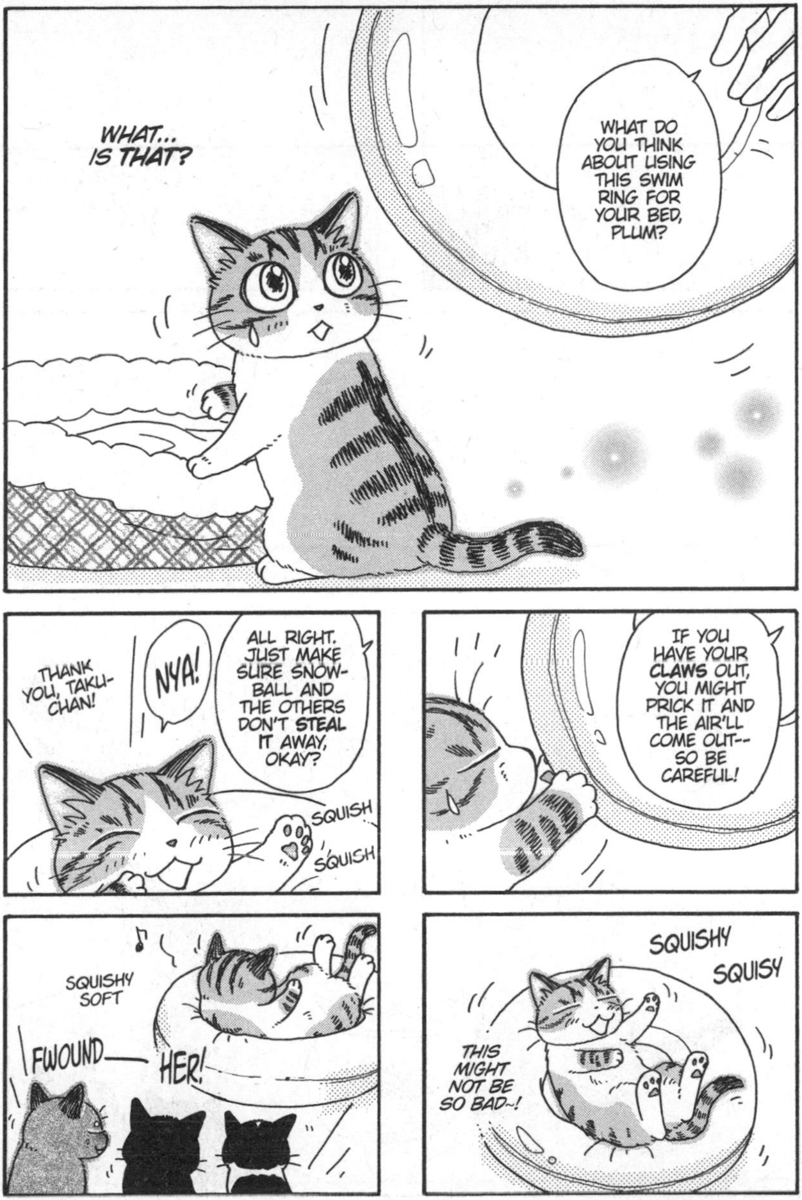
WHAT DO YOU THINK ABOUT USING THIS SWIM RING FOR YOUR BED, PLUM?
WHAT... IS THAT?
IF YOU HAVE YOUR CLAWS OUT, YOU MIGHT PRICK IT AND THE AIR'LL COME OUT-- SO BE CAREFUL!
ALL RIGHT. JUST MAKE SURE SNOW-BALL AND THE OTHERS DON'T STEAL IT AWAY, OKAY?
NYA!
THANK YOU, TAKU-CHAN!
SQUISH
SQUISH
SQUISHY
SQUISY
THIS MIGHT NOT BE SO BAD~!
SQUISHY SOFT
FWOUND—
HER!

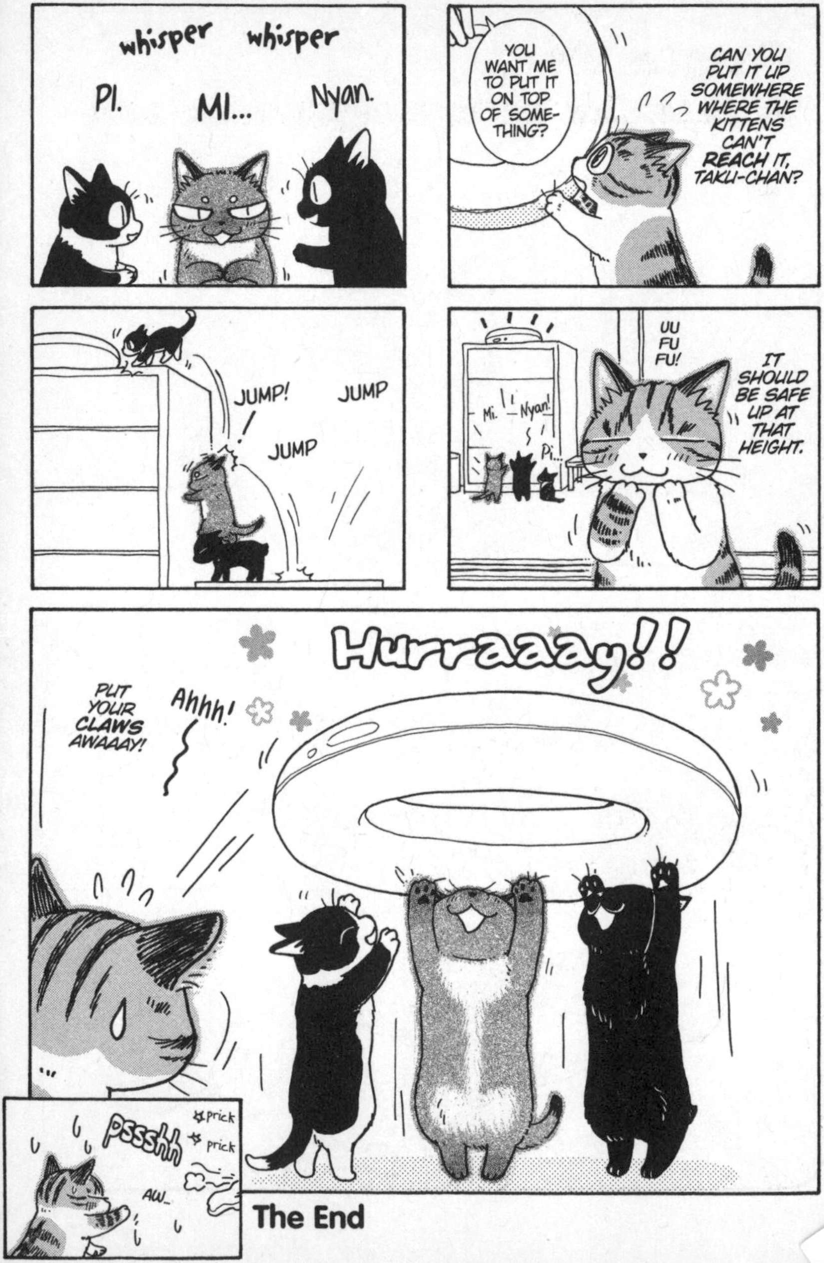
CAN YOU PUT IT UP SOMEWHERE WHERE THE KITTENS CAN'T REACH IT, TAKU-CHAN?
YOU WANT ME TO PUT IT ON TOP OF SOME-THING?
whisper whisper
Nyan.
MI...
PI.
IT SHOULD BE SAFE UP AT THAT HEIGHT.
UU FU FU!
Nyan!
Mi.
Pi...
JUMP
JUMP!
JUMP
Hurraaay!!
Ahhh!
PUT YOUR CLAWS AWAAAY!
prick
prick
Psssshh
AW...

The End

Chapter 19
A Close Call for Squeaky Mouse-san!

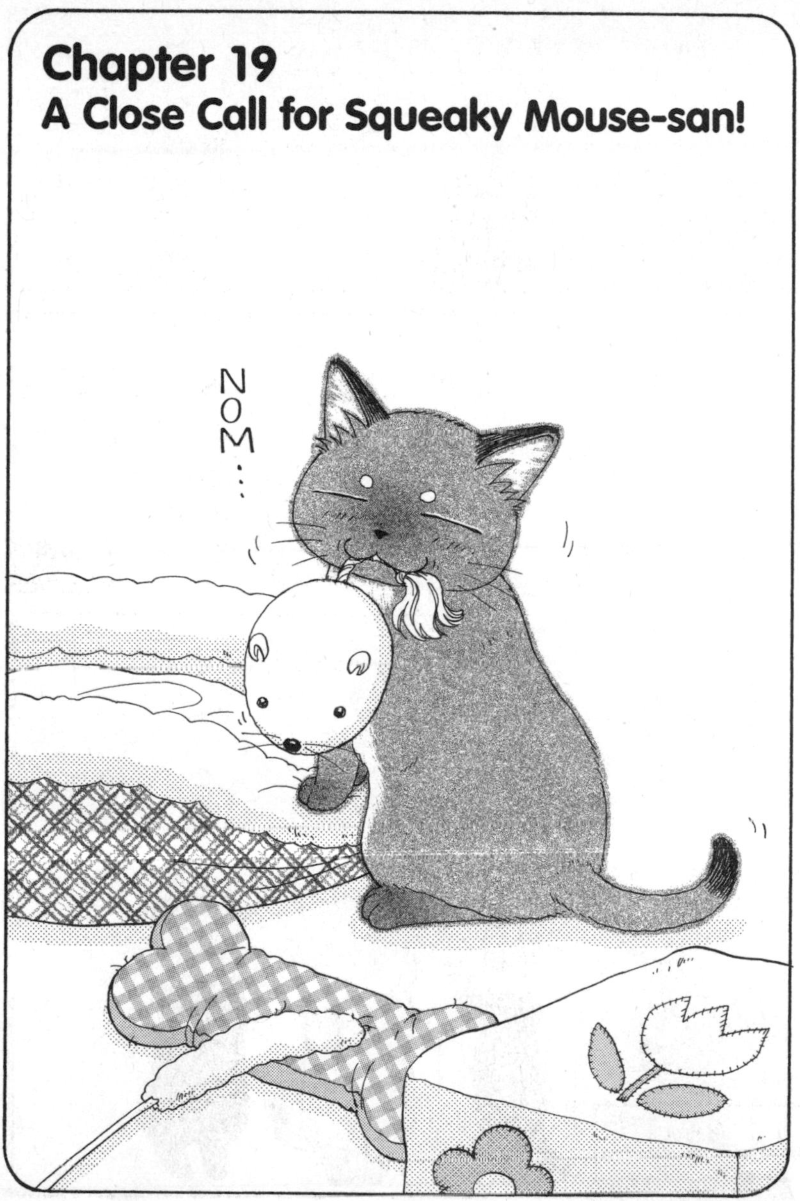
NOM...

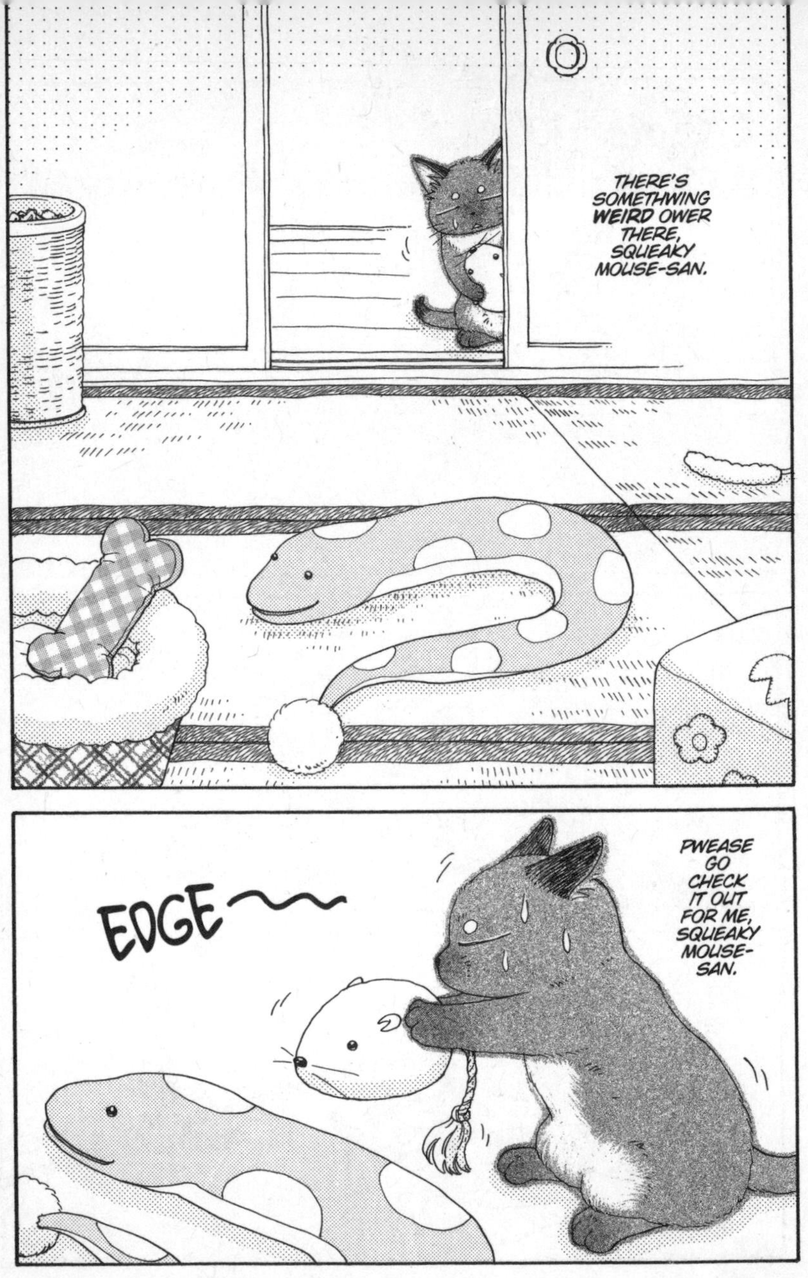
THERE'S SOMETHWING WEIRD OWER THERE, SQUEAKY MOUSE-SAN.
PWEASE GO CHECK IT OUT FOR ME, SQUEAKY MOUSE-SAN.
EDGE

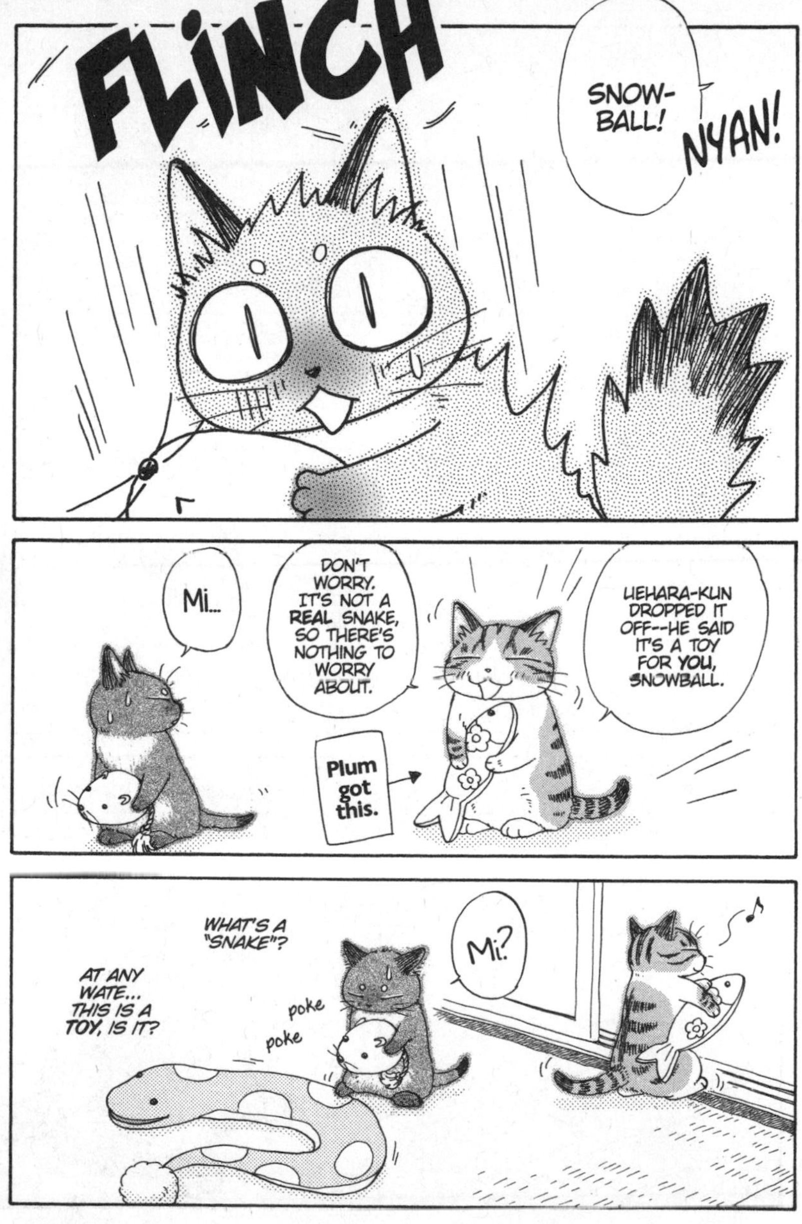
SNOW-BALL!
NYAN!
FLINCH
UEHARA-KUN DROPPED IT OFF--HE SAID IT'S A TOY FOR YOU, SNOWBALL.
DON'T WORRY. IT'S NOT A REAL SNAKE, SO THERE'S NOTHING TO WORRY ABOUT.
Plum got this.
Mi...
Mi?
WHAT'S A "SNAKE"?
AT ANY WATE... THIS IS A TOY, IS IT?
poke
poke

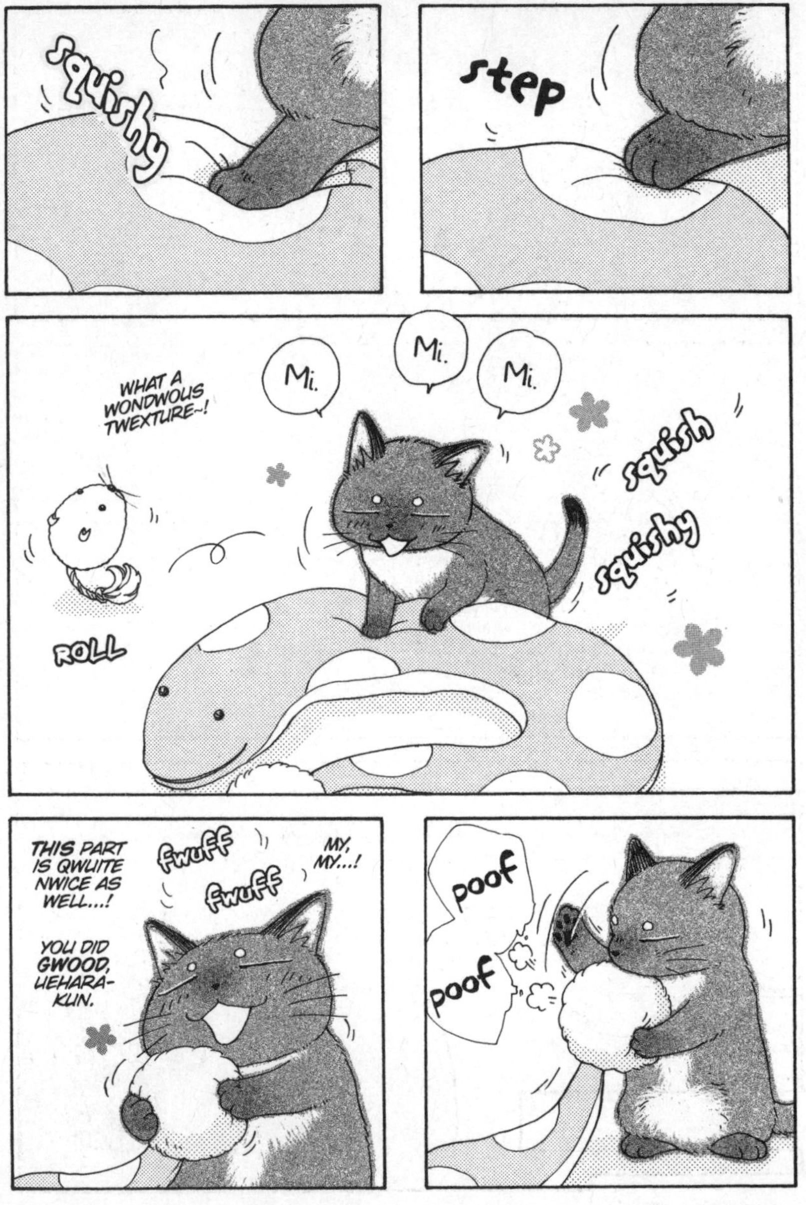
step
squishy
Mi.
Mi.
Mi.
squish
squishy
WHAT A WONDWOUS TWEXTURE~!
ROLL
poof
poof
MY, MY...!
fwuff
fwuff
THIS PART IS QWUITE NWICE AS WELL...!
YOU DID GWOOD, UEHARA-KUN.

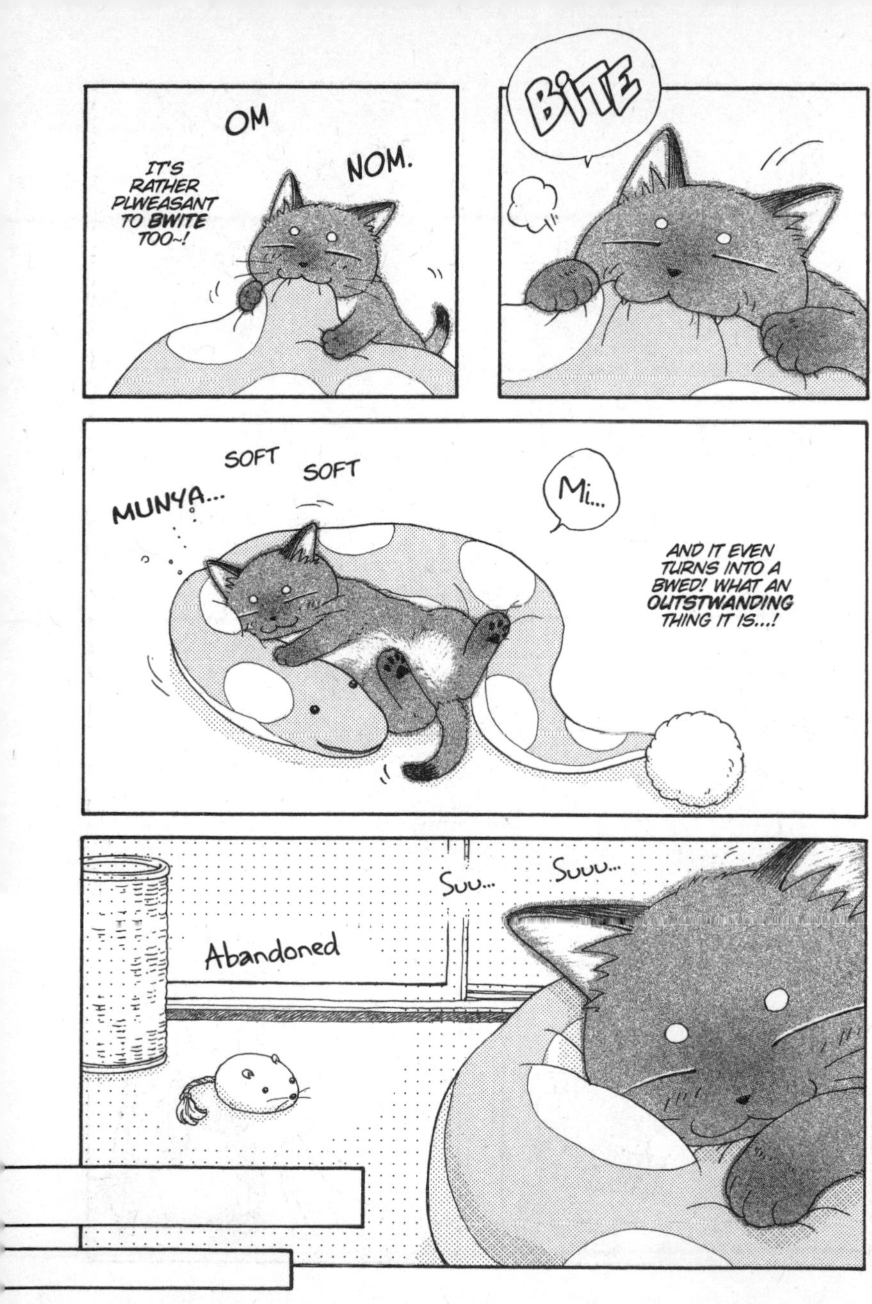
BITE
OM
NOM.
IT'S RATHER PLWEASANT TO BWITE TOO~!
Mi...
AND IT EVEN TURNS INTO A BWED! WHAT AN OUTSTWANDING THING IT IS...!
SOFT
SOFT
MUNYA...
Suuu...
Suu...
Abandoned

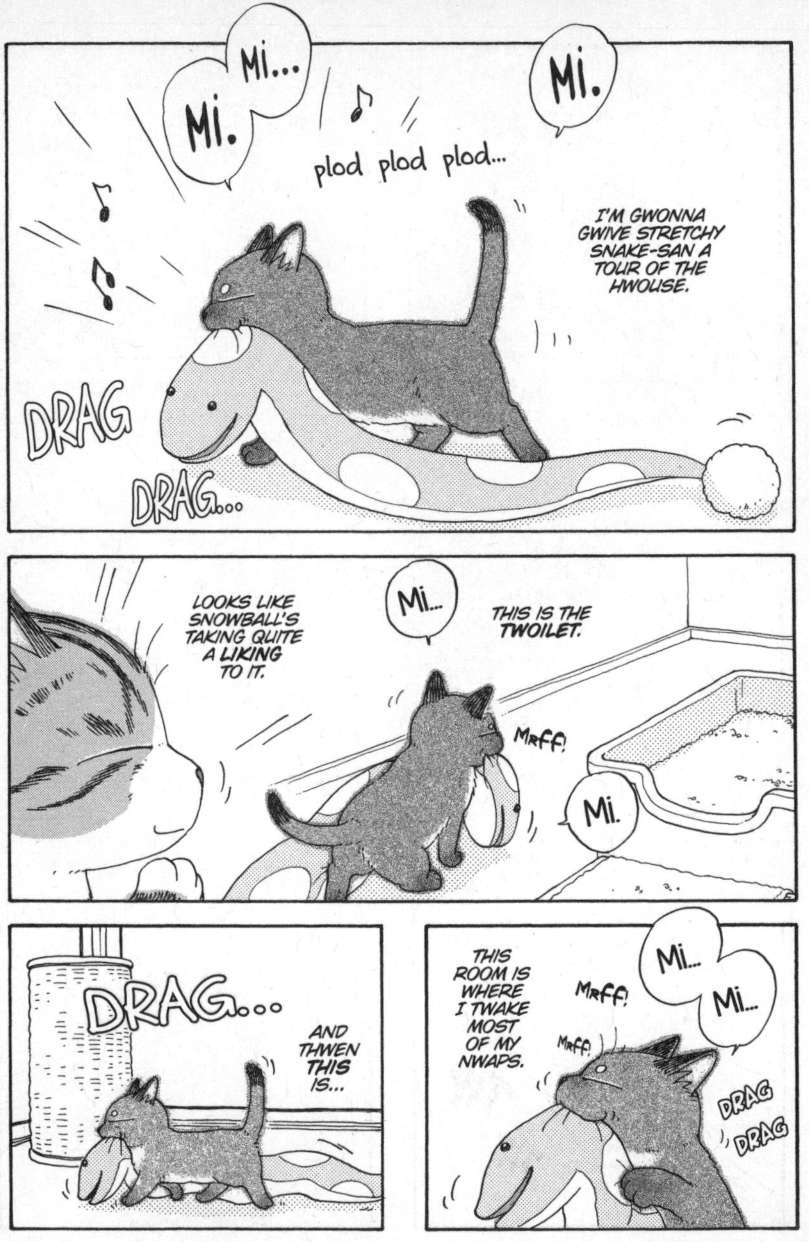
Mi.
I'M GWONNA GWIVE STRETCHY SNAKE-SAN A TOUR OF THE HWOUSE.
plod plod plod...
Mi...
Mi.
DRAG
DRAG...
THIS IS THE TWOILET.
Mi...
Mrff!
Mi.
LOOKS LIKE SNOWBALL'S TAKING QUITE A LIKING TO IT.
Mi...
Mi...
THIS ROOM IS WHERE I TWAKE MOST OF MY NWAPS.
Mrff!
Mrff!
DRAG
DRAG
AND THWEN THIS IS...
DRAG...

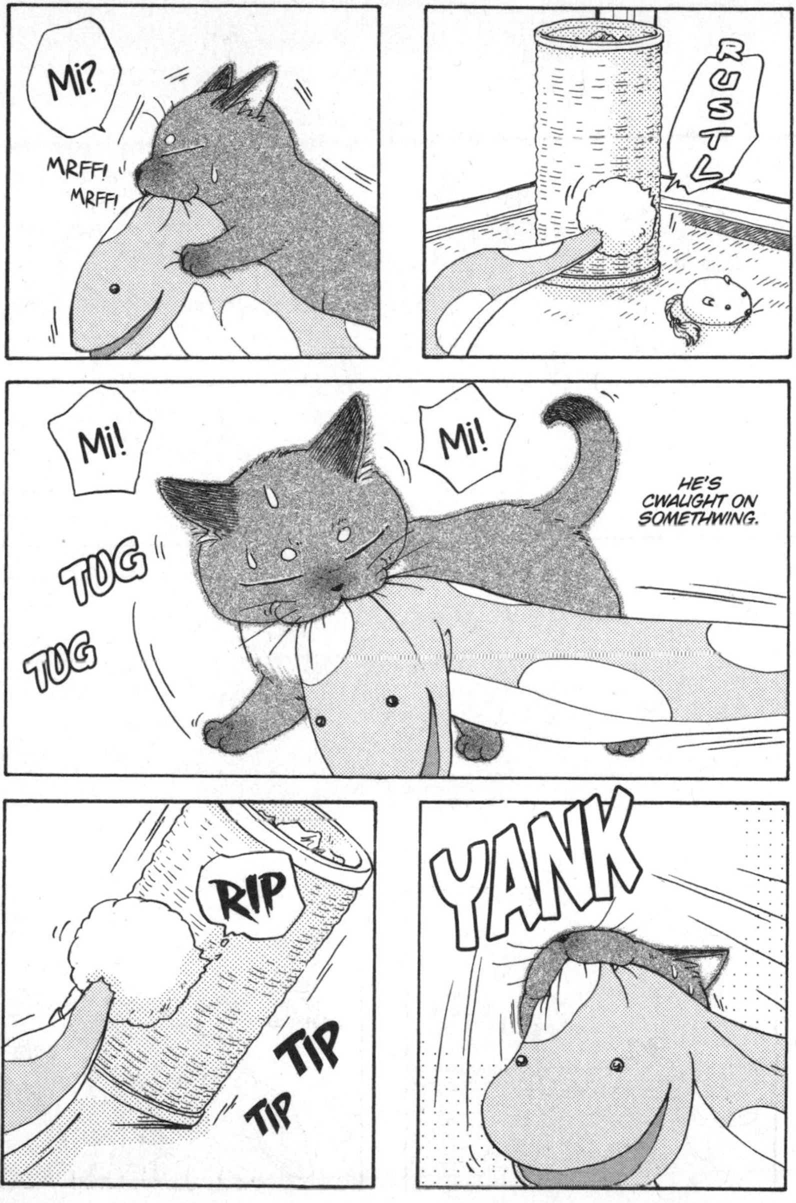
RUSTL
Mi?
MRFF!
MRFF!
HE'S CWAUGHT ON SOMETHWING.
Mi!
Mi!
TUG
TUG
YANK
RIP
TIP
TIP

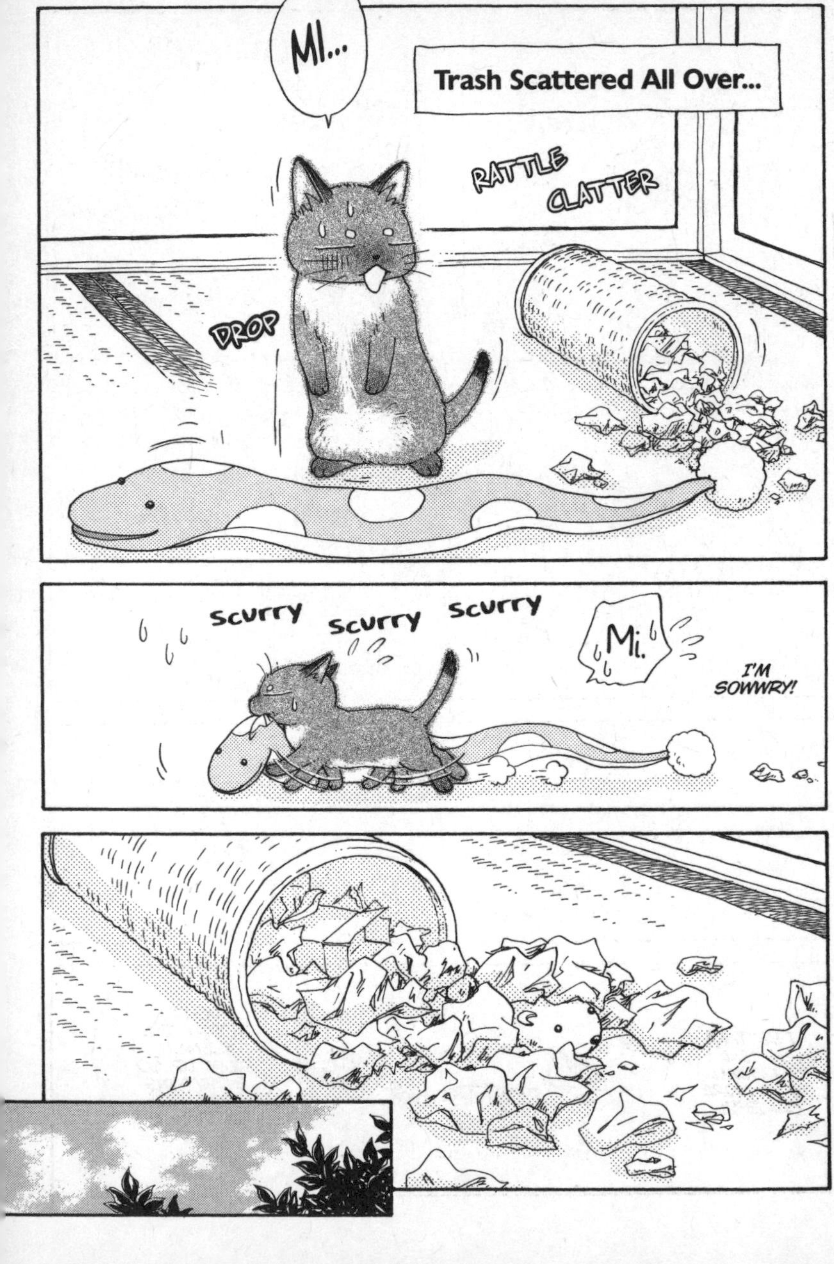
Trash Scattered All Over...
RATTLE
CLATTER
MI...
DROP
Mi.
I'M SOWWRY!
scurry scurry scurry

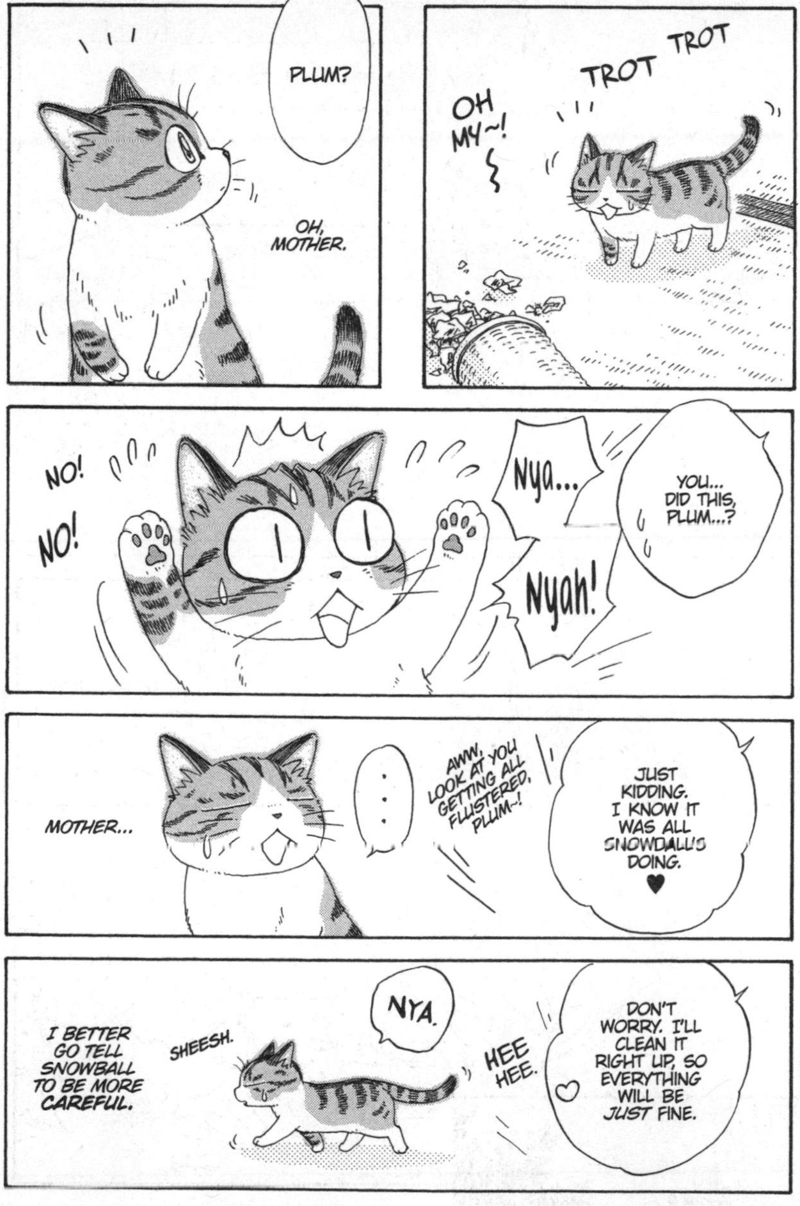
TROT TROT
OH MY~!
PLUM?
OH, MOTHER.
YOU... DID THIS, PLUM...?
Nya...
Nyah!
NO!
NO!
JUST KIDDING. I KNOW IT WAS ALL SNOWBALL'S DOING. ♥
AWW, LOOK AT YOU GETTING ALL FLUSTERED, PLUM~!
...
MOTHER...
DON'T WORRY. I'LL CLEAN IT RIGHT UP, SO EVERYTHING WILL BE JUST FINE. ♡
HEE HEE.
NYA.
SHEESH.
I BETTER GO TELL SNOWBALL TO BE MORE CAREFUL.

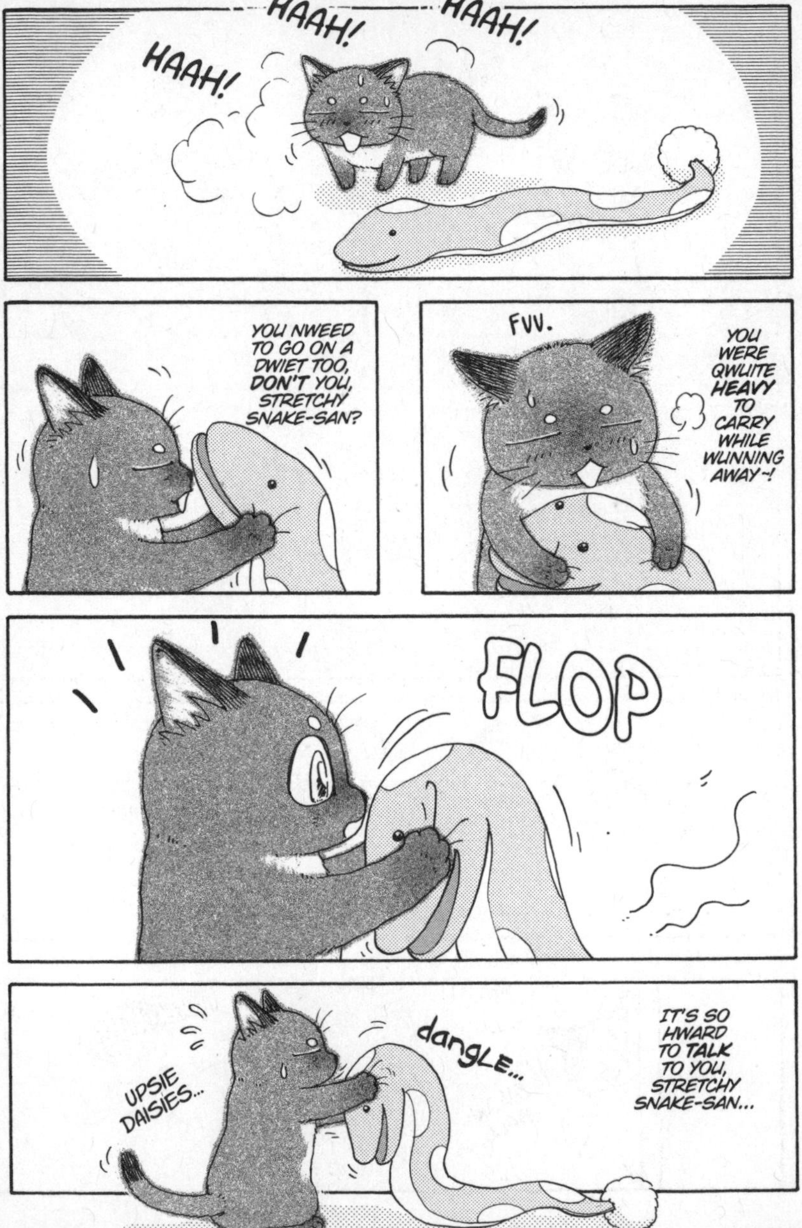
HAAH!
HAAH!
HAAH!
FVU.
YOU WERE QWUITE HEAVY TO CARRY WHILE WUNNING AWAY~!
YOU NWEED TO GO ON A DWIET TOO, DON'T YOU, STRETCHY SNAKE-SAN?
FLOP
IT'S SO HWARD TO TALK TO YOU, STRETCHY SNAKE-SAN...
dangLE...
UPSIE DAISIES...

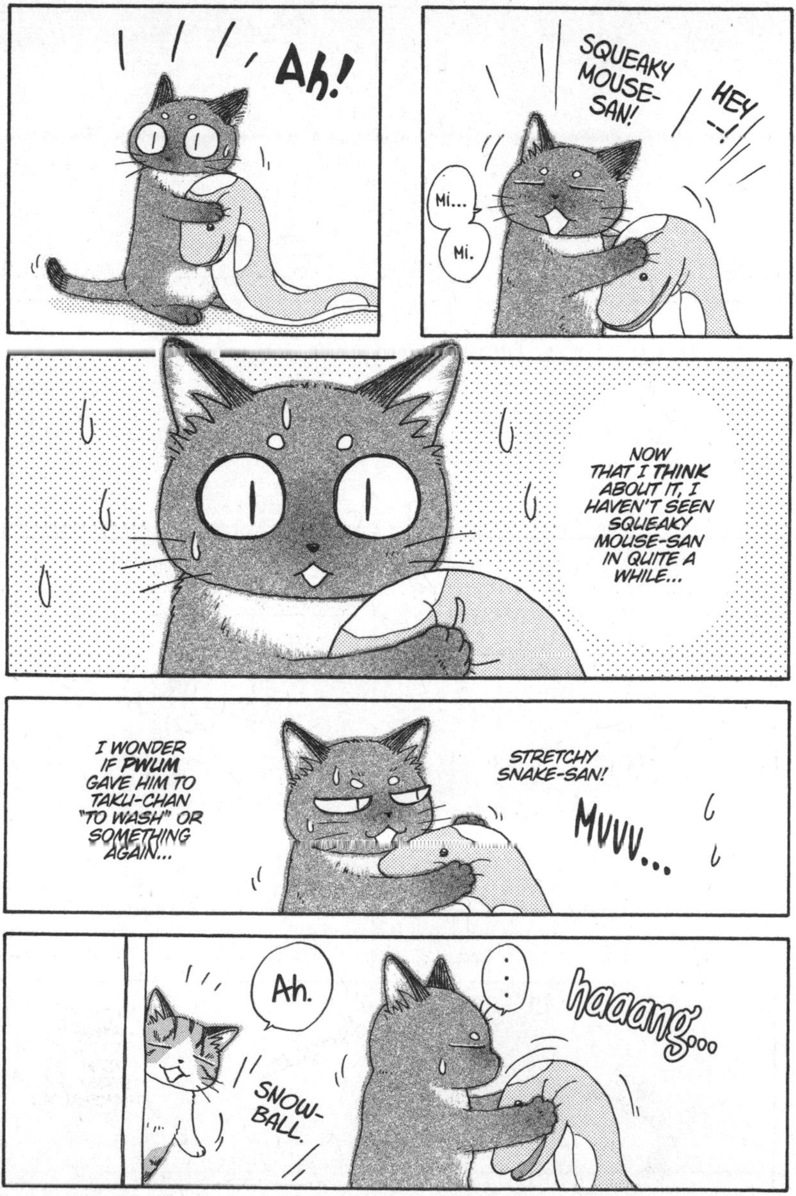
SQUEAKY MOUSE-SAN!
HEY--!
Mi...
Mi.
Ah!
NOW THAT I THINK ABOUT IT, I HAVEN'T SEEN SQUEAKY MOUSE-SAN IN QUITE A WHILE...
MVVV...
STRETCHY SNAKE-SAN!
I WONDER IF PWUM GAVE HIM TO TAKU-CHAN "TO WASH" OR SOMETHING AGAIN...
haaang...
...
Ah.
SNOW-BALL.

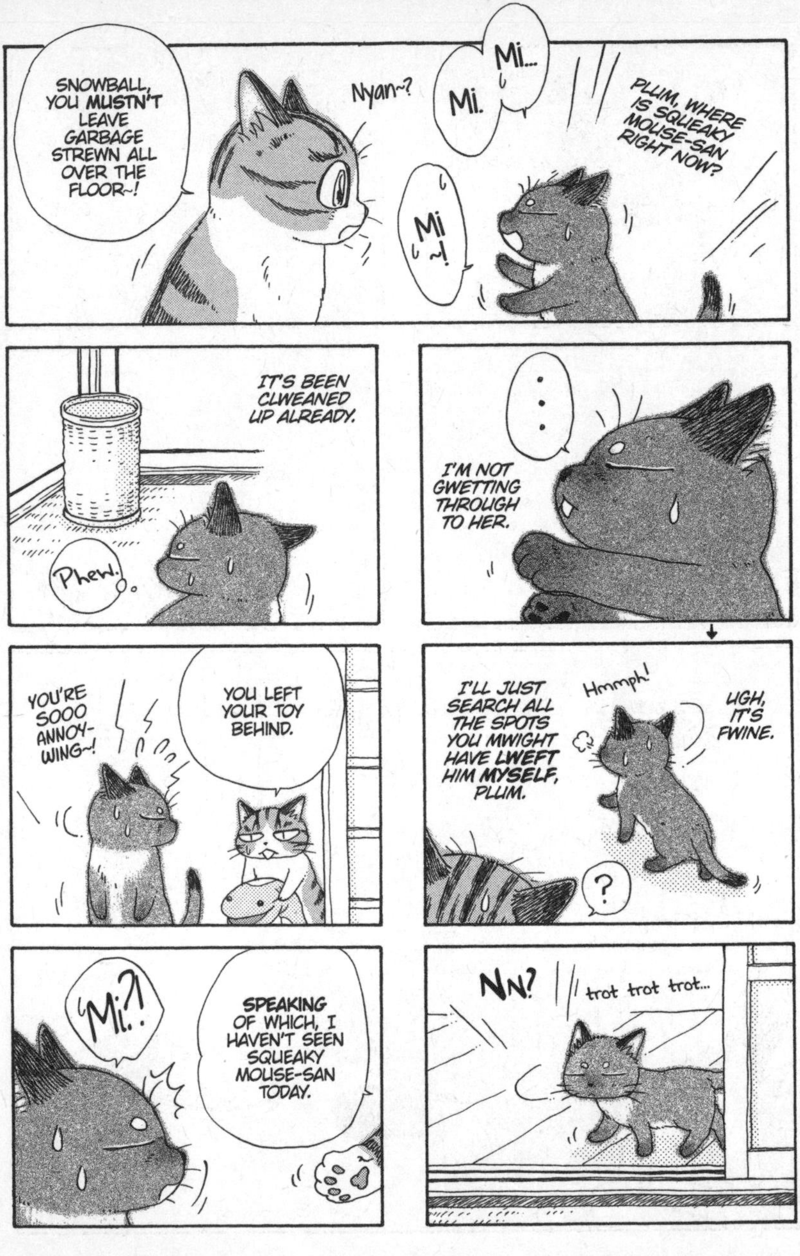
PLUM, WHERE IS SQUEAKY MOUSE-SAN RIGHT NOW?
Mi...
Mi.
Nyan~?
Mi ~!
SNOWBALL, YOU MUSTN'T LEAVE GARBAGE STREWN ALL OVER THE FLOOR~!
...
I'M NOT GWETTING THROUGH TO HER.
IT'S BEEN CLWEANED UP ALREADY.
Phew.
UGH, IT'S FWINE.
Hmmph!
I'LL JUST SEARCH ALL THE SPOTS YOU MWIGHT HAVE LWEFT HIM MYSELF, PLUM.
?
YOU LEFT YOUR TOY BEHIND.
YOU'RE SOOO ANNOY-WING~!
trot trot trot...
NN?
SPEAKING OF WHICH, I HAVEN'T SEEN SQUEAKY MOUSE-SAN TODAY.
Mi?!

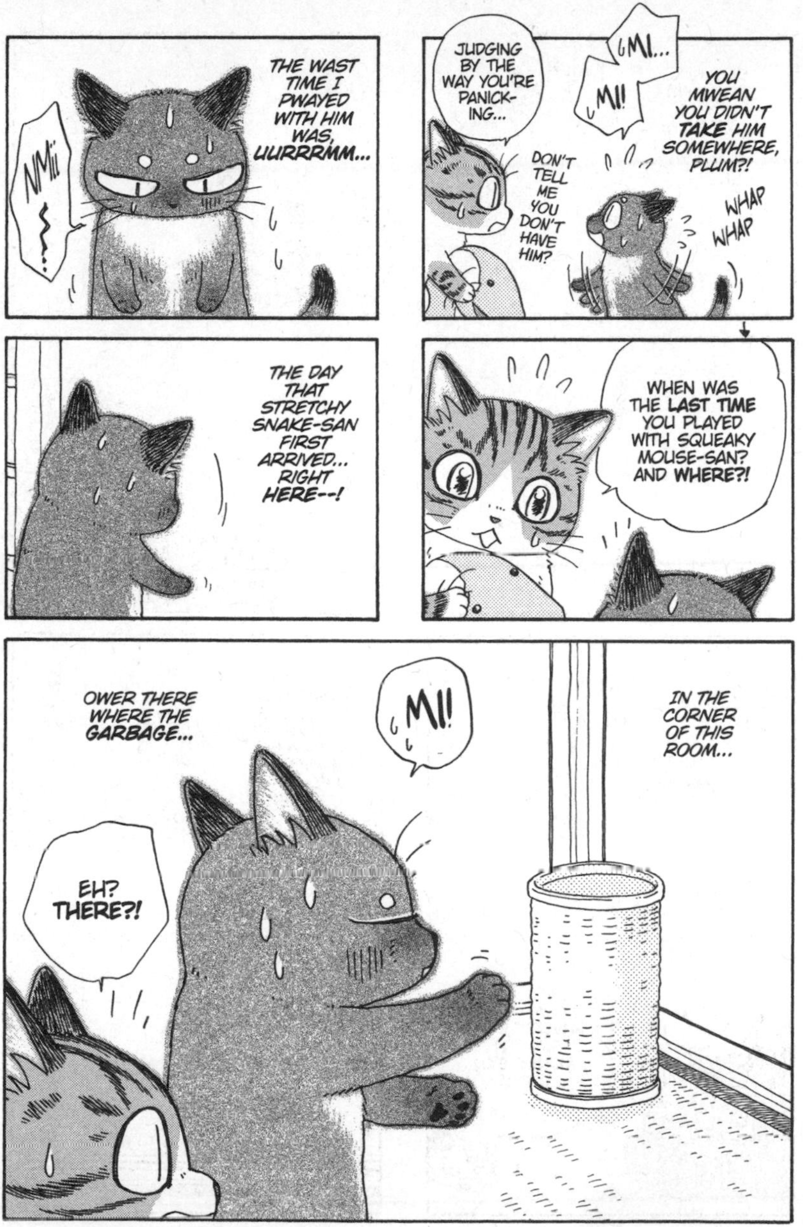
MI...
MI!
YOU MWEAN YOU DIDN'T TAKE HIM SOMEWHERE, PLUM?!
JUDGING BY THE WAY YOU'RE PANICK-ING...
DON'T TELL ME YOU DON'T HAVE HIM?
WHAP WHAP
THE WAST TIME I PWAYED WITH HIM WAS, UURRRMM...
NMii~...
WHEN WAS THE LAST TIME YOU PLAYED WITH SQUEAKY MOUSE-SAN? AND WHERE?!
THE DAY THAT STRETCHY SNAKE-SAN FIRST ARRIVED... RIGHT HERE--!
IN THE CORNER OF THIS ROOM...
MI!
OWER THERE WHERE THE GARBAGE...
EH? THERE?!

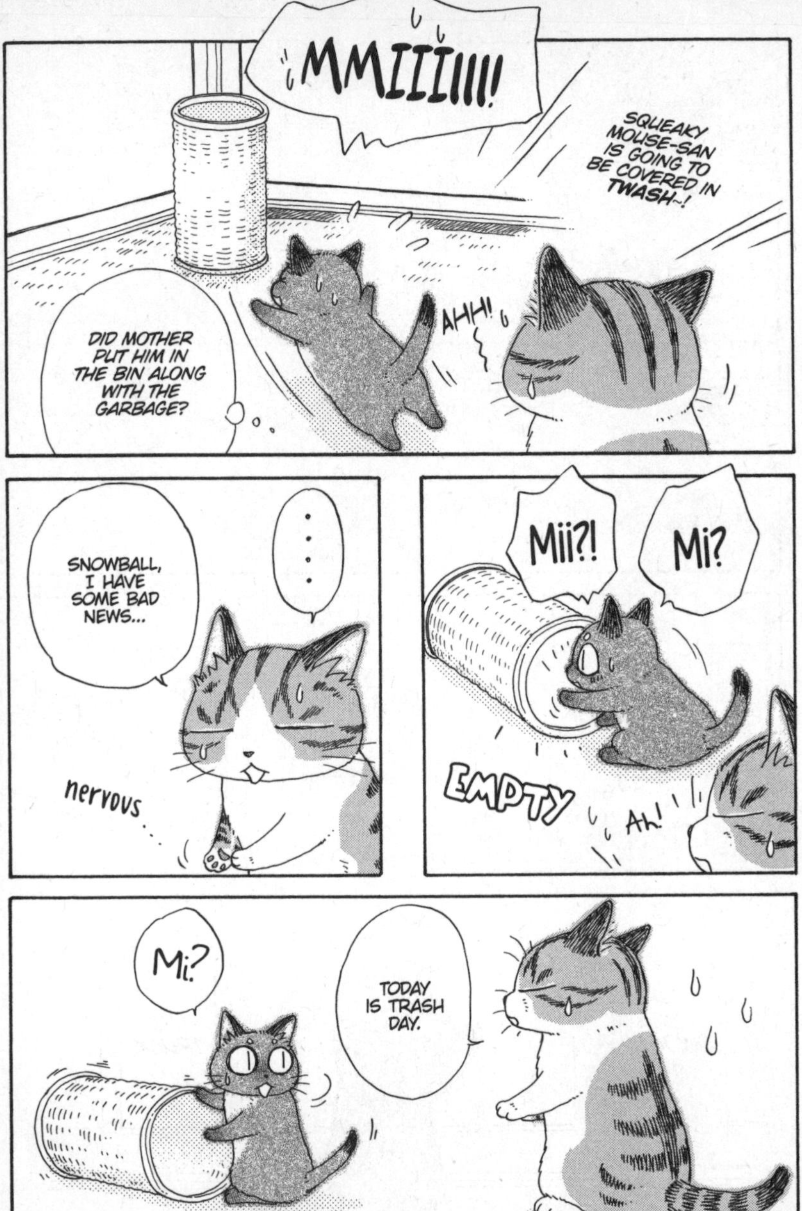
MMIIIIII!
SQUEAKY MOUSE-SAN IS GOING TO BE COVERED IN TWASH~!
AHH!
DID MOTHER PUT HIM IN THE BIN ALONG WITH THE GARBAGE?
Mi?
Mii?!
EMPTY
Ah!
....
SNOWBALL, I HAVE SOME BAD NEWS...
nervous...
TODAY IS TRASH DAY.
Mi?

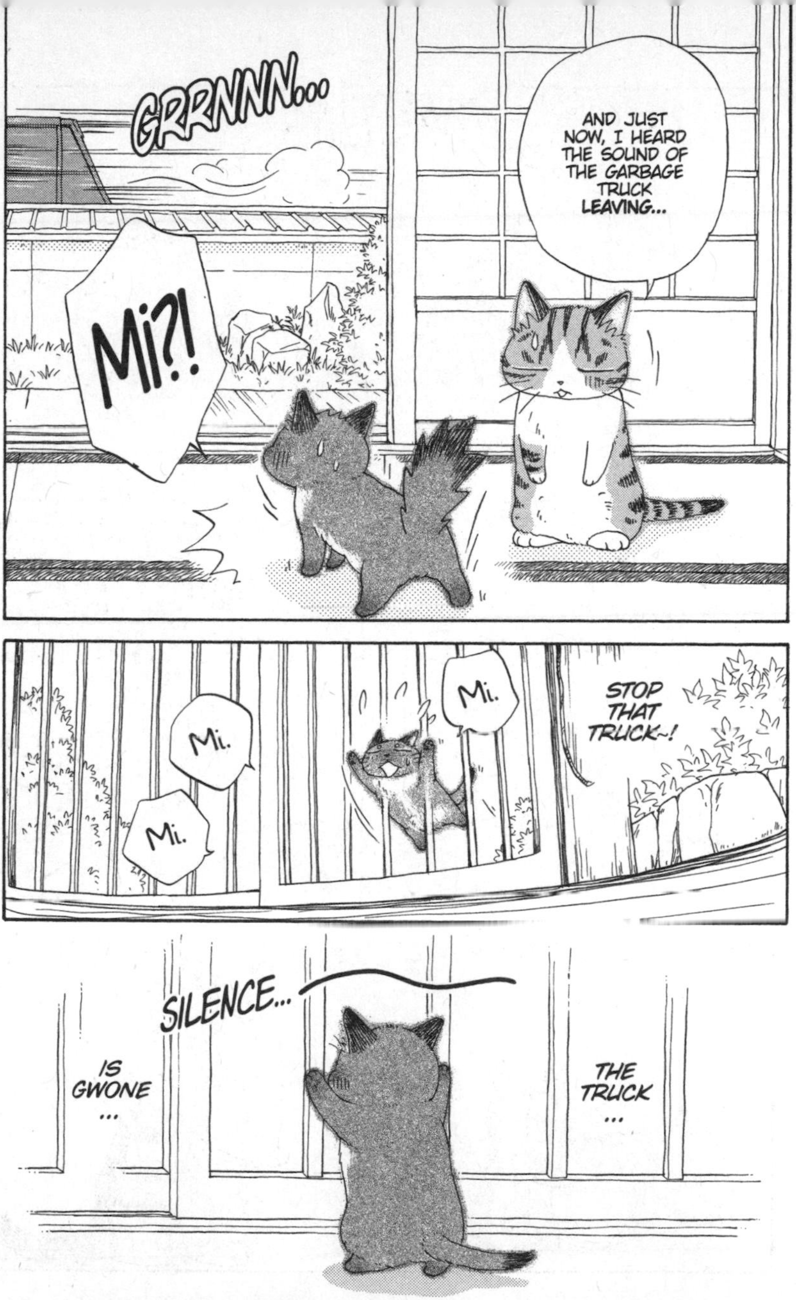
AND JUST NOW, I HEARD THE SOUND OF THE GARBAGE TRUCK LEAVING...
GRRNNN...
Mi?!
STOP THAT TRUCK~!
Mi.
Mi.
Mi.
SILENCE...
THE TRUCK...
IS GWONE...

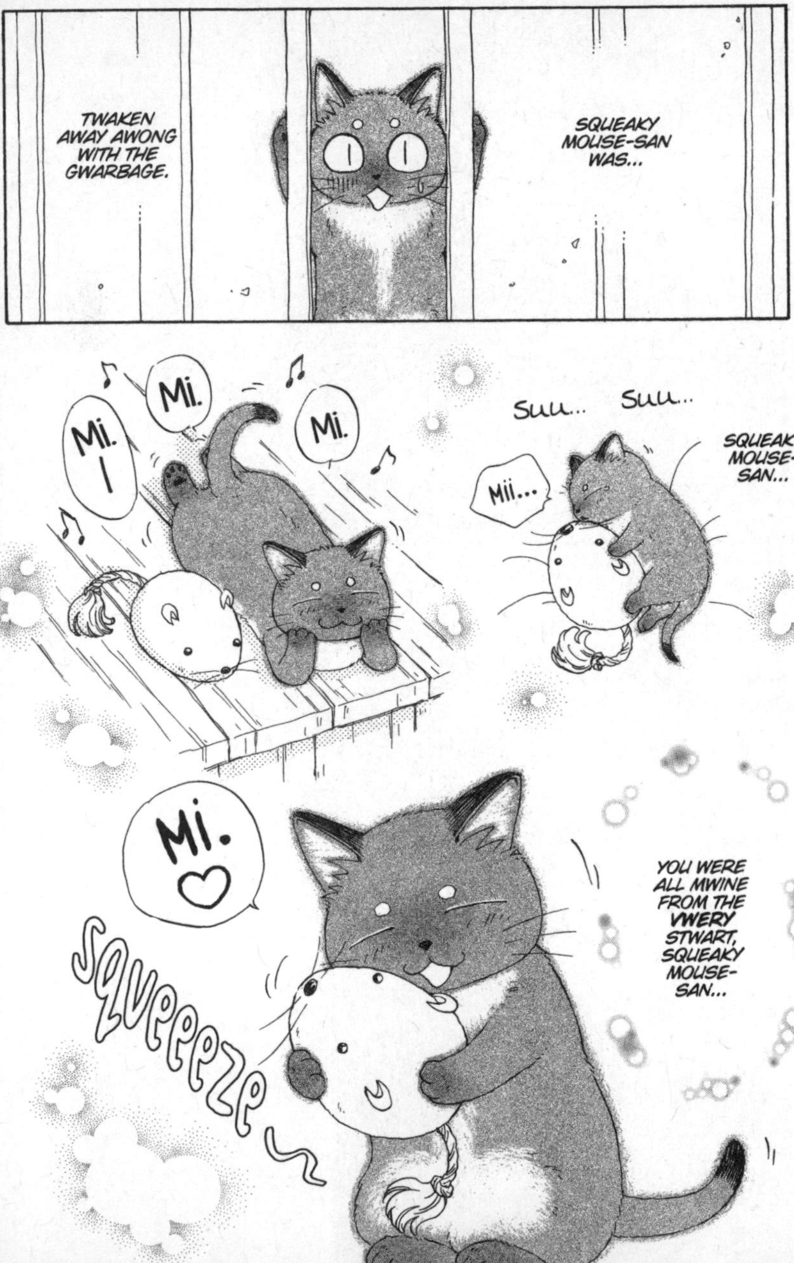
SQUEAKY MOUSE-SAN WAS...
TWAKEN AWAY AWONG WITH THE GWARBAGE.
SUU... SUU...
SQUEAKY MOUSE-SAN...
Mii...
Mi.
Mi.
Mi. !
YOU WERE ALL MWINE FROM THE VWERY STWART, SQUEAKY MOUSE-SAN...
Mi. ♡
squeeze~

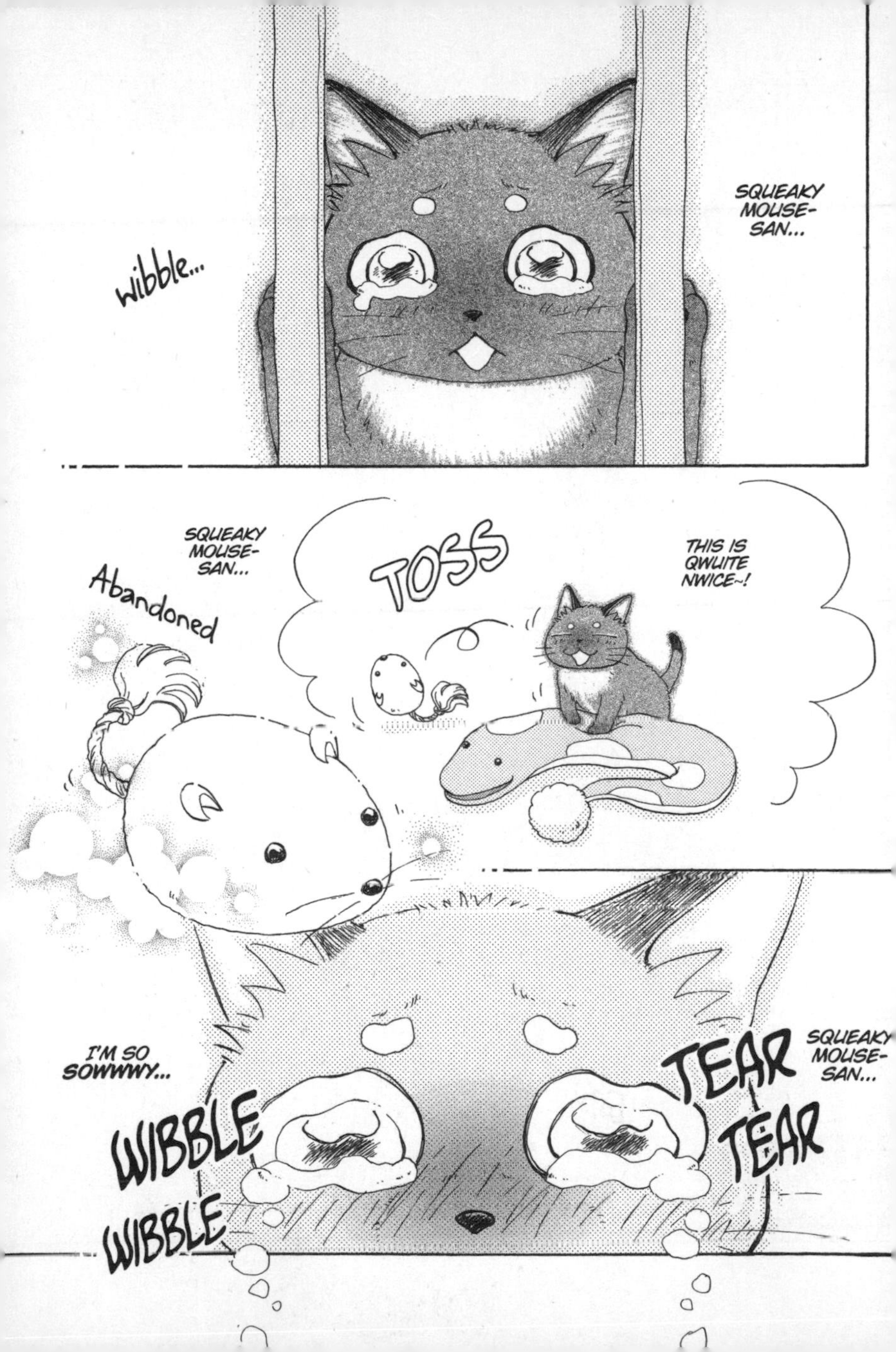
SQUEAKY MOUSE-SAN...
wibble...
THIS IS QWUITE NWICE~!
TOSS
SQUEAKY MOUSE-SAN...
Abandoned
SQUEAKY MOUSE-SAN...
TEAR TEAR
I'M SO SOWWWY...
WIBBLE WIBBLE

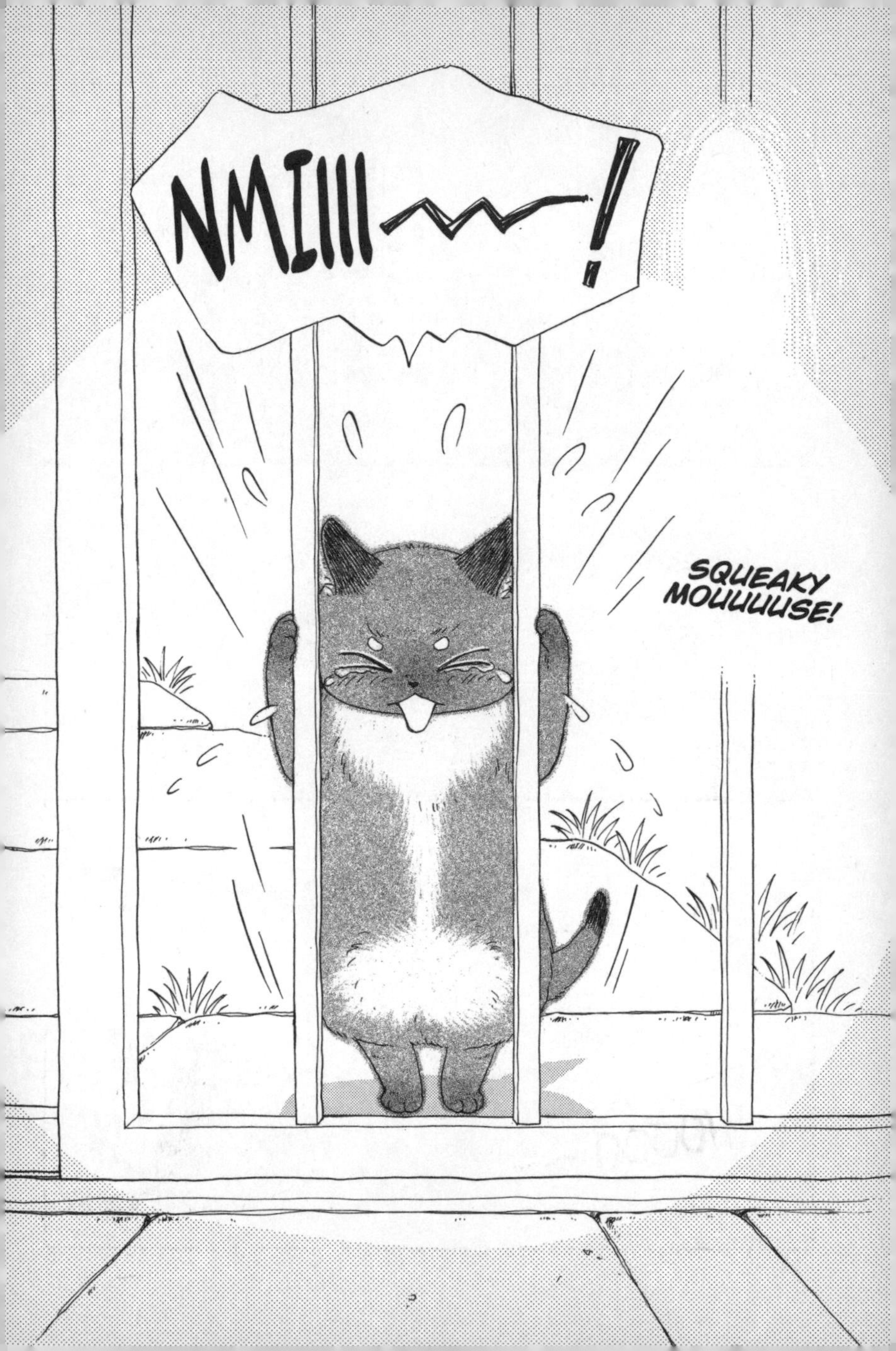
NMIIII~~!
SQUEAKY MOUUUUSE!

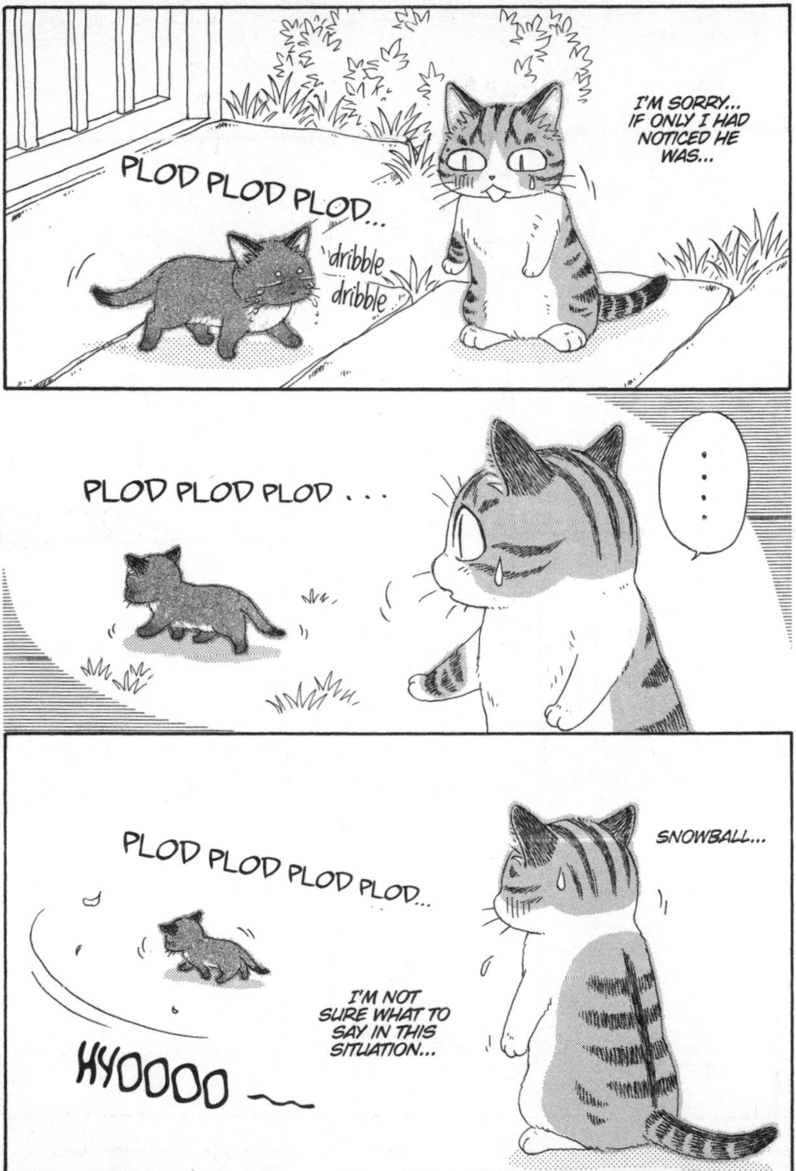
I'M SORRY... IF ONLY I HAD NOTICED HE WAS...
PLOD PLOD PLOD...
dribble
dribble
.....
PLOD PLOD PLOD ...
SNOWBALL...
I'M NOT SURE WHAT TO SAY IN THIS SITUATION...
PLOD PLOD PLOD PLOD...
HYOOOO ~~

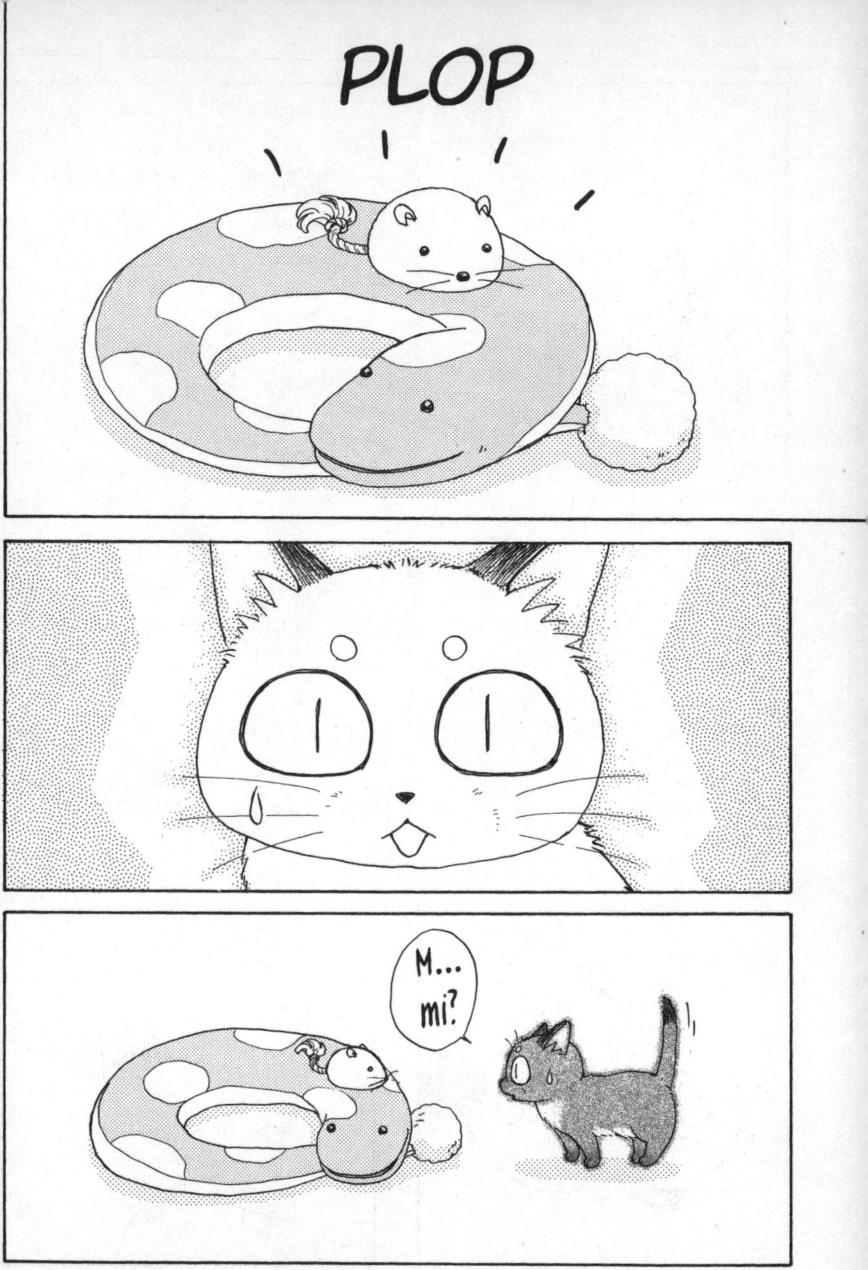
PLOP
M...
mi?

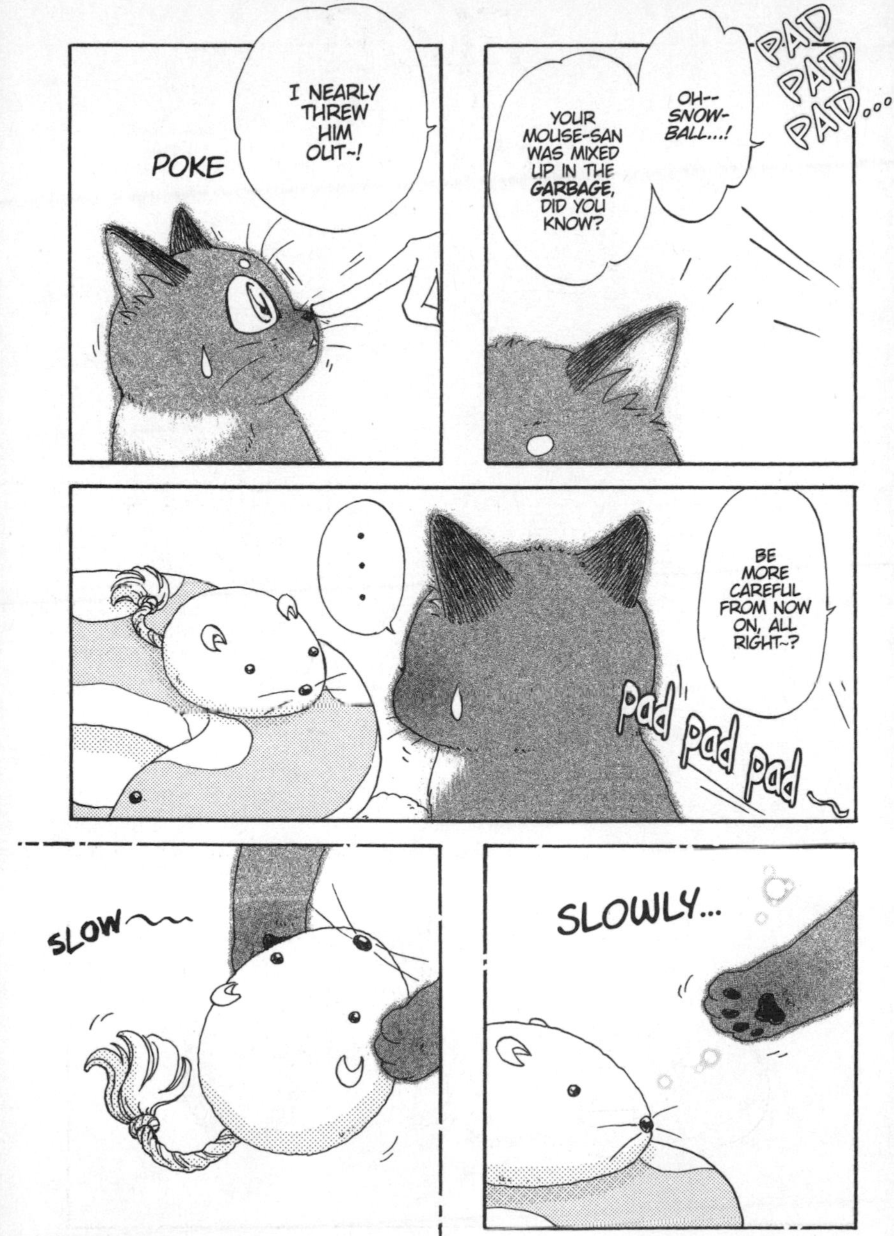
PAD PAD PAD...
OH-- SNOW-BALL...!
YOUR MOUSE-SAN WAS MIXED UP IN THE GARBAGE, DID YOU KNOW?
I NEARLY THREW HIM OUT~!
POKE
BE MORE CAREFUL FROM NOW ON, ALL RIGHT~?
pad pad pad
...
SLOWLY...
SLOW~~

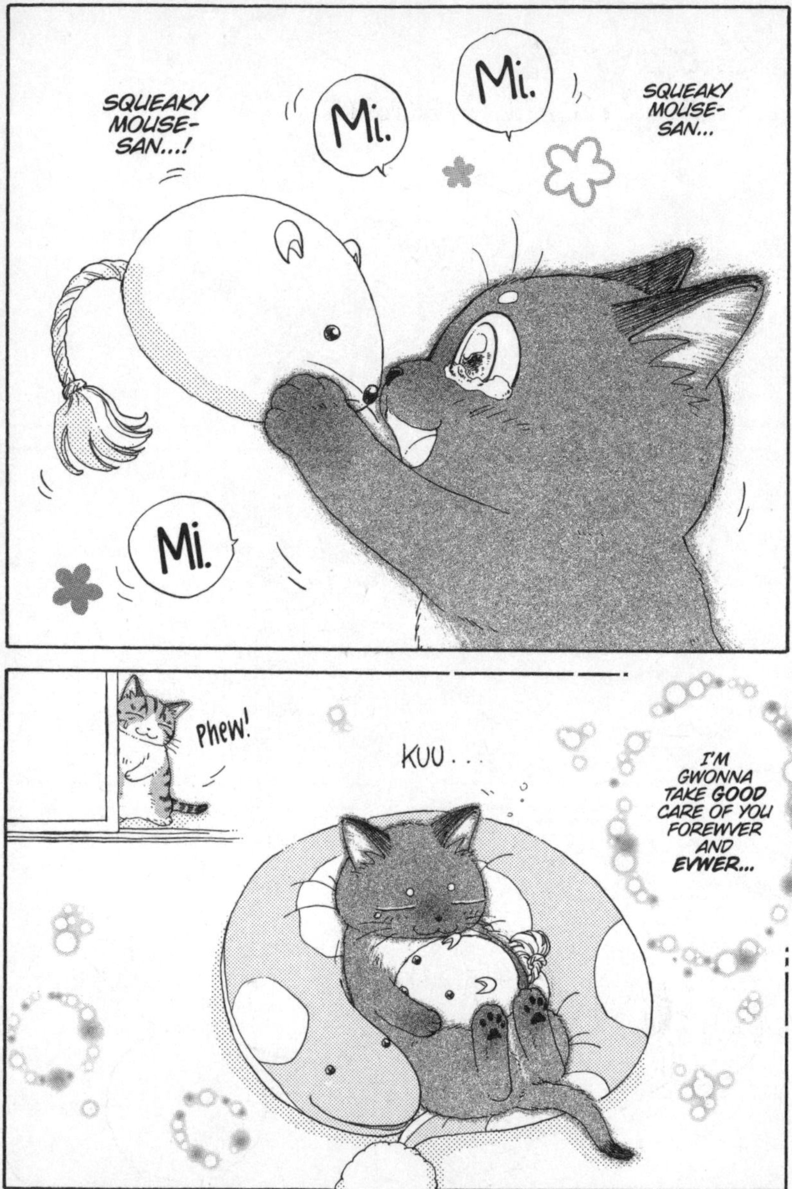
SQUEAKY MOUSE-SAN...
Mi.
Mi.
SQUEAKY MOUSE-SAN...!
Mi.
I'M GWONNA TAKE GOOD CARE OF YOU FOREWVER AND EVWER...
KUU...
Phew!

(19) The End

Chapter 20
Plum Has a Dream

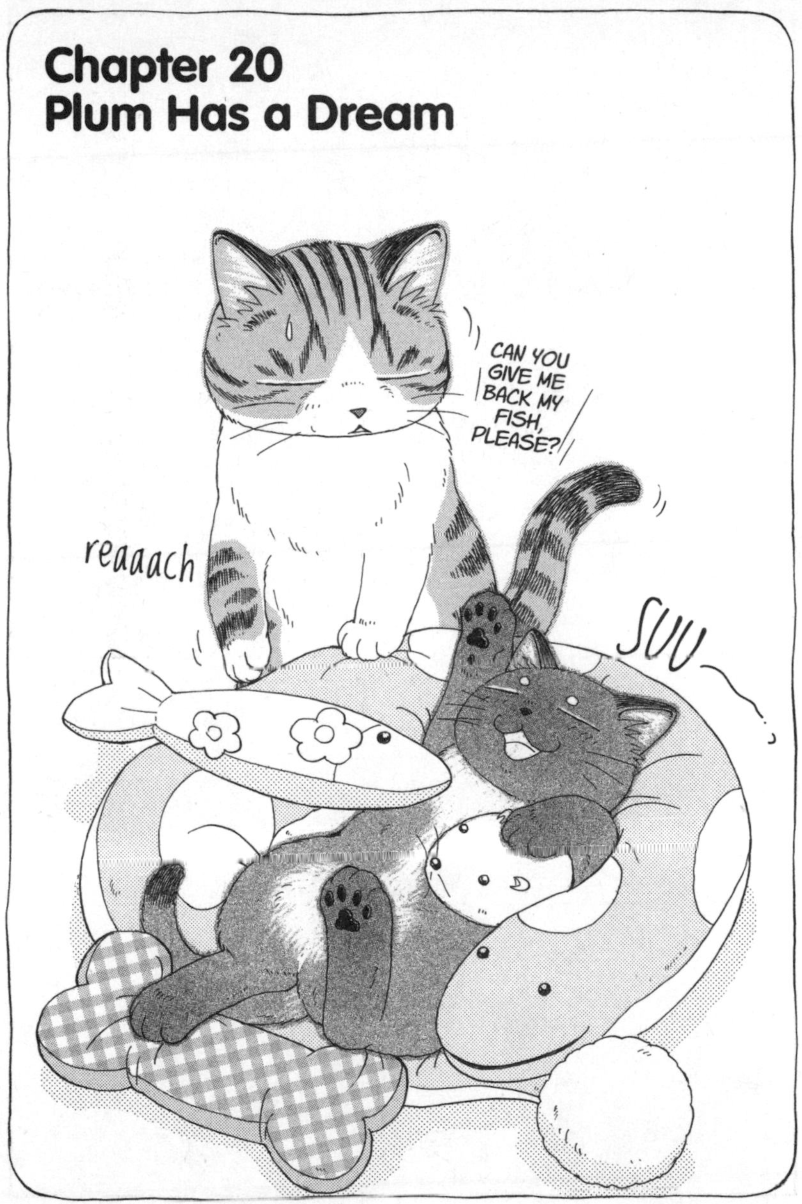
CAN YOU GIVE ME BACK MY FISH, PLEASE?
SUU
reaaach

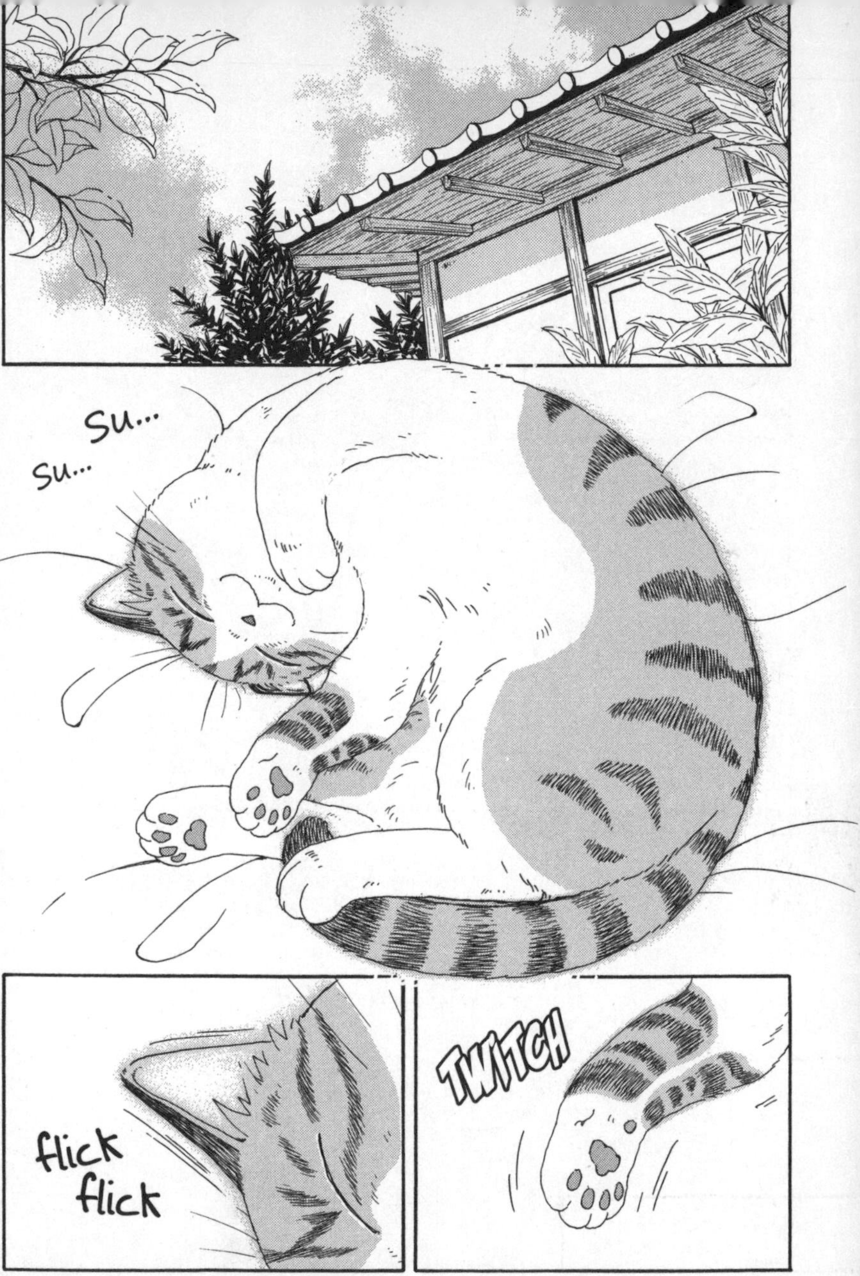
su...
su...
TWITCH
flick
flick

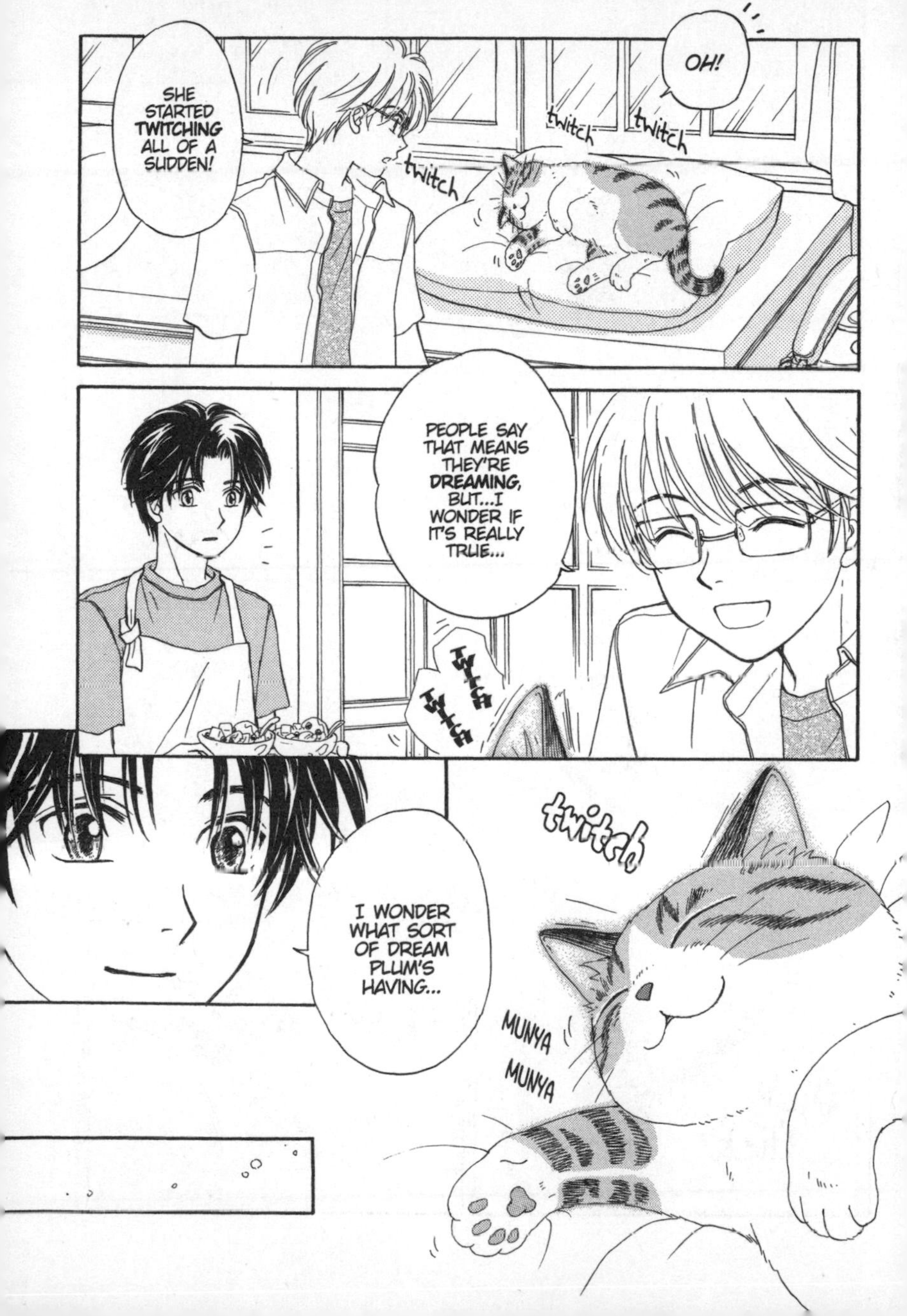
OH!
twitch twitch
twitch
SHE STARTED TWITCHING ALL OF A SUDDEN!
PEOPLE SAY THAT MEANS THEY'RE DREAMING, BUT...I WONDER IF IT'S REALLY TRUE...
TWITCH TWITCH
twitch
MUNYA MUNYA
I WONDER WHAT SORT OF DREAM PLUM'S HAVING...

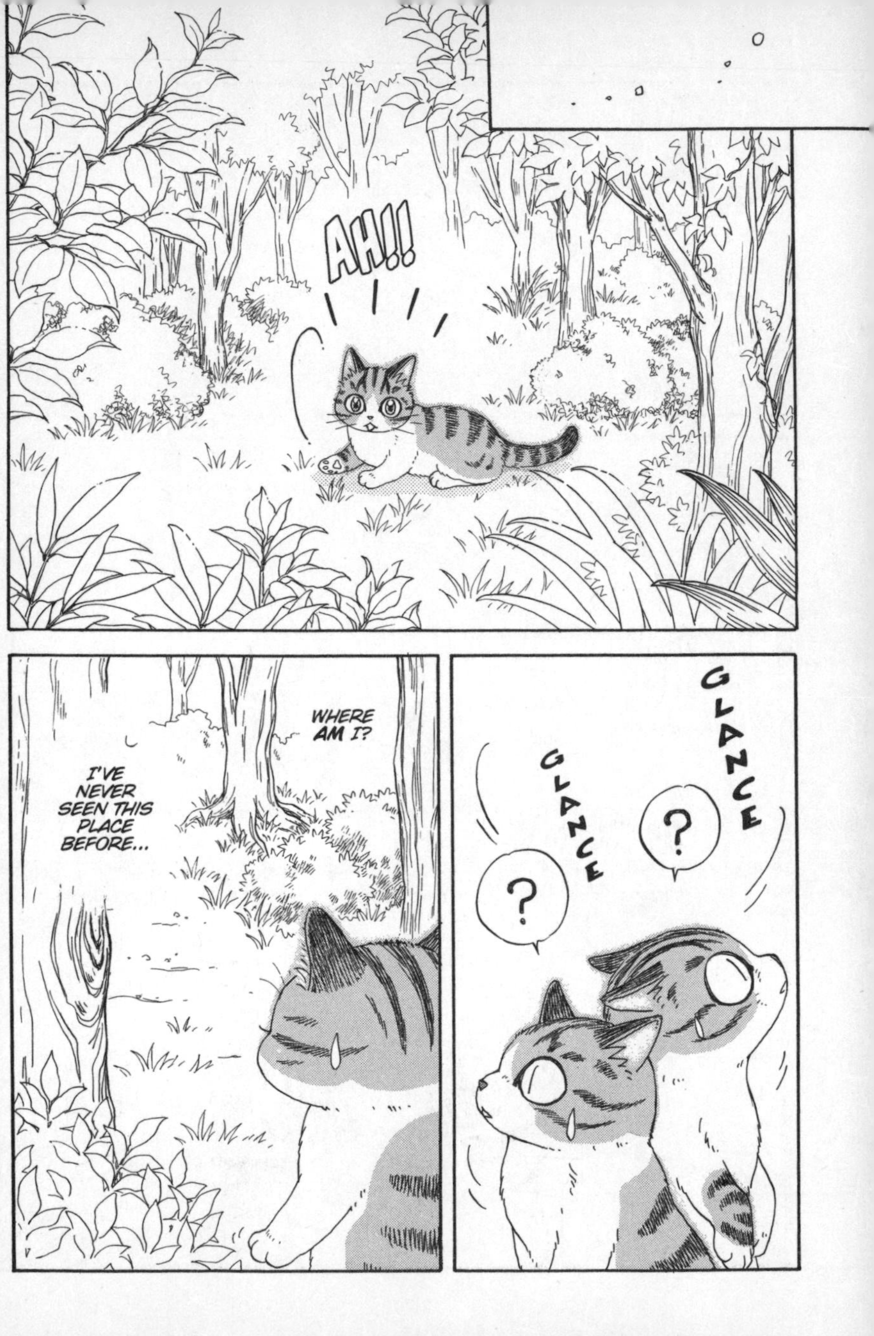
AH!!
GLANCE
GLANCE
?
?
WHERE AM I?
I'VE NEVER SEEN THIS PLACE BEFORE...

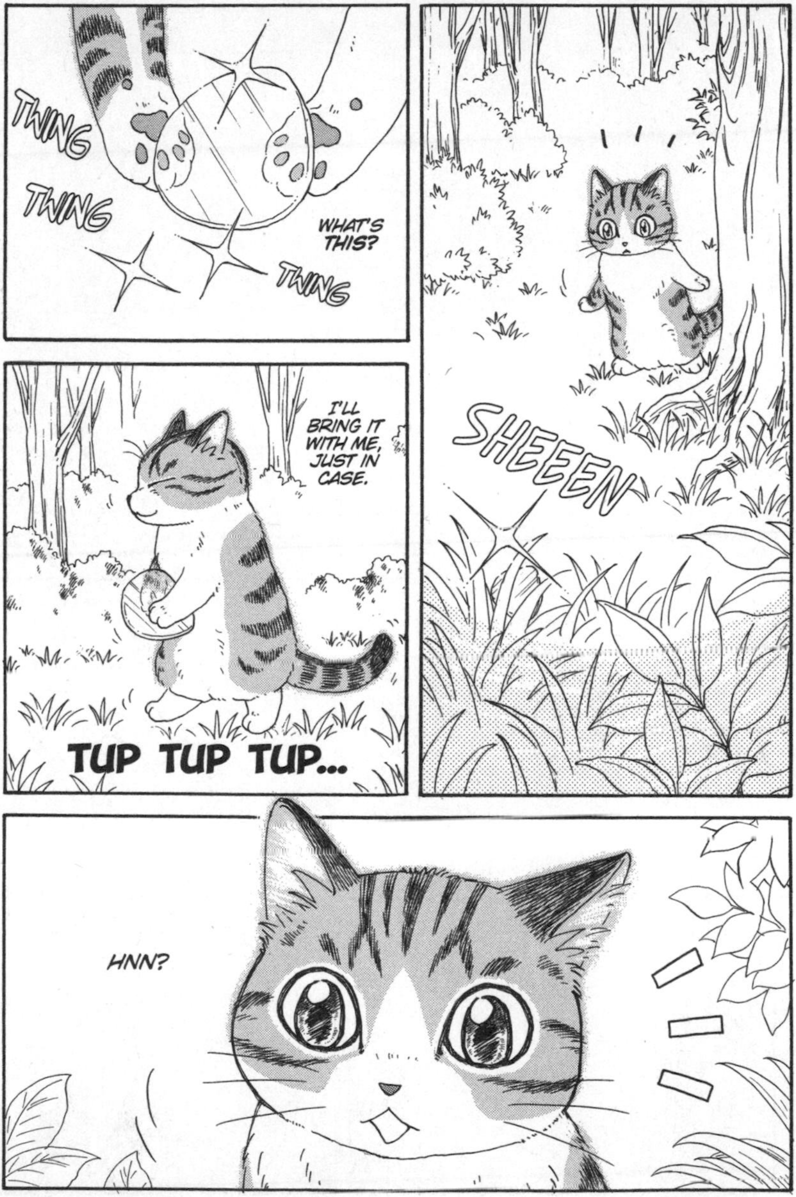
SHEEEN
TWING
TWING
WHAT'S THIS?
TWING
I'LL BRING IT WITH ME, JUST IN CASE.
TUP TUP TUP...
HNN?

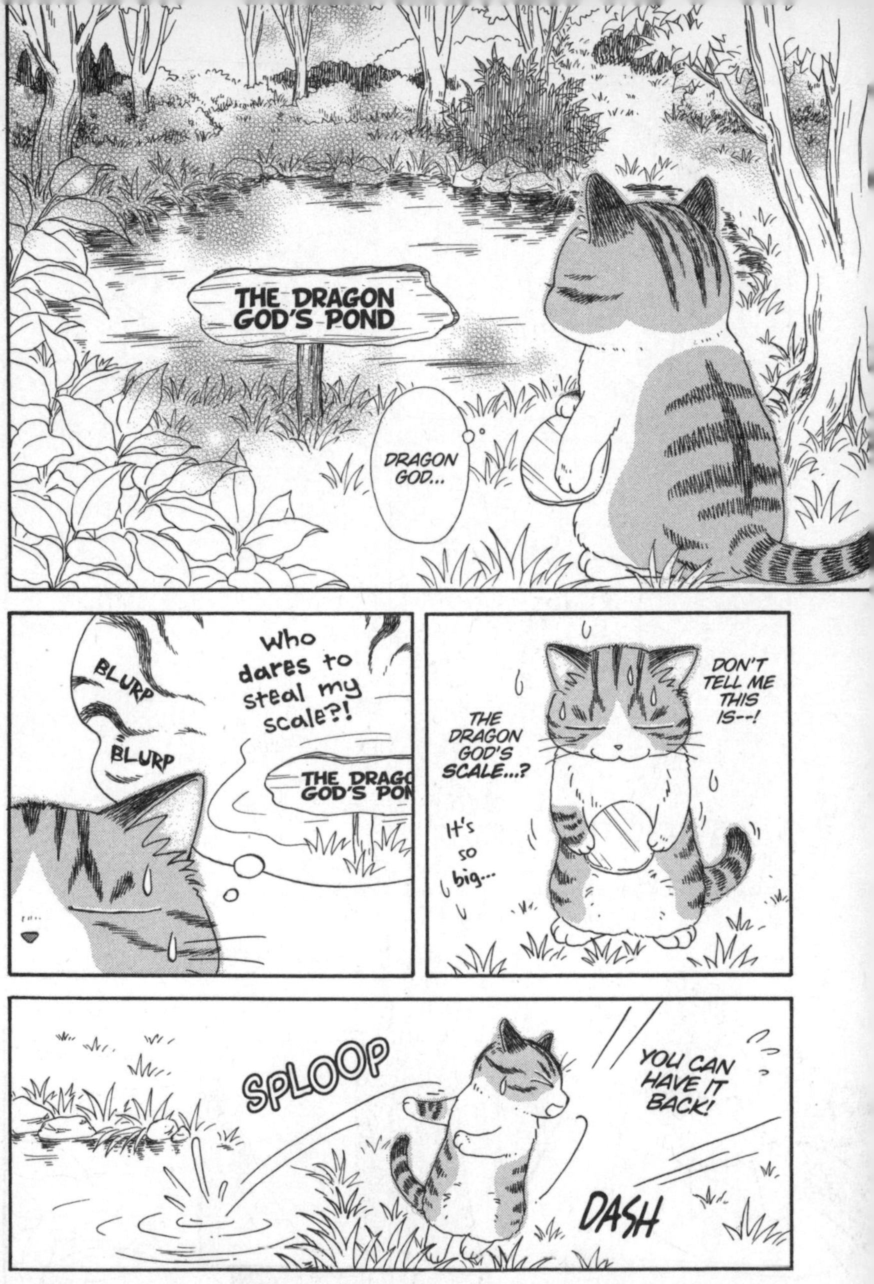
THE DRAGON GOD'S POND
DRAGON GOD...
DON'T TELL ME THIS IS--!
THE DRAGON GOD'S SCALE...?
It's so big...
Who dares to steal my scale?!
BLURP
BLURP
YOU CAN HAVE IT BACK!
DASH
SPLOOP

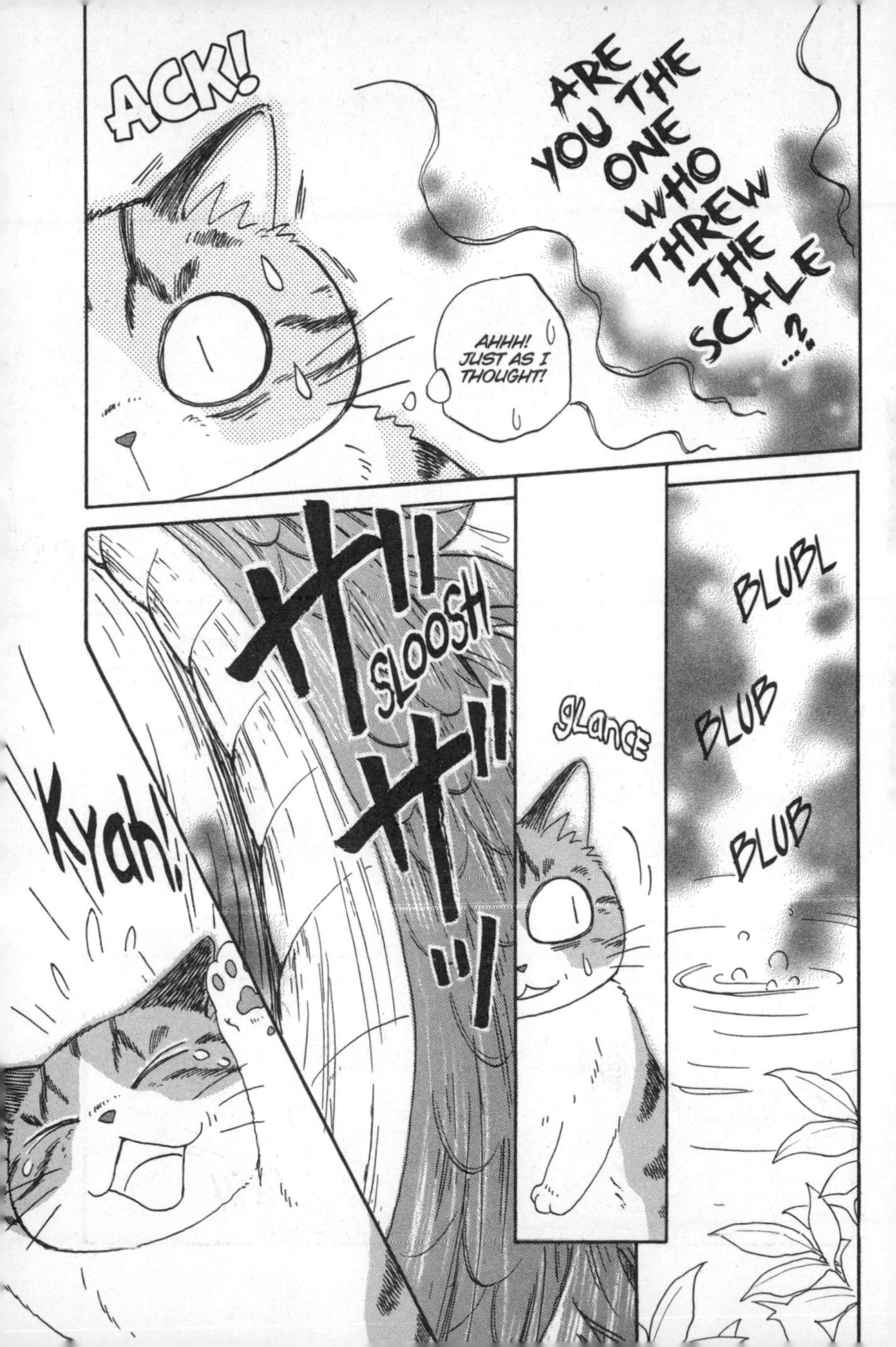
ARE YOU THE ONE WHO THREW THE SCALE ...?
AHHH! JUST AS I THOUGHT!
ACK!
BLUBL
BLUB
BLUB
gLance
SLOOSH
Kyah!

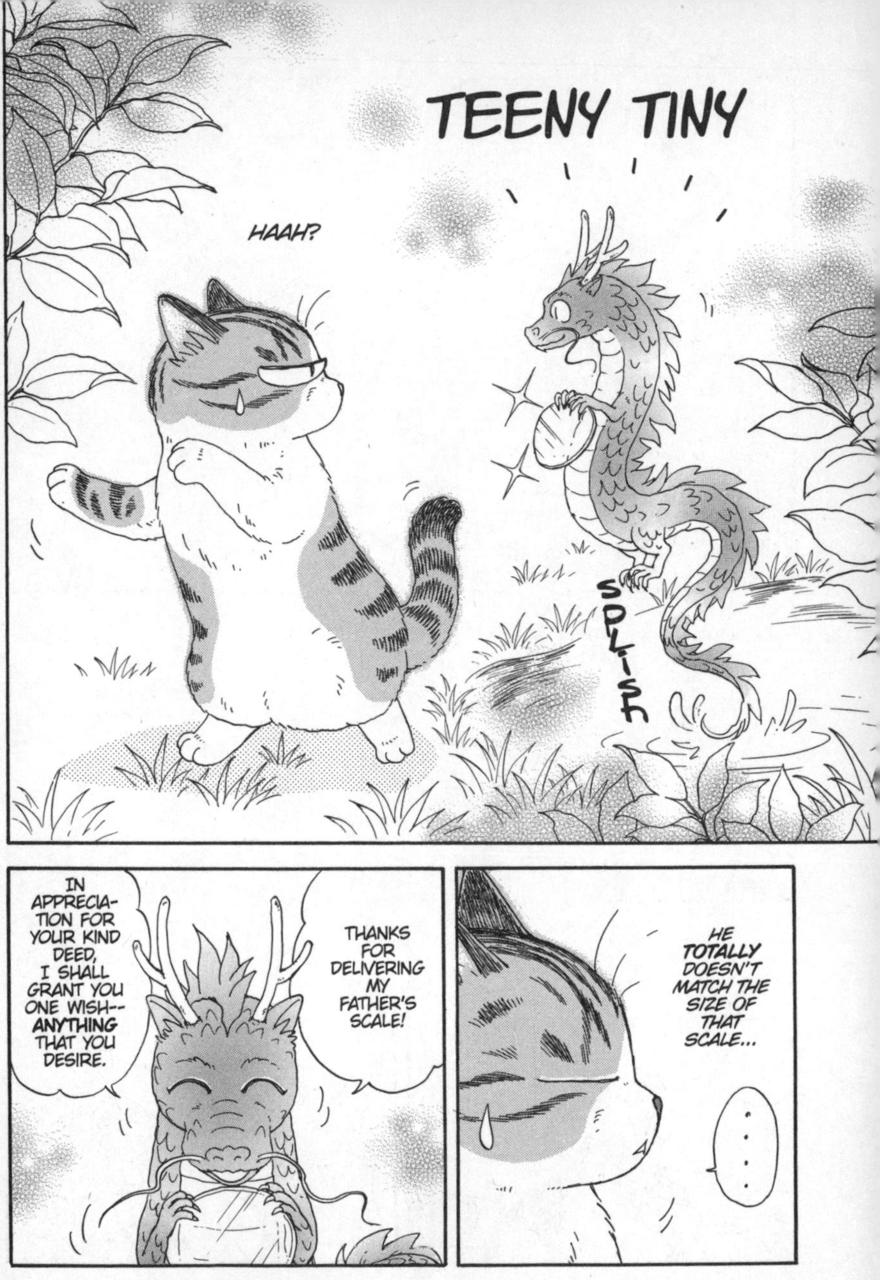
TEENY TINY
HAAH?
SPLISH
HE TOTALLY DOESN'T MATCH THE SIZE OF THAT SCALE...
...
THANKS FOR DELIVERING MY FATHER'S SCALE!
IN APPRECIATION FOR YOUR KIND DEED, I SHALL GRANT YOU ONE WISH--ANYTHING THAT YOU DESIRE.

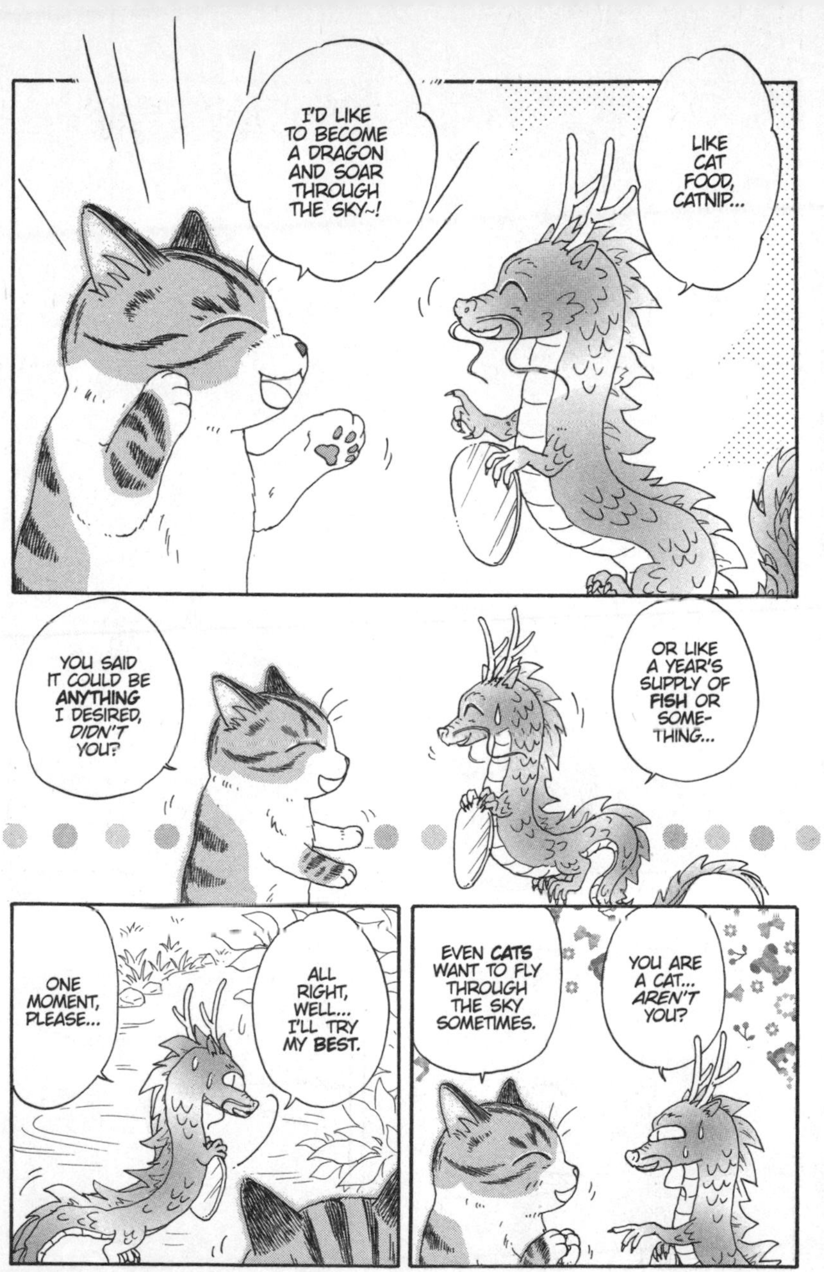
LIKE CAT FOOD, CATNIP...
I'D LIKE TO BECOME A DRAGON AND SOAR THROUGH THE SKY~!
OR LIKE A YEAR'S SUPPLY OF FISH OR SOME-THING...
YOU SAID IT COULD BE ANYTHING I DESIRED, DIDN'T YOU?
YOU ARE A CAT... AREN'T YOU?
EVEN CATS WANT TO FLY THROUGH THE SKY SOMETIMES.
ALL RIGHT, WELL... I'LL TRY MY BEST.
ONE MOMENT, PLEASE...

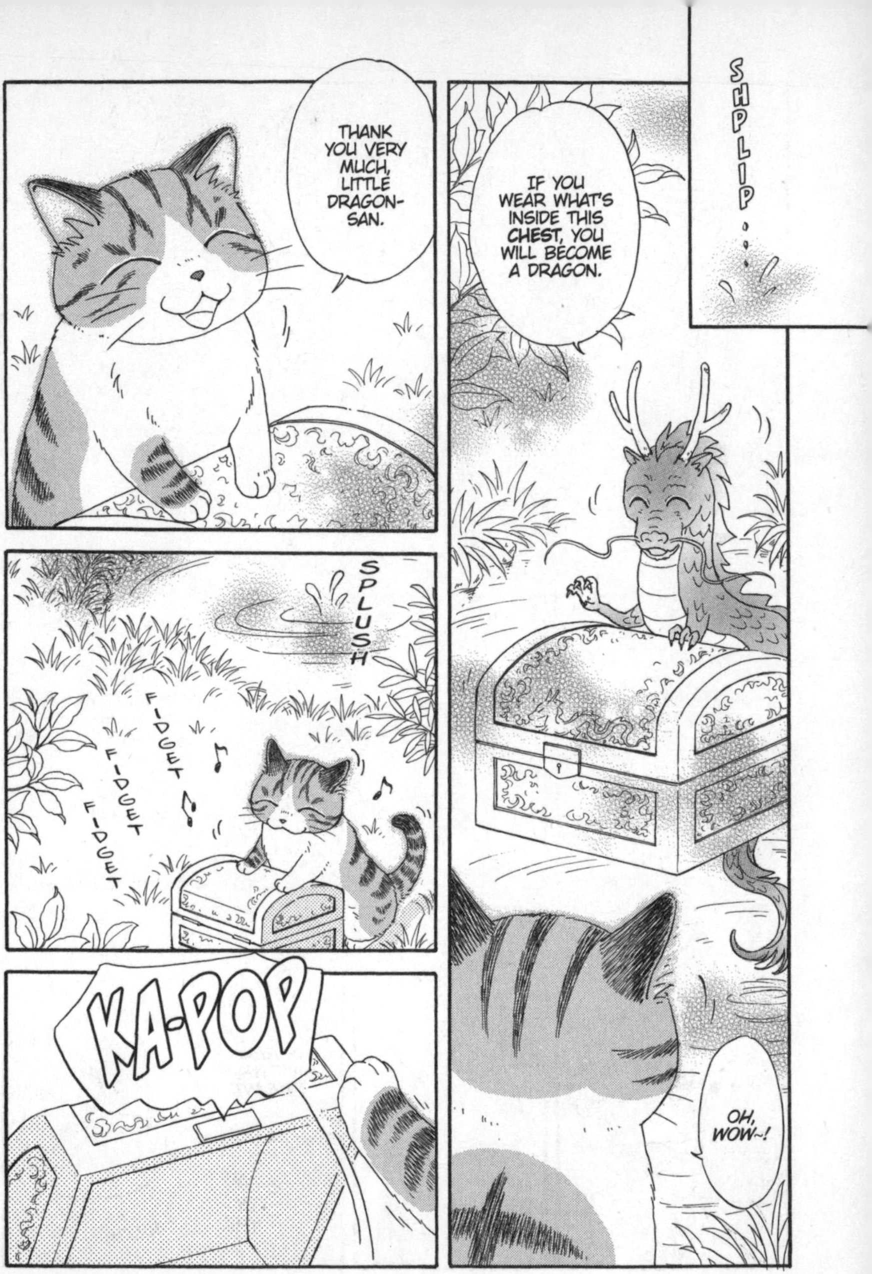
SHPLIP...
IF YOU WEAR WHAT'S INSIDE THIS CHEST, YOU WILL BECOME A DRAGON.
OH, WOW~!
THANK YOU VERY MUCH, LITTLE DRAGON-SAN.
SPLUSH
FIDGET
FIDGET
FIDGET
KA-POP

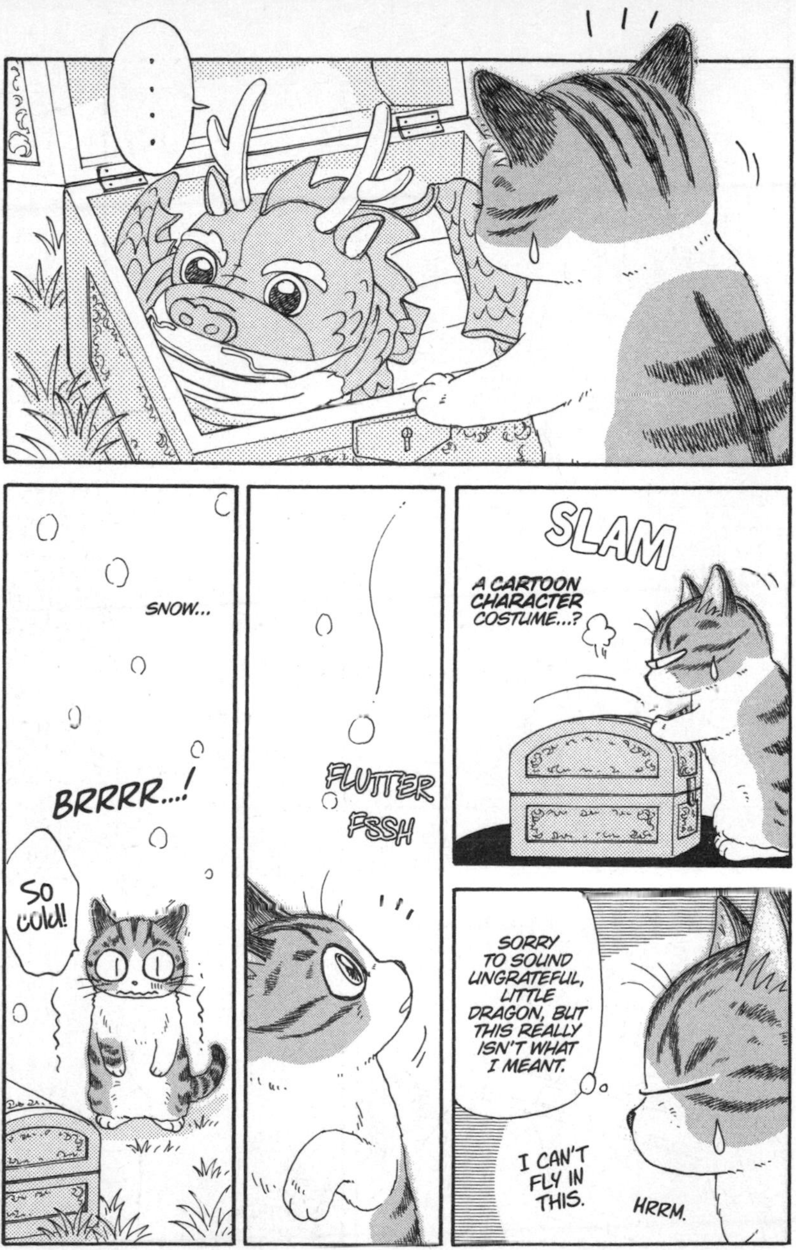
.....
SLAM
A CARTOON CHARACTER COSTUME...?
SORRY TO SOUND UNGRATEFUL, LITTLE DRAGON, BUT THIS REALLY ISN'T WHAT I MEANT.
I CAN'T FLY IN THIS.
HRRM.
FLUTTER
FSSH
SNOW...
BRRRR...!
SO COLD!

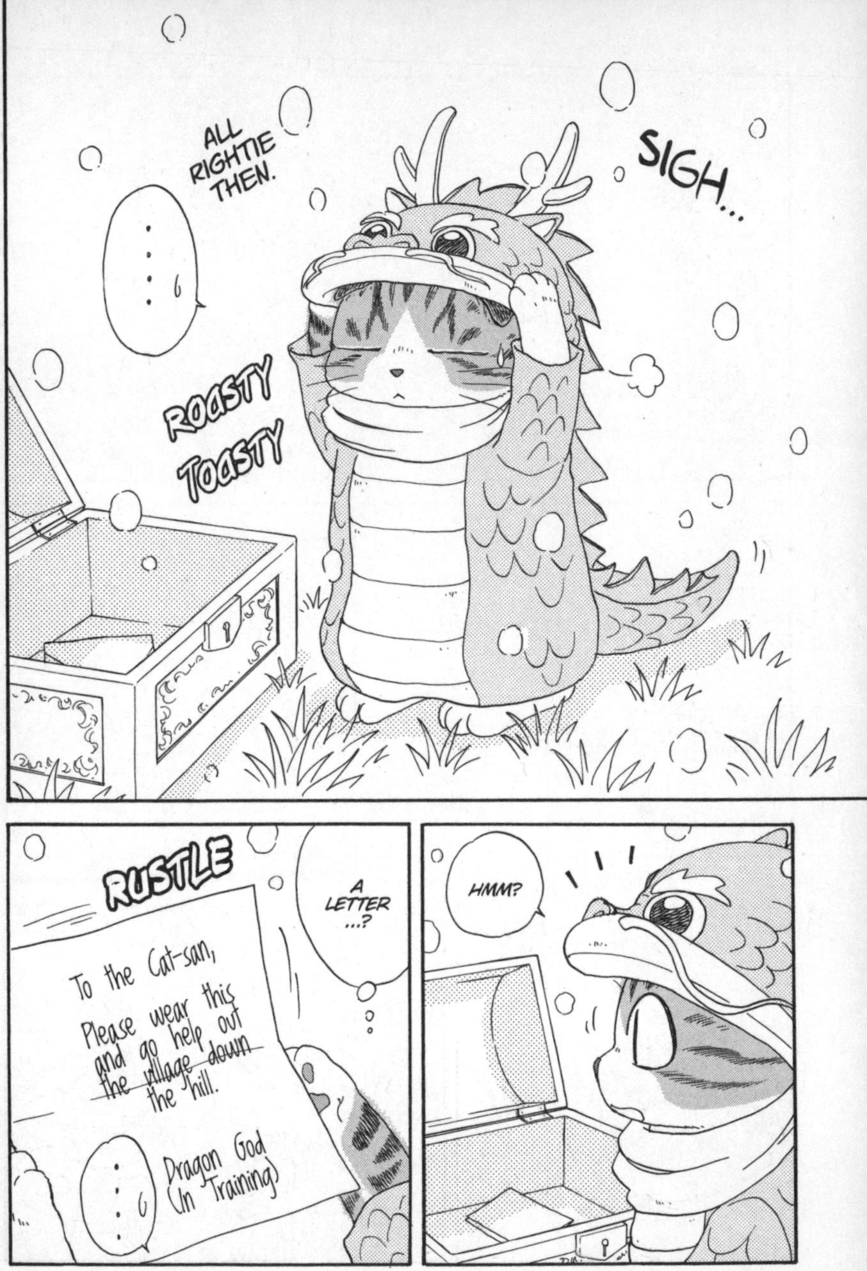
SIGH...
ALL RIGHTIE THEN.
....
ROASTY TOASTY
HMM?
A LETTER ...?
RUSTLE
To the Cat-san,
Please wear this and go help out ~~the village down~~ the hill.
Dragon God (In Training)
....

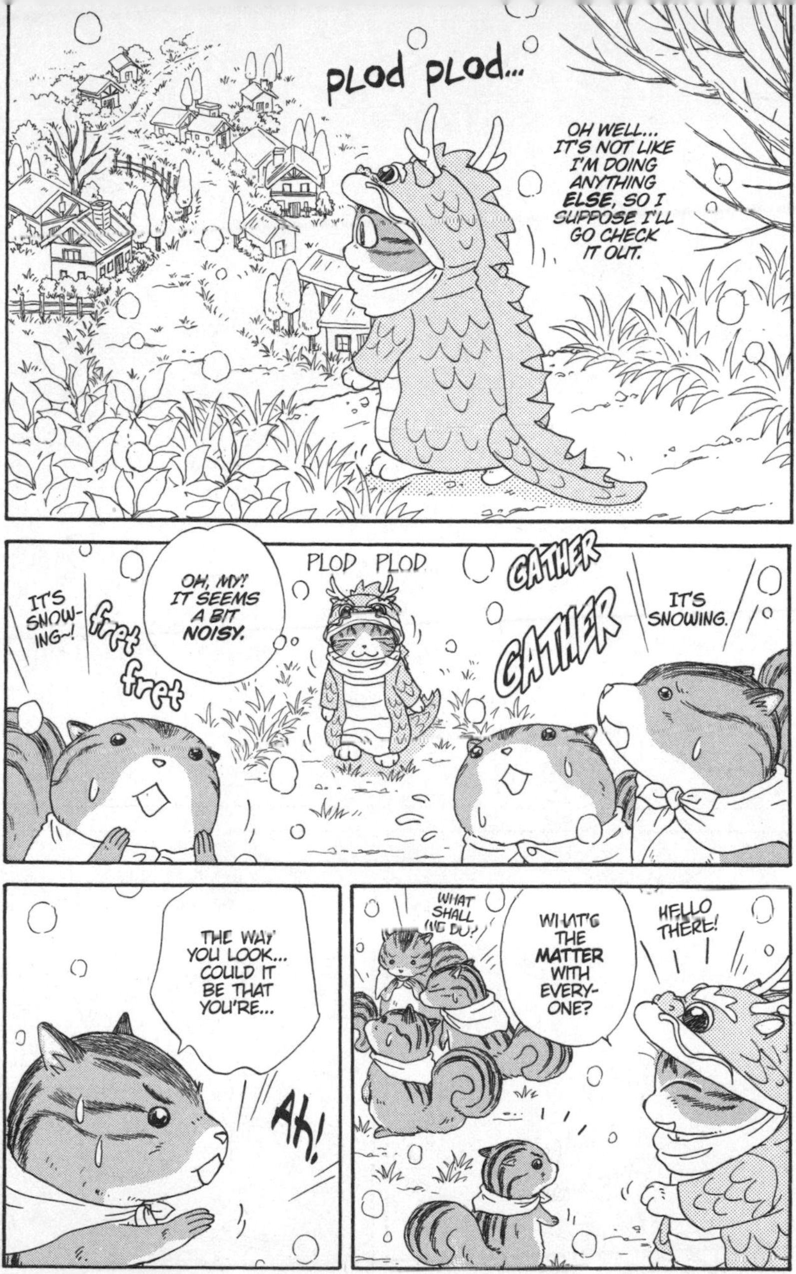
PLOD PLOD...
OH WELL... IT'S NOT LIKE I'M DOING ANYTHING ELSE, SO I SUPPOSE I'LL GO CHECK IT OUT.
IT'S SNOWING.
GATHER GATHER
PLOD PLOD
OH, MY! IT SEEMS A BIT NOISY.
IT'S SNOWING~!
fret fret
HELLO THERE!
WHAT'S THE MATTER WITH EVERY-ONE?
WHAT SHALL WE DO?
THE WAY YOU LOOK... COULD IT BE THAT YOU'RE...
Ah!

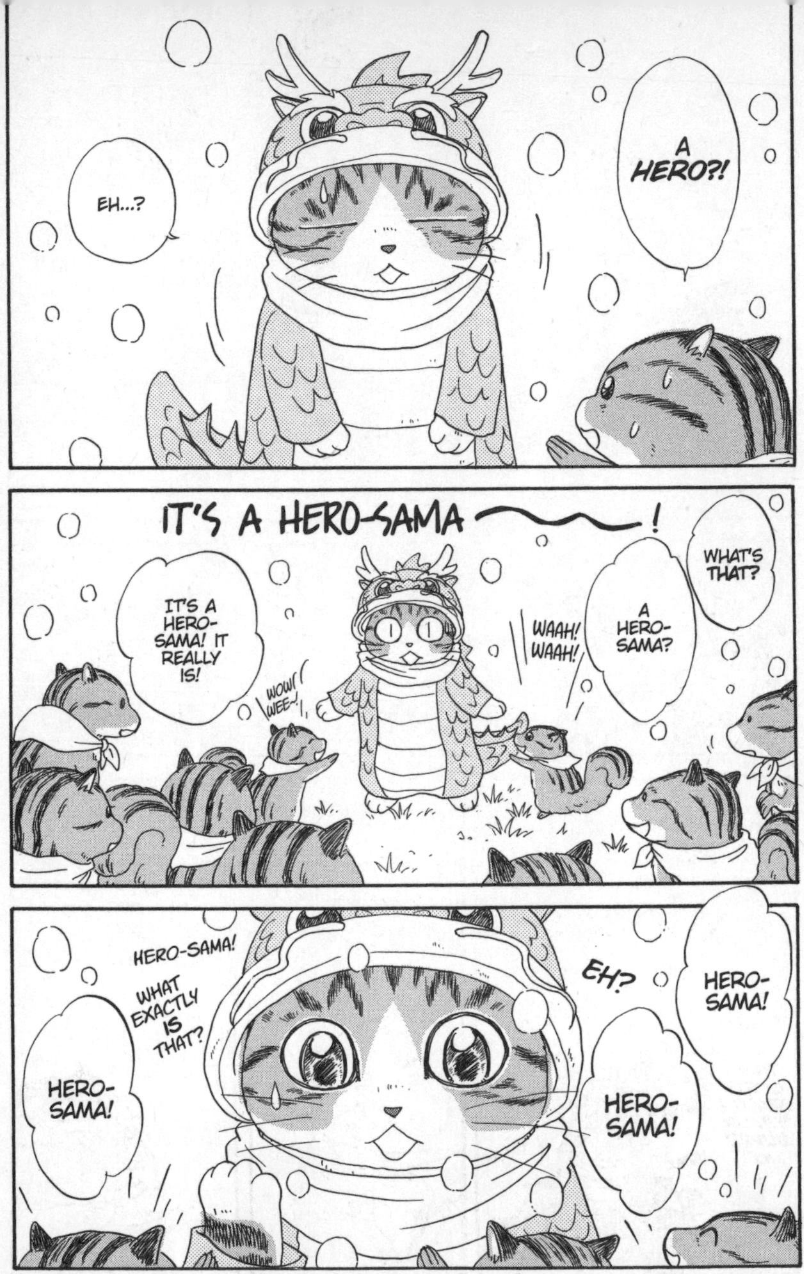
A HERO?!
EH...?
IT'S A HERO-SAMA~~!
WHAT'S THAT?
A HERO-SAMA?
WAAH! WAAH!
IT'S A HERO-SAMA! IT REALLY IS!
WOW WEE~!
HERO-SAMA!
EH?
HERO-SAMA!
HERO-SAMA!
WHAT EXACTLY IS THAT?
HERO-SAMA!

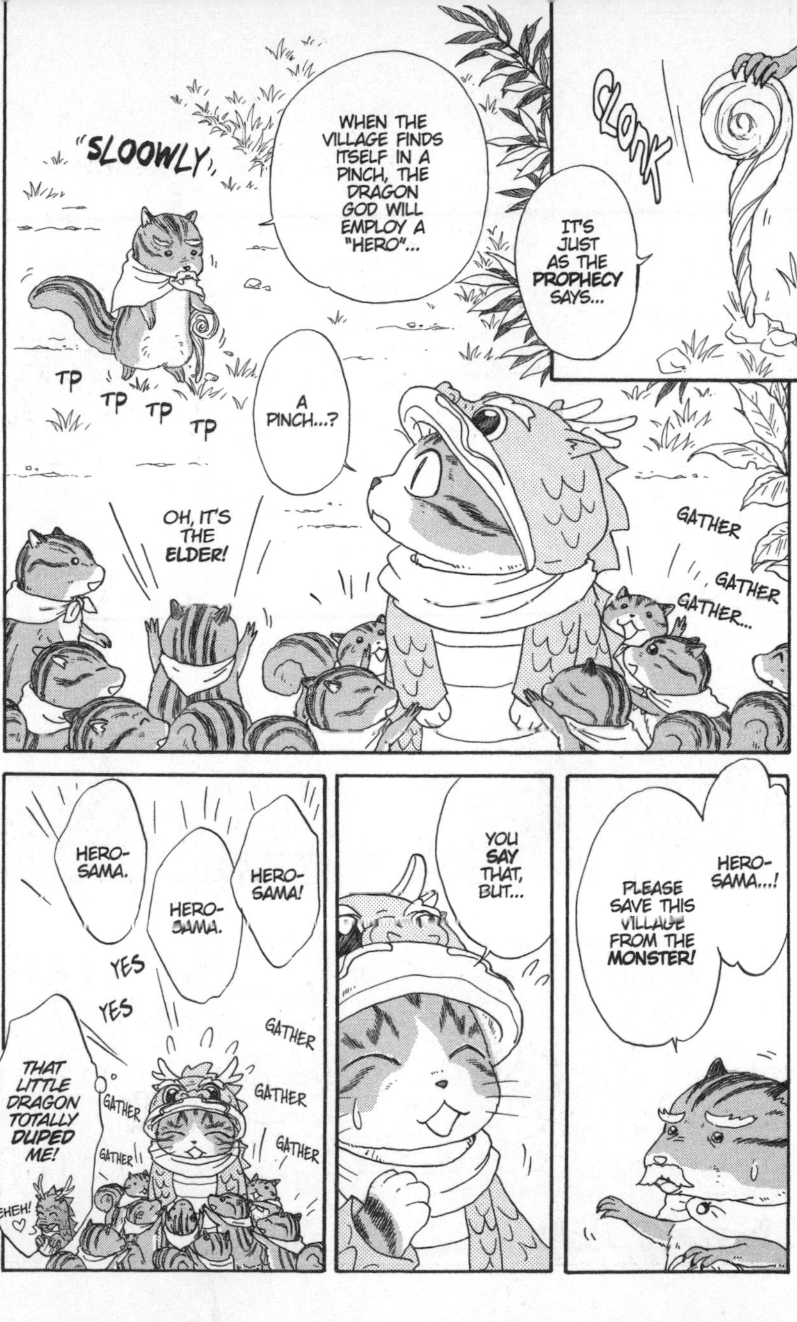
CLONK
IT'S JUST AS THE PROPHECY SAYS...
WHEN THE VILLAGE FINDS ITSELF IN A PINCH, THE DRAGON GOD WILL EMPLOY A "HERO"...
SLOOWLY
TP TP TP TP
A PINCH...?
GATHER GATHER GATHER...
OH, IT'S THE ELDER!
HERO-SAMA...!
PLEASE SAVE THIS VILLAGE FROM THE MONSTER!
YOU SAY THAT, BUT...
HERO-SAMA!
HERO-SAMA.
HERO-SAMA.
YES
YES
GATHER
GATHER
GATHER
GATHER
GATHER
THAT LITTLE DRAGON TOTALLY DUPED ME!
EHEH! ♡

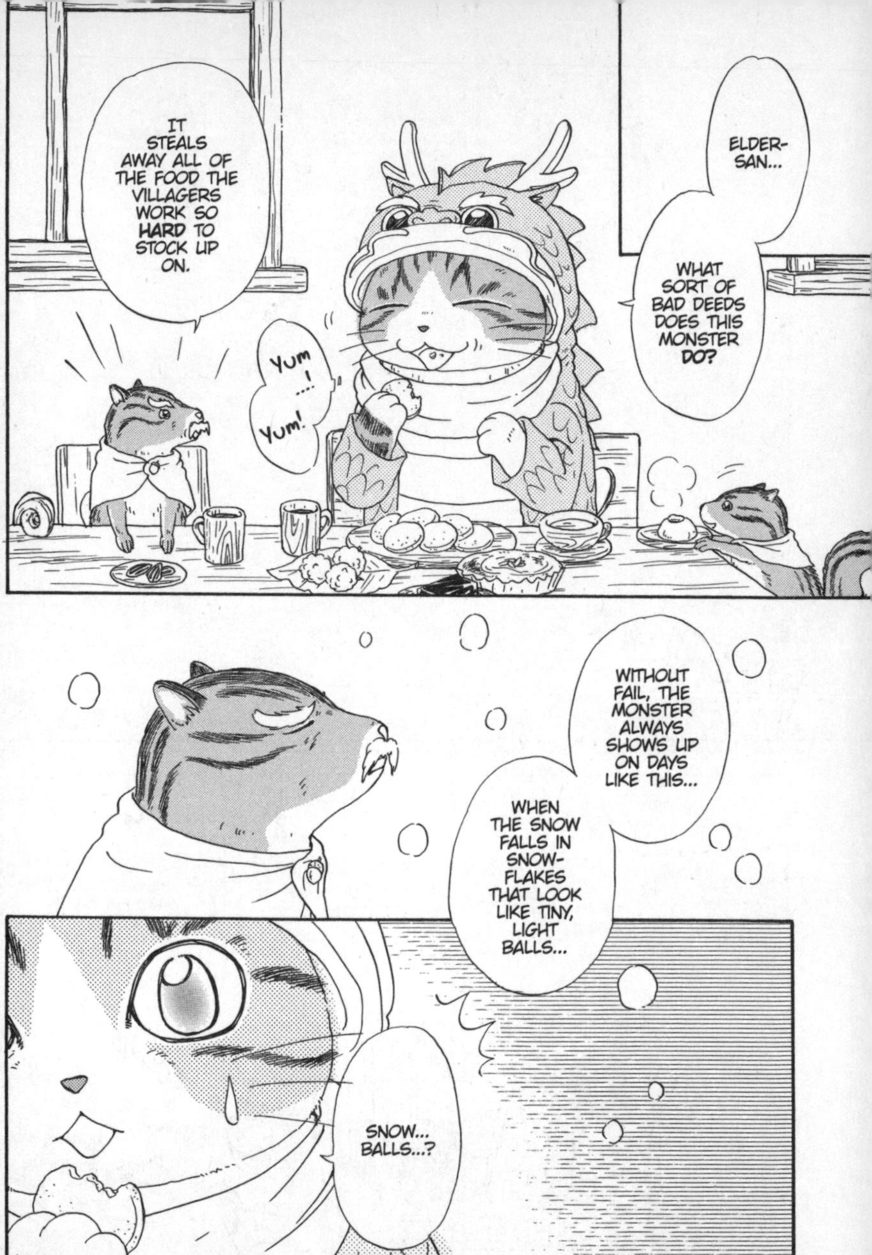
ELDER-SAN...
WHAT SORT OF BAD DEEDS DOES THIS MONSTER DO?
IT STEALS AWAY ALL OF THE FOOD THE VILLAGERS WORK SO HARD TO STOCK UP ON.
Yum ...! Yum!
WITHOUT FAIL, THE MONSTER ALWAYS SHOWS UP ON DAYS LIKE THIS...
WHEN THE SNOW FALLS IN SNOW-FLAKES THAT LOOK LIKE TINY, LIGHT BALLS...
SNOW... BALLS...?

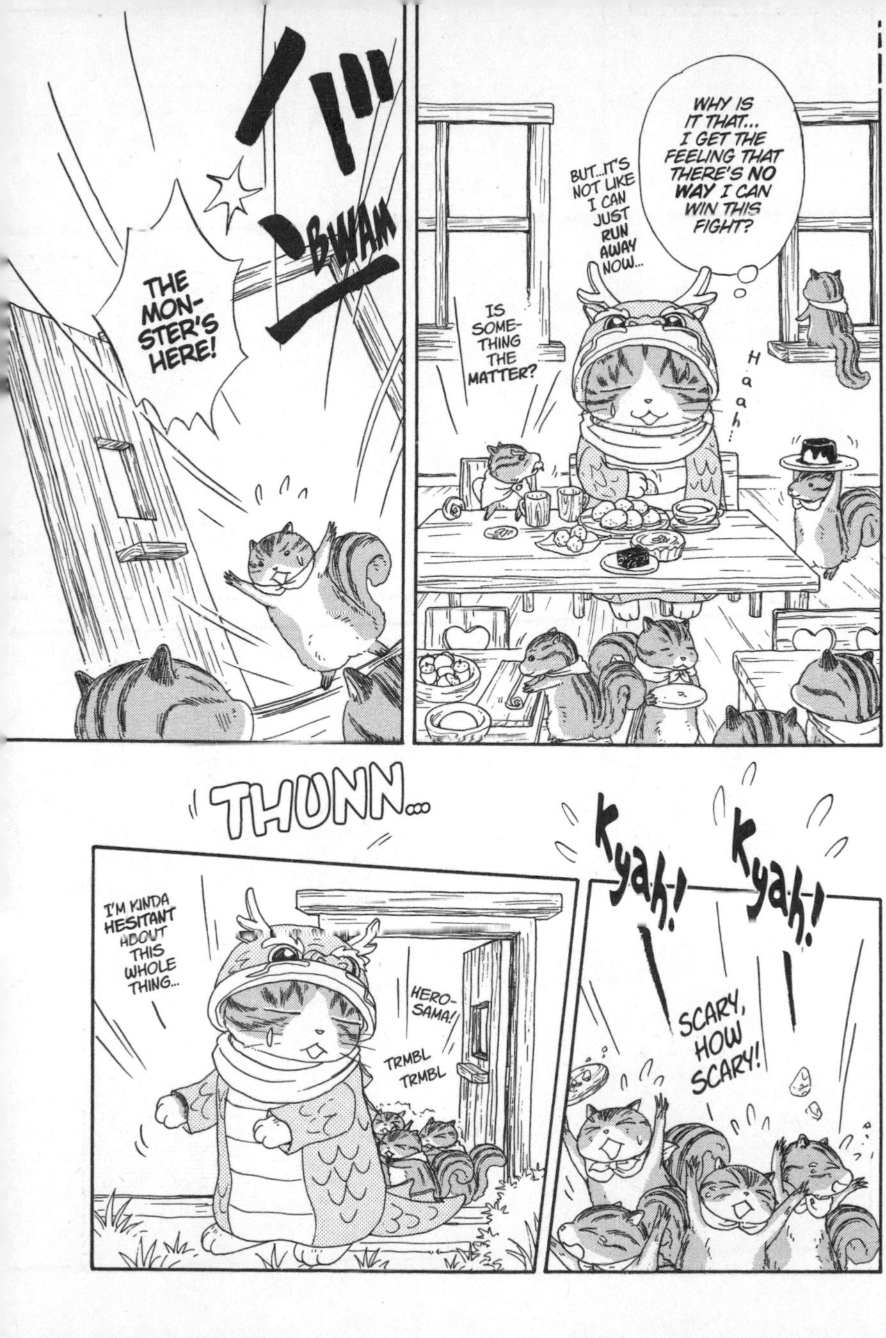
WHY IS IT THAT... I GET THE FEELING THAT THERE'S NO WAY I CAN WIN THIS FIGHT?
BUT...IT'S NOT LIKE I CAN JUST RUN AWAY NOW...
Haah...
IS SOMETHING THE MATTER?
BWAM
THE MONSTER'S HERE!
Kyah! Kyah!
SCARY, HOW SCARY!
THUNN...
HERO-SAMA!
TRMBL TRMBL
I'M KINDA HESITANT ABOUT THIS WHOLE THING...

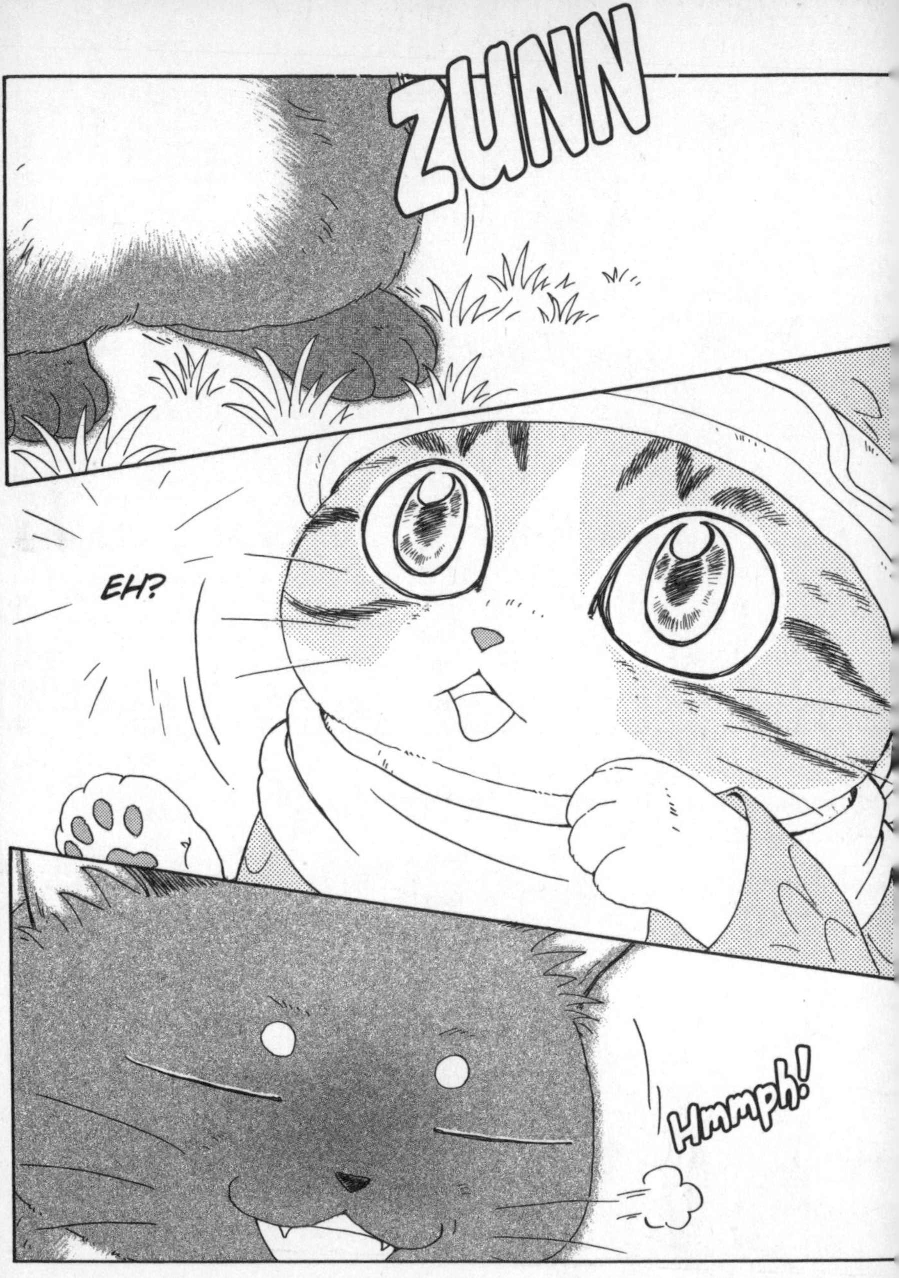
ZUNN
EH?
Hmmph!

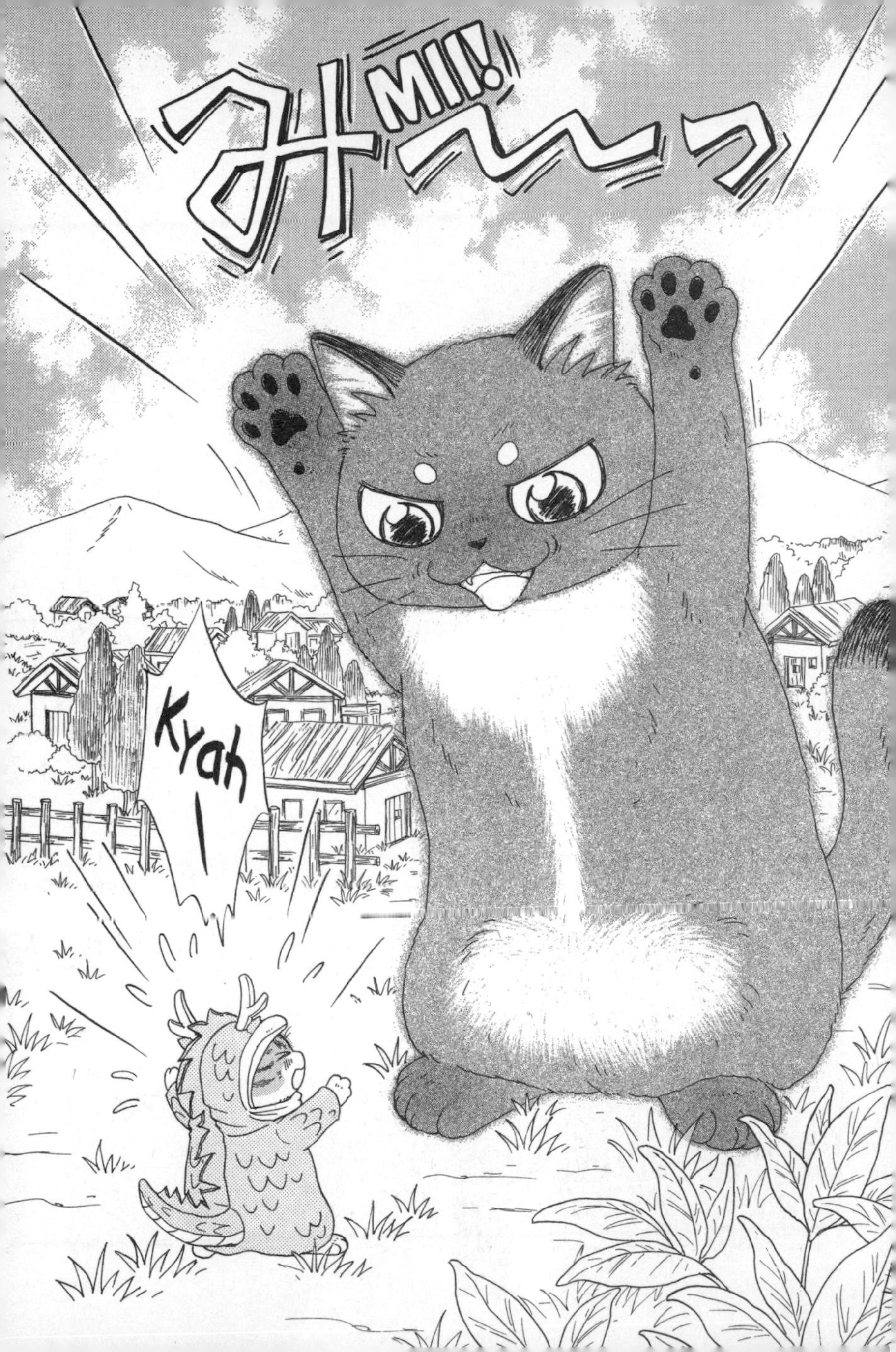
みーっ
MII!
Kyah!

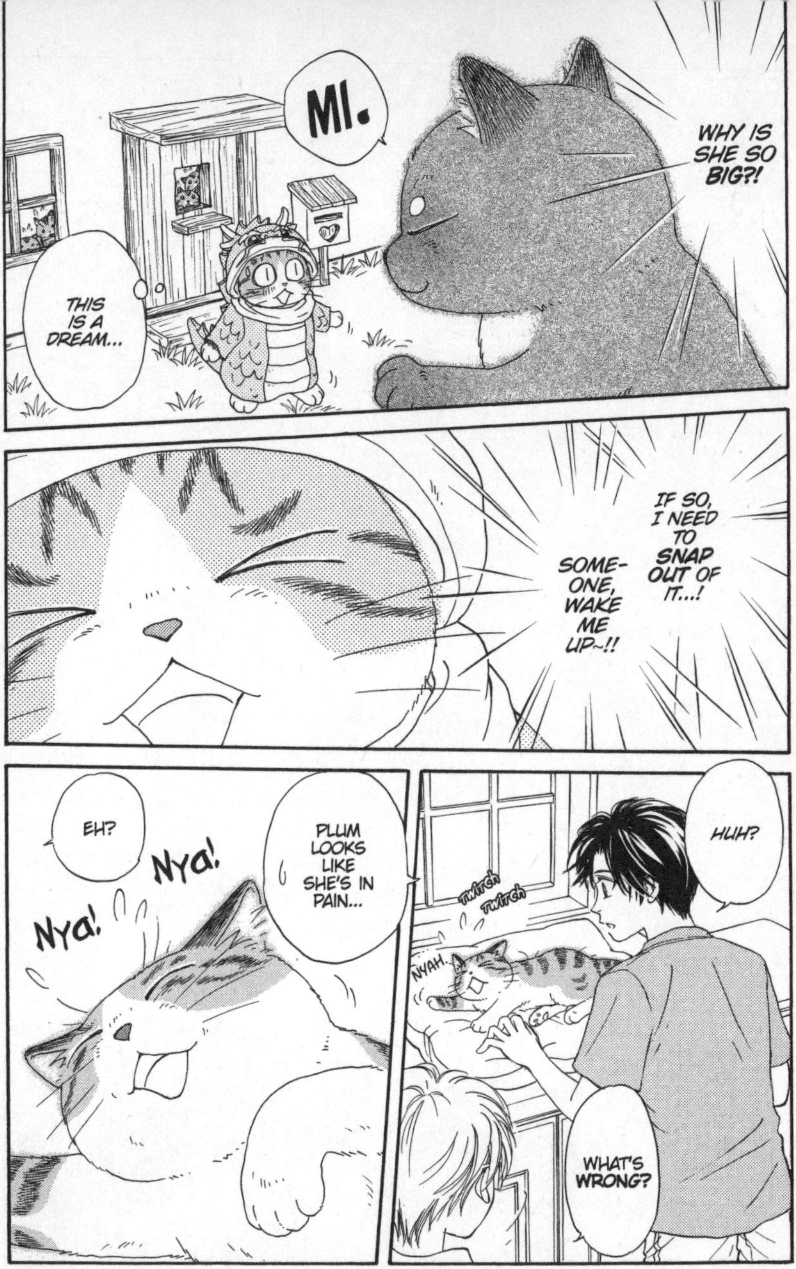
WHY IS SHE SO BIG?!
MI.
THIS IS A DREAM...
IF SO, I NEED TO SNAP OUT OF IT...!
SOME-ONE, WAKE ME UP~!!
HUH?
TWITCH TWITCH
NYAH.
WHAT'S WRONG?
PLUM LOOKS LIKE SHE'S IN PAIN...
EH?
Nya!
Nya!

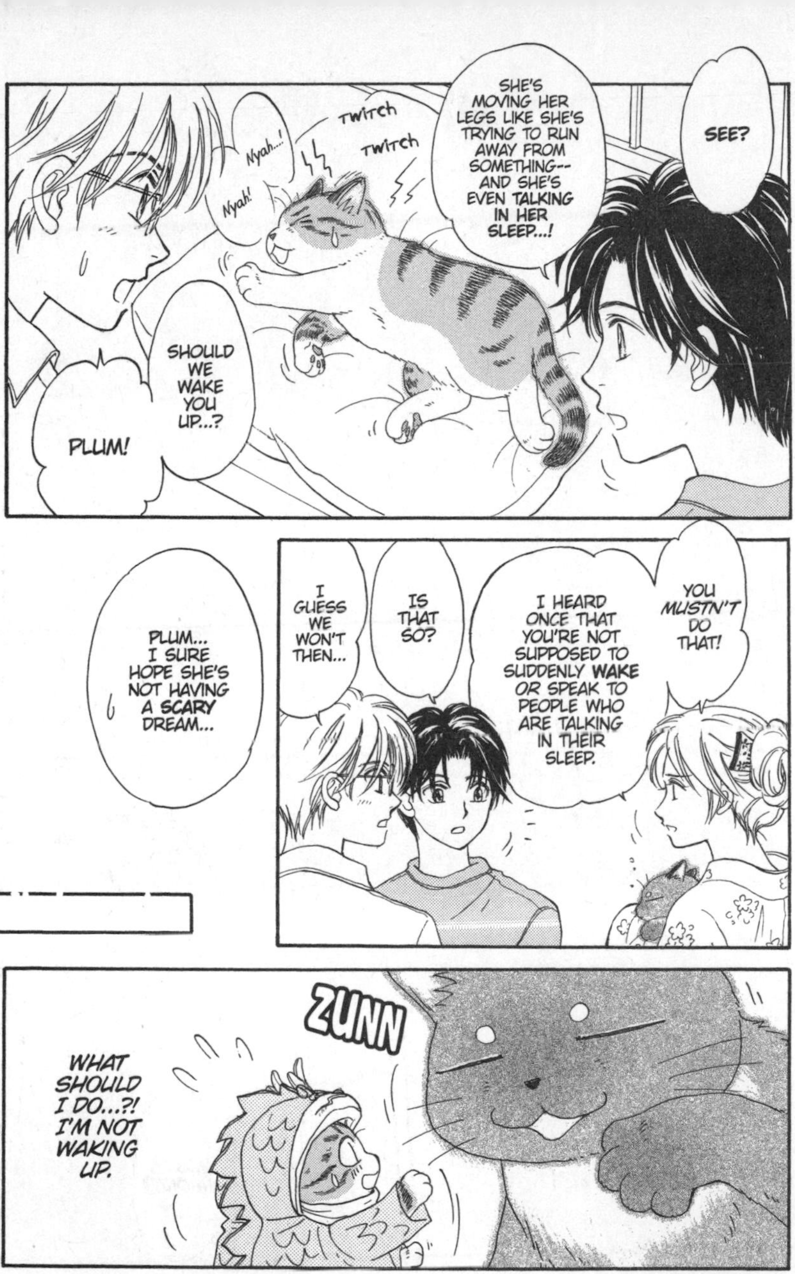
SEE?
SHE'S MOVING HER LEGS LIKE SHE'S TRYING TO RUN AWAY FROM SOMETHING-- AND SHE'S EVEN TALKING IN HER SLEEP...!
TWITCH
TWITCH
Nyah...!
Nyah!
SHOULD WE WAKE YOU UP...?
PLUM!
YOU MUSTN'T DO THAT!
I HEARD ONCE THAT YOU'RE NOT SUPPOSED TO SUDDENLY WAKE OR SPEAK TO PEOPLE WHO ARE TALKING IN THEIR SLEEP.
IS THAT SO?
I GUESS WE WON'T THEN...
PLUM... I SURE HOPE SHE'S NOT HAVING A SCARY DREAM...
ZUNN
WHAT SHOULD I DO...?! I'M NOT WAKING UP.

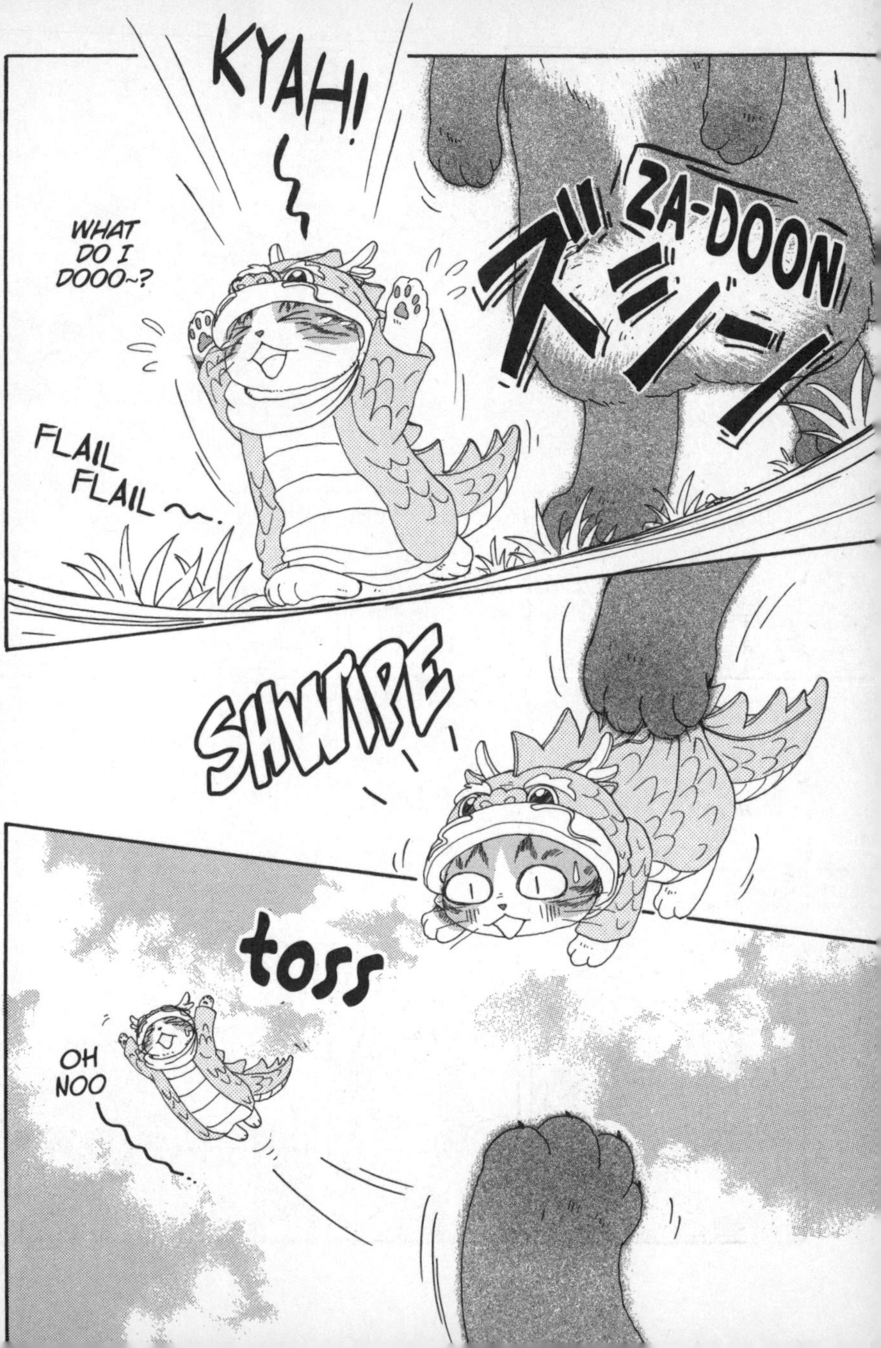
ZA-DOON
KYAH!
WHAT DO I DOOO~?
FLAIL FLAIL~.
SHWIPE
toss
OH NOO~...

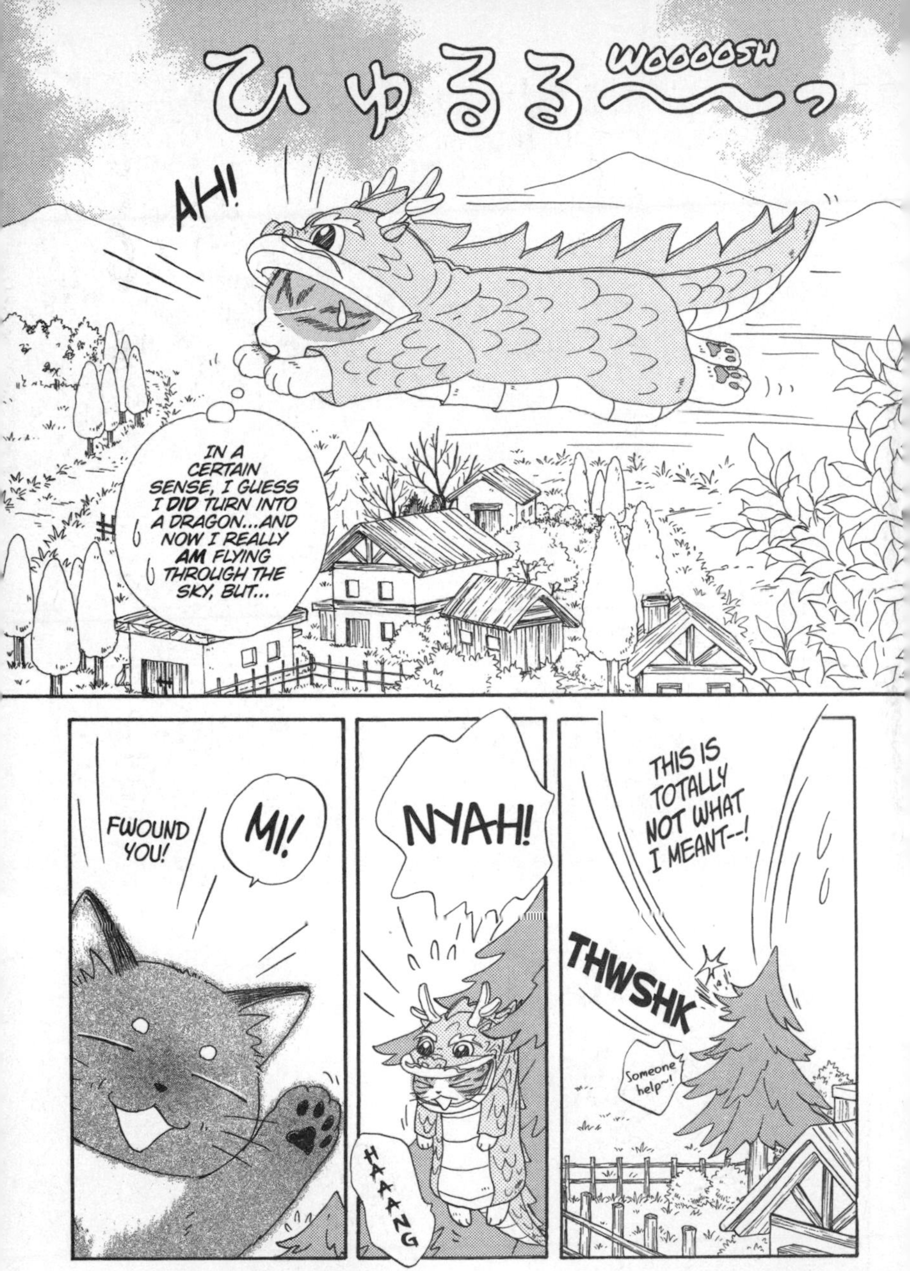
ひゅるる〜〜っ
WOOOOSH
AH!
IN A CERTAIN SENSE, I GUESS I DID TURN INTO A DRAGON...AND NOW I REALLY AM FLYING THROUGH THE SKY, BUT...
THIS IS TOTALLY NOT WHAT I MEANT--!
THWSHK
Someone help~!
NYAH!
HAAAANG
MI!
FWOUND YOU!

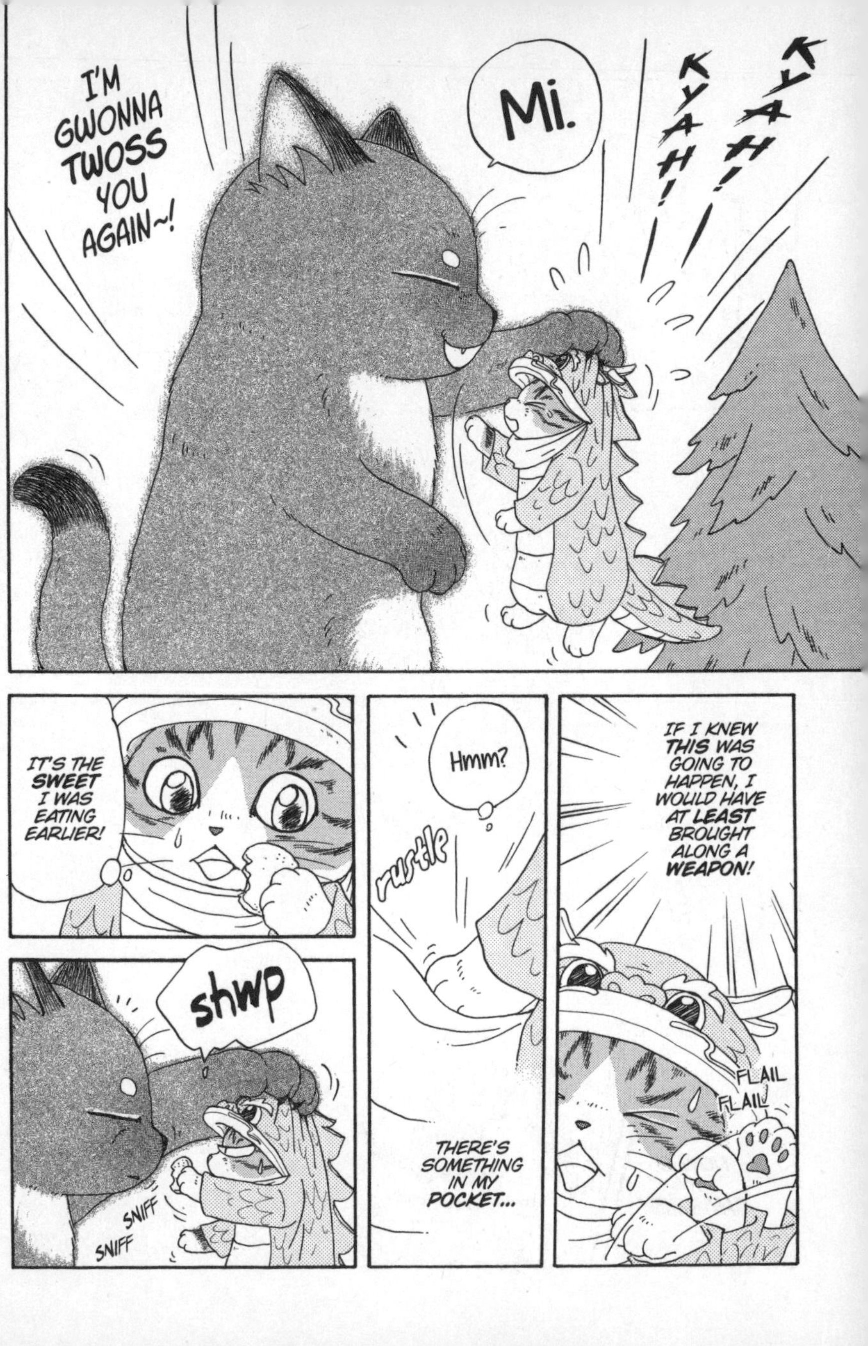
KYAH!
KYAH!
Mi.
I'M GWONNA TWOSS YOU AGAIN~!
IF I KNEW THIS WAS GOING TO HAPPEN, I WOULD HAVE AT LEAST BROUGHT ALONG A WEAPON!
FLAIL
FLAIL
Hmm?
rustle
THERE'S SOMETHING IN MY POCKET...
IT'S THE SWEET I WAS EATING EARLIER!
shwp
SNIFF
SNIFF

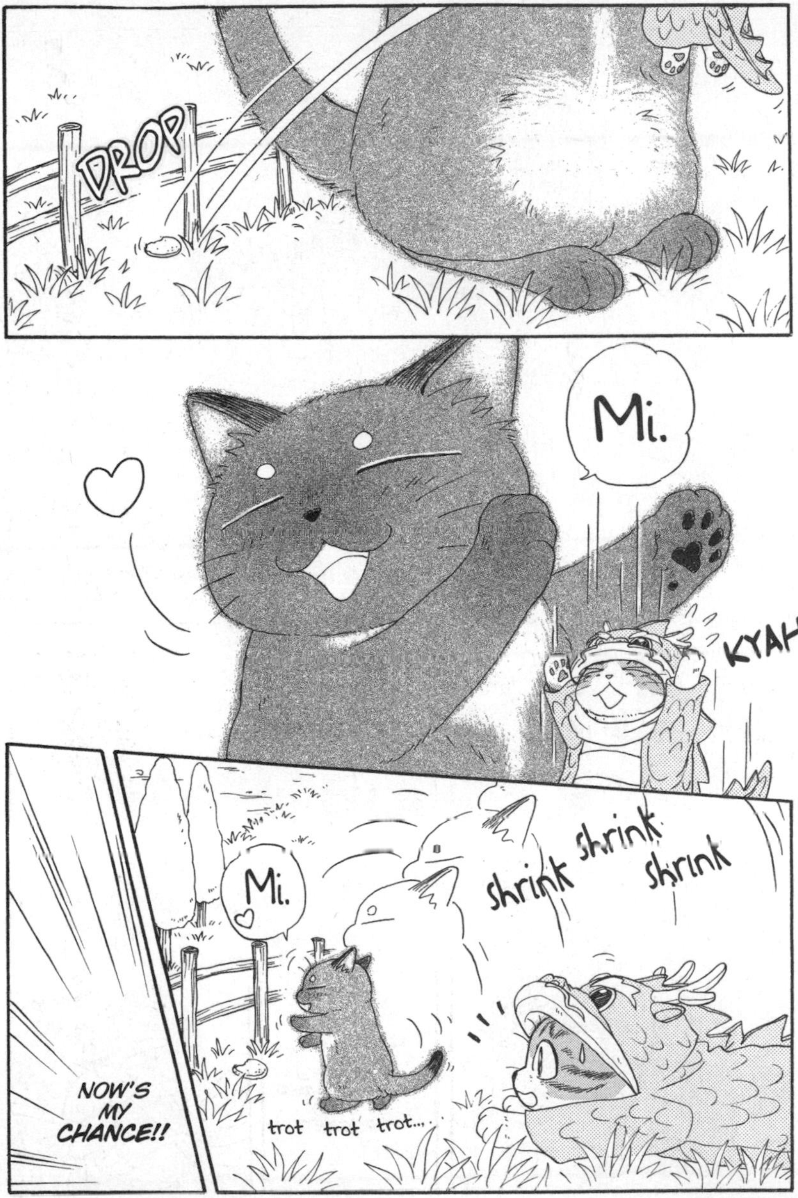
DROP
Mi.
KYAH!
shrink shrink shrink
Mi.
trot trot trot...
NOW'S MY CHANCE!!

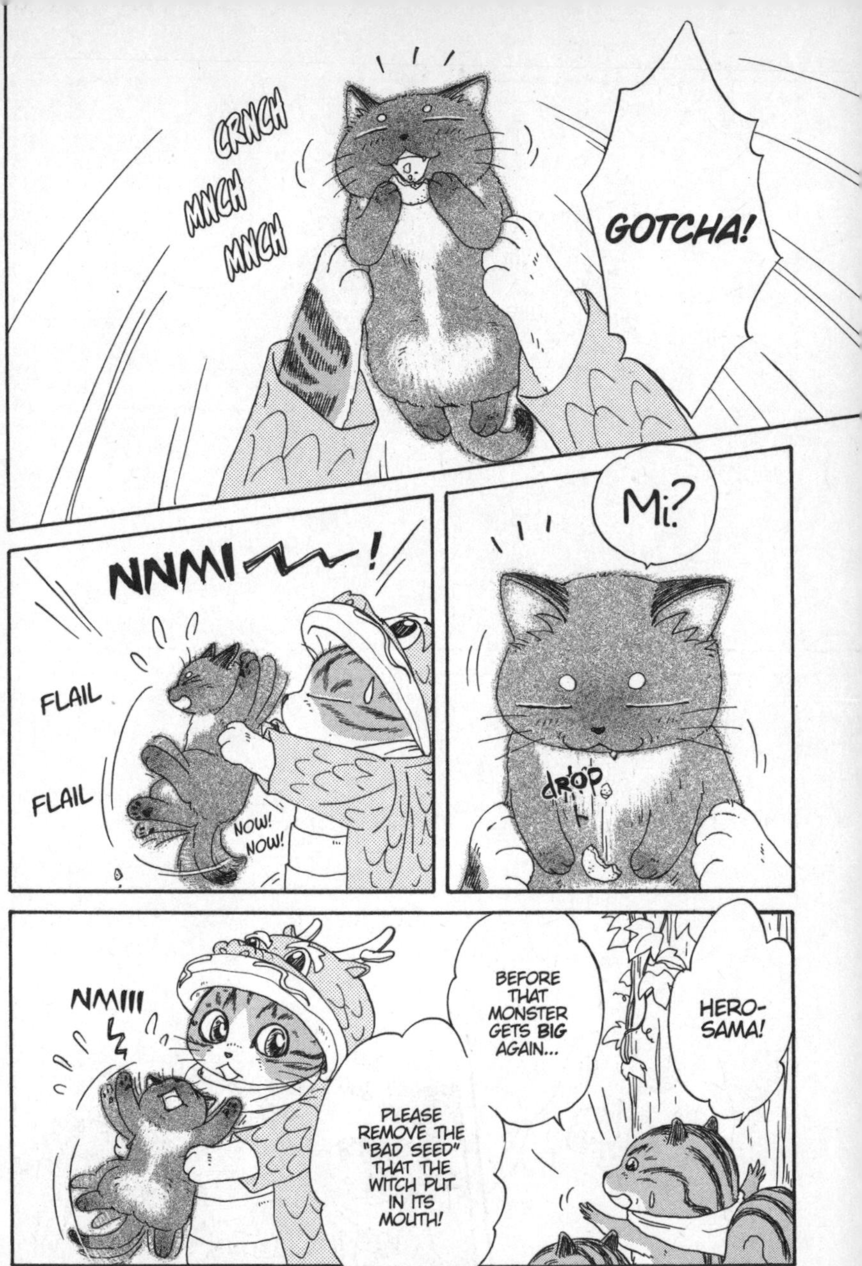
GOTCHA!
CRNCH
MNCH
MNCH
Mi?
dROP
NNMI~!
FLAIL
FLAIL
NOW! NOW!
HERO-SAMA!
BEFORE THAT MONSTER GETS BIG AGAIN...
PLEASE REMOVE THE "BAD SEED" THAT THE WITCH PUT IN ITS MOUTH!
NMIII

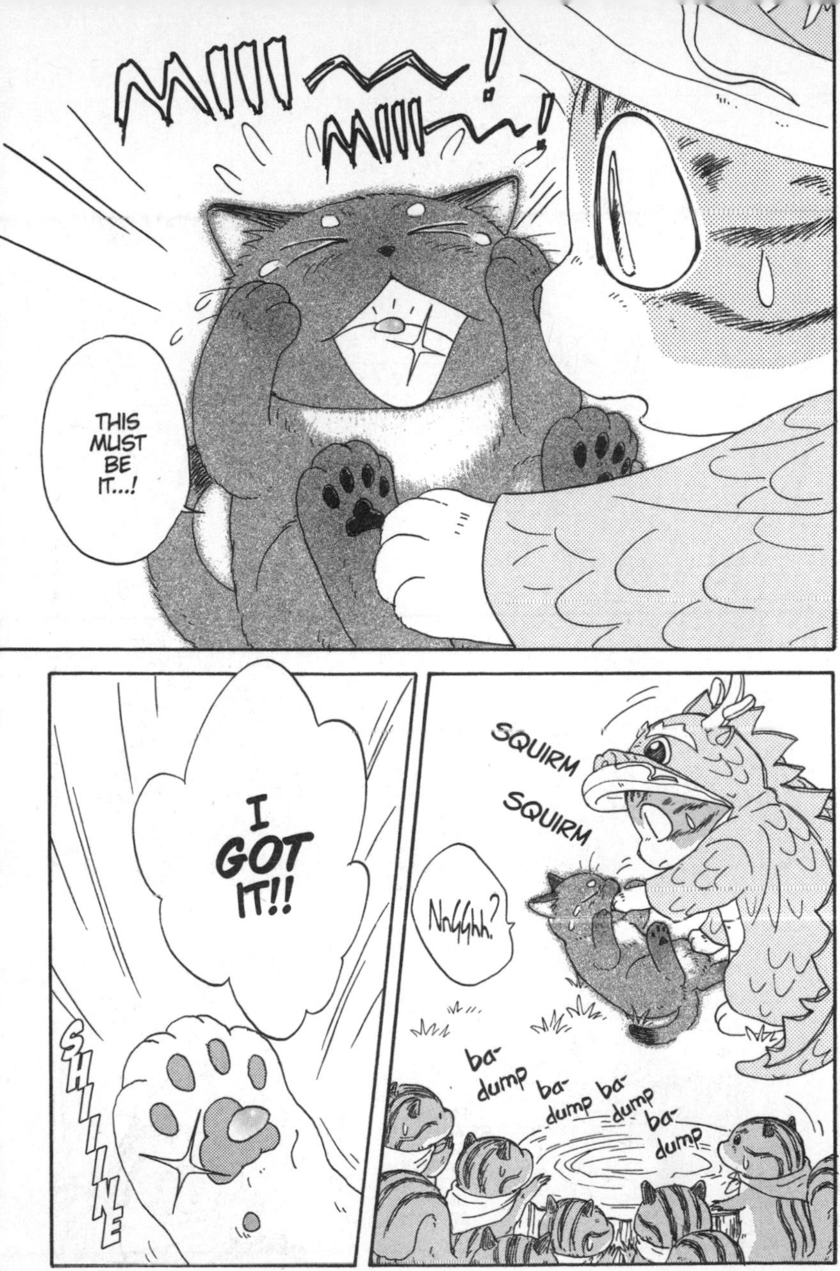
MIII~~!
MIII~~!
THIS MUST BE IT...!
SQUIRM
SQUIRM
NnGGhh?
ba-dump
ba-dump
ba-dump
ba-dump
I GOT IT!!
SHIIINE

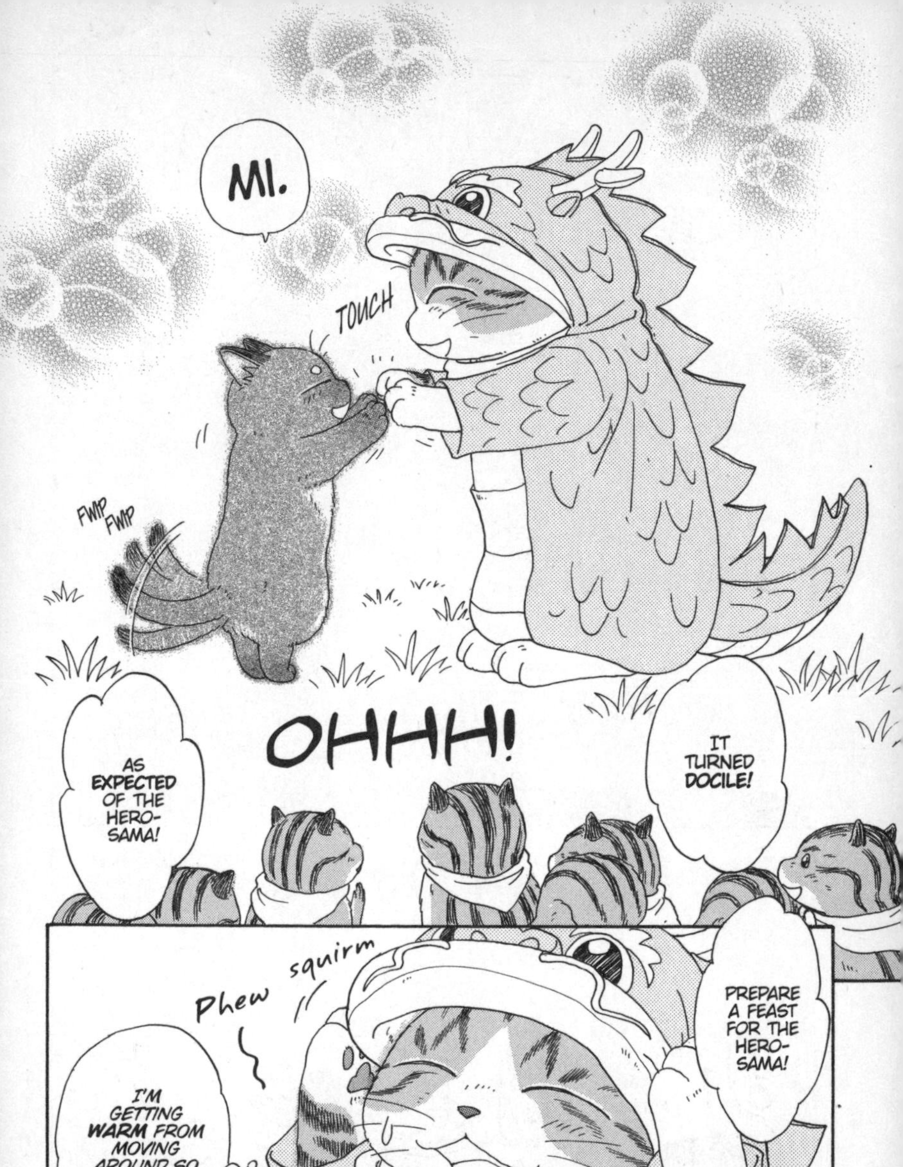
MI.
TOUCH
FWIP FWIP
IT TURNED DOCILE!
OHHH!
AS EXPECTED OF THE HERO-SAMA!
PREPARE A FEAST FOR THE HERO-SAMA!
squirm
Phew
I'M GETTING WARM FROM MOVING AROUND SO MUCH~!

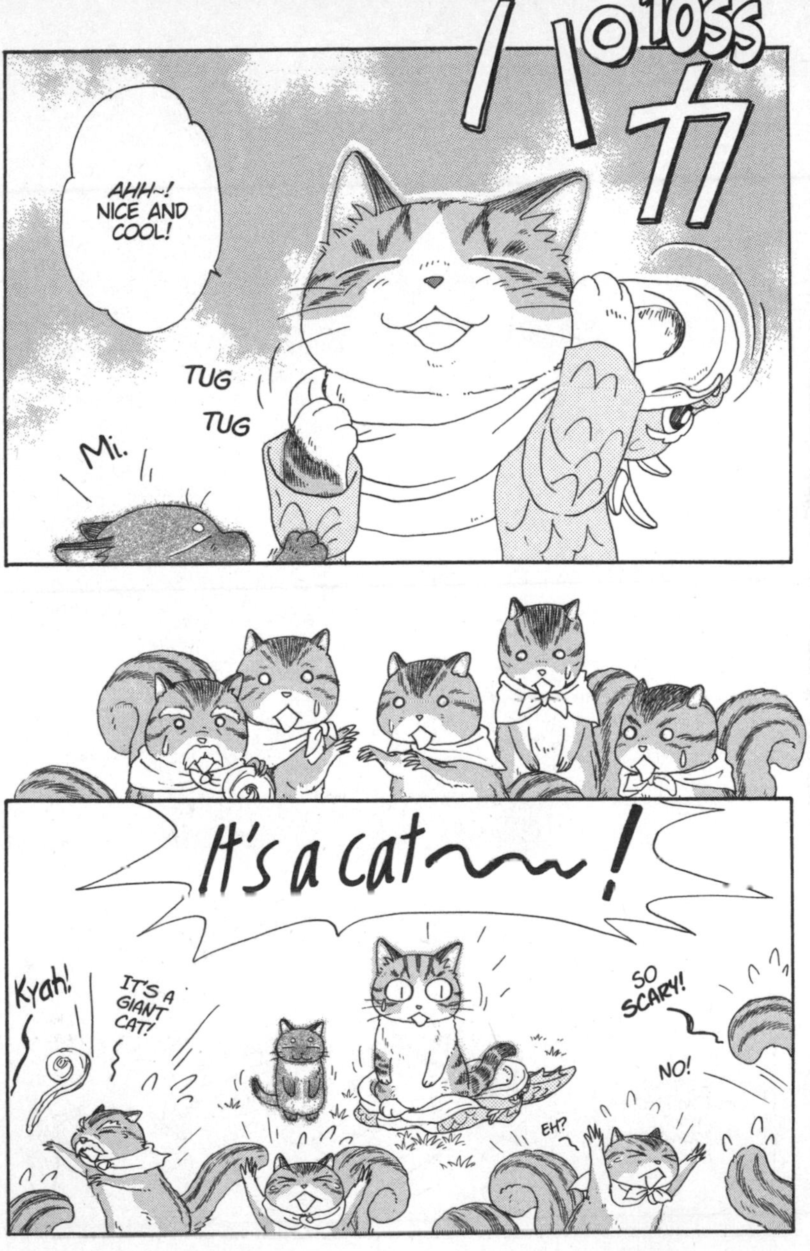
TOSS
AHH~! NICE AND COOL!
TUG
TUG
Mi.
It's a cat~~!
SO SCARY!
NO!
EH?
IT'S A GIANT CAT!
Kyah!

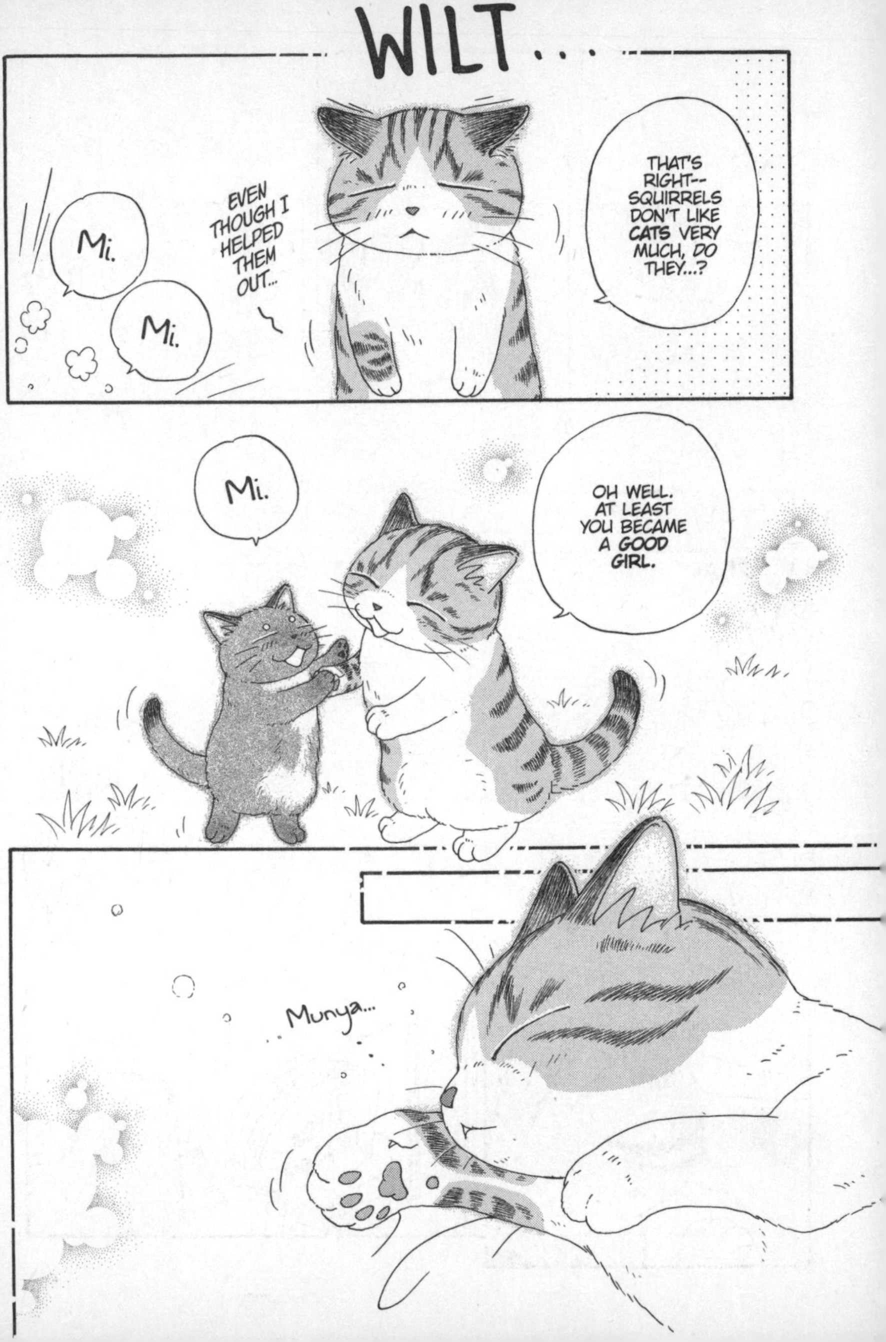
WILT...
THAT'S RIGHT-- SQUIRRELS DON'T LIKE CATS VERY MUCH, DO THEY...?
EVEN THOUGH I HELPED THEM OUT...
Mi.
Mi.
OH WELL. AT LEAST YOU BECAME A GOOD GIRL.
Mi.
Munya...

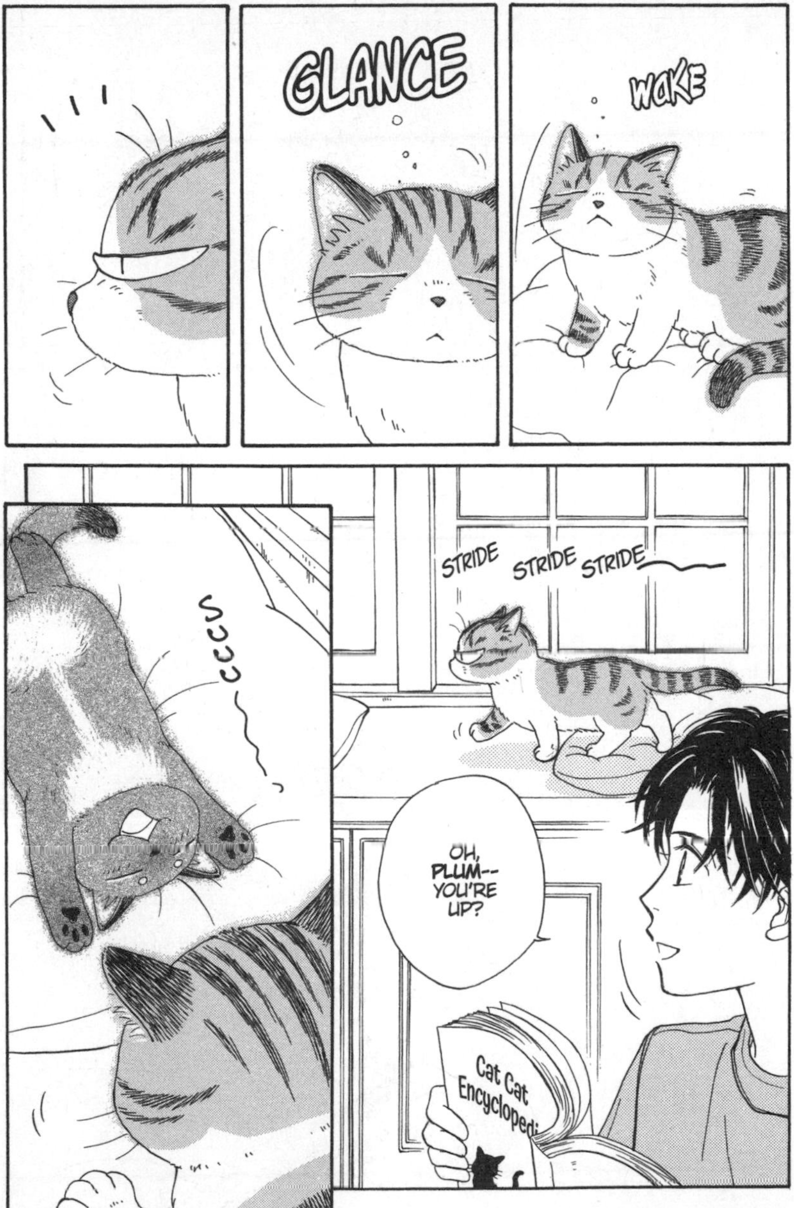
WAKE
GLANCE
STRIDE STRIDE STRIDE
OH, PLUM-- YOU'RE UP?
Cat Cat Encyclopedi

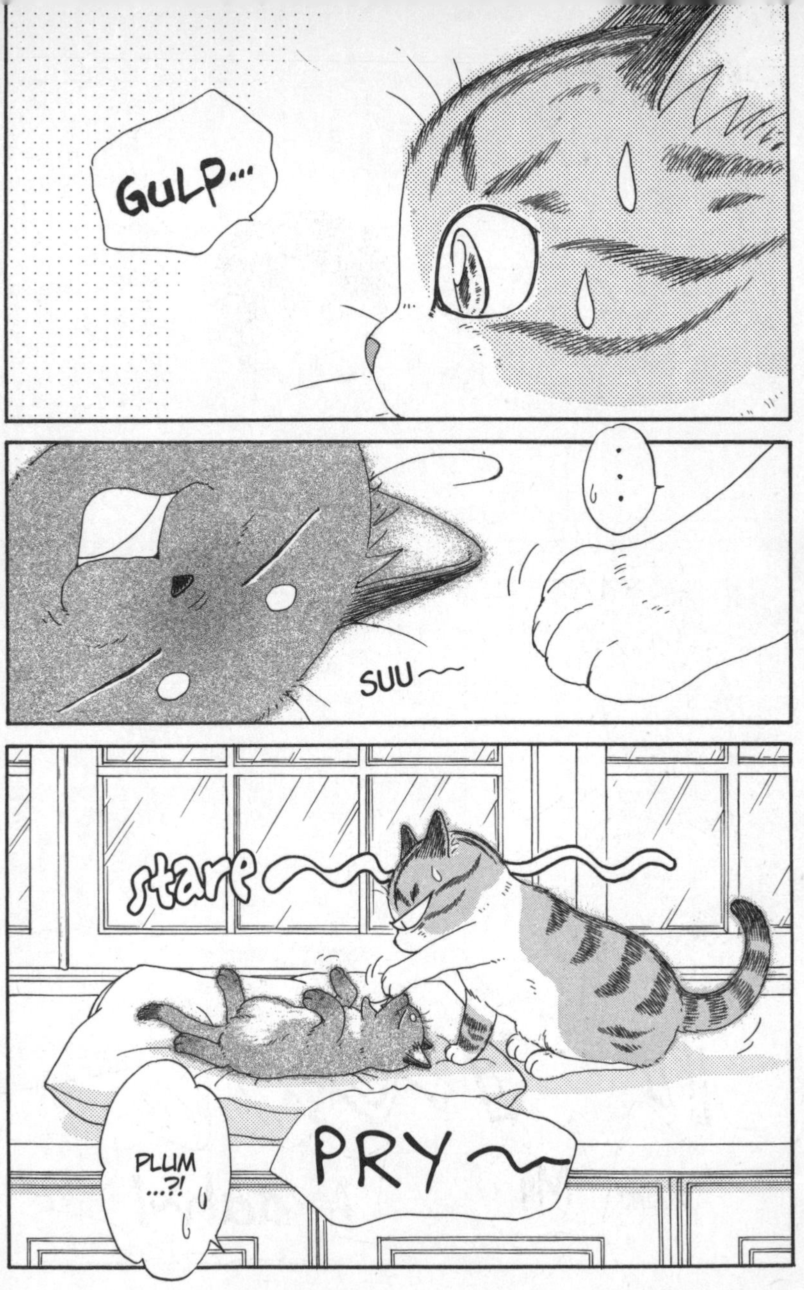
GULP...
...
SUU~~
stare~~
PRY~
PLUM ...?!

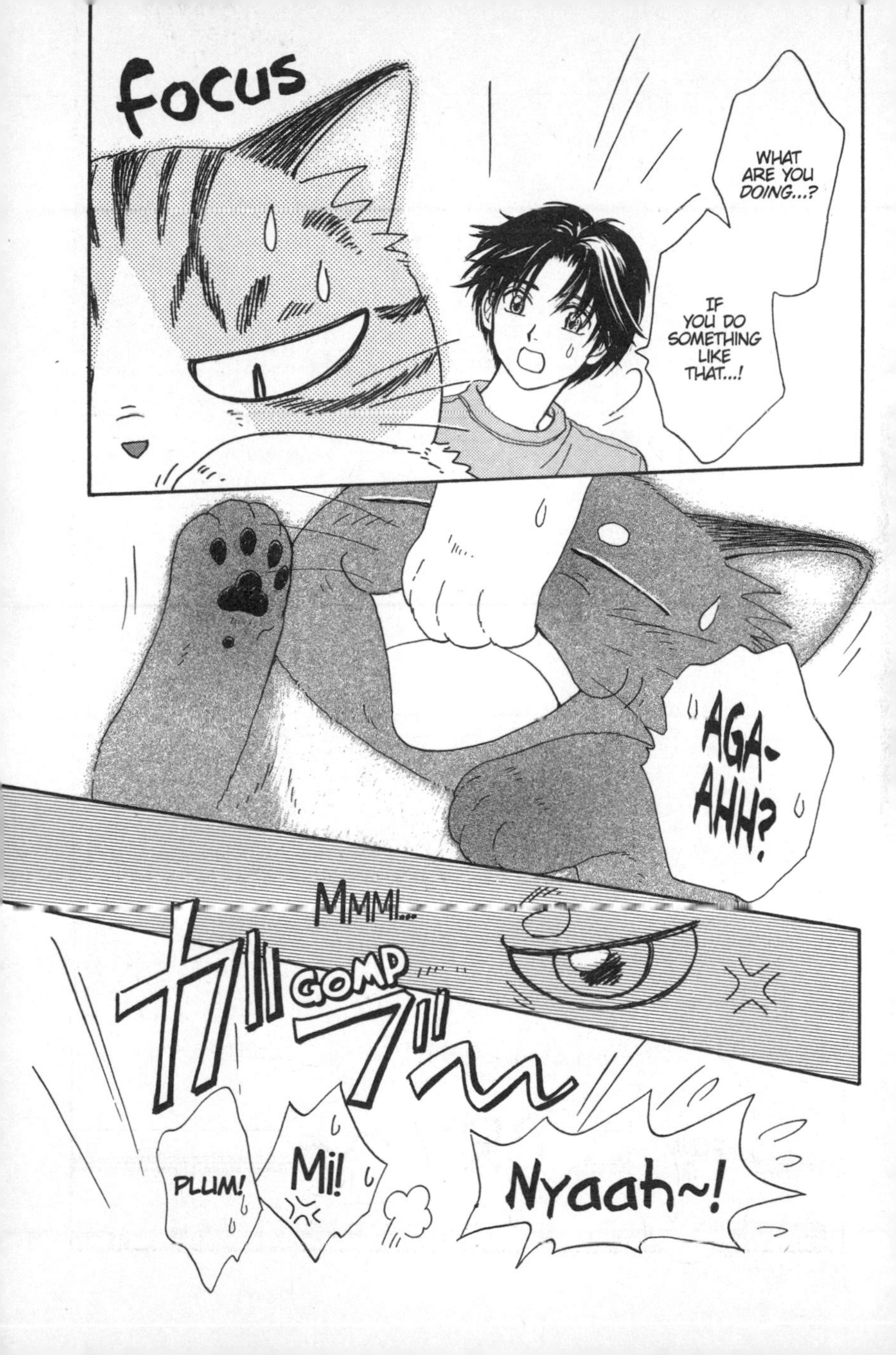
WHAT ARE YOU DOING...?
IF YOU DO SOMETHING LIKE THAT...!
focus
AGA-AHH?
MMM...
GOMP
ガブ
Nyaah~!
Mi!
PLUM!

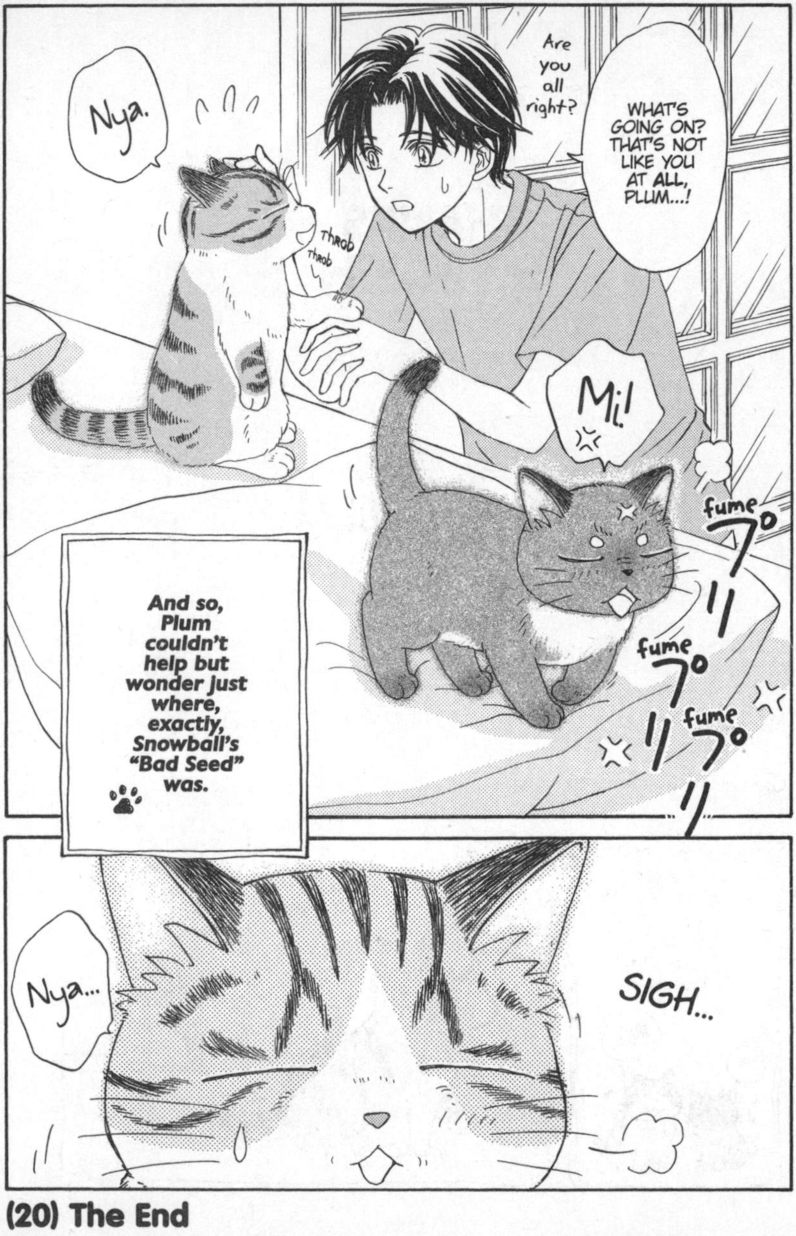
WHAT'S GOING ON? THAT'S NOT LIKE YOU AT ALL, PLUM...!
Are you all right?
Nya.
Throb throb
Mi!
fume fume fume
And so, Plum couldn't help but wonder just where, exactly, Snowball's "Bad Seed" was.
SIGH...
Nya...

(20) The End

THANKS SO MUCH FOR READING!

SEE YOU NEXT TIME-!

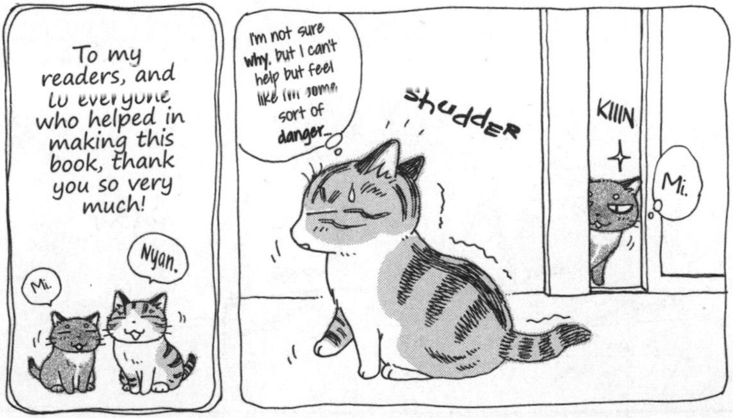
I'm not sure why, but I can't help but feel like I'm in some sort of danger...
SHUDDER
KIIIN
Mi.
To my readers, and to everyone who helped in making this book, thank you so very much!
Nyan.
Mi.

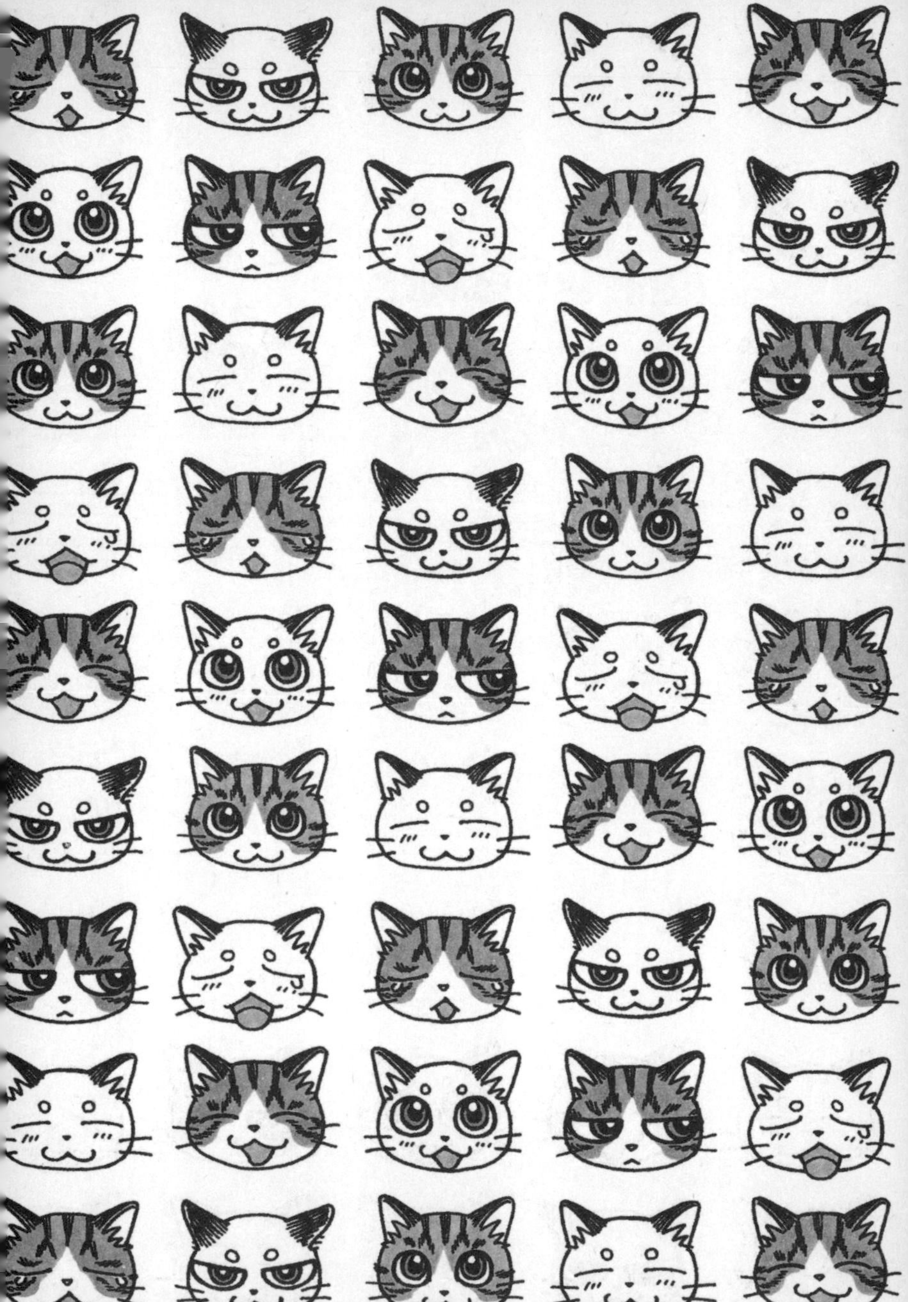

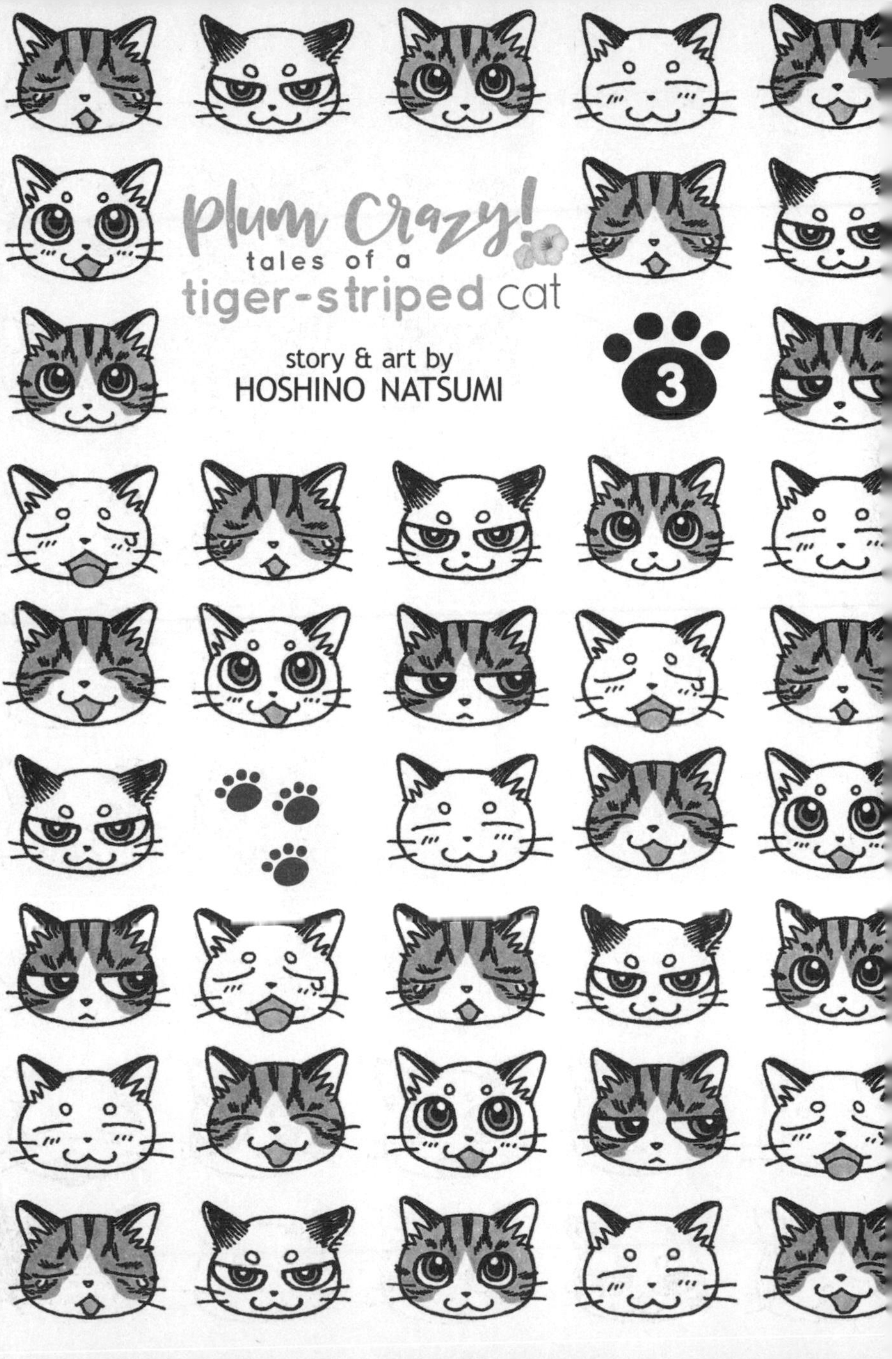
Plum Crazy!
tales of a tiger-striped cat
story & art by
HOSHINO NATSUMI
3

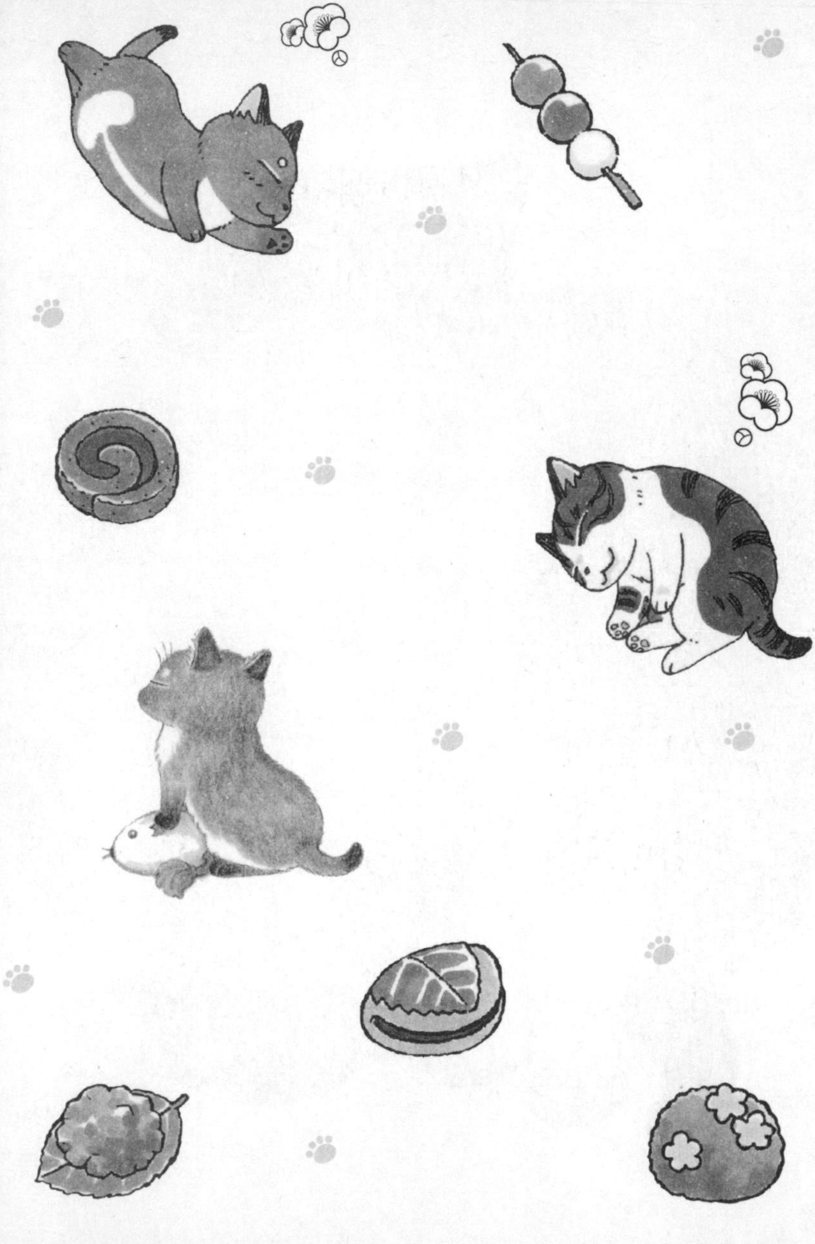

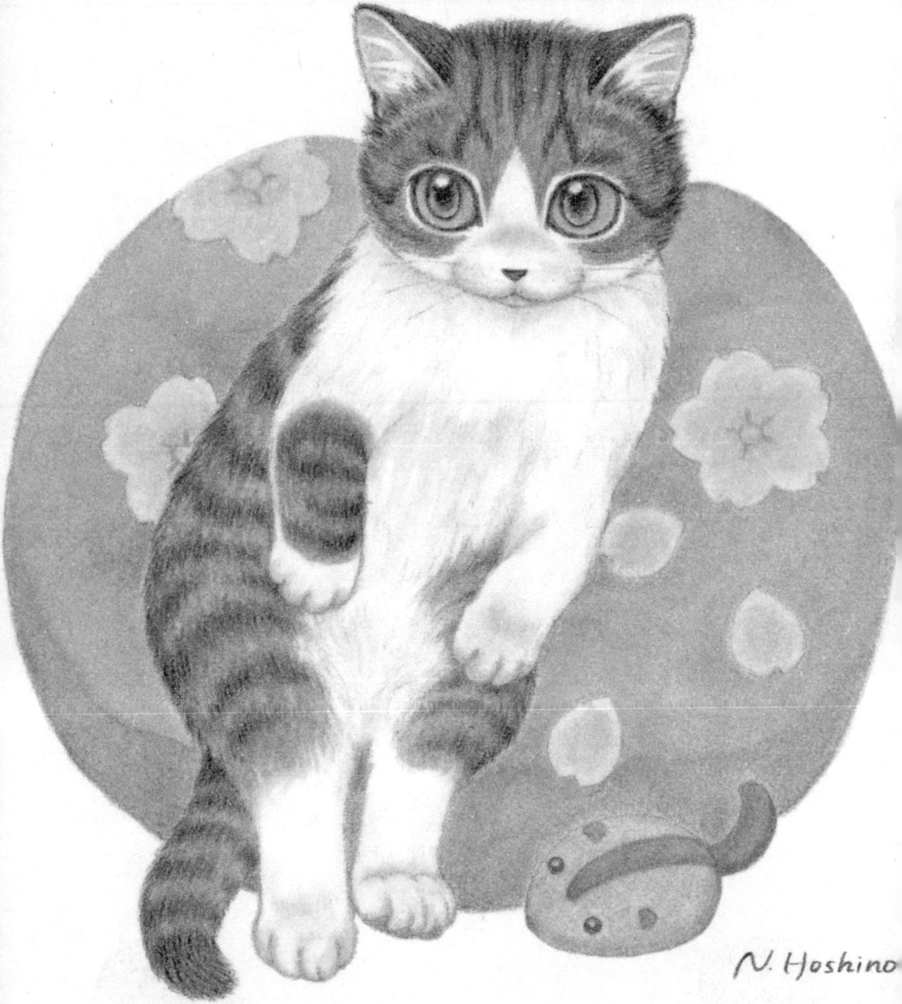
N. Hoshino

plum Crazy!
tales of a
tiger-striped cat

SEVEN SEAS ENTERTAINMENT PRESENTS

Plum Crazy! tales of a tiger-striped cat

ZRJC
3/19

story and art by NATSUMI HOSHINO VOLUME 3

TRANSLATION
Nan Rymer

LETTERING
Ray Steeves
Lune Moon

COVER DESIGN
Nicky Lim

PROOFREADER
Katherine Bell
Brett Hallahan

ASSISTANT EDITOR
Jenn Grunigen

PRODUCTION ASSISTANT
CK Russell

PRODUCTION MANAGER
Lissa Pattillo

EDITOR-IN-CHIEF
Adam Arnold

PUBLISHER
Jason DeAngelis

PLUM CRAZY! TALES OF A TIGER-STRIPED CAT VOLUME 3
© Hoshino Natsumi 2010
Originally published in Japan in 2010 by SHONENGAHOSHA Co., Ltd., Tokyo.
English translation rights arranged through TOHAN CORPORATION, Tokyo.

No portion of this book may be reproduced or transmitted in any form without
written permission from the copyright holders. This is a work of fiction. Names,
characters, places, and incidents are the products of the author's imagination
or are used fictitiously. Any resemblance to actual events, locales, or persons,
living or dead, is entirely coincidental.

Seven Seas books may be purchased in bulk for promotional, educational, or
business use. Please contact your local bookseller or the Macmillan Corporate
and Premium Sales Department at 1-800-221-7945, extension 5442, or by
e-mail at MacmillanSpecialMarkets@macmillan.com.

Seven Seas and the Seven Seas logo are trademarks of
Seven Seas Entertainment, LLC. All rights reserved.

ISBN: 978-1-626925-82-3

Printed in Canada

First Printing: November 2017

10 9 8 7 6 5 4 3 2 1

FOLLOW US ONLINE: *www.gomanga.com*

READING DIRECTIONS

This book reads from *right to left*, Japanese style.
If this is your first time reading manga, you start
reading from the top right panel on each page and
take it from there. If you get lost, just follow the
numbered diagram here. It may seem backwards at
first, but you'll get the hang of it! Have fun!!

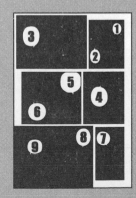

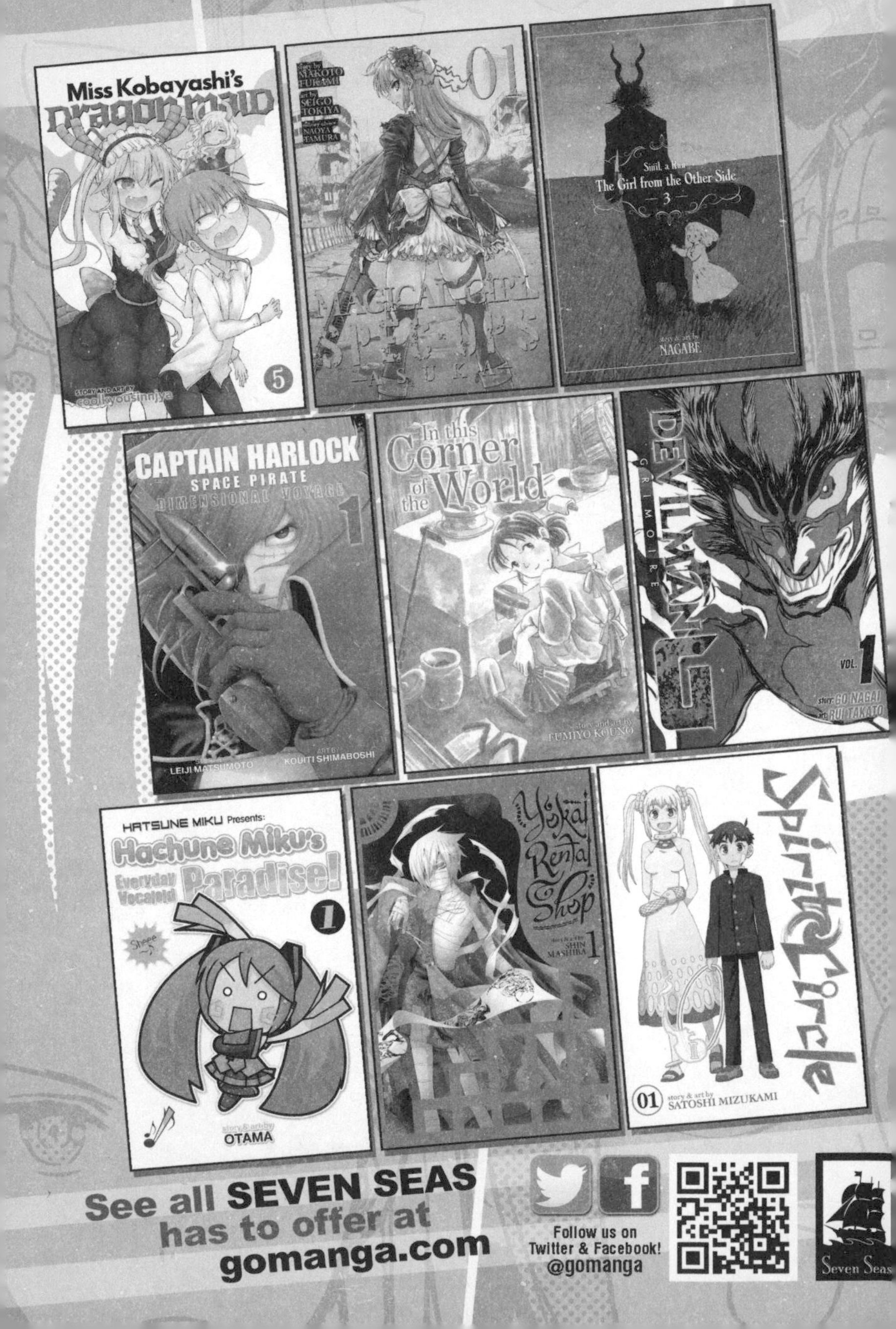
Miss Kobayashi's Dragon Maid
5
STORY AND ART BY coolkyousinnjya
story by MAKOTO FUKAMI
art by SEIGO TOKIYA
01
MAGICAL GIRL SPEC-OPS ASUKA
Siúil, a Rún
The Girl from the Other Side
3
story & art by NAGABE
CAPTAIN HARLOCK
SPACE PIRATE
DIMENSIONAL VOYAGE
1
LEIJI MATSUMOTO
ART BY KOUITI SHIMABOSHI
In this Corner of the World
story and art by FUMIYO KOUNO
DEVILMAN G GRIMOIRE
VOL. 1
story: GO NAGAI
art: RUI TAKATO
HATSUNE MIKU Presents:
Hachune Miku's Everyday Vocaloid Paradise!
1
story & art by OTAMA
Yōkai Rental Shop
story & art by SHIN MASHIBA
1
Spirit Circle
01
story & art by SATOSHI MIZUKAMI